# Making Trouble for Muslims

This edition is dedicated to
Professor Mohammed Aman, friend and scholar

# Making Trouble for Muslims

## A. Rawlinson's
*Adventures in the Near East, 1918-1922*

Edited and introduced by
Paul Rich

WESTPHALIA PRESS
An imprint of Policy Studies Organization

Making Trouble for Muslims
A. Rawlinson's
*Adventures in the Near East, 1918-1922*

All Rights Reserved © 2012 by Policy Studies Organization

Westphalia Press
An imprint of Policy Studies Organization
dgutierrezs@ipsonet.org

*All rights reserved.* No part of this book may be reproduced or transmitted in any form or by any means graphic, electronic, or mechanical, including photocopying, recording, taping, or by any information storage or retrieval system, without the permission in writing from the publisher.

For information:
Westphalia Press
1527 New Hampshire Ave., N.W.
Washington, D.C. 20036

ISBN-13: 978-0944285688
ISBN-10: 0944285686

Updated material and comments on this edition can be found at the Policy Studies Organization website: http://www.ipsonet.org/

# Preface to the New Edition

## Making Trouble for Muslims:
## A. Rawlinson's *Adventures in the Near East*, 1918-1922

Alfred Rawlinson's book about his World War I adventures includes personal experiences in what is now Iraq, where his father had a distinguished archaeology career, and about his encounters with the Assyrian diaspora, Turkish empire, Russian interest in the region, and the Kurds. He was a swash-buckler out of a British boy's magazine.

The same events he recounts in the following pages enabled Major A.J. Smithers to write an entertaining account (Toby: A Real Life Ripping Yarn, Gordon & Cremonesi, London. 1978), described in its jacket blurb: "Toby, the Duke of Westminster, and a bunch of fellow madcaps all dashed off to the Front in their Rolls Royces with their chauffeurs to the astonishment of both sides. So began a tense engaging series of adventures of espionage and death-defying escapades through Europe which eventually took him to the Middle East."

Major Smithers reminds us that Rawlinson had many claims to fame: "He devised a new gun for the British to repay German mortar fire, modified a stethoscope to detect zeppelins, dashed off to Turkey for a spell in prison after adventures in Persia where he scared off a vast Russian armed detachment with a cardboard tank."

Great entertainment, but possibly less fun for the Muslims as the soldiers marched back and forth. Ever since Edward Said's seminal study *Orientalism* appeared in 1978, we have been on notice to read between the lines in accounts such as Rawlinson's. He touches on many border and ethnic disputes that are still with us, and the fact that he encountered them one hundred years ago should be a cause for wondering why the same problems remain on the agenda. The blood and treasure he witnessed being spent so lavishly accomplished naught.

Western interventions seemingly have made a lot of trouble for a lot of people without resolving much. Based on living in the Middle East for many years, I feel that one reason Western relations with the

Muslim world have been so frustrating is the frequent failure of all concerned, Muslims and Westerners, to acknowledge the degree of cultural and racial diversity in the region. Alongside the war, which is of course central to Rawlinson's narrative, the sheer number of different stakeholders he mentions should be a useful reminder of the actual pluralism of the region.

Historically, for decades we have seen consequences of a mindset on the part of Western policy makers that at best sees a few divisions such as Sunni and Shia and simply ignores how many competing groups are involved. People who would never dream of considering the United Kingdom without reference to its different historic components will do that with offhand abandon in describing Turkey, Iraq or Iran.

That, then, gives an additional value to A. Rawlinson's book. A number of the volumes that I have written or edited about the Arabian or Persian Gulf have helped to show a cultural diversity of what is often regarded as a monolithic area. I have found that authors like Rawlinson inadvertently provide valuable evidence for this cultural approach. The part played by diverse parties is an aspect of my research in *Creating the Arabian Gulf* (Lexington Books, Lanham, Maryland, 2009). Appreciation of the number of different groups in the Middle East has important political consequences, and translates into workable policy suggestions.

Readers, no matter how they feel about imperialism and its legacy, will inevitably admire Rawlinson for his fortitude and daring. While a prisoner of the Turks, he teaches chess to the enlisted men imprisoned with him: "Oxo cubes as Castles, corks as Knights, large revolver cartridges as Bishops, machine-gun cartridges as Queens, and big Russian cartridges as Kings, small revolver cartridges being the Pawns. With these rather 'explosive' chess-men we had many an interesting game." (p.294) Lieutenant-Colonel Sir Alfred Rawlinson, CMG, CBE, DSO, died 1 June, 1934. He was the third baronet. The current and fifth baronet, Sir Anthony Henry John Rawlinson, is a well-known photographer with work in the National Portrait Gallery in London and, possibly unsurprisingly, an inventor.

Paul Rich, *George Mason University*

Col. Rawlinson and "George" at home in England

*Frontispiece*

# ADVENTURES IN THE NEAR EAST

## 1918—1922

BY
A. RAWLINSON, C.M.G., C.B.E., D.S.O.
Late Lt.-Col. R.G.A., and Commander R.N.V.R.

INTRODUCTION BY
ADMIRAL SIR PERCY SCOTT

NEW YORK
DODD, MEAD AND COMPANY
1925

# AUTHOR'S PREFACE

For some time past many friends have been at some pains to impress upon me that, having had so many adventures in so many queer places, and having now come out of them alive and, if a bit knocked about, yet "still kicking," I ought to write down some account of my experiences, as they might prove of interest to many people who have had no knowledge of the kind of life which it has for the last few years been my lot to lead.

I therefore start by relating here that portion of my adventures which took place subsequent to the spring of 1918, when I went East once more after many years in other parts of the world.

Knowing nothing of how such a story ought to be written, I hope my readers will bear with my inexperience of "writing," in consideration of the variety of experiences of other kinds which this book endeavours to put before them.

Political questions have been avoided wherever possible, and only introduced where some knowledge of the actual conditions obtaining at the time becomes necessary to enable the reader to appreciate the incidents related.

I am anxious to express my very grateful thanks to my late Commanders, Major-General Dunsterville, General Sir George Milne, and Lieut.-General Sir Charles Harington, for their uniform kindness to me at all times, and particularly for the great honour they have done me in contributing the introductions to the various parts of this book, of which they have each such special knowledge, and I am more than satisfied if, when serving under them, I have been able to carry out their orders in a manner which has met with their approval.

My thanks are doubly due to my old friend and chief, Admiral Sir Percy Scott, both for his general introduction to this book and for his great kindness to me on many other occasions.

A. RAWLINSON.

LONDON,
*January* 15, 1923.

# GENERAL INTRODUCTION

By ADMIRAL SIR PERCY SCOTT, Bart.,
K.C.B., K.C.V.O., LL.D.

I first met the author of this book at the Admiralty early in 1915. I had then just been given the task of defending London against attacks from the air, and Mr. (now Lord) Balfour informed me that, while presenting me with this appointment, he could not give me the means necessary to protect London. It did not sound a very nice job, but in war-time one has to take anything.

Although I had never met Toby Rawlinson before, I was acquainted with part of his career. I knew that he had been in the Seventeenth Lancers and had played polo for England on many occasions, and that he gave up a soldier's life to let his mechanical knowledge make a fortune for him in the early days of motor-car racing.

This exciting amusement did not appear to offer Rawlinson sufficient chances to break his neck; flying was more dangerous, so he took to that new pastime, and his International Pilot's Certificate was the third one issued. He represented the British Aero Club at the earliest International meetings on the Continent, and he and Rolls were considered the most daring of fliers; they both crashed at the International races at Bournemouth in July, 1910. Rolls was killed, but Rawlinson recovered. He then went back into business, but gave it up on the outbreak of war, and in August, 1914, put himself, his motor-car, and his machine-guns at the disposal of General Headquarters in France as a volunteer. From that time the tale of his adventures, until I had the pleasure of meeting him, would fill a big book. Eventually he got blown up, and ought to have been killed, but he was not.

Knowing much about the character and ability of Toby Rawlinson, and as I had got a job of building bricks without straw, I thought that he was the man to help me, so I took him into the Anti-Air Defence, and the inhabitants of London owe him a debt of gratitude for his assistance in the defence of their city against attacks from the air. For my own part, I can truly say that I could not have had a more charming officer to deal with; the more difficult the job I gave him, the more he seemed to like it.

Colonel Rawlinson remained in the Anti-Air Service until a more important and more dangerous work was found for him. The ability with which he carried out this work was signified when from a volunteer driver he eventually became a Lieut.-Colonel and was awarded the C.M.G., the C.B.E., and the D.S.O., being also four times mentioned in dispatches from the front.

His book tells the story of his adventures in the Near East in a singularly attractive form; his account of capturing a Bolshevik ship and piloting her out of Baku Harbour under very difficult circumstances will astonish many sailors. Four men against ninety-six enemy, with the only alternative of blowing up himself, his four men, the ninety-six enemy, and the ship, with dynamite, is a position that not many would enjoy; but it appeared to suit Rawlinson's constitution, for he remarks that after thirty-six hours of it he enjoyed a very good dinner.

There is, however, a very sad side to his story, which, I am afraid, will very much distress many men and women of this country. Colonel Rawlinson put his uniform on in 1914, and did not take it off until March, 1923. He was cast into a Turkish prison for twenty months, and all but starved to death, as a consequence of which his health is impaired for life. He was also stripped of all he possessed by the Turks, including his two machine-guns which cost him over £500 in 1914, and which had done such valuable service all through the war. His grateful country, however, is now paying him 57s. 8½d. per week for a limited number of months only, and he has been refused any kind of compensation either for his imprisonment or for the loss of his property.

It appears to me incredible that in a civilized country this should be considered as an adequate recognition of such good and brave active service for over seven years, and if such is the treatment laid down by the military regulations for men who have readily given all they had to give for the service of their country, I feel convinced the British public will not rest satisfied until the regulations are altered and adequate compensation made.

# CONTENTS

|  | PAGE |
|---|---|
| AUTHOR'S PREFACE | v |
| GENERAL INTRODUCTION | vii |

## PART I

### THE "HUSH-HUSH" ARMY
(*May to November*, 1918)

WITH INTRODUCTION BY MAJOR-GENERAL L. C. DUNSTERVILLE, C.B., C.S.I., GENERAL OFFICER COMMANDING DUNSTERFORCE, 1918

### CHAPTER I

#### EASTWARD BOUND TO THE TIGRIS

The War Office—the Fourth Army Headquarters before Amiens—The "fast" convoy—Submarine attack—Malta—Alexandria—Cairo—The Australian Cavalry—Suez—The Red Sea—Aden—Captain Cockman—Muscat—The Straits of Ormuz—The mouth of the Euphrates . . . . . . . . . . . . . . . . . . . . . . . . 5

### CHAPTER II

#### MESOPOTAMIA, THE LAND OF THE RIVERS

The great Euphrates River—German obstruction of navigation—Bussrah—The port and its growth—The I.G.C.—Reflections on past prosperity and present prospects of the country—The river steamer—The rivers—Their transport value and difficulties—Troops' accommodation—The junction of Tigris and Euphrates—The Garden of Eden—Ezra's Tomb—Amora—Loss of a man overboard—The desert Arabs and their camps—Their horses—Distant mountains of Persia—Kut—River windings—Report G.H.Q.—Bagdad—Orders to leave at night—Hospital—Convalescent home—Commander-in-Chief's house—Town and bazaars of Bagdad—**Army Boxing Final—Departure by Decauville Railway** . . . 23

# CONTENTS

PAGE

## CHAPTER III
### PERSIA: THE ROAD AND THE FAMINE

Railhead camp at Ruz—The Foot-hills—Khanikin—A.S.C. post—Entry to the mountains—The Tek-i-Gehri Pass, Ascent of—Convalescent camp—Dinner on edge of precipice—The upland country—Brigand-infested country round Kirmanshah—Camp at Kirmanshah—The convoy—The Rock of Bisidun—Darius cuneiform inscription—Modern lorries and ancient bridges—Bivouac in the open—The Asadabad Pass—Oil deposits—Russian preparations for defence—Hamadan—Famine horrors—Relief work—Persian gunfire—Biblical scenes—The site of the Book of Esther—Ancient Ecbatana of Herodotus, Alexander the Great, Ruth, and Boaz to-day—Burning of the petrol dump—Road to Kasvin—G.H.Q. Hush-Hush Army—Billet—Ordered to relieve Armenians surrounded 300 miles west—Build armoured car—Jungalis—Battle of Menjil—Ordered to command convoy to force the passes to Caspian Sea . 39

## CHAPTER IV
### THE CASPIAN SEA—ADVANCE TO, AND RELIEF OF, AND SIEGE OF BAKU

The convoy—The upper pass—Through the Jungalis in the lower pass—The sea at last—Kazian, the end of the road—Sickness—An oil tank as a transport—Bad weather—Bolshevik gunboat—Baku Harbour—The city—Preceding events—Services lent to Caspian Republic—The Government appoint me Controller of Ordnance—Difficulties—The arsenals, armament, and ammunition—The Armenians—Project to cut Turk communications—Constant attacks—Decide to withdraw—Government refuses to consent—Prospects of capture—Plan to blow up ammunition—Turks hesitate—Resistance continued—I acquire a German flat—The end approaches . 61

## CHAPTER V
### EVACUATION: THE STEAMER "ARMENIAN"

Enemy shelling—Work of the *Armenian*—Preparations for raid on enemy communications—Turk deserter's information—The final attack—Preparations for evacuation—State of the quays—Guarding the arsenal pier—I traverse the quays to obtain reinforcements—Our H.Q. sentries—Permission to shift for myself—Arrangement of signal—The Commissaire—His treatment—Getting the breech-blocks—Massacre by Tartars—Withdrawal of our last pickets—The Turks in the town—Withdraw my guard from pier—

## CONTENTS

Another Commissaire—The *Armenian* casts off—The hospital ship passes—The anchor is lost—Find and speak the *Kruger* at last—Follow her out—Trouble on board—Challenged by the guardships—They open fire—Trouble with the captain—Trouble with the crew—At sea—Triumphal entry into port—The Chief's congratulations . . . . . . . . . . . . . . . . . . 83

### CHAPTER VI

#### HOMEWARD BOUND—THE ARMISTICE

The cargo of the *Armenian*—Kasvin—Journey to Bagdad—The order of the day—Journey to Bussrah—To Suez—To Taranto—Paris on Armistice Day—Fourth Army Headquarters—London . . . . 102

## PART II

### INTELLIGENCE IN TRANSCAUCASIA

(*February to August,* 1919)

WITH INTRODUCTION BY GENERAL SIR G. MILNE, G.C.M.G., ETC., COMMANDER-IN-CHIEF, ARMY OF BLACK SEA

### CHAPTER I

#### "EAST AGAIN"—SALONIKA, CONSTANT, AND BATOUM

Rationing at home—Meet Sir G. Milne—Appointed Special Service "Intelligence" Officer to G.H.Q., Constantinople—Morris left in England—Railway journey during French demobilization—Rome—Rest camp at Taranto—Grecian Archipelago—Mount Athos—Salonika—Kit lost—Journey from Salonika to Constant—Catalja Lines—Constantinople—Palace of Constantine—Old Stamboul—Galata—The Grande Rue of Pera—St. Sophia—Adrian's Roman Wall—Carnival in Pera—Down the Bosphorus—Varna—Samsun—A mine at sea—Batoum . . . . . . . . . . . . 119

### CHAPTER II

#### THE CAUCASUS—AFTER THE ARMISTICE

The Czar's Imperial train—Party on board—Journey to Tiflis—Georgia and its capital—British Advanced Headquarters—My duties and establishment—The Azerbaijan frontier—Tartar brigands—Conditions in Tiflis—The main chain of the Caucasus—The Georgian Road—Queen Tamara's summer palace—The Russo-Georgian frontier—Russian brigands—The Ingoush tribe—Orders to equip a train and go to Kars—Snowed up—Conditions at Kars—Escape from Kars—Report to Commander-in-Chief at Batoum—Further orders . . . . . . . . . . . . . . . . 135

## CHAPTER III

### EASTERN ANATOLIA—TREBIZOND AND ERZEROUM

Orders—Appointment with Commander-in-Chief at Kars—Leave Tiflis—The Advent of "George"—The Rion Valley—Batoum again—Landing at Trebizond—The Zigana Pass—The Kharshut Valley—The Vavok Pass—Baiburt—The Khop Pass—Bivouac in snow—The Upper Euphrates—Erzeroum—The Kars Road—The Russo-Turkish frontier—The Saganli Mountains—Kars again—Return to Erzeroum—The fortress town—Kiazim Karabekir—Difficulties—"George" and the camel—Reinforcement reaches Trebizond . . 157

## CHAPTER IV

### THE RUSSO-TURKISH FRONTIER—TROUBLE BREWING

Visit from General Beach—Interview with Kiazim Karabekir Pasha—Plans for repair of railway—Our supplies looted—Start for Trebizond—Beautiful camp—Our reinforcements—Hidden guns discovered—Return to Erzeroum "sick"—Our party augmented—Plans for removing armament—Arrival of Mustapha Kemal—Reports of trouble on frontier—Joined by Russian officers, also American naval officer and others—Leave for the frontier—Railway blocked—Night journey on a trolley—Armenian Generals at Kars—Leave for the South—Hussein, the Kurdish Mountain Chief—The race down the pass . . . . . . . . . . . 177

## CHAPTER V

### THE RUSSO-TURKISH FRONTIER—KURDS AND ARMENIANS

Cross the Aras—Reception at Khagizman—The town—The general situation—Omar Aga, the Kurdish brigand—Interview—We run out of petrol—Return to Zivin—Position in Olti District—Camp in the Olti Hills—Eyeeb Pasha—His troops—Moslem refugees—Robbers' punishment—Machine-gun practice—Kurdish national game—Kurds going into action—Our car attacked and corporal shot—Return again to Zivin . . . . . . . . . . . . 198

# CONTENTS

## CHAPTER VI

### THE TURKISH ARMISTICE A FIASCO—FOUNDATION OF THE NATIONALIST PARTY

Arrangements for evacuation of Turkish armament—Rumours of Erzeroum Conference—Turks refuse consent—Proceed to Erzeroum—Cable Commander-in-Chief, Constant—Cable Tiflis *re* Armenian atrocities on Moslems—Meet Commission appointed to investigate—Taken prisoner by Kurds—The armament is stolen—Commander-in-Chief's cable order to evacuate my men from Turkey—Proceed to Erzeroum—Interview with Kiazim and Mustapha Kemal—Result of Conference—The Nationalist Pact—Halt at Sarikamish—Ordered to Constant—Tiflis and Batoum—An American destroyer—Report to Commander-in-Chief—Orders for home—Dinner at Therapia—The Turkish train—Roumania and Bucarest—Journey to Trieste, Paris, and London . . . . . . 216

# PART III

## IN KEMALIST TURKEY

(*October, 1919, to November, 1922*)

WITH INTRODUCTION BY LIEUT.-GEN. SIR CHARLES HARINGTON, G.B.E., K.C.B., ETC., COMMANDER-IN-CHIEF, ALLIED FORCES IN THE NEAR EAST

## CHAPTER I

### LONDON AND CONSTANTINOPLE

Interview with Sir Henry Wilson—Interview with Lord Curzon—Reception of my reports—My instructions—Journey via Paris and Rome to Taranto—Embark on a hospital ship—Call at Salonika—Passage of the Dardanelles—Orders to fit out a new party at Constant—"A" mess—Organization of my Mission—Their training—Adrian's Aqueduct—The Forest of Belgrade—General Sir Tom Bridges—General Sir Henry Wilson—Admiral Webb—Admiral de Robeck—Dinner on the *Iron Duke*—Fox-hunting—Golf—A fireship in the Bosphorus—Loading mules on the transport—Sail for Trebizond—Landing in Anatolia . . . . . . . . . . . 237

# CONTENTS

## CHAPTER II

### ANATOLIA IN WINTER

Trebizond in winter—Camp at Hamsikeui—The Zigana Pass—Our house at Gumush Khaneh—Visit of Greek Bishop—The Vavok Pass—Persian travellers—My men exhausted—Bivouac in the snow—Reach Baiburt—Start for the Khop—Our Turk mountaineers—Their Chief and their oxen—The climb—Ankers' good work—Bivouac on the summit—Christmas night—Sunrise amongst the peaks—Casualties on the road—Reach Erzeroum . . . . 251

## CHAPTER III

### ERZEROUM IN 1920

Our house—The Army Commander—His orphan military school—The climate—The food—The wolves—I send some of my party in sledges to the coast—Our arrest—Destroy my papers—Surrounded by a mob—Play chess—Turk preparation for a military offensive—Kiazim Pasha leaves for the front—He is succeeded by Kiazim Bey—Teach the men Morse signalling—Make and plant a garden—Peace terms are announced—Our cars are taken—Our officer is withdrawn—Our guards steal our food—We become ill and weak—Our Irish driver joins the Turks—Our Christmas festivities—We receive a box from the Americans at Trebizond—We are removed to the prison . . . . . . . . . . . . . . . . 267

## CHAPTER IV

### THE PRISON

Some reflections—Armenian prisoners—The building—The new Commander—Our fellow-prisoners—The Armenian officers—Salah-a-din—A letter—My answer—Outside assistance—Another letter—The surprise—The search—Its result—Deprived of all literature—Salah-a-din's kindness—His books—Rumours of exchange—Visit of Headquarters Staff Officer—Order for our march to the coast—Our preparations—Lieutenant Hairie—Our lack of resources—Obtain credit from the "jobmaster"—Our departure—Ilija—"George's" lameness—The hovel at Pernikapan—The Khop—Baiburt—Khadrak—Gumush Khaneh—Zigana Khan—The pass—Hamsikeui—Trebizond—Our good treatment there . . . . . 289

# CONTENTS

## CHAPTER V

### PRISON AGAIN

The Fort at Trebizond—Good treatment—We are told we are to return to prison—Our officer's offer to send a letter to Constant—My dispatch—Our departure—Americans at Gumush Khaneh—Erzeroum Prison again—Kindness of the officer commanding the prison—My accounts and precautions—We are searched for money—Prince Toumanoff and his family—My model house—My dictionary—Permission to sit in the prison yard—The Bulgarian officer—The letter in a cigarette—Sketch of ancient mosque—Moonlight music—Visit from Nouri Pasha—Other visits—Ordered to the coast—Fighting on the Khop—"George's" speech—Billet at Trebizond—Maman—Colonel Baird arrives—We are taken on board H.M.S. *Somme* . . . . . . . . . . . . . . . . 308

## CHAPTER VI

### EXCHANGE AND HOME

Turks return my papers and box—Arrangements for exchange—British expect to receive 140 prisoners—Three only are forthcoming besides ourselves—I board the cruiser—The High Commissioner cables authority to exchange—Constantinople once more—Colonel and Mrs. Gribbon's hospitality—Admiral Sir Reginald Tyrwhitt—His invitation—The Chief—Our interview—Dinner with Embassy Staff—Accumulated correspondence—The men are entertained at the Embassy—Luncheon with Sir Charles and Lady Harington—Chief's cable to War Office—Reasons for refusal to see reporters—Sail for Malta in the *Centaur*—The Achi Baba position in the Gallipoli Peninsula—Full-speed trial of *Centaur*—Malta—Lord and Lady Plumer's kindness—The Palace at Valetta—The castle—Cable from General Harington—Dinner with Sir John de Robeck—The *Somme* takes us to Naples—Entertain our liberators—"George's" railway tragedy—Paris "George" rejoins—Arrive in London—Recommendation of men—Sir Henry Wilson—Collapse—Medical board's recommendations—New regulations—Visit to South of France—His Majesty receives our party at Buckingham Palace—Interviews with Lord Curzon at Foreign Office—Demobilization—Pensions . . . . . . . . . . . . . 334

# ILLUSTRATIONS

| | |
|---|---|
| Colonel Rawlinson and "George" at home in England . *Frontispiece* | |
| | FACING PAGE |
| Travelling on the Tigris, June, 1918 | 24 |
| The Tigris River from the Convalescent Home near Bagdad | 25 |
| The Rock of Bisidun | 40 |
| The panel showing Darius with the captive kings | 41 |
| North-western Persia | 62 |
| The Bolshevik steamer "Armenian" | 100 |
| Map of the Near East showing route in "red" | 108 |
| The Bosphorus at Constantinople | 120 |
| Sketch-map of the Russo-Turkish Frontier | 136 |
| The Georgian Road, the only Pass for wheeled vehicles over the main Caucasus Mountains | 150 |
| The Georgian Road (*continued*) | 151 |
| The Zigana Pass over the coast range of eastern Anatolia on the southern shore of the Black Sea | 160 |
| The Khop Pass | 170 |
| The Khop Pass (*continued*) | 171 |
| The coast country round Trebizond | 178 |
| The Russo-Turkish Frontier | 179 |
| Hussein Bey's country—Upper Aras valley | 194 |
| Eyeeb Pasha's Olti country | 200 |
| Eyeeb Pasha's country (*continued*) | 201 |
| Frontier scenes | 218 |
| Return to Constantinople | 219 |
| The Allied fleets in the Bosphorus seen from Galata Hill | 246 |
| Landing at Trebizond | 247 |
| The coast range | 252 |
| The road inland | 253 |

xviii ILLUSTRATIONS

| | FACING PAGE |
|---|---|
| The Khop Pass | 264 |
| In confinement in our house | 268 |
| Erzeroum | 269 |
| Colonel Rawlinson | 278 |
| At Erzeroum before arrest | 279 |
| Photograph of wooden model | 286 |
| Plan of wooden model | 287 |
| The Erzeroum prison | 290 |
| On the road to the coast | 304 |
| Coming down to the sea | 305 |
| Awaiting exchange | 310 |
| The journey back to prison | 311 |
| Wooden model of house with plans of each floor, made by Colonel R. in prison | 320 |
| Sketch of the ancient mosque on the eastern side of the prison yard at Erzeroum | 321 |
| Last journey to the coast | 330 |
| The party at Trebizond before exchange | 331 |
| The entrance to the Dardanelles from the Ægean Sea | 336 |
| Released | 337 |
| The party at Baron Robert de Rothschild's house in Paris | 348 |

# MAKING TROUBLE FOR MUSLIMS

## PART I

### THE "HUSH-HUSH" ARMY
(*May to November*, 1918)
WITH INTRODUCTION BY MAJOR-GENERAL L. C. DUNSTERVILLE, C.B., C.S.I., GENERAL OFFICER COMMANDING DUNSTERFORCE, 1918

# INTRODUCTION TO PART I

BY MAJOR-GENERAL L. C. DUNSTERVIILE, C.B., C.S.I.,
G.O.C. DUNSTERFORCE, 1918

In his account of his share in the fortunes, or misfortunes, of the Dunsterforce, Lieut.-Colonel Rawlinson offers the reader a very vivid picture of various incidents in which he was the chief person concerned, and of which he can therefore speak with the fullest knowledge.

The circumstances in which the force was involved in Persia and Baku led to the situation that borders on burlesque, though we knew that tragedy was followng very closely on the heels of comedy.

Lieut.-Colonel Rawlinson dwells on the comic side of the episodes, realizing that the reader will not fail to appreciate the tragedy of it all. It was on July 7th, 1918, that he reported to me at Kasvin. I must admit that I was astonished to find that his bedding appeared to be used chiefly as a wrapping for assorted weapons of war. I seem to remember that a machine-gun or a portion of one, peeped from beneath his pillow. I instantly realized that I was confronted with a personality that was not of a usual type, and one that was likely to impress itself upon others. I well remember the construction of an armoured car out of a Ford van. I see he says it was constructed of "solid" materials. Either my memory plays me false or he and I differ as to the meaning of the word "solid." As far as I can recollect, the materials were mostly tissue-paper and gum, perhaps some cardboard, and these are undoubtedly "solids" not usually employed in armoured-car construction. Whatever the material was, the car was the most terrific thing to look at and might possibly have been even superior to the real article, in a land where looks go for much.

The description of the last days in Baku and the final flight gives a very real picture of the happenings of those stirring days.

I liked Colonel Rawlinson sufficiently to dislike his scheme for blowing up a bridge on the Turkish lines of communication, because the chances of his returning alive were extremely remote; but it was a bold sheme, well worked out to the last detail, and had some prospect of success in the hands of a leader to whom the danger was the chief attraction. One finds so many people, not only in war-time, but in peace-time, who are quite reckless of other people's lives, that it is a pleasure to find a man who confines his recklessness exclusively to his own life.

I am glad that he has been persuaded to describe some of his many adventures, and I wish the book the success it deserves.

*(Signed)* L. C. DUNSTERVILLE.

Isle of Man,
*November* 22, 1922.

# CHAPTER I

### EASTWARD BOUND TO THE TIGRIS

The War Office—The Fourth Army Headquarters before Amiens—The "fast" convoy—Submarine attack—Malta—Alexandria—Cairo—The Australian Cavalry—Suez—The Red Sea—Aden—Captain Cockman—Muscat—The Straits of Ormuz—The mouth of the Euphrates.

In April, 1918, I received notice that my application to be relieved of my command in the Anti-Aircraft Defence of London had been acceded to, and shortly afterwards I was instructed to attend at the War Office for an interview with the C.I.G.S. (Sir Henry Wilson), whom I had had the advantage of knowing for many years—both before and during the war.

He received me with great kindness, and, in his own peculiarly abrupt and jerky manner, the conversation was pretty well as follows:

C.I.G.S.: Well, Toby, what are you going to do now?
SELF (*with great diffidence*): I hope, sir, I may be able to be of service somewhere.
C.I.G.S.: Would you go to Persia?
SELF: Certainly, sir.
C.I.G.S.: When could you leave?
SELF (*with more confidence*): What time does the train start?

That made him smile his unforgettable, whimsical smile, and all was well.

I was then passed on to quite a different class of person—to wit, a Colonel of G.S.—who made the part of the world in question his particular study at that time.

This gentleman, who looked and acted as if he even *slept* in his "brass hat," was pleased to be extremely patronizing, and opened: "*I* am going to send you to Persia." I replied to the effect that I considered it an honour to go, and after a few remarks about the country generally, I was given a packet of papers to study, and dismissed. And thus commenced my connection with what was known as the "Hush-Hush Army."*

The packet of papers is worth description.

The preamble was to the effect that, as officers selected for this particular service would experience arctic temperature in the snows as well as tropical heat in the plains, it was necessary to warn them that they would require fur coats and caps, snow-shoes, fur sleeping-bags, snow-goggles, and a variety of special outfits for temperature below zero, in addition to drill clothing, tropical gauze, sun-topees, spine-pads, mosquito-nets, and sun-goggles, for extreme heat. Then followed an elaborate list of all these articles as understood by the gentleman describing them in London, and doubtless furnished to him by enterprising firms of outfitters. This was studied by me with the attention the subject demanded, and with considerable amusement.

The next paper, however, was of a nature to eclipse entirely the first in interest, and was to the effect that, as officers detailed for this special service would be called upon to provide themselves with a considerable extra outfit as set forth above, it had been decided that certain financial assistance should be afforded them to enable them to do so. To this end they were authorized, on producing the necessary certificates of their orders, to draw from the pay office for that purpose a special grant of five pounds!

Having duly studied this through a magnifying-glass, it became necessary to devise some means of finding a practical solution to this problem—with which, however, previous experience in a somewhat more modified form had not left me entirely unfamilar. The solution was quickly arrived at, in that all above outfits were for the purpose of protecting the miserable human form of the offcer in question—and the gracious grant of five pounds had the same generous intention.

I therefore concluded that if I got the five pounds inside me in the form of food and drink, it would answer the pur-

---

* The "Hush-Hush" or Phantom Army was known to exist from the fact that officers had been asked to volunteer for it, mostly from the French front, and, having been carefully selected, from that moment they disappeared. All that was known by their friends was that they had gone East on some rather desperate but unknown enterprise.

pose more effectively in either climate than it was likely to do in the form of inadequate *external* protection, and it was at once duly drawn and so expended—with quite satisfactory results.

On May 2nd I left London for the East, having with me one kit-bag, two automatic pistols, my camera, and my two faithful private machine-guns, which had been with me everywhere since August, 1914. On my way across France I stopped and spent the night with my brother, * who had then just been relieved from his rather uncongenial task of British Member of the Allies' Supreme War Council at Versailles, and sent back to reorganize the old Fourth Army to defend Amiens, after the Boche had broken through Gough's Fifth Army.

I found Fourth Army H.Q. in the fine château at Flexicourt, close to Amiens. The old Army staff had been reassembled from the various different posts they had gone off to on the breaking-up of the original Fourth Army, and all were hard at work, and as pleased to be back working with all their old colleagues and friends again as a lot of schoolboys are when they find themselves together again after the holidays.

They were all very well aware how serious and how "tough" was the job in front of them, and all realized the **responsibility** which lay on the Fourth Army to show an impassable front and to hold up the German advance at Amiens, upon which, indeed, the whole future course of the war depended. How well their work was done is now a glorious page of history.

Motoring to Paris, I left for Marseilles on May 7th, arriving next morning to find what was known as the "fast" convoy assembling. This consisted of seven large liners, all about 10,000 tons; these were to be convoyed by five Japanese torpedo-boats, and it was well known that submarine attack was to be expected at any moment.

The *Omrah*, of the Orient Line, was the senior officers' ship, and I was booked for passage on her, and slept that night at the Hôtel Splendide, preparatory to going on board next morning. Marseilles, a town I have known well for a long time, was at that time very interesting, being full of troops of many nations, and odd lots of officers from all parts going

* Then General Sir Henry Rawlinson, commanding the Fourth Army; now Lord Rawlinson, Commander-in-Chief in India.

in every direction; whilst the port was full of shipping and the quays crammed from end to end with all kinds of munitions.

Next day I got my kit and gear down to go on board the *Omrah*, but at the last moment received orders to go and take command of the troops on board another large vessel of 12,000 tons, where I was told things needed "straightening out," as we were to sail at night, and the Boche was waiting outside!

On arriving on board my ship about 4 P. M. I found it a magnificent vessel, and was allotted palatial quarters as O.C. troops; but the rest of the show was not so promising. There were 375 young officers, all full of life and courage, and other things which were less desirable at the moment. However, having had plenty of experience of transports, things soon began to get into shape, and, after selecting an Adjutant, closing the bars, and addressing the gentlemen in very straight terms, we were successful in getting them all told off to their boat-stations and watches before dark; and after calling them to those stations at various times during the night, and going all round myself, impressing on them the vital necessity which existed for them to get to their stations quick, they were capable of making quite a decent show before daylight, when we went out of port. Anyway, once it was understood that it was no pleasure cruise we were going for, but the real thing, with the enemy waiting for us, all turned to with a will and showed the really good stuff of which they were made.

We lay all next day in the roadstead, and were there joined by our five Japanese destroyers. These were smart ships and not to be distinguished from British torpedo-boat destroyers, except by the flag they carried. I was told by those who had been with them before that they could be relied upon to keep at sea in any weather our own destroyers could stand, and probably to keep it up longer, as they carried a complement of seven officers to the British destroyers' three at that time. All being in order, soon after nightfall on May 10th the convoy got under weigh and stood away south on a course to take us west of Corsica and Sardinia, the pre-war course for Malta, passing, of course, *east*, not west, of those islands, so that a considerable detour was made, with the object of avoiding, if pos-

## THE "HUSH-HUSH" ARMY

sible, the cordon of German submarines which was known to be awaiting our very valuable and important convoy.

During the night, no lights being shown, it was impossible to make out in what formation the convoy was steaming, but at daybreak next morning I spent a long half-hour studying our neighbours and our destroyers before calling our troops once more to their stations and then going round the whole ship, including our battery, to make sure that all was in readiness for the attack which might take place at any moment.

The convoy, when the sun finally rose, was a most impressive sight, all the transports being first-class ocean liners, none under 10,000 tons, and all capable of easily maintaining the 15 knots which was our minimum regular speed. We steamed five liners abreast at two ship's length interval, with two destroyers on each flank, the second line, quite closely following, consisting of two more liners and another destroyer. Needless to say, all eyes were everywhere on the look-out for the least "feather" on the surface, which we knew would be first and about the only thing we were likely to see of the attack that was quite certain to come.

Soon after seven my steward brought me tea, and whilst I was drinking it I heard the unmistakable "toot" of a whistle coming from one of the Japanese destroyers on the left flank, we being the second ship from the left. The "toot" is the signal "Can see danger," and on that I made one leap from my bunk into my flannels, grabbed my money first and then my tunic, scarf, tobacco, and glasses, in that order, and raced for the bridge, the captain hailing me as I ran up the deck to come up and stand by him to give orders to the troops.

I was, as may be imagined, moving pretty quick, but a "toot" from the ship immediately on our left made me move smarter still, and I was on the bridge in less than two seconds from the first "toot." Of course, once there, I could see everything, and it was "some" sight. This is what my letter, written the same day, says about it:

"The 'toot' from the left-flank destroyer was followed by a 'toot' from the ship on our left, and immediately after *we* could see the torpedo coming, and we 'tooted' too, as that's the fashionable thing to do when you *see* it. We saw it first about 100 yards away, coming past the stern of the ship on our left; it was coming from the rear of our left flank, and apparently going to hit us straight amidships on our port or left side. It was not coming fast (perhaps 20 miles an hour), and had therefore come at least 2,000 yards, and was slowing down rapidly.

"You could see the 'feather,' a kind of little wave on the surface showing where it was, and also the wake behind showing where it had passed; it appeared quite certain to get us somewhere about amidships, and all the boys on deck stood fast for the 'bump!' Meanwhile the captain and his merry men were putting in some pretty strenuous work, swinging the ship to port—that is, to the left, for all they were worth. They say this ship 'turns quick,' and it was turning its best then, without any manner of doubt. I saw the d——d thing till it went out of my sight behind the deck-house on the bridge, when I couldn't see it any more, and I stood, like everyone else, stock-still, not because I wasn't interested, but for the sake of example, and after what seemed *hours* I was immensely relieved to hear a 'toot' from the ship on our right, which, of course, meant that *they* could see it, and that it had gone past without hitting us. Our people on the aftergun-platform right at the stern tell me it missed our rudder by feet only (some say 5 and some 9 feet), but it passed right under our counter, which is quite close enough for me.

"In the meanwhile the *Omrah,* on our right, couldn't see it until it had *passed us,* as we were in the way, and so *she* had no time at all to turn, and, though it was then going quite slowly, it hit her 'smack' just forward of the bridge, and there was a tidy explosion and a lot of black smoke. The hatches were blown off the fore-hold and all the wreckage fell on the bridge; but we don't know how many were hurt—anyway, she began to settle down by the head pretty well at once, and her stern got higher and higher in the air. All the rest of the convoy cracked on their best speed and began zigzagging about in various directions on the look-out for the next one. Our Japanese destroyers turned round like eels, and the nearest one was off to the place the torpedo came from like lightning, and dropped a 'depth charge,' which exploded under the surface and sent up a great mushroom of water, but I don't know if it got the submarine. The ship on our left fired a couple of rounds from her stern battery, but I couldn't see where the shells went, and I don't suppose they could see any target to shoot at. It was a lovely morning, quite calm, and a wonderful sight. Two destroyers stood by the *Omrah* and commenced to take the people

# THE "HUSH-HUSH" ARMY

off at once, whilst she fell rapidly astern of us, with her stern coming higher and higher out of the water.

"It was a pathetic sight to see this magnificent vessel all down by the head like a wounded thing, and the last we could see of her as she dropped rapidly astern was that she was heading due east (we were steering south), in a quite hopeless endeavor to make the coast of Sardinia, 30 miles away, before she sank. Our people thought she would float, as if the foreward engine-room bulkhead held she could go a long way in that condition; but we had a wireless later to say she had sunk, and that the water got to the furnaces and so finished her off. It was a sad end indeed to such a fine vessel, but it has a side also of which they may well be proud—namely, *that the last boat had left the ship within six minutes (as timed from here by me)*, so there were no casualties other than those due to the explosion, and we hear all are safely on the destroyers, and they will be all right; but, of course, they will lose all their kits, and have a roughish time on the island if they go there.

"Not the least sign of hurry or disturbance either there *or here,* and all as steady and cool as possible, *which is good to see.*

"The result of this morning is we have been sent an extra escort. We have now seven destroyers to six transports instead of five to seven as it was before, and have also had an air-ship with us the greater part of the day. It is also likely more ships will be sent out to meet us from Malta.

"I don't think I have ever seen a more impressive sight than the whole convoy this morning, but far the finest part was the perfectly calm and natural behaviour of one and all. *It was fine.*"

That letter was written on the same afternoon, and the next afternoon Malta came in sight, where we were to coal. As we were stringing out to enter Valetta Harbour, the two destroyers with the complement and passengers of the *Omrah* came by, and we gave them a rousing cheer to buck them up a bit, which was needed, I suspect, as they were packed like sardines in a tin, many, including one General, still in their pyjamas, with bare feet. However, they were sure of a good reception on landing, and things might have been much worse.

The entry of such a large convoy in Valetta Harbour was a most interesting affair, the harbour not being by any means famous for spacious anchorage, and six liners over 10,000 tons and proportionate draft is apt to tax the accommodation of most harbours, even if not already crowded, as Valetta was on this occasion. The great ships came in, one by one, of course, and each had in turn to be "swung"—*i.e.*, turned completely round—to be ready to start again. This operation was most smartly and successfully carried out, and I proceeded ashore, hoping to find Lord Methuen, the Governor, and his wife, my first cousin, whom I had not seen for a long time.

On landing I proceeded to the Palace, where the Governor resides when in Valetta, which is the capital of the island. This Palace is a most famous and interesting building and merits a description all to itself; but as I was later on fortunate enough to stay there as Lord Plumer's guest, it will be more suitably described in a later chapter. On this occasion, to my great regret, I heard that Lady Methuen was absent from the island, organizing hospital accommodation elsewhere, and that the Governor was then at one of the two country palaces which are at the Governor's disposal. A telephone message produced a kind and cordial invitation to go out there (8 miles) to dinner; this was most gratefully accepted, as a ship "coaling" in harbour is a poor place for any man, and I was looking forward to seeing Lord Methuen again and giving him the latest news from the French front, even more than I was to seeing the Palace and enjoying his liberal hospitality. It is a beautiful drive of about 8 miles out to the Palace, and on arriving I had time to go round the wonderful gardens before dinner.

Although the Palace is in itself very interesting, it is the gardens surrounding it which are the feature of the place. Everywhere is running water in old stone water-courses and fountains, and the whole effect is most cool and restful, more like some of the better class of Persian gardens than anything I have seen elsewhere.

At dinner I met the three shipwrecked Generals, and heard at first-hand what had happened on the *Omrah*. Two of the Generals had some clothes of their own, but the third had only some khaki "off the peg" in Valetta, having come ashore in his pyjamas, with bare feet. It appeared they never saw the torpedo coming at all, as our ship blocked their view, and although she actually floated one hour and forty minutes before finally sinking, yet they were all in the boats in six minutes, but being unable to go back for anything, everyone had lost all they had. It was, however, a very cheery dinner, and, of course, my late news of the reorganization of the Fourth Army before Amiens was a joy to everyone. The moonlight drive back to Valetta was a dream of beauty, and I got on board in the small hours to find coaling nearly finished and every prospect of sailing next day.

We sailed from Malta on the 15th, and had an uneventful voyage in very hot and calm weather to Alexandria, the only incident of interest being the forming of the convoy into what they call "line ahead," so as to go single file through the mine-fields outside Alexandria. The sea there is so shallow and the mine-field begins so far out that we formed in single file before the shore was in sight at all, and, to show how intricate the passage was, I have a note that we formed up at 12.15 and did not get alongside till 5 P.M., so taking four and three-quarter hours to come through. This struck me as a very deep defence, and indicated how "unhealthy" these waters were then considered to be!

During the passage I had been suffering from a bad arm, which was getting rapidly worse; it resulted from a pretty severe inoculation at Marseilles, the same being intended to guarantee me against small-pox, enteric, typhoid, and cholera for a start, and I don't know how many other things incidentally. But, anyway, it insured my having a dose of some of those complaints, and I felt ill enough to be having them *all* at the same time, and my arm swelled so I could not put on my tunic on landing.

Having seen the ship clear of troops and signed all the thousand and one necessary papers, I went up next day and reported at Headquarters, and found an old friend in the G.O.C., who said I could go right on via Cairo, so I telephoned to another old and good friend, Major Fred Stern, who was then doing D.A.Q.M.G. at Cairo, to say I was coming, and he asked me to stay at his house there, which I was very glad to do, especially as I much feared I was going to be pretty bad. I got on to Cairo in the afternoon, and Fred Stern met me in his car and took me to his charming house on the island in the Nile. On arrival I had to go to bed and send for the doctor, as it looked as if I was going to be laid up, which would have been terribly hard, when so much interesting work lay immediately before me.

The doctor pulled a very long face when he saw my arm, which he said was the worst he had ever seen. He seemed to think it would have to be cut off! But I was d——d sure it would have to be "left on," as I'd had surgeons proposing to cut limbs off me before, and thus far had always been able successfully to resist their anxiety to operate. Anyway, it looked bad enough, being terribly swollen right up to and into the shoulder, a horrible colour, and quite dead to the touch, and more like a bit of pretty hot metal, or the branch of a tree with some tiny little fingers at the end, than an arm of flesh and blood. My temperature, meanwhile, was threatening to burst the thermometer—a bad state in which to face the Red Sea, Persian Gulf, Mesopotamia, and Persia, and I believe my friend Stern thought I was "for the box," which is the expressive military term for a fatal casualty. However, we set to work and poulticed and massaged, and after about three days in bed I heard there would be a ship at Suez next day, and I rose up and "hopped it" to the station—a bit shaky and unable to wear a coat, but not in the least disposed to give in. My good and most kind friend Stern, I feel sure, thought he would never see me again; and as yet he has not, but I hope he soon will now, that I may have an opportunity to thank him for his kindness, which quite certainly saved my arm and quite likely my life.

The rail journey from Cairo to Suez via Ismalia is no joy-ride in summer, even in peace-time, and rail travelling is certainly no *more* comfortable in war-time. However, on this occasion I was lucky in that I enjoyed a perfectly unique military show from the train between Ismalia and Suez. Somewhere in these parts the Australian cavalry were training, and soon after leaving Ismalia I became aware that a cavalry advance in line, on a large scale, was in progress parallel to the railway and about level with the train. This was the Australians training for the advance which they eventually made against the Turks, with the results that prove beyond dispute the value of cavalry in open country, as they fairly put the fear of God into the Turks, and so started the *débâcle* which, spreading to other fronts, finally showed the war was won.

Having as a young officer done regimental duty through several cavalry camps of exercise in the East, I was quite competent to judge of the remarkable show I was fortunate enough to be so well placed to see. It was in every way excellent, better than anything of the kind I had ever seen before, and covering a much greater distance at a much faster rate than I had hitherto thought possible; while the general control of the advance and the individual horsemanship and initiative was a revelation indeed.

The country in the neighbourhood of the Canal and railway is sandy, scrubby desert, with frequent groups of sandhills, and in places quite dense scrub. The line extended as far as I could see on either side, a front of a good many miles; the troops engaged, therefore, could not have been *less* than a brigade, and were more likely a cavalry division.

In spite of all obstacles, the very long general line was excellent throughout, and although all scrubby ground was gone through and made good wherever I could see it, yet by hard riding the line was kept, and the speed of the general advance exceeded the speed of my train—which, if it was not a Scotch express, kept, all the same, moving decently along *all the time*—and at the end of quite 10 miles the line halted *in advance of the train*.

I would have liked—and, in fact, I longed—to see those concerned and to congratulate them on the show; also to see their horses and their methods in the lines, as only first-class horsemanship in camp can produce such excellent work in the field. I went on my journey with the confidence that men that could *train* like that in that country were liable to make the Turk "smell hell" in about the same fashion as he had been in the habit in the past of making others smell it; and when they got the chance they did just that. I remember well how sad I felt that I was not to have any such troops along with me; however, they were best where they were, and would have been wasted elsewhere.

We reached Suez at midday, and it looked as uninviting and hot as ever. I was fortunate to get a ramshackle Egyptian cab and pair of ponies to take me to the Embarkation Officer's office, as walking at all during midday in those parts is not a good kind of medicine for a sick man. However, on arrival I found that estimable officer was not there, and wouldn't be till about 4 P. M. So I adjourned to a fifth or tenth class café near-by, where I waited his convenience, and as soon as he went by, returning from his lunch, about three hours later, followed him to find out when the ship was due. He was in his office when I got there, and as I could not wear a coat, and had therefore no badges on, he had no idea who I was, and, being much impressed by the fact that he ranked as a Major, took no notice of me, and continued his conversation with some of his friends who had come to assist him to pass the "working" hours. This was illuminating, and explained much that I had heard as to embarkations at Suez. However, in due course he ascertained who I was, and was then as civil as he knew how—being, I judged, a bit out of practice. The ship, I learned, was alongside the pier and was not to sail for two days, as she was waiting for Army Service Corps drafts, and I was to be O.C. troops. The ship was a P. and O., *Kashgar* by name, still running in their Eastern service in 1922—a splendid vessel, commanded by Captain Cockman, D.S.C., one of the best fellows it has ever been my good fortune to meet. But about him more later.

On going on board, I found my quarters on the boat deck aft very comfortable, but no one about. I had a solitary dinner with the skipper, and made friends in exchanging a very wide and varied lot of experiences, turning in about 10 P. M. Night very hot, not to say sultry, and my arm very painful.

The troops duly arrived on board next day, and we started, at daylight on the 27th, down the Red Sea.

It was my fifth trip through that very trying part of the world, and much the worst of the five.

The Red Sea, in my experience, is always *hot*, and no adjective I can write here can properly describe the heat. There is occasionally a wind, and often a calm; you may therefore either *meet* the wind, in which case it is pleasant, or you may (rarely) have a beam wind, in which case the heat is bearable, or, if it is calm, you get a draught from the speed of the vessel through the still air; but occasionally you get a *follow-*

*ing* wind, which is the very devil, and it was so in this case—and we *gasped*. I have a note that I couldn't write without a separate piece of paper under my hand, which otherwise wouldn't slide along when writing, and that the thermometer was 92° at midnight, with all the doors open and electric fans going, and everything soaking wet from the moisture.

We rigged up a great sail as a bath for the men, and they were in it all day and all night, in batches of twelve at a time, and enjoyed it thoroughly.

Aden, generally a most dismal place, was reached on the 28th. It was at this time more interesting than it has ever been, either before or since, as the Turks were besieging the town. The siege was somewhat of the comic opera kind, as the belligerents fired at each other occasionally only, and that at excessive range, and this firing was said only to take place when the Turks did not allow the fresh vegetables to be brought in from the mainland! This was the report, for the accuracy of which I cannot vouch. However, the siege made no difference to our coaling there. The coaling was done from lighters by "Seedi boys." These are African natives, who made such a noise in their hundreds, by all shouting at the same time at the top of their voices, that on board one could hardly hear oneself speak. However, they were extremely efficient, and the job was done quickly and well, and we were away again at daylight on the 30th, on the long, hot, and tedious passage through the Arabian Sea and Persian Gulf to the mouth of the Euphrates.

On May 31st we had wireless news that the Bosche submarines had sunk another of our "fast" convoy on their return passage from Alexandria to Marseilles, so it appeared they were keeping pretty busy, and it was a relief to us all to hear that, as far as was known, there were no German submarines east of Suez.

Going still east, on leaving Aden we found so much moisture in the air that it amounted to a regular fog, an unusual phenomenon in these latitudes, where the sun usually reigns supreme. No doubt people accustomed to our old English climate will think that, there being no sun, the weather would be cooler! But that's just where they would be wrong, as our young soldiers soon began to find out. The heat was stifling on this occasion, and, everything being wringing wet, our soldier-boys began to find out something about "prickly heat," a most unpleasant experience which most people have at one time or another in those parts.

Prickly heat, for the information of those who are fortunate enough not to have made its acquaintance, is an excessive irritation of the pores of the skin from continuous perspiration, and the effect of it is a terribly trying and intolerable itching, which causes an overwhelming inclination to scratch. This one has to learn to resist, and about the only way to learn that hard but necessary lesson is *to scratch,* and see what happens! Having done so once, it is extremely unlikely that you will do so again, as it only increases the irritation. We had a good few of our men in hospital on that account in a very short time, whilst the rest were all each one more uncomfortable than the next all the way round the ship. To add to their discomfort, as we began to get out towards the Indian Ocean we began to get the ocean roll caused by the monsoon, which had already (May 31st) begun to blow across the other side on the Indian coast. So we had a glassy sea, a temperature of 96° on the bridge, a flat calm, a heavy fog, and a real ocean swell, and I note without surprise in my letter written at that time that the captain and I dined *alone!*

This Captain Cockman was a splendid fellow in every way. I believe he was about the senior of the P. and O. captains at that time, and was and is known and liked far and wide by all who have met him. He told me of his experiences of torpedoes, and no one was better qualified to do so, as his experience was, if not unique, yet certainly as glorious as any one else's; and here it is as I wrote it down that day.

This old hero, who had been many years in H.M.'s Navy and retired as a Commander, found himself in command of a P. and O. in 1915, and when about to enter Plymouth Harbour his ship was struck by a Bosche torpedo, which sank her. Whilst *he* was sinking, however, he was *fighting,* not squealing, and he *sank the submarine* from his own sinking ship before she finally went down; for which he received a thoroughly well-deserved D.S.C. from His Majesty at Buckingham Palace.

The eastern coast of Arabia is very rarely seen by any one, as ships don't often coast along there, all regular commercial traffic going east to Bombay or Karachi when coming out of the Persian Gulf, and therefore it was interesting to see the coast, which is quite different and much more inviting than the Red Sea coast, though that does not in consequence make it any "oil-painting!" Down the Red Sea from Sinai to Aden there is not one blade of any kind of grass, shrub, or vegetation, but all is sand and rocks, and over the whole is a quivering heat which makes all objects dance about as you look at them. The eastern coast, however, is better, due, I suppose, to its getting a share, though a small one, of the annual monsoon wind. I don't think it gets any of the "rain" which the monsoon brings, and upon which India depends for its fertility; but no doubt there is a freshening moisture in the wind itself, blowing up from the south-west, which suffices to clothe the slopes from the high desert uplands down to the coast with pretty dense scrub of sorts, so that the quivering glare of the red-hot, naked rocks is absent, and does not recur till round the eastern point the cliffs begin again.

We rounded that point about midday on June 3rd, in a damp heat as bad as ever, and stood up the coast north-west to pass close to Muscat on our way to the straits at the entrance to the Persian Gulf. Muscat is worth a word or two; it is said to be the hottest place on earth. That may be so to sailors, few of whom have ever seen the Caspian Sea, to which I am prepared unhesitatingly to give the prize. However, in the meanwhile Muscat will do to go on with, as it certainly has no chance as a pleasure resort.

The town, such as it is—just a very old Arab pirate fortress—stands at the foot of sandstone cliffs on which are cut the names of many ships which have had the misfortune to be stationed there. The cliffs are from 500 to 800 feet high, in a little bay facing south, so that they are exposed to the sun all day, and get pretty well red-hot. The reader, therefore, may *try* to realize what the atmosphere is like in the little narrow donkey-paths which are the only streets in the old town.

At Muscat lives an Arab Sheikh—descended, curiously enough, from an Englishman—whose history makes a rather interesting tale. It appears that in Elizabethan days, when the first British adventurers reached those seas, having sailed round the Cape of Good Hope with the intention of establishing trade with Persia, they found that Muscat was the home of the *élite* of the pirates of those days. These gentlemen (the Arab pirates) appear to have been very powerful, and, from the tales which are still told in the bazaars about them, they were in the habit of "drinking blood," and had many other even less attractive habits. However, on its arrival, the English ship and crew promptly disappeared, and how much blood was drunk on that occasion was not recorded. The only outstanding fact which is on record is that the ship's barber alone was kept alive, as a slave, owing to his proficiency with his razor, upon which the somewhat peculiar customs of the Arabs led them to place a high value.

In due course the barber, making adequate use of his exceptional opportunities, became extremely popular with the numerous and influential female occupants of the zenana, or harem, of the pirate King, or Sheikh, and with such success did he wield his razor that the ladies soon saw to it that he was afforded an opportunity of exercising his skill upon the pirate chief's throat. The barber, being, apparently, in no way lacking in enterprise, took instant advantage of his opportunity, and promptly and effectually cut the throat that in the past had ordered so many others to be similarly treated. His friends and supporters immediately placed the barber on the throne, to fill the vacancy created by his razor, and he reigned over the whole coast long and gloriously, and there his descendants reigned after him, and do so reign to this day!

On reflection it will doubtless be appreciated that in those parts the barber's trade is indeed an influential one, and the reason for this is in no way difficult to understand if it is borne in mind that in those parts of Arabia, as in most Eastern countries, the men usually remain unshaved.

Leaving Muscat at 4 P. M. on June 3rd, and steering northwest, we continued to experience all the delights (?) of a truly tropical voyage, and as we approached the Straits of Ormuz at the entrance to the Persian Gulf, the mountains, which now commenced to come right down to the sea, got barer of scrub and hotter and hotter, till the cliffs were a good thousand feet high, quite bare of vegetation, quivering with heat in the daytime and retaining the heat at night, so that as we approached them such air as there was came off the cliffs like the blast of a furnace.

I have a note written that night to the effect that the thermometer on the bridge registered 98° at midnight, and that I sat there to get the draught caused by the ship's travelling through the soaking air, with a pair of tropical drill shorts on —nothing else at all—and streaming with perspiration! Needless to say, there was no sleep for any one. Stopping on the bridge all night, the scene at daylight was well worth much of the discomfort which we had been experiencing. As the day broke, the Straits of Ormuz came in sight, and the sun-baked mountains became bolder, grander, and many thousand feet higher, whilst the sea became dotted with many rocky and precipitous islets of all sizes, through which we threaded our way up to the extreme north-eastern point of Arabia. This ends in a sheer cliff of several thousand feet, with deep water close in, and the coast of Persia showing up a few miles away in the form of a great bay into which the great rocky mountain cape of Arabia juts out, making a most impressive gateway to the sea and country which challenge old Egypt's claim as the *oldest* and, in dim antiquity, the *richest* country on the earth.

We had a pleasant trip up the gulf until nearing the mouth of the Euphrates, when we hit a dust-storm straight from the desert, and the air so full of sand you couldn't see your hand before your face, and hardly breathe. It was the first dust-storm most of our men had seen, and they didn't like it. However, they were learning something every day, and we had them trained to a much more amenable frame of mind than when they came on board at Suez.

We poked about trying to find a lightship which should have been somewhere about those parts, at the mouth of the great river; but we had no luck with it in the dust-storm, and so as soon as we got into soundings (*i.e.*, shallow water) down went the anchor, at midnight, June 5th, to wait for daylight.

Mesopotamia at last, 3,350 miles, and 14 days out from Suez, and 5,500 miles, and 32 days out from London.

We lay at anchor till daylight, and got wireless orders during the night to keep on up the river next morning. So the anchor was weighed as soon as we could see to get our bearings, and I said good-bye to the sea and salt water till I could pick up the Caspian Sea, a good 700 miles away as the crow flies, and more than double that distance by the way I should have to go, across as wild a country as any one can wish for—*through* one enemy in arms, then to take ship and tackle another and stronger enemy on the far side of the great inland Caspian Sea.

# CHAPTER II

### MESOPOTAMIA, THE LAND OF THE RIVERS

The great Euphrates River—German obstruction of navigation—Bussrah—The port and its growth—The I.G.C.—Reflections on past prosperity and present prospects of the country—The river steamer—The rivers—Their transport value and difficulties—Troops' accommodation—The junction of Tigris and Euphrates—The Garden of Eden—Ezra's Tomb—Amora—Loss of a man overboard—The desert Arabs and their camps—Their horses—Distant mountains of Persia—Kut—River windings—Report G.H.Q.—Bagdad—Orders to leave at night—Hospital—Convalescent home—Commander-in-Chief's house—Town and bazaars of Bagdad—Army Boxing Final—Departure by Decauville Railway.

At 7.30 A. M. on June 6th we entered the great Euphrates River, one of the mightiest of the great rivers of the earth.

The value of this river to the countries it traverses is comparable only to the Nile, as in each case the waters are the life-blood of vast tracts of land on either side, which by irrigation have from time immemorial been transformed from a burning desert into the great corn-bearing lands known to the ancient races whose home they were in the dim ages of antiquity.

There is, however, and always has been, a fundamental difference between Egypt, the land of the Nile, and Mesopotamia, the valley of the Euphrates; for whereas the Nile by its annual floods causes an automatic irrigation and fertilization of the country, the Euphrates has no such regular annual flood, and the spreading of its fertilizing waters over the land has ever been dependent on the skill and labour of the inhabitants. In ancient days that skill and labour were always forthcoming, until the advent of the Turk effectually put a stop to any such useful enterprise or labour, and allowed the ancient irrigation works to decay and fall in ruins, as had already fallen the great Empires of Assyria and Babylon.

The crumbling ruins of the great irrigation works of a bygone age, and the shapeless mounds of sand, standing as they do to-day in an uncultivated plain, are all that are now left to mark the sites of Nineveh, Babylon, and other great cities, each in their way the wonder of the ancient world, where a thriving and industrious population devoted all their energies to the intelligent cultivation of the land, and, by their labour alone, for centuries made of that now unproductive plain "the granary of the human race." What a pathetic commentary is here upon the blighting effect of the old Turkish Imperial rule—which effect has been unfailingly reproduced in every country where that curse has fallen, whatever may before have been the industry of its people or the wealth of their prosperity!

The Euphrates River during the last 70 miles of its course from Bussrah to the sea is about the width of the Thames at Gravesend, and ships of 10,000 tons, or even more, can ascend it with ease. The land on either bank is a flat, marshy plain, but the banks everywhere are lined with plantations of date-palms, which, being evergreen, show up well against the sandy and monotonous background, and tend to give a general impression of fertility and cultivation.

The most interesting sight after leaving the coast was the ships sunk in the river by the Germans at the outbreak of the war. I examined them as we passed with great curiosity, as I could see at once that they must have been previously specially loaded with rocks and prepared for the purpose, and it was yet one more sign of the thoroughness of German preparedness, that they had ready beforehand in this remote spot the means of blocking the river to British vessels; and though, of course, no such defence could last long, yet they considered even the small delay that might result was worth the trouble it cost.

We saw nothing more of interest until entering the long, straight reach of the river, where the great British base at Bussrah has grown like a large mushroom in so short a time, from an insignificant old native river town.

We anchored our great ship a mile or more above the British Military Headquarters, and I got a launch of sorts and went down and across the stream to report and take orders.

The Headquarters, presided over by Major-General Sir George MacMunn, the I.G.C. (as is called the Inspector-General of Communications), was in a large and well-planned brick building of two, if not three, floors facing the river, with many clerks and offices on the ground floor and large rooms and spacious

## TRAVELLING ON THE TIGRIS, JUNE, 1918

A troop steamer with double-decked barge lashed alongside

British troops on the barge

## THE TIGRIS RIVER
### From the Convalescent Home near Bagdad

View down-stream

View up-stream towards the city

verandahs in the Chief's own quarters on the first floor. I got a most courteous and hearty reception from all the H.Q. staff, from the Chief himself downwards, and an invitation to move over there as soon as I squared up my returns and handed over my troops. And so back to the ship, to spend the last night on board, after a pretty tough trip of sixteen days from Suez.

Next day I got all my work done and handed over my troops in time to get to H.Q. to lunch with the I.G.C. All were too busy for much talk at lunch, but I was given a hut in the garden for quarters, and the loan of a car to have a look round and fit myself out with tropical gear from the military ordnance stores at the base.

Sallying forth in a car about 6 P. M., I got all I needed in the way of tropical kit of the right sort, signing for it against future "emoluments"—*i.e.*, pay—which was a whole heap better than buying quite likely unsuitable stuff, to the value of £5, in London—at London prices, and for *cash*.

In due course I got back to dinner at Headquarters, which was presided over by that most interesting and enlightened personality, the I.G.C.

I remember that dinner well, and that, after I had given them the latest news from the French front and answered a small proportion of the many questions fired at me, I was tackled by the I.G.C. generally, on the ancient history of this most ancient country. My father\* having spent many years here and having been the recognized authority on Nineveh and Babylon antiquities, I conclude I was expected to possess a considerable portion of the knowledge it had taken him a large slice of a lifetime to acquire; and though, of course, I was pretty familiar with the subject—in that stories of Sennacherib, Nebuchadnezzar, Darius, and such-like, had formed the greater part of my entertainment in my nursery days— yet I was astounded to find the vast amount of knowledge and information which was fluently disclosed by my host, and his practical views of possible future developments based upon his own experience of the country at the present day.

I should consider it very unlikely he retains those views

---

\* Major-General Sir H. Rawlinson, Bart., G.C.B., the famous archæologist, the original decipherer of the dead cuneiform language and the last surviving director of the old East India Company.

to-day, but *I* retain the most vivid recollection of the impression his stores of accurate information of the past and his confidence as to the future left on my mind. Here, again, was a quite exceptional personality, holding a peculiar and important post, and evidences of his energetic activity were to be seen then, and are still, everywhere throughout the country to which he has striven so hard to restore some portion of its ancient prosperity.

It was hot at this time even for Mesopotamia, being 104° in the first-floor verandah overlooking the river, after sundown, at 8.30 P. M., and about the same all night, and 120° to 130° inside during the day, with the electric fans going, so that I was glad indeed when all my preparations were made and I was ready to start up the great river at daylight next morning, and so enter a country of the greatest interest, but one which was then quite new to me.

Soon after daylight on June 8th I embarked on the river steamer which was to take me up the great Tigris River to Bagdad, and here was "novelty" indeed, as there was nothing anywhere which was like anything I'd ever seen before.

The first outstanding object to absorb my attention was the steamer itself—an absolutely new type of vessel to me. In order to adequately appreciate by what chain of circumstances it came to be here at all, it is necessary to bear in mind the peculiarities of the river itself, and the events for which it had provided the "setting" and been itself the "scene" during the two immediately preceding years of war.

In marked contrast to the Euphrates, which is a "slow" and "sluggish" river, the "Djala Zu," or Tigris, runs fast, through the sandy plain in which its course is constantly changing, sandbanks being quickly formed in some places, and as quickly swept away in others, so that a shallow draft is as indispensable to a steamer to enable her to keep afloat as are powerful engines to enable her to ascend against the stream. Add to this the fact that during the British advance to Bagdad the river formed practically the main and only means of transport in bulk for the supply of the troops, and it is not hard to realize the exceptional transport difficulties with which our forces were confronted, but which were in the end, as usual, satisfactorily overcome.

The immediate result of these exceptional requirements was a great search and requisitioning of all the shadow-draft steamers which could be found in every hole and corner of the Dominions. The steamer upon which I now found myself had quite lately been tackling the equally difficult waters of the Irrawady, the great river of Burmah. She was, it seems needless to observe, hardly a *Lusitania*, and sleeping-cabins, except two small box-like erections on the upper deck, were conspicuous by their absence. However, she had good engines, by Denny of Dumbarton, perhaps the most satisfactory part of the whole show, and their regular and unfailing power was transmitted to the water by a method quite new to me—namely, a "stern-wheel."

Another striking novelty was the fact that two great flat-bottomed barges, nearly as broad and long as the steamer, were lashed one on each side of her. The object of this somewhat unusual form of "rig" is that when, as she often does, the steamer bumps the bank, it is the barge that takes the bump or goes aground, the steamer itself being spared that very searching trial. This considerably improves what chance there may be of continuing the passage without spending many hours aground, or, in the even worse case, of being stopped entirely by some structural injury to the vessel. Although those very unsightly barges form in the first instance shields for the steamer, yet incidentally they also form transports, and on this occasion were packed with troops, both British and Indian natives, whilst the officers only were accommodated—that is, could, and did, sit and lie—on the deck of the steamer itself.

On this in no way spacious deck, on this occasion, were "parked" over seventy officers, with all their kits and belongings, and though we frizzled there for ten solid days, no one had a word of grumbling to say about it, and all were content, as we were moving on towards our goal, and as long as we moved we got some air. But when we got aground and stood still it could be remarked what a wealth of variety of anathema the English language is capable of producing—to say nothing of the very considerable amount of "chat" emanating from the native troops, who were so closely packed on their barge alongside that they were obliged to take it in turns to "sit down!"

The first day out of Bussrah we passed the junction of the Euphrates and Tigris; but as the country there is a huge marsh —which, in fact, is the form in which the Euphrates joins the Tigris—the actual junction was not apparent and did not in any way attract attention. During the night we passed through the "Garden of Eden," or rather the place where tradition has placed the earthly paradise of the ancients. We have been brought up to think of this as having been a most desirable retreat, the outstanding feature of which was that no clothes were worn there. Well, in those days it may, or may not, have been a pleasant retreat, but I have no doubt at all that no clothes were ever worn there, as certainly when we went through even the Biblical fig-leaf would have seemed like "winter clothing," the damp heat was so oppressive.

About midday on our second day we passed Ezra's Tomb, a very ancient holy place, now maintained by subscriptions from Jews in all parts of the world. Here is the ancient tomb, surrounded by several courtyards of rather pretentious buildings of mud bricks, with a tower in the centre crowned by a remarkable Oriental dome of ancient construction, whose surface is entirely covered with the real old sky-blue glazed tiles which were a beautiful feature of the famous buildings of Babylonian days, and are still to be found scattered about on the most venerable relics of past ages which are the salient features of this otherwise most monotonous country.

The tomb in these days forms in reality a kind of hotel, presided over by a Jewish priest, whose staff consists entirely of experienced midwives—although exactly in what the priest's own particular speciality may consist I was unable to discover. However, it appears Jewish women, who are about to have the great honour of "doing their bit" towards the continuance of the chosen race, are in the habit of retiring to this spot as the critical moment approaches, in order that the future "Ikey" may get his first view of the world from the precincts of the holy place, and it may be presumed, under the auspices of the expert priest, which combination they are taught will insure that a child so born will lead a specially holy and successful life!

However, whether that may be so or not, the old tomb, with its sky-blue dome sparkling in the Mesopotamian sun, forms the most prominent feature of the otherwise sadly monontonous landscape for many miles.

After passing old Ezra's somewhat remarkable resting-place, the river becomes narrower and the eternal groves of date-palms come nearer together, the river about here being about the width of the Thames at Richmond.

About halfway between Bussrah and Kut is Amora. This is quite a decent-sized place, with now a railway station and a depôt for stores, with the usual hospitals, rest-camps, etc. The great feature, however, is the bridge of boats, the first yet seen, and the *only* one from Bagdad to the sea, a distance of quite 400 miles as the crow would fly if he was there—which he is much too wise to be—and quite three times as far following the interminable windings of the river, as we were perforce obliged to do.

The reach at Amora is long and straight, the river being much broader there than for many miles below, and on leaving this reach the width compared with the Hudson River above New York; but at the same time became very shallow in places, with low banks and many sandbanks. Our course therefore zigzagged about from one side to the other, the course being steered according to indication-posts placed on either bank, and constantly changed as the sandbanks formed or disappeared, to give the pilots a reasonable chance of keeping afloat —which, in our case, we duly proceeded *not* to do. However, even this had its compensations at that particular moment, for as the banks got lower and the country marshier, the groves of date-palms which had covered the banks all the way up from the sea now disappeared, and let us get a breath of a God-sent breeze, blowing south over the marsh from the distant mountains which bound the high uplands of Persia and now appeared like a dim, dark cloud far away to the north. The only happening of interest about here was the loss of one of the native troops overboard. They had been warned again and again not to sit on the side, but they would still do so, with their legs hanging over to get the splashing of the water; and a sudden bump pitched this poor fellow overboard, where he had no chance at all, and the stern-wheel promptly "ate him up." However, this incident had more effect on the others than all the orders I had published, and sitting on the side became, for a time at any rate, a much less popular pastime.

We now began to leave the country where any cultivation is done in these days, and opened out the pasture country, the true home of the real nomadic, or wandering, Arabs. The wealth of these tribes lies to-day entirely in their flocks and herds, as has always been the case since the days of old Abraham; but above all in their horses, which are well enough known and valued the world over to need no praise from me.

The villages or camps of these wandering Arabs are queer places. We saw and passed close to many on the river-banks in crossing these great open plains. They consist of just a small collection of tents or hovels, just sticks stuck in the ground and covered with reeds cut on the river-bank and plastered with mud. Sometimes, in the case of a Chief or Sheikh, his home will consist of a great sheet of cloth woven from the hair of his camels, which sheet will also be plastered with mud, to give it weight in the wind and keep off the fierce rays of the Mesopotamian sun, the one great force which dominates every form of life in those parts.

These hovels slope up from the back over a cross-pole, or, in some cases, over two cross-poles, and are invariably in a position facing and close to the river-bank, and are open at the sides, to get all the benefit possible of the cooler air off the water. In most cases the front can be lowered at night, and so give some small amount of privacy, upon which, however, the Arab sets small value. Again and again, in passing close inshore, I was able to study through my excellent field-glasses the minutest intimate details of the Arab's home-life in his tent, cooking, eating, sleeping, and bathing, without such curiosity causing either the Arab himself or his wives, daughters, and dependents generally, the smallest concern. The thing that struck me most amongst the habits of these communities was the position occupied by the horses in the home circle. This is such as is hardly to be realized by those familiar with the horse as he is known in any country.

From the time of his birth the Arab's steed is a respected

and most highly valued member of the family circle, the foals as well as their parents sharing in the family meals in the tent and being at all times as free to take advantage of its invaluable shade during the day as of its equally welcome protection from the dew at night. The insult of a bridle is one that many of them never experience, and the Arab Chief would be far more likely to tie up his *wife* or *daughter* than he would be to offer his *horse* such an insult—in which conclusion it is quite probable that his experience of *both* affords him ample justification.

It is this treatment for centuries past which gives to the Arab horse his supreme confidence in himself and makes him what he is, the king amongst the horses of all countries, as he knows not, nor ever *has* known, fear, neither of his master nor of anything else. He behaves himself, accordingly, with uniform reason and propriety, and his general behaviour and self-control might be imitated with advantage by many so-called "civilized" human beings elsewhere.

These encampments, so inimitably and immortally described as "the tents of the Arabs, which they silently fold when they steal away," are always pitched where the pasture at the moment is best and the water plentiful and easy of access, and are moved frequently and without difficulty as the feed offered for the flocks by the surrounding country becomes better in other sites. The flocks which constitute the sole wealth of the Sheikhs consist of horses, in the first place, and also of camels, cattle, sheep and goats, and donkeys, and these wander at their own sweet will around the encampments, all coming readily at their master's call, at daybreak and sunset, to give their milk, which is the greatest luxury of the true desert.

I was on several occasions fortunate in seeing an Arab, wakened fresh from sleep by the passage of our steamer, come from his tent and, calling his horse, leap on its back, where he sat entirely and obviously at home, without thought of saddle or bridle. They then together proceeded at a canter, with equal grace and mutual confidence, to make the round of the flocks to see to their welfare, such being the daily and exclusive occupation of the true Arab and his desert steed.

Hereabouts we obtained our first clear view of the Persian mountains, which were now seen rising sheer out of the plain about 30 miles north of the river. They looked very high, though I knew they were not more than 5,000 feet, and therefore babies compared to the snow-topped giants of more than three times that height amongst which my path would lie 500 miles or more farther on. We here passed through the Turkish lines which were laid out by the German staff of the Turkish Army. These trench systems extended for miles on either side of the river, and fulfilled the object of their construction, which was to hold up the British force which was rushed up the river to the relief of Kut.

The town of Kut is by no means impressive, being a collection of mud hovels surrounded by a mud wall, the whole lying within a large loop of the river, which offered the only feature of any military defensive value. It was obvious at first glance that nothing but dire necessity could have occasioned its selection for the last and gallant stand the British troops made there before their ultimate and disastrous, though unavoidable surrender.

On leaving Kut the course of the river becomes, if possible, even more sinuous than before; so much so that one spot, marked by a small mound crowned by a permanent if humble building, was approached by us quite closely from three different directions in turn. To illustrate further the nature of the country and the rapidity of our progress in the true direction of our goal, there were in sight at this place at the same time three different steamers ahead of us and three behind us in the various loops, though each was separated from the other by many hours of river travel!

In the early morning of June 15th the minarets of Bagdad became visible. At 12 noon that day we tied up at a military wharf, after eight days of the Mesopotamian river in June, a two days quicker passage than we expected, but one which provided me with all the experience I shall ever require of that form of travel.

Leaving the disembarkation to be superintended by others, I got a launch and went 5 miles up the river to report at G.H.Q., but found that the Commander-in-Chief, Lieut.-General Sir W. Marshall, to whom I had several letters and whom I was most anxious to meet, was absent, organizing the final advance, which was then being prepared for, with the great secrecy indispensable to its success.

At Headquarters I heard I was detailed to leave that same evening for the wilds, in command of a convoy of 300 cars, which left me only a few hours to get all my kit, and that with a temperature of 115° in the hotel courtyard, the coolest place to be found, seeing it had a fountain in the middle and punkahs and fans all round, and in any case no sun could ever penetrate there. However, as there was no moment to spare, and so much to do, I was forced to go to work in the heat of the day, when all others were resting in the cool, and, worst of all, though I was promised a car, yet, as it did not turn up quickly, I had to start out on my feet—an unheard-of proposition at midday in midsummer in these parts.

I did my best, but within an hour I was gasping for breath and "down and out," so that when the car *did* come I was just able to tell the driver to go for a doctor. This he did, and brought him "on the run." The doctor had one look at me and one at his thermometer, giving my temperature, and phoned straight to the hospital for an ambulance, which got me there in double-quick time. I just remember that, and then a blank for some days, during which time I lay unconscious; and an official telegram was sent to the War Office, and forwarded by them to my wife and brother, saying: "General hospital announce Col. R. dangerously ill." My brother, getting that, knew well it meant "No hope," as no such wires are sent whilst a chance remains. However, my wife, thanks to some special gift which God has given her, and of which, without the least understanding it, I have had conclusive evidence on subsequent similar occasions, entirely refused even to consider the possible accuracy of such a statement, and maintained stoutly that, though I might be "looking dead," yet in fact I wasn't, which was actually the true state of the case; though how she could *know* it with certainty, not even knowing what might or might not have happened to me, is one of those cases which I make no pretence of understanding or explaining, but am content to give the bare facts.

After being unconscious in hospital twenty-four hours, my temperature came down and not much harm had been done, but I was very weak and tottery, and was kept lying down for three more days, without being allowed to get up. I was, no doubt, in a very weak state, my over-inoculations having left me far from fit to come through as I had, at such a time of year; but the fever appeared to have mostly attacked my "inside," and all the time I was tied down in bed I was given nothing to eat, and my drink appears to have alternated between milk in plenty and castor oil. This, though it does not sound appetizing, was none the less very effective, and in a week I was considered fit to move, and *did* move, to the convalescent home on the river-bank, 5 miles down-stream—a bit weak and very thin, but being otherwise all right.

In my letter from the home is noted the fact that the temperature in the verandah and balcony of my room, there looking over the river, was 113° at 8 A. M., before the sun got its power at full blast, and 130° at 5.30 P. M. in the same place; though what it was when the sun was hottest at midday, I had not apparently had the strength or courage to go and see. It appears that, having had no mosquito-nets coming up the river, I had been pretty badly stung by sand-flies—that curse of Mesopotamia—which brutes had inoculated me with their own special form of fever, about the only one my friends at Marseilles had omitted from their otherwise very complete assortment of inoculations.

My own recollections now of that time are that the rest and comfort of the hospital, and the care, skill, and attention of the nurses, were heavenly, and only marred by the rather brutal statement of a very self-satisfied junior medical officer, whose experience of the East certainly did not equal my own, that I should never be any good in that climate as I was too old, and ought therefore to be sent home at once! If that same gentleman had repeated that same remark to me a little later on, when I was a bit stronger, it would have afforded me the very greatest satisfaction to demonstrate his error to him without delay in a thoroughly effective manner.

At lunch on second day of my stay at the convalescent home I was called to the phone to speak to the Commander-in-Chief's house. I rushed to the phone, and was told the Chief had just returned, and had got the letter I had brought him from

Sir H. Wilson, and that if I would come and stay with him at his house he would send an A.D.C. with his own launch to fetch me at once, and also a car for my kit and a servant to look after it! No doubt of my answer to such a glorious invitation, and within an hour down came the launch and car, and I went off in state to his lovely house, built right on the river, with great big rooms, cool courtyards, and a spacious terrace with steps to his private pier and landing-stage!

This was luxury indeed for me, and I knew well that I should have, thanks to his kindness, the best chances of "picking up" quickly and so getting on up-country at the earliest moment. In the big house all was in the highest state of efficiency—no kind of ostentation, but everything was the best of its kind: electric fans, ice, a first-class cook and servants, a launch on the river, and cars for the city.

The party in the house consisted only of the Chief himself, his Chief of the Staff, the military secretary, two aides-de-camp, and myself; and of course I got all the latest information from Persia, and was able to give them what was of perhaps even more interest to them than their news was to me—that is, a first-hand account of how things were going "before Amiens" at the real heart and vital centre of the war.

The three days which I passed as the Chief's guest were spent in laying in stores of every description, as on once leaving Bagdad I should be unable to obtain any stores of European origin, and very little, if anything, of any other kind. It was therefore necessary to provide myself with all requisites, from a tent and saddlery down to lamps, cooking-pots, and as many tinned provisions as I could run to. And at the same time I was anxious to see as much as possible of Bagdad itself, the famous "City of the Caliphs," where my father had spent twelve of the most interesting years of his life.

Bagdad, to which the Great War has brought more change and progress in its short course of years than had been produced by three times that number of centuries previously, lies chiefly on the northern bank of the Tigris River, here a broad, shallow, and fast-running stream of which the real bed is about half a mile in width, but which is full of sandbanks, some of which are frequently exposed, and greatly detract from the effect which would otherwise be produced by that expanse of water.

I took great pains to discover if my father's house was still standing, but after many inquiries I at last learned that it had been pulled down more than twenty years ago to make room for more modern buildings upon its splendid site on the river-bank at the apex of its northern bend, from whence both reaches of the river are commanded and a fresh breeze off the water is obtained during the winds usually experienced in the time of the great heats.

All the life and interest of the Oriental inhabitants of Bagdad has always centred round the bazaars, and though there are now many counter-attractions of Western origin to be found elsewhere in the town and suburbs, yet here in the bazaars is to be found the true and unchanging "East," where the merchant and his ways are as crafty and torturous as they ever were in centuries long passed away. It must be borne in mind that Bagdad is still as much the centre of all the transcontinental and caravan trade of Asia as it was in the days of the Caliphs, and here to-day come caravans from the Arabian Desert and from Syria, Palestine, and Egypt, as they also come from Asia Minor, Persia, Mesopotamia, India, Central Asia, and far-off China, just as they did in the time of Haroun-al-Raschid in the days which are so vividly put before us in the "Arabian Nights."

All the types rendered familiar to us all by these famous tales of old are still before us here to-day, and, last but not least, "The Forty Thieves" are conspicuous in every direction, and my own abiding wonder was at once aroused as to what possible object the old chronicler could have had in *limiting their number to forty!*—a figure which gives an entirely erroneous idea of their multitude, and therefore tends to be misleading and costly to the stranger!

On entering the bazaars one understands at once why so little is to be seen outside, as these centres of commerce teem with life and echo with an incessant and high-pitched jabbering which is the native merchant's invariable method of doing business; and the Westerner, on first entering this remarkably hungry and active collection of merchants, will be irresistibly reminded of our own London Stock Exchange!

Not that the individuals who frequent these two famous markets in any way resemble each other, but that it is impossible not to recognize that the spirit which moves and excites the Stock Exchange jobber is an exact reproduction of that which moves the Bagdad merchant, and that the result is in each case exactly the same, and produces the excitedly jabbering and excessively noisy crowd which is the salient feature in each case!

The bazaars themselves are in all cases covered in, as a protection from the heat of the sun outside, but this protection is entirely ineffective against the heat generated by the excited and perspiring crowd who are thus sheltered, and the atmosphere so created and "bottled" is such that the European in his haste to escape therefrom becomes a more ready prey to the Eastern chafferer than he perhaps otherwise would be.

The bazaars themselves in their structure remind one irresistibly of the Burlington Arcade, with the exception that the female portion of the community in Bagdad are invariably hidden under voluminous coverings which leave their age and personal attractions to the imagination—an ideal of female attire with which our European experiences render us strangely unfamiliar! Here are shown every kind of Oriental merchandise, and incidentally as fine a collection of Persian carpets, both ancient and modern, as could be found anywhere, whilst the flowing white robes of the Arabs and the many-hued costumes and turbans of other Eastern peoples make a mass of vivid and striking colouring, constantly changing in its combinations and presenting a kaleidoscopic effect which is unique.

In the evening, after dinner, we attended the finals of the Army Boxing Competition, 5,000 British soldiers being present, who made the most enthusiastic and interested audience imaginable. A Canadian shoeing-smith was the winner of the heavyweights, beating a sergeant of British cavalry, who was much the better boxer of the two, in the final. The Canadian got a great reception both before and after his effort, and was evidently a well-known character and very popular. He knew very little of the skilful part of the game, but his strength was colossal and he hit, when he did hit, like a cart-horse kicking; however, he was most diffident of his powers, and showed the greatest anxiety throughout in case he should be tempted to hit *too hard*, and so hurt his opponent seriously. This accident, it appeared, had once before happened to him, and in consequence it had only been with the greatest difficulty that his admirers had succeeded in persuading him to enter the competition at all. However, one or two red-hot punches delivered in quick succession and with great skill on the end of his nose by his expert cavalry opponent soon rendered him much less diffident, and in the end he hit out "good, hard, and plenty," and the cavalry-man promptly acknowledged his powers by duly relapsing into immobility on the floor. On this climax being reached, the huge Canadian delighted the whole assembly by showing signs of the liveliest concern for the well-being of his erstwhile antagonist, and, dashing across the ring, picked him up in his arms like a baby and carried him off as fast as he could run to the ambulance post near-by, amongst the wholehearted and deafening applause of all present.

Immediately on the close of the boxing I went straight to the little station of the Decauville Railway, and left for the 60 miles' journey to railhead, after a total stay in Bagdad of ten days only. Here the real "road" was to begin, and the frontier of Old Persia would at last be close at hand.

# CHAPTER III

### PERSIA: THE ROAD AND THE FAMINE

Railhead camp at Ruz—The Foot-hills—Khanikin—A.S.C. post—Entry to the mountains—The Tek-i-Gehri Pass, Ascent of—Convalescent camp—Dinner on edge of precipice—The upland country—Brigand-infested country round Kirmanshah—Camp at Kirmanshah—The convoy—The Rock of Bisidun—Darius cuneiform inscription—Modern lorries and ancient bridges—Bivouac in the open—The Asadabad Pass—Oil deposits—Russian preparations for defence—Hamadan—Famine horrors—Relief work—Persian gun-fire—Biblical scenes—The site of the Book of Esther—Ancient Ecbatana of Herodotus, Alexander the Great, Ruth, and Boaz to-day—Burning of the petrol dump—Road to Kasvin—G.H.Q. Hush-Hush Army—Billet—Ordered to relieve Armenians surrounded 300 miles west—Build armoured car—Jungalis—Battle of Menjil—Ordered to command convoy to force the passes to Caspian Sea.

In the small hours of the morning of June 26th, fifty-seven days out from London, the little baby Decauville train arrived at the railhead camp of Ruz, 60 miles north-west of Bagdad, which then formed the base for the Hush-Hush Army, as well as for the rail-construction department.

This was just a canvas camp pitched in very orderly fashion, each tent being sunk about 4 feet into the earth in an endeavour to obtain extra shelter from the sun. Quite a good breakfast was forthcoming, and two Ford vans were produced, with which I was to endeavour to catch up the convoy of which I should have taken command ten days before, and which was to be found somewhere ahead of me in the mountains. Having loaded up, we got away about 9.30 on our long and, as it turned out, eventful journey.

Immediately on leaving Ruz the first foot-hills begin, which, although at first quite low, cause many windings and difficulties for the road, of which the surface was then uniformly bad, although ultimately it became, if possible, worse, before reaching that part, much farther on, which had received the attention of the Russian engineers during the earlier part of the war.

Our first halt, about midday, was at an old ruined pilgrim caravanserai, in a curious old town, now three-parts ruins, called Khanikin. Here was quartered a party of A.S.C. mechanics, whose arduous duty it was to repair breakdowns in the Mechanical Transport using the road, upon which the phantom force ahead of us was entirely dependent for supplies of all kinds. Their post was indeed no sinecure, and most effectually was their work carried out throughout, thus rendering possible what had often been asserted to be imposible—that is, maintaining of a European force in the interior of Persia in time of war and famine.

A good A.S.C. meal, and we started again, the hills getting ever higher and the road ever rougher, whilst the country, although at one time it had obviously been thickly inhabited, now showed nothing but ruined villages and had become an uninhabited wilderness. All day, in the distance ahead, we could see the bold outlines of the higher mountains of Persia which bound the upland plains which were our goal; but darkness was creeping on ere we could distinguish the particular gorge which was to give us access to the pass, and this we first distinguished in the otherwise apparently impassable cliffs, from a distance of 4 or 5 miles, where we spent some time in mending our seventh puncture of the first day.

Passing through a V-shaped gorge, we found ourselves in a narrow valley with a swift-running stream, and after ascending this for nearly 10 miles the valley abruptly ended in an apparently impassable cliff of 2,000 feet of sheer perpendicular rock, and we were face to face with the famous pilgrim pass, the Tek-i-Gehri, which gives access to Persia proper, and is the only pass negotiable by wheeled vehicles for some hundreds of miles on either side.

At the foot of the cliffs is the small old native village of Pai Tuk and there was posted a party of British troops to control the ascent of the pass, which latter, however, was at first sight nowhere to be distinguished, although some hundreds of feet overhead, in a horseshoe cleft in the rocks, we saw a kind of ledge which slopingly ascends, and from below appeared to hold out some small hope of a footing on the otherwise sheer face of the cliff. On further examination it was seen that in the slope of rubble and débris at the cliff foot on the

## THE ROCK OF BISIDUN

From the Kirmanshah Road (16 miles distant)

X——X the cuneiform inscription of Darius (Hystaspes)
The panel illustrating Darius and the conquered kings
is enclosed within □

## THE PANEL

Showing Darius with the captive kings

The height of the panel is 10 feet and its width is 18 feet. The figure in the centre, amongst the cuneiform inscriptions above the heads of the captive kings, is the Sun God worshipped by the Persians in the time of Darius

## THE "HUSH-HUSH" ARMY

left side of the road zigzags had been cut, and here lay our "road!"

Before starting our ascent, however, it was necessary to telephone to the summit to ascertain if anything was coming down, as in the upper portion of the pass the track is far too narrow to permit of vehicles passing each other, and, in fact, there is only the barest room for one vehicle, with nothing to spare on either side, on the left being the sheer perpendicular cliff rising upwards, and on the right the awe-inspiring emptiness of the equally sheer abyss. On receiving the assurance from the post at the summit that nothing was coming down, nor would anything be allowed to start until we had reached the top, we started the ascent, which presented no difficulties whilst ascending the zigzags, but only became interesting when we embarked on the ancient track following an insignificant ledge in the sheer wall of rock, and so rising as it makes the circuit of the horseshoe recess of cliff forming the actual "head" and end of the valley.

Here the tract consists of the live rock itself, worn smooth by the feet of the countless thousands of pilgrims who have passed up and down this same narrow pass for many centuries; for every pilgrim from Persia and all the lands of Central Asia must pass and repass this same narrow track if he desires to earn the crown of Moslem sanctity, which is the reward of those who have carried out the pilgrimage to the Holy Shrine of the great Prophet Mahomet at Mecca.

In addition to the difficulties of the extremely narrow track, we became aware as we went of the much more serious one presented by the fierceness of the slope. The immortal Henry Ford, when designing the only less immortal vehicle with which he has endowed mankind, took account in his design of almost every slope he knew of, and made it master of all; but though he knew much, yet his knowledge was, it appears, even then incomplete, as he was unacquainted with the Tek-i-Gehri and its slope. The pilgrim climbs this with more or less ease, according to his age and figure, but its gradient effectually brought both my Fords to an uncompromising halt at the most critical part of the ascent, and thereby augmented the already sufficiently excited state of nervous tension with which we were then all struggling manfully.

The first step and most necessary precaution was to insure against any involuntary retrograde movement on the part of the vehicles; this was quickly and most effectually secured by rocks of quite uncalled for weight and solidity which we hastily placed behind each car. The next step was to concentrate the entire man-power of the party to assist the horse-power of each vehicle in turn, and so, by fits and starts, to effect the ascent of one vehicle at a time. A minor difficulty was experienced owing to the impossibility of squeezing *past* the cars from back to front between the wheels and the cliff, for there was no room to do so; and as the drivers' nerves were not equal to passing on the outside (hanging over space), they both elected to crawl underneath. This method, though extremely effective, appealed so irresistibly to our sense of humour that the old rocks rang and echoed again and again with the hearty laughter of the whole party.

In the very heart of the cleft and the middle of the ascent is a hollow, in which stands the venerable shrine of an unknown saint, and there we found room to halt and drink from a true mountain spring which proved equally refreshing both to our own parched throats and to the hissing radiators of our mechanical comrades. With this relief, the summit was eventually reached as night was upon us. A first day's trip of 100 miles, with a rise of 4,000 feet, in just over twelve hours—very good going, under the conditions.

Arrived at the summit, we found quite a large convalescent camp established there. This camp had nothing much to do with our Hush-Hush Army, but owed its existence in the first instance to the necessity of providing some place in the hills to which convalescents from the various parts of the Mesopotamian plain could be sent during the summer, to escape the great heat. As this plateau is quite 4,000 feet above the plain below, the difference in temperature is very considerable, and the instant relief we experienced on safely arriving there was even more considerable.

I found General Champain, the Brigadier in command, was the younger brother of an old friend of mine of my Sandhurst days, and on our arrival I enjoyed an excellent dinner with him, amidst surroundings of wonderful beauty.

Our table was set out on a natural platform of rock on the

very edge of the horseshoe precipice we had just climbed, and whilst all round us were trees and scrub, in front of us was just empty air, with the tinkle of falling water coming up from the depths far below. Over all shone a bright full moon, causing all the higher hills around us to stand out as clear as day; but in front of us, over the burning plains below, there was only a quivering haze of heat, somewhere below which, we knew, lay and sweated and suffered those of our comrades less fortunate than ourselves.

Afoot next morning well before daylight, we were on the road again as soon as there was light enough to see our way—a very necessary precaution in the case of the road which lay immediately in front of us; for here we were in a rocky and difficult country, and the ever-winding hill-track was everywhere obstructed by the huge rocks and stones which are constantly falling from the mountains towering on either side of the route.

After 12 miles or more constant climbing we at last reached the ridge which forms the boundary of the upland plateau, and from there followed an easy and gradual descent for another 25 miles, the valley opening out to a long, narrow plain, marshy in places, but with fair signs of cultivation, and the scattered villages which form the usual landscape of the richer pastures of the Persian uplands plains.

Over this country, as the valley widened, we were able to travel at a much better average speed than we had hitherto been able to achieve, for the road, although only a dirt one and innocent of "metalling," yet had a hard and dusty but fairly level surface, and punctures became rarer.

After being twice bogged at marshy crossings of small streams, there being no bridges, and crossing two ranges of mountains by most indifferent passes, towards late afternoon we came in sight of the higher and more continuous ranges encircling the ancient town of Kirmanshah, where we hoped to spend the night and catch up the convoy we were in pursuit of. The country in these parts, in normal times, is fairly well cultivated and populated in the plains, but the mountains have always borne an unsavoury reputation amongst travellers as the resort of the dreaded Bactiari tribes, the brigands *par excellence* of the Persian mountains.

Although the march of my isolated party of two cars was against all the standing military regulations, yet my two faithful machine-guns gave us every confidence, and they were ready and loaded all the way, so that, if the truth is to be told, it was with a sad feeling of disappointment that we topped the last ridge, at over 6,500 feet, as night was falling, without having had any opportunity of trying conclusions with the famous Bactiari brand of brigand, and from there we could see the town and camp of Kirmanshah lying in the valley far below.

At this moment, on the very last ridge, where the road was at its very worst and steepest, we had the misfortune to break a wheel; and as we had no spare one, there was nothing for it but to continue with one car and to leave the other till we could send back a wheel for it. I well remember impressing on the two men I left the beauty of the view to be obtained from the unpleasantly prominent spot where they would have to wait, and from whence they could not fail to be seen by every robber in the surrounding country. Having given them plenty of ammunition for the one machine-gun which I left with them, and having also abstracted from their car all the portions of my kit which I considered most valuable, we hoisted a British flag on the hood and hurried on, followed by the most plaintive glances from the somewhat pale and startled heroes, who had watched our proceedings with deeply interested curiosity, and who appeared much more interested in keeping their eyes on the forbidding-looking rocks in their immediate vicinity than in admiring the panoramic view of the country farther off, to the beauty of which I had been at such pains to draw their attention!

At Kirmanshah we found a good-sized camp and transport depôt, and having at once dispatched a wheel and relief car to bring in the other car, I pitched my tent and got a fair dinner at the A.S.C. mess, learning at the same time that, although my original convoy had broken up, or rather down, on the road, through a variety of mechanical casualties, yet I should be able to continue my journey with some twenty-five American lorries at daylight next morning. And so to a well-earned rest, having covered a good 120 miles since daylight, the latter part through what was at this time a quite desolate and very "ambushy"-looking country, where we had made no voluntary halt

## THE "HUSH-HUSH" ARMY

all day, in our anxiety to get into camp before dark to avoid having to bivouac in the open in such an unhealthy locality.

On mustering our convoy at daylight next morning, we found we had only eighteen lorries in condition to take the road. The greater part of these were of American construction, and in a state of mechanical efficiency which reflected the greatest credit on their designers and manufacturers, in view of the difficulties of the country over which they were daily called upon to travel.

The road at first was very good, though it was unmetalled, the surface being much superior to the rocky tracks over which we had travelled the previous day, and the first 20 miles, over a flat plain, with a view of snow-capped mountains in all directions around us, was quite pleasant driving, the society of a Mechanical Transport officer, now with me, being also much appreciated.

As on crossing each range we had found the plain beyond higher than the one behind us, we had by degrees reached an elevation of about 5,000 feet on the plain of Kirmanshah, and the air was infinitely cooler, though the sun promptly burned the skin off any part left exposed to its rays.

At once on leaving the camp we could see the famous Rock of Bisidun, close under which our road would pass. The base of the rock is actually 20 miles from Kirmanshah, but such is the height of which it rises, a sheer 4,000 feet above the plain, that it appears quite close at hand when viewed from the town itself, and at 10 miles' distance appears to be only half a mile away.

The summit even in late June had still some snow, but when we finally reached the base, the rock itself, where exposed to the sun, was too hot to bear one's hand on. Here we found the most delightful spring of ice-cold water running from an ancient stone fountain dating back to the days of Darius, nearly 3,000 years ago. This rock was the lodestone which retained my father in those parts for twelve long years, and on its surface is the famous cuneiform inscription which had remained unread and undecipherable for 2,500 years, till he determined he would persevere until he achieved the success which was his at last, when, after twelve years' continuous study, he gave the long-lost language back to the world, with alphabet, grammar, dictionary complete, and so laid bare to history the records of Darius, the King of Kings.

I was familiar from childhood with the great cliff, and many tales of my father's efforts to climb up to and obtain tracings of the old writings high upon its rocky face were fixed ineradicably in my memory. I therefore gazed up at the great rock, expecting to see at once their familiar form; but it was only after a hard climb of 100 feet or more over the hardest and sharpest of rocky débris that I at last reached a spot from whence the inscription could be seen. I gazed at it as much astonished at the terrible difficulties he must have overcome in obtaining his tracings as I had ever been amazed at his success in his apparently impossible task of afterwards deciphering them.

The inscription itself, which consists of a quantity of panels (over thirty, I believe), is as clear to-day as when first cut, and in a very few places only has any crumbling taken place. The labour entailed must have been colossal, as the hardness of the quartz rock is quite remarkable, and when the inscription was completed, presumably at what was at that time the base of the great cliff, the rock itself was then scarped away below so as to continue the perpendicular cliff for a further 100 feet at least to the level of the plain below, and so render the inscription inaccessible to all for ever.

The writing is mostly extremely well preserved, and the picture of the great King, with prisoners bound and kneeling before him, is remarkably well drawn, the figures, with their hands tied behind their backs, being much less "wooden" than most ancient figures, while Darius himself looks (as my note says) the "hell of a swell, with his square beard and his hair all beautifully and elaborately 'crimped' in the fashion of that day." *

The general impression carried away is (1) that the labour of those days must have been excessively cheap; (2) that the

---

* The means by which Sir Henry Rawlinson achieved the apparently impossible task of deciphering an unknown language, written in strange characters which presented no resemblance to any known form of writing, can hardly fail to be of general interest. At a spot some hundred miles north of Behistun he discovered two inscriptions in the unknown writing, obviously proclamations by the great kings of those ancient days.

great King's draftsmen were very skilful; and (3) that he certainly chose the most prominent site in his whole vast dominions to write his diary on, for the benefit and instruction of future ages.

Close to the foot of the rock runs a river of fair size, over which is an ancient bridge of good design built, to my surprise, of *bricks* of a quality at that time new to me. No doubt the engineers of those far-off days never contemplated their work being called upon to carry a convoy of 5-ton American motor-lorries loaded to their utmost capacity, for the "crown" of the bridge offered such an excessively steep ascent that it was necessary for each individual lorry to charge it in turn at full speed in order to "get over." This very modern and violent form of attack proved altogether too much for the venerable construction, which had for so many centuries withstood every kind of strain with which its designers were familiar, and in the middle of the attack it was suddenly discovered that the crown of the

He observed that each was headed by two separate groups of signs. These were in the first inscription:

(a) 𒀭𒁹𒀸 *? Darius*

(b) 𒀭𒁹𒀸 *? Hystaspes*

and in the second:

(c) 𒀭𒁹𒀸 *? Xerxes*

(d) 𒀭𒁹𒀸 *? Darius*

As he was well aware the name of a king was invariably followed in ancient times by the name of his father, he inferred that the first inscription was by a king represented by group (a) whose father's name was represented by group (b), and that the second inscription was by a king whose name was represented by group (c) whose father was the author of inscription (a). From his profound knowledge of the history of the ancient Persians he presumed that the three kings in question were probably Darius, the son of Hystaspes, and Xerxes, the son of Darius; and assuming group (a) to represent Darius, group (b) to represent Hystaspes, and group (c) to represent Xerxes, he was able to fix the meanings and values of certain characters. From this small beginning, with infinite toil and astounding ingenuity, after twelve years of study he eventually succeeded in evolving every detail of the long lost language, and supplied the key which has unlocked the door closed for over 2,000 years, and placed at the disposal of the modern world the written records of the great empires of the ancient East.

arch was no longer there! We were therefore forced to complete the passage of our convoy by the still more ancient custom of fording the stream, a both difficult and tedious undertaking, which occupied the greater part of the day, so that darkness eventually overtook us many miles short of our destination, in the open country, 20 miles from the great Asadabad Pass, itself 20 miles from the old city of Hamadan we had been hoping to reach that night. Having started at 6 A. M., and halted only half an hour, we had done fifteen hours' continuous driving, during which we covered 85 miles, an average of under 6 miles per hour, from which the difficulties presented by the road may be imagined.

Bivouacking with a car convoy is a very simple proceeding, and consists in halting at any convenient spot where water can be obtained, the cars being drawn up one behind the other and close together; sentries are then posted, and each man proceeds to look after himself, a matter of no difficulty, as all carry a primus stove and a ration of some kind, according to the supplies obtainable. Tea being then made on the step or footboard of each lorry, a meal of sorts is soon eaten, and each man seeks whatever corner of his heavily loaded lorry offers the least uncomfortable prospect for the night. At the first sign of drawn primus stoves are going again, and after the invariable tea and a wash in whatever water can be found, engines are started, and the convoy moves off again.

Our actual start on this occasion took place at 5.30 A. M., and we reached the foot of the great Asadabad Pass, 20 miles away, in two and a half hours. Here, knowing the climb that was in front of us, we halted and filled every vessel in our possession which was capable of holding water, as there is little or none to be obtained in the pass, and hot engines were a certainty during the severe climb.

The Asadabad Pass is the highest in this part of the country, being nearer 9,000 than 8,000 feet above the sea, and the road over it has been well and only lately made by Russian engineers, the old road from Kirmanshah to Hamadan being thereby shortened by a good 70 miles. The rise in the main pass is 2,000 feet in $3\frac{1}{2}$ miles, a practicable but severe gradient all the way, and of course the road turns and twists incessantly as it follows the "trace," being everywhere cut out of the terribly steep hillside.

The surface is fair and the track everywhere broad enough for two cars to pass, and I noted with great interest that the greater part of the ascent is made through oil-bearing rock very similar to the oil-bearing shale with which I had been familiar in Scotland, and I had the curiosity during one of our numerous stops to climb down to inspect a mountain stream, finding, as I expected, that in any pool where the water was more or less at rest, it was covered with a film of oil, a matter which I made a point of subsequently reporting in the proper quarter. The view looking back south-east from the summit of the pass was most characteristic of the Persian uplands, showing a great amphitheatre of rocky ranges with snow-covered peaks, surrounding the plain in every direction and distant from 30 to 60 miles, whilst 20 miles to the east the ridge on which we stood culminated in a lofty peak, with at least 1,000 feet of snow, which I knew at once to be Mount Elvand, the highest peak until the Caspian ranges are reached. At this high altitude I found my Mesopotamian shorts and drill clothing somewhat chilly, and my thoughts flew irresistibly back to the gentleman in Whitehall with his printed paper of extremes of temperature and his five pounds!

However, I was more interested in the extremely elementary trench defences which had evidently been recently laid out on the summit. These had been prepared by the Russians with the idea of holding the position against the Turks—on whose arrival at the foot, however, the Russians promptly bolted, leaving the indifferent trenches as the only evidence that they had ever been there, for they were such as could never have been dug, or rather scratched, by any other troops. The descent was easy and the road pretty good, and we arrived at Hamadan at 2.30 P. M., with all our cars, almost as much relieved at doing so ourselves, as were those waiting for the supplies we carried to see us arrive safely.

Hamadan, the ancient Ecbatana, the great treasure-city of the Achæmenian Kings, lies some 200 miles north of the "shushan" of the Bible, and is full of interest. The population, laregly Armenian, was, before the famine resulting from the war, probably more than 50,000 but at the time we are dealing with can hardly have reached 10,000, the majority of whom were in the last stages of starvation. The old town lies at an elevation of 6,500 feet above sea-level, and the Headquarters of our force was on the eastern side, at least 500 feet higher up the slopes of the great mountain—a pleasant enough position in summer, but one which must indeed be arctic in winter.

Here, in a pleasant and almost European house standing in its own grounds, was quartered the Brigadier-General commanding the line of communication of our famous Hush-Hush Army; and, having reported to him, I received a cordial invitation to pitch my tent in his garden and to mess with him, both of which suggestions I was very glad to fall in with. At dinner that night I learned the news with respect to local conditions and as to our chance of being able to keep Persia from the Turks, which was the real object of the existence of our "phantom" army.

The first and most pressing need was to alleviate the famine from which hundreds were then dying daily throughout all the upland country, and to this work my host had been devoting his energies, with a success so considerable that the general feeling towards the British, which on our arrival had been most antagonistic, was already showing signs of veering round in our favour.

At this time literally thousands of starving people were daily fed by our force, and the great stores of grain accumulated and kept off the market by the Persian dealers, with the object of selling it at high prices as the famine became more general and acute, were freely requisitioned and distributed by us, with the result that many thousands of lives were saved and much abject misery and suffering averted.

The whole position was typical of the Persian character, and could hardly have existed in any other country, for the Persian's indifference to suffering in others is a national characteristic mercifully unique. Without having seen such things personally, it is almost impossible to realize that a wealthy Persian will enter his house without giving a moment's thought to the dead and dying who may have congregated at his door in the hope of relief, and of whose dying misery it does not occur to him to take the least notice.

Nor, even when they are dead, does he trouble to remove or bury their corpses, which at this tine were constantly to be seen lying unnoticed in the streets of the native city, and in even greater numbers on the roads leading to that haven of mercy where the British fed the starving, but which hundreds of the poor country people were without the strength to reach, and so fell and died by the roadside, where were none to bury them.

The terrible conditions of famine, with the awful misery, protracted suffering, and eventual heavy death-roll which at this time existed in Persia, were subsequently reproduced amongst the Armenian population in the districts of Alexandropol, Erivan and Kars in Anatolia. In Anatolia, however, such horrors served as a dark background against which the glorious work of the great American organization of Near East Relief stood out even more clearly than would have otherwise been the case.

With the unique opportunities which it has been my lot to experience of the horrible sufferings of the population in both these countries, I have often regretted that the conditions in Persia in 1918 were unknown to the great American public. In the light of the subsequent action taken by the Relief Organization established in the United States by which literally hundreds of thousands of lives were saved, there can be little doubt that, had the state of affairs in Persia at that time been known in America, such an appeal for relief of suffering humanity would in this case also have met with the instant and cordial response which has in every case been unfailingly forthcoming and which commands the admiration of all other nations.

My note written at the time says that "in the villages of the plain there are never as many as twenty inhabitants where two to three hundred formerly throve, and thousands die of starvation every week, whilst the dead lie in the streets and the living are spectres which it is terrible to behold." It was here, at this time, that I came across the only case, of any individual being "stoned to death" in public, of which I have ever heard outside the Bible. But, that at least one such case occurred at Hamadan, either during or immediately prior to our occupation, I am in a position to know as a fact. The crime which called forth this punishment is so unnatural that I am not prepared to allow that, under the circumstances and in that country, it was not an effectual, and possibly the only effectual, method of putting a stop to such crimes, which, if unchecked, are apt to spread.

My refined European readers, used to the customs and laws of civilization, may wonder at this, and conclude that I must be myself a barbarian to hold any such opinion. But pause, please, before coming to any such hasty conclusion, and reflect; for the punishment was ordered by the mullahs (priests) and the crime was that of a *mother eating her child*—an almost inconceivable crime, I think it will generally be agreed, even after making every allowance for the extremities of suffering and starvation!

Under these circumstances it is not to be wondered at that murder, robbery, and many crimes of violence, were of daily occurrence, and all British officers went armed, both day and night, by order. Every night and at all hours of the night rifle-fire was to be heard, which is somewhat disconcerting to the Western mind, but to which, however, one soon becomes accustomed, as the Persian, like many of his Eastern neighbours, has a weakness for letting off his rifle at odd times, for no particular purpose except to let all and sundry know he has one.

I could find no buildings of interest, though no doubt such must exist; but I saw the huge mound which is all that remains of the great city and palace which the first, and greatest, of all historians, Herodotus, describes as having "seven encircling walls, each within and commanding the next, and all of different colours, the first five being white, black, scarlet, blue, and orange, and the sixth coated with silver, whilst the palace in the centre was similarly covered with gold."

This was the palace where Alexander the Great held his great drunken feasts when he halted there in his all-conquering campaign, during one of which orgies he, to his own subsequent regret and everlasting shame, murdered his greatest friend and foremost General.

At Shushan lived King Ahasuerus, who married Esther the Jewess, whilst her uncle Mordecai sat at the gate as a beggar; and here also, by Esther's influence, the great captain Haman was hanged by the King's order on the high gallows he had erected for Mordecai. The massacre of all the Jews in the country, which had been ordered by the King, was thus averted by Esther, as may be read in the Book of Esther, in the Old Testament of our Bible.

The most striking part of this old country is the absence of any change or progress during the lapse of the 3,000 years with respect to which we have reliable information as to the habits and customs of its inhabitants. All the old characters of the Bible are here met in everyday life, exactly the same in every respect as their prototypes of ancient times; and here we find the same vineyards, gardens, and cornfields, the same old one-pronged wooden plough drawn by oxen, and the ubiquitous ox also treads the corn (instead of threshing), exactly as was the case in Biblical days. Also the young girl gleaners can be seen following the reapers in the field, and the modern Ruth varies not at all from her ancestress. Infallibly to-day, as of old, will also be found a modern, elderly Boaz, following the young girls at their gleaning, wearing precisely the same expression which must have distinguished his Biblical prototype as described in the Book of Ruth. It requires, however, a considerable stretch of imagination to anticipate that the production of another King David will result to-day, as was formerly the case, from this very ordinary pastoral incident.

A very few days at Hamadan, where it was necessary to wait for transport, convinced me that the question of the possibility of any effective action by our "skeleton army," or even its ability to exist at all, was entirely dependent upon the efficiency of our motors, and I therefore took every means of informing myself with regard to their mechanical condition and the means of repair available. The results of my inquiries were not inspiring, as I found that, although our mechanics were more than fair in their skill and experience, and the Mechanical Transport officers most efficient, yet spare parts were hard to come by, and, above all, our supply of petrol was extremely precarious. All petrol had to be brought at that time from Bagdad by road; the amount, therefore, was limited by the transport available, which was already inadequate for the supply of the other requirements of the troops. This unfortunate state of affairs could not be remedied until a direct and regular supply could be established over the Caspian

Sea from the wells at Baku. This, however, did not appear at all imminent in the face of the conditions then existing in the Jungali country between Persia and the Caspian coast.

A petrol dump had been established at Hamadan, which at this time, therefore, constituted the most vital link of our very precarious chain of communication. Having had much experience of the storage of petrol, I was struck with horror when I inspected our store of this invaluable fuel, the first and worst part of the business being that the most elementary principles of safety had been neglected, the whole of or supply having been collected at one spot, so that any accident which might set it alight would infallibly consume the entire reserve. The tins also, having travelled 500 miles over the worst of roads, were all leaking badly, so that the danger of fire was imminent, and, once alight, nothing could possibly save any part of our priceless stock.

It was soon after midday when I first saw the dump, and even from a distance it could be seen that the atmosphere above it consisted mostly of petrol gas, which was rising freely from the leaking tins. I therefore hastened back to the General's house and told him my fears. I am afraid I was too guarded in my language, as he failed to appreciate the danger; however, he readily agreed that he would come out to the dump with me before sundown, and would give orders as to the immediate rearrangement of the whole system, and he then retired to his room, and I to my tent, till the worst of the heat of the day should be past.

I had not been five minutes in my tent, however, and certainly had not yet got my boots off, which is the very first step towards an Oriental siesta, when I became aware the sun no longer shone with its usual power on the tent, and I therefore promptly went out to see if a dust-storm was coming on. One glance at the sky was sufficient, and started me at my best speed towards the house, to waken the General, for from the direction of the petrol dump (providentially far from any buildings) was rising a dense cloud of smoke, which already had obscured the sun, and which, to any one who had ever seen such a sight before, at once told its own tragic story—continuously confirmed and emphasized by a succession of explosions caused by the bursting of the petrol tins as the heat increased.

The General leapt up on my shout, and together we ran the half-mile or more to the scene of the catastrophe, at which we could only gaze, and that from a good hundred yards' distance, the heat effectually preventing any nearer approach. A tragedy indeed, but if, as I make no doubt, its lessons were well learnt by all concerned, one that would prove of great value in the future.

At this time a good deal of trouble and delay was caused to the Hush-Hush Army by the difficulty in obtaining stores, and assistance generally, from Headquarters at Bagdad, which was easy to understand, as many of the demands made were of a quite unexpected nature, and in consequence they were often met in rather a "querulous" spirit by the General Staff. One case occurs to me especially, as illustrative of this state of affairs. When steps were first being taken to alleviate the famine at Hamadan we were called upon to produce bread and to provide meat in entirely unforeseen quantities, and in face of this urgent demand a telegram was sent to Bagdad asking that a "butcher" and a "baker" might be sent up at the first opportunity. It must be remembered that this telegram had to be sent over 100 miles to Teheran, and then via Ispahan and Shiraz to Bushire on the coast of the Persian Gulf, and then across to Bussrah and up the river, well over 2,000 miles in all. So that when, after waiting a week or ten days, the reply eventually arrived our state of mind may be conceived when we read the following message: "It is not understood for what purpose the services of a 'butcher' and 'baker' are required!"

As I had been rather defending the attitude of Bagdad Headquarters in the face of the many demands made on them, this was handed to me to read on its arrival, and my opinion as to a reply was asked. There appeared to be only one possible answer that could meet the case, and I wrote it out and handed it in, but I much fear it was never sent; it was: "A Butcher is required to Bake the Bread, and a Baker to cut up the Meat!" Perhaps it was a pity if it was never sent, as it would quite probably have produced the men at once, and relieved the somewhat strained relations.

A few days more at Hamadan and on July 7th two Ford vans became available for the 140-mile journey to Kasvin. The road was a good one, and as we got farther north the misery, and the evidences of it by the roadside, became fewer. We had one pass to cross, the Sultan Bulak Gedik, just over 50 miles north of Hamadan, and in spite of its somewhat evil reputation for brigand "hold-ups," I and my small party crossed it without incident, and although our guns were ready we had no occasion to use them. This was most probably because they were, and were known to be, constantly ready for use, as well as skilfully handled—under which circumstances good machine-guns will always command considerable respect in all countries. We arrived at Kasvin the same evening, at 5.30 P. M., and on reporting at our G.H.Q. I got a billet with the British officer commanding the town and arranged to mess with him during my stay.

Kasvin is a large town, about the same size as Hamadan, but more pretentious, with some streets of considerable breadth and a certain sprinkling of shop windows of more or less European appearance. The famine was less apparent here, though the familiar corpse and dying beggar were both occasionally to be observed in the side streets.

The city, one of the many old capitals of Persia, lies 10 miles south of the foot of the great Elburz Range, and 80 miles west of the Shah's capital of Teheran. The main western road divides west of the city, the northern branch leading to the port of Enzeli on the Caspian Sea, and the southern to Tabriz by the ancient caravan route from Persia and the East generally, through Anatolia to the Black Sea, or through Tiflis and Georgia to Southern Russia. The town is at an elevation of only 4,000 feet above sea-level, and is therefore considerably hotter in summer than Hamadan, which is a good 1,500 feet higher. The houses, though mostly of the universal mud, are typically Persian, being built for the most part round a sunk court and garden, in which is usually found a fountain or running water of some kind. These courts provide a cool retreat in the heat of summer, as well as efficient shelter from the icy blasts of the severe gales which are the curse of these uplands in winter.

Our little mess of four occupied a native house of the above description, and consisted of the town Commander, Lieut.-Colonel Warden, D.S.O., a British Columbian, and two Captains forming his staff—the one an Australian and the other the son of an English father and Russian mother, brought up in Russia. So that when we forgathered at our frugal meals in the courtyard much cosmopolitan and interesting conversation ensued.

On the morning after my arrival I made the acquaintance of General Dunsterville, the famous Commander of the Hush-Hush Army, for the first time, and never in the course of a very varied career have I met any personality so instantly claiming or so permanently retaining my respect and sympathy. Possessed of an exceptional sense of humour, no difficulties were ever so great, nor situations so hopeless, that he could not, and did not, see and appreciate the brighter side of every event, however tragic. Himself possessed of the great and inestimable gift of courage in the face of adversity, he knew how to communicate to others, less gifted than himself, that confidence in themselves to which is due the measure of success achieved by the force under his command in the face of the apparently impossible task with which they found themselves confronted.

I learned from him the whole difficult and complicated position of affairs, and he also told me he should require me to take charge of a column proceeding at once to the west, to relieve a force of Armenians and Assyrians who were in a pretty bad way some 300 miles west of us, on the western shore of the great freshwater lake of Urumia. It appeared that there were collected there about 80,000 Christians, who had put up a good fight during the four previous months against the Turkish divisions surrounding them, but were now sadly in want of ammunition and in imminent danger of massacre. The intention was to force a passage through the Turks and renew the Christians' ammunition; and on this being effected, I was to send back the relieving column and to remain myself to organize the further defence, and to occupy the attention of as mnay Turkish troops as possible, and thereby divert them from their scheme of again over-running Persia.

I thanked the Chief very heartily for the very honourable task he had allotted me, but next day, when I heard he had been called to Bagdad, and that the expedition was postponed, I heaved a deep sigh of relief, feeling sure that events in other parts would now move too quickly for it to be worth while to lock me up in such an infernal spot, where I could have effected little or nothing, and about which there appeared to be only one outstanding certainty, and that was that my return would be more than doubtful!

In the meantime, on my suggestion, he agreed that I should at once undertake the construction of an armoured car, of quite novel design, the chief characteristic of which would be the absence of armour; so that, whilst to all appearances it would be the real article, and as such strike terror into all and sundry, yet, as the armour would consist of paint only, applied to very thin planking, the car, upon which my own machine-guns would be mounted, would be so light as to be capable of travelling at high speed, and over country which would be quite impassable to the genuinely armoured vehicle.

My time, therefore, day and night during the next fortnight was concentrated on the production of such a vehicle, having at my disposal none of the material, skilled labour, or mechanical equipment which such a construction would, under ordinary conditions, require.

It was, however, completed within a fortnight, and in such a solid form that it carried me many thousand miles in the next ten weeks, over every conceivable and inconceivable obstacle, and was still running efficiently when I at last handed it over at Bagdad in October.

The design itself was an affair of hours only, and the next step, which was to obtain a fairly serviceable Ford chassis and to dismantle it, was comparatively easy. From that point the construction presented many difficulties, chiefly with regard to material. I had, however, observed on entering the town a vast heap of remains of Russian vehicles of every description, abandoned by the Russian troops in their retreat, and this became my gold-mine, from which I drew, if not all my requirements, at any rate substitutes for them, so that on the Chief's return I was able to present for his inspection a most efficient-looking vehicle, of which he immediately appreciated the value.

During this period, the later part of July, the tribe of the Jungalis, who occupy the wooded northern slopes of the great range through which passes the road from Kasvin to the Caspian, had been giving considerable trouble, led by their chief, Kuchi Khan, supported by the Bolsheviks, and encouraged, armed, and, as far as they could be, trained by German officers.

On June 12th, under their German Commander, Von Passchen, they had put up a formal resistance to the Russians under General Bicherakov, who were on their way home to Russia, and were accompanied by what British and native troops could be spared to hold the road to the sea. The site of the battle which ensued was Menjil, at the commencement of the lower part of the pass leading from Kasvin to the shores of the Caspian Sea. The result was the complete discomfiture of the Jungali force, which forthwith retreated into the thick forests of their native hills, leaving the road in the possession of our pickets. A force of about 400 British and Gurkha troops then passed down the pass, and subsequently held the town of Resht, in the marshy country between the mountains and the sea, whilst a further detachment held the port of Kazian on the sea-shore, about 30 miles farther north.

This position was not at all to the liking of the German officers, whose plans for the penetration of Persia, by means of the Jungalis, were entirely defeated by the interposition of this small force, which threatened to insure access to the Caspian Sea for any number of British troops which might presently become available. Taking, therefore, their courage in both hands, which after-events showed cannot have constituted a very severe burden, and urged on by the German officers and Turks, who were together exploiting and arming them, the Jungalis, on July 20th, launched an attack in force on our troops in Resht and on our posts on the road. This attack met with a certain measure of success, in that certain posts on the road were driven in, the troops in Resht itself were reduced to defending themselves in their quarters, and the control of the road temporarily passed into the enemy's hands. The only surprise was that the insignificant British force was not entirely wiped out.

Such was the position at the end of July, when General Dunsterville returned from Bagdad. It was at once decided to force the pass and open the road to the sea; and to my great delight I was notified that I was to command the convoy, and that my newly constructed dummy armoured car was thus to have a chance of demonstrating its utility. On receipt of this most welcome news. I promptly sallied forth with my car into the open country, and commenced a fusillade at any kind of prominent object which offered itself as a target in the surrounding country, with the double object of testing all my gear and at the same time creating an impression upon the many spies who I knew would be on the look-out, and who could not fail to report the existence of this new and awe-inspiring vehicle, which crossed the fields with ease and jumped the ditches like a horse, vomiting bullets all the while unceasingly!

This was, in fact, what happened, and by the time the news of its existence reached the enemy Headquarters, my dummy car appears to have been magnified into a brigade of tanks at the very least, as the sequel will show. Anyway, having passed quite an enjoyable evening, I had the still more pleasant sensation of some good work done, and was all ready to start next morning.

# CHAPTER IV

### THE CASPIAN SEA—ADVANCE TO, RELIEF OF, AND SIEGE OF BAKU

The convoy—The upper pass—Through the Jungalis in the lower pass—The sea at last—Kazian, the end of the road—Sickness—An oil tank as a transport—Bad weather—Bolshevik gunboat—Baku Harbour—The city—Preceding events—Services lent to Caspian Republic—The Government appoint me Controller of Ordnance—Difficulties—The arsenals, armament, and ammunition—The Armenians—Project to cut Turk communications—Constant attacks—Decide to withdraw—Government refuses to consent—Prospects of capture—Plan to blow up ammunition—Turks hesitate—Resistance continued—I acquire a German flat—The end approaches.

On August 3rd, having been warned to "stand by" some days before, I received orders to muster my convoy outside Kasvin City, at the Enzeli (the Caspian road) Gate at daybreak on August 7th, and to halt and camp for the night at Menjil, about 80 miles below, at the commencement of the second and lower half of the pass, where also I was to collect some more cars and men and carry on next day to the sea.

Accordingly, at daybreak we mustered, and I could then see what kind of an outfit I was going to have. It was ever so much better than I was expecting, as sixty to eighty cars turned up, each with at least two rifles and some with three, also one *genuine* armoured car, which was, of course, a tower of strength in itself. And I further found there were several other machine-guns scattered about the column, so that we had, roughly, about 120 men—and a pretty tough lot they looked—good British troops with a sprinkling of Gurkhas amongst them, who are great fellows in a hill scrap, or, indeed, in any other, and whose "kukris," or Nepaulese knives, had already established a most valuable reputation among the Jungalis.

The first 20 miles was over rolling uplands, by a good Russian-made road, to the head of the pass, where we must have been quite 6,500 feet above sea-level. It was quite refreshingly cool before the sun got its full power, and, to my surprise, in this part I saw a quantity of partridges, and no corpses. I remember well, when we halted at the top of the pass to collect stragglers, remarking to the officer in the armoured car, what a great country this would be for partridge-driving. Having closed up the column, we got on down the pass, finding the road good, though steep, and the country changing rapidly as we went down, till we found ourselves in a deep, rocky gorge, with the hills rising in sheer cliffs many thousands of feet above us all round, and the road winding constantly and following insignificant-looking ledges on the face of the precipitous rocks. The mountain torrent whose course we were following was often lost to view, though it could be plainly heard roaring through the gorge hundreds of feet below us, to reappear a few moments later alongside the road on the same level at the foot of the next steep descent.

About 15 miles down the pass we halted again to close up stragglers, and the men ate their rations; whilst there, to my surprise, the Chief joined us in his car, and, having talked a few minutes and had a look round, he went on down the pass in front, entirely without escort. I supposed he knew all about it—as in fact he did—but it seemed to me to be an unhealthy kind of spot for him to be driving about without any form of escort, and I therefore handed over the control of the convoy and pushed on after him as hard as I could go; this entailed some very fast and rough driving, which tested all my dummy car construction most effectively. He was, I remember, driving a 35-h.p. Vauxhall, with a good driver who knew the pass, and my Ford, light as it was, wanted a good deal of shaking up to keep in sight of him. However, we did keep him in sight, although it necessitated such hard and dangerous driving that even my cast-iron mechanic squirmed more than once—the only time I ever knew him to do so, though subsequently he certainly had plenty of other excellent opportunities.

We caught the Chief at the river crossing three-parts down the first half of the pass, where he had halted to eat what he had with him, and we did likewise, having explained to him the reason of our having followed him so hard. He then informed me that our halfway post was only about 10 miles in front, and that all this upper part of the pass was clear of

## NORTH-WESTERN PERSIA

The Pass through the Jungali country to the Caspian Sea

The dummy armoured car after the campaign
(Pte. Morris, M.M., R.A.S.C., in front)

the enemy. So we waited there for the convoy to come in, and, having closed up the cars, we all got into camp together at dusk, on the site of the Battle of Menjil, which had taken place six weeks before.

Menjil will always remain in my recollection as the most uncomfortable spot it could be possible to select for a camp. Lying, as it does, at the junction of three valleys, there is in summer, not a wind only, but a perfect hurricane, invariably blowing up the main pass from the sea. So strong and continuous is it that the trees and shrubs are all permanently bent over by the force of the wind. Pitching a tent under those conditions becomes a matter of the greatest difficulty and of very doubtful permanency; and once having pitched it and got inside, it is a sheer impossibility to keep a primus stove alight to do, even elementary, cooking. However, there were more interesting things to think of just then than personal comforts or discomforts, and we got what rest we could, turning out again at daylight to find our party nearly doubled, so that we had about 135 cars and from 200 to 300 men to start away with down the lower pass.

The first portion of the lower pass, for about 30 miles, presented no difficulty, though the surrounding mountains, reaching, as they do, nearly perpendicularly up to 11,000 and 12,000 feet, or even more, appeared to get higher and higher as we went down. However, the road was good and accidents few, and we halted at an old Russian military post halfway down about midday, having thus far seen no sign of an enemy. Here the danger-zone began, and the slopes became covered with thick forest jungle, so that we could only see a few yards from the roadside, and were absolutely at the mercy of any force firing upon us from the impenetrable thickets.

It was in this part that many convoys had been held up and parties, both British and Russian, wiped out by the Eastern gentlemen who, we felt sure, were now observing us from the thick undergrowth on both sides of the road. Nowhere in any part of the world have I seen a road which lent itself so well to defence, nor where an attempt to force a passage had less chance of success in the face of any determined opposition. For not only was it impossible to see in any direction on the hillside out of which the road was cut, but the road itself was absolutely commanded from the woods on the steep slope across the river, hardly a quarter of a mile distant, where a few machine-guns would have been very difficult to locate, and could have made it impossible for any one to live for five minutes on the road we were to follow.

Such was, then, the appetizing prospect before us after lunch!

Before starting, I went all round the convoy, impressing upon all hands, in the first place the necessity of keeping "closed up," with no gaps in the column, and in the second that in the event of our being attacked advantage should be instantly taken of any place where the road was in the nature of a "cutting," and the cars then run in close under the banks, and as soon as might be possible an advance could then be made into the scrub, which it would be necessary to clear by hand-to-hand fighting.

This having been thoroughly explained and understood, I sought out the Chief, and, reporting "All ready," got his order to proceed. Having loaded my guns, I then drove slowly along the whole length of the column, from rear to front, and took my place at the head to lead them through. It was indeed a glorious moment, and I had no doubt at all that at last I had reached the fighting front again, although many thousand miles from where I had left it in France, and I know I *felt*, and was told afterwards that I *looked*, proportionately "elated."

Off we went, very slowly at first, but after a while faster, until the speed was as great as could be maintained without "opening out" the column. We soon began to come on signs of the fate of previous convoys—in the shape of remains of cars and lorries, scattered cartridge-cases, a few corpses, and all the usual signs of a scrap. However, as we got deeper and deeper into the jungle without any sign of an enemy, a certain disappointment began to creep over us all, until, halfway up a very steep hill in the middle of the very densest part of the forest, I suddenly stopped short! In a second every car behind edged to the bank and every rifle was at the ready. As I jumped out, the General's car tore up from its position just behind my advance-guard of six cars, and he very unconcernedly asked me, "What is it you see?" and when I said, "Nothing, sir," he said, "Why, then, do you halt in this infernal position?" I replied, "*I* don't halt, sir, but my *car* does, and won't go on"; and, so saying, I jumped into the next car following; and off we moved again, leaving my mechanic, much to his disgust, to see what the matter was, and to bring the car and guns on after us as soon as possible.

After about 20 miles of these densely wooded hillsides, we reached a large open space at the foot of the hills, and halted there for about half an hour to receive reports from the forest plain in front, where scouts had been sent out from our posts at Resht. Everything appearing satisfactory, we carried straight on through a densely wooded country, seeing many traces of fighting, burnt buildings, etc., till at last the country, becoming sandy, gave evidence of the proximity of the sea, and finally we saw the blue, blue waters of the Caspian shining brightly in the evening sun. We halted on the banks of the harbour of Enzeli-Kazian about an hour before sunset, after an interesting but entirely uneventful drive of about 80 miles from Menjil through seemingly impossible country. It appears that the fame of our armoured (?) cars and machine-guns had preceded us, and that the wild Jungalis were actually present in force in the woods through which we had passed. Yet because of the exaggerated tales they had heard, and the apparent strength of our party, their "discretion," let us call it, got the better of their valour, and not one of them had ventured in any way to betray his presence!

The port of Enzeli-Kazian is the only port on the Caspian coast of Persia, or at any rate the only one of any importance, and its situation is rather peculiar. The high mountains here recede from the coast, leaving a strip of marshy and extremely fertile but unhealthy plain, averaging about 40 miles deep, between the mountains and the southern shore of the sea, for a distance of over 100 miles. This is the Persian province of Gilan; and though it has at various times since the days of the earlier Czars been occupied by the Russians, yet it has always in the end been evacuated on account of its pestiferous climate, which renders any lengthy residence fatal to Europeans. The port itself is nothing but a narrow channel which connects a large lagoon, many square miles in extent, with the sea, and the old town of Enzeli and the more modern Kazian lie respectively on the western and eastern points of the two spits of land which enclose the lagoon, the modern Russian road (by which we had come) following the eastern spit of land to Kazian, whence the old town of Enzeli is seen across the narrow waterway.

Before the road was made the oversea traffic from Persia to Baku and the other Caspian ports was conducted by lighters, which traversed the lagoon from Resht at its southern shore to Enzeli, where their cargoes were shipped on sea-going vessels. To-day, however, this form of transport is comparatively neglected, and such trade as may be carried on uses the road.

Within the few preceding weeks the Armenians in Baku had succeeded in ousting the Bolsheviks from power in that city, and were now even more anxious to procure what assistance might be obtainable from us than the Bolsheviks had previously been to prevent our advance. Under these circumstances it was decided to do what might be possible for their assistance, and a small body of about seventy British troops had, when we reached the coast, already crossed the sea as an earnest of further assistance, and more were to follow as and when opportunity offered.

On arrival at Kazian I pitched my tent under a clump of trees in what had once been a garden, some 200 yards from the banks of the harbour, and here at once experienced a bad "go" of fever, with exceptionally high temperature; this lasted about a week, and left me feeling a very poor specimen, though anxious as ever to proceed.

Kazian in August remains always in my mind as the hottest place I have ever been in, and also the most unhealthy. The cause is probably the breeding in vast numbers on the stagnant lagoons of every kind of venomous and fever-carrying insect. I find my notes say: "Here (at Kazian) is found every kind of venomous bug which is known to exist on earth, and they all bite, and kept on biting all the time." If it is borne in mind that whilst absorbing all this poison one also has to resist the very worst form of damp heat (in the only concrete building in the place I have seen the thermometer at 138°, with the moisture streaming down the walls), it will surprise no one to learn that sickness was rife, and that many cases had serious results, which sadly depleted our already very limited resources of man-power, and so made our difficult task even more arduous.

One most acceptable item of news we learnt on arrival—namely, that the Baku Bolsheviks had consented to supply us with, and had actually forwarded for our use, large quantities of petrol in exchange for quite a small number of motor-cars which were to be forwarded from Bagdad. This was good news indeed, and the cars forming my late convoy left at once, on their return journey, each carrying a load of 50 gallons of petrol in a good steel drum, so that we could now expect that our much-needed reinforcements and stores would speedily appear on the scene.

On the night of August 14th I was shown an empty oil-tank steamer and given charge of a detachment of about seventy British troops to get on board and across to Baku as quickly as might be possible by that means. We got them all on board that night, and I could well understand the surprised expression which showed itself on every countenance when they saw the transport so different from any other of which they had had experience.

Our tank was, indeed, just an iron tank, more or less in the shape of a ship, with some indifferent engines at the stern. The iron top of the tank itself formed the deck, and also the entire accommodation for passengers, or anything else, with not even an apology for a bulwark round it to prevent men, kit, or animals slipping over the side into the sea. Also, whenever the sun shone, which was pretty nearly all the time, the iron became too hot to bear one's hand on, and rendered sitting on it a delicate and far from comfortable proceeding. This contrivance was said, in a calm sea, to be capable of about 5 knots per hour as a maximun speed, which optimistic estimate I very much doubt the truth of, although we were, on this trip, never in a position to verify or refute the statement, the "calm sea" being conspicuous by its absence during this passage. In fact, it blew so hard on the first day that we could get no pilot to undertake to take our crazy conveyance over the nasty "bar" at the harbour mouth. When at daylight of the 16th we did finally get "out" the seas ran so high that even the pilot's frantic desire to return to his family and friends ashore was not a sufficiently powerful inducement to persuade him to take the chance of drowning by getting into a boat, and he therefore was obliged to accompany us on the 300-mile crossing to Baku.

The iron deck, such as it was, was liberally furnished with rings and "cleats" of various kinds, and we got some "poles" on board, not of the human, but of the forest variety, and these we securely lashed to the deck, and everything movable, including my two cars, was firmly lashed to them. After that operation had been satisfactorily concluded, we proceeded to see to what provison had been made for rations for the men.

I found some terribly disconsolate-looking faces, the owners of which pointed out three sheep which had been driven on board at the last moment, saying they didn't know what they were for, and they had had no rations issued for the journey except some local black bread! This and their hopeless expression of countenance when I told them the sheep were their rations tickled my sense of humour, so that I laughed heartily, and said if they'd bring one along to my car, which had now become my cabin, I'd show them how to skin and cut them up, of which very ordinary operation they were profoundly ignorant. The sea, however, was getting worse and worse, and the men getting greener and greener, so that it became evident that the question of eating would be subordinated to the endeavour to *retain* what they had eaten bebore starting. In the meanwhile it rained torrents, and as the weather got worse rather than better those sheep were not touched till we reached Baku on the morning of the third day. We had a really bad passage, in which the only incident was the passing during the night of a Bolshevik gunboat steering an opposite course to ourselves, no doubt going to investigate the state of affairs at the port we had just left. It was a great relief when she passed us without notice, taking us for an empty oil-tank only—for had they come on board things would have been very nasty, the men being far from fit to take on a scrap.

The Caspian Sea is, roughly, 750 miles long and averages about 350 miles in width, and as unpleasant rough weather is to be found there as in any other sea that I have experience of. It does not, of course, compare with the long swell of the ocean, but being "shorter"—that is, the waves being nearer together—it is even more unpleasant, and in our exposed position on our wallowing tank we got the full benefit of it, and my car also underwent a trial of a kind I had never contemplated when constructing her, as she was called upon to resist the waves breaking over us. However, she stood it well, a fact of the utmost importance to myself, as I was camped inside of her and never moved out during the passage.

Baku Harbour is as fine an anchorage as exists anywhere, and all the fleets in the world could easily lie comfortably there in any weather. The main harbour is a deep bay running inland about 15 miles, the mouth of the bay being a little less than that distance across, blocked up by a large island which leaves only a narrow channel at either end, the southern entrance only being used for navigation, and this affords, as we were to find out later on, a passage, only a quarter of a mile wide, of deep water.

The town, a somewhat pretentious one, in European style, with many fine modern buildings, occupies low-lying ground gradually sloping upwards from the sea-front to the sharp ridges which encircle the town at a distance of from 2 to 3 miles inland. The sea-front is well supplied with piers and quays, and the front itself extends about 4 miles. We came in at daylight, and moored alongside a pier, on August 17th, and the men joined their units at once, whilst I reported at Headquarters for duty. A few words will here be necessary to describe the actual position of affairs in the town of Baku at that time, and the manner in which that situation had been brought about.

Previous to the final success of the Bolshevik movement in Russia, a very considerable proportion of the arms and munitions obtained by the Czar's Government from the Allies had been transported to the Caucasus, with the double object of supplying the Grand Duke Nicholas' force operating in Persia and Anatolia, and at the same time of keeping the armament out of the hands of the Bolsheviks in Central Russia, as it was believed that there were great chances of the Transcaucasian provinces holding out against the Bolshevik movement. This belief, however, proved to be a delusion, and the Bolsheviks, under Comrades Shaumian and Petrov, obtained control in Baku. This state of affairs continued until the end of July, when a revolution took place in the town, and the Bolshevik Government was replaced by another body calling themselves the "Central Caspian Dictatorship," who had invited us to come to their assistance in resisting the Turkish attacks on the city. Comrades Shaumian and Petrov, the defeated Bolsheviks, on the overthrow of their Government, seized thirteen ships in the harbour, and having loaded them with the entire contents of the arsenals and all the munitions and other loot that they could lay hands on, embarked their Red supporters and set sail for Astrakan, at the mouth of the great Volga River, at the northern extremity of the Caspian, which was then the great Bolshevik centre in Southern Russia.

The new Government in Baku, however, succeeded in prevailing upon the gunboats guarding the port, who were manned by Bolsheviks of a different brand, to intercept the thirteen ships, and eleven of them were obliged to return and disgorge their cargoes of munitions and general loot. These, at the time of arrival, were lying heaped in inextricable confusion upon the quays at the custom-house.

The new Government consisted of five Dictators, and relied upon the support of the more moderate Russians and the Armenians in approximately equal numbers, the very considerable Tartar (Moslem) population looking on only, but with very strong Turkish sympathies.

In the meanwhile the Turks, with the assistance of a German Commander and many German staff officers, were investing the whole peninsula, and at the time of our arrival some kind of resistance had been organized by the new Government, and a line occupied resting its left flank on the sea, 3 or 4 miles south of the town, and extending a distance of about 12 miles in a northerly direction. This line, although it covered the actual town, still left a gap of about 7 miles between its northern end and the sea, and therefore did not adequately defend the peninsula and the oil-wells which form its greatest asset.

The troops or, more properly, the local levies available to hold this line were, when we arrived, about 6,000 men, in some twenty battalions of 200 to 400 men each, consisting of Armenians and Russians entirely wanting in discipline, experience, and, most important of all, any fighting instinct. The investing force consisted of two regular Turkish divisions and about an equal number of irregulars, the whole amounting to a force of about 30,000, with artillery which, if not numerous, was yet extremely efficient, the force being well armed throughout and well supplied with German machine-guns and ammunition.

Such, then, was the problem before us as our small force came dribbling into the beleaguered city.

Upon reporting at our Headquarters, I was asked if I would undertake the duty of enumerating and organizing the ordnance resources of the new Republic. This included armament of all kinds, ammunition, explosives, and every variety of equipment, and in view of the absolute state of chaos existing at the moment, it appeared to be an almost impossible undertaking in the short time during which it seemed likely we should be able to defend the town. However, I immediately expressed my readiness to undertake anything, and to do my best; so it was agreed that my services should be "lent" to the new Caspian Government for this special service, and a note to that effect was forwarded to the Dictators, with the result that within an hour I found myself in the presence of General Bogratouni, the "Minister of War."

This officer (an Armenian, and the only one of that race for whom I have, at any time, entertained any respect) had served in the Imperial Army of Russia, in which he had attained the rank of General. He was at this time suffering severely from the after-effects of an indifferently performed amputation of the leg, which had been seriously injured by shell-fire some time previously.

In spite of his suffering, he was doing heroic work, and was the only man of decision whom I came across, and his orders were obeyed promptly, which is more than can be said of those of any of his colleagues. He invested me with the proud title of "Controller-General of the Ordnance," and gave me the fullest powers of control over all arsenals, factories, and stores of all kinds, at the same time placing the Russian General acting as Director of Artillery under my orders. I received within half an hour of our interview a commission from the Government to the above effect, signed by all the Dictators and Ministers and by the Commander-in-Chief, and so promptly got to work, reporting progress personally to the

Minister of War at 7.30 each evening from that time onwards, and always being able to count on his effective support.

The first step was to inspect what resources might exist in the town in the way of factories capable of producing shells, fuses, explosives, etc. Having had a rapid and general look round, I came at once to the conclusion that there would be nothing to be done in the way of the manufacture of anything in the time at my disposal, which I felt certain would be very limited. The town, however, I found to be full of ammunition, armament, and military equipment of all kinds, all scattered about in various places in hopeless confusion, for the safe keeping of which, apparently, no one had hitherto been responsible, no lists of it being in existence.

The next step was to get the whole lot of miscellaneous material together in one place. For this purpose I selected the custom-house on the sea-front, some 2 miles from the main piers, and began assembling the material there on the first day after my arrival, continuing day and night till I had collected there at least the greater part of it. The custom-house had many advantages, as it lay on the sea-front, with three piers of its own, the railway from the terminus being extended to it, and small trolley lines running within its gates and so out on to the various piers.

The building itself was of one story only, and though large and straggling, yet enclosed a considerable space, within a solid wall which was capable of good defence, except to artillery fire. The best feature, however, was that, being in the very centre of the perimeter of the outside trench-line, it would be the last place to become accessible to the shell-fire which was to be expected as the enemy's lines approached the city.

The eleven ships which the Bolsheviks had been obliged to return had been brought back to the custom-house piers and made to unload all the munitions, with which they had tried to get away, on to these piers. There they still lay, including guns of all kinds, and an enormous quantity of high-explosive ammunition, which, being without any guard, constituted a very real danger to the whole town.

In the face of all this confusion and without any assistance, it may be imagined that the task with which I found myself

## THE "HUSH-HUSH" ARMY

confronted was one to fill me with despair; but fortunately that vice was omitted when my allowance of vices was served out, and therefore I returned forthwith to the Minister of War and asked for as many men as could be raised, not less than 200, anyway, of any sort or description, to handle the material, and as many reasonably competent Russian or even Armenian officers as could be spared, to be placed under my orders at once. Having immediately obtained a Russian officer as A.D.C. and a Russian barrister (who smelt of drink) as a secretary, I returned to my new-found arsenal to await events, and towards late afternoon a few, about six or eight, Russian and Armenian officers and N.C.O.s turned up, and we got to work. In the meanwhile, a crowd which defies description began to assemble at the gates, and these were the men procured to assist! They were all more than half-starved, and were of all nations: Russians, Armenians, Kurds, Tartars, Turcomans, Mongols, Persians, Dagistanis, and many more cross-bred by every description of cross-breeding between these races. All were in the last state of destitution, in rags and starving. The most pressing need, therefore, was first of all to feed them.

I had been fortunate enough to obtain the use of a few Russian lorries to bring in the munitions from other parts of the town, and as they came in and unloaded they were immediately dispatched for bread, whilst I explained to my newly organized Ordnance Corps of astounding appearance that they would be promptly *fed,* which statement was received with much emotion. When, however, I went on to say that their pay would in future consist of *food,* and not money, the majority dissolved into tears, for food at that time was very hard indeed to come by, whereas money they all habitually stole, and they had never expected such consideration. The results were invaluable; work went ahead at an astonishing rate, and order soon began to evolve out of chaos.

There were, at the time I took over, about ten or twelve guns of various calibre and undoubted antiquity actually mounted in the line of defences, but I found scattered about approximately 120 others in various states of inefficiency, some wanting breech-blocks, others sights, and all with some indispensable portion missing. However, by improvising parts, rectifying adjustments, etc., we were soon successful in getting upwards of fifty guns in action, and before the final evacuation we actually had eighty-six guns in action in the line.

In the meanwhile the question of ammunition and its supply to the batteries and firing-line became acute. For though a colossal store of ammunition had been accumulated in the town, yet it had been under no sort of control, and not even listed or checked, so that every regimental or battery commander had both taken and fired or "sold" whatever he wished, and the waste had been terrible. Now, however, I got it all counted and classified, and was truly astonished at its quantity and origin, which same remark applied to the guns themselves.

Amongst the guns were none larger than 6-inch, and this calibre was represented by the very best form of Krupp (German) mobile Q.F. howitzer. There was also, to my astonishment, a battery of four of the latest 1916 Creusot (French) long-range Q.F. 105-millimetre field-guns sighted to 14,500 metres, as fine a modern mobile gun as was to be found on any front at that time; and last, but not least, two of our own 4.5 howitzers, made by the Coventry Ordnance Works in 1916. This principal armament, with an infinite variety of Russian guns and howitzers and machine-guns of every kind, constituted, of course, our main means of defence, and the report I sent in, after going through these resources, had a very stimulating effect on the spirits of the Central Caspian Republic generally, which, indeed, was the principal intention with which it was prepared.

The ammunition amounted, without doubt, to a considerably greater quantity than could be found in the whole of Mesopotamia for the use of our troops. I counted up to well over 100,000 rounds of gun ammunition, mostly high explosive, of English and French manufacture, and many milions of rounds of small-arm ammunition, much of which was manufactured by Rimington in U.S.A. and marked with a broad arrow, "Re-examined in England," the total amount being so great that it was useless to contemplate the moving of the vast quantities still lying on the pier into the arsenal, and it had therefore to lie where it was—under guard, indeed, but exposed to every kind of danger both from theft or detonation.

In the meanwhile the British Headquarters had been established in the Hôtel de l'Europe, a large European hotel in the centre of the town, and the Chief had come over from Kazian, and, though generally to be found on board his ship, the *Kruger*, moored at one of the town piers, was always at some time every day at the hotel, where I daily went to get a most indifferent meal and, more particularly, to keep in touch with our own people.

Without going into details, it can be understood that attacks, more or less severe, were pretty frequent, and our line gradually fell back, as it was impossible to keep the town levies in the line. Though they would be there if there was any question of rations being issued, yet the moment they received them they slunk off back, by twos and threes, to the security of their various cellars and "funk-holes" in the town. It is hard to describe the Caucasian Armenian's attitude towards fighting, as he seems incapable of grasping the possibility of himself actually fighting, even in defence of his life; but an incident which actually happened may convey the correct impression.

On one occasion the Turks were threatening an attack on a portion of the line held by these heroes, who, as usual, executed a brilliant *feu de joie* by discharging their rifles with great gallantry into the empty air, from a position already well behind the line, as a preliminary to carrying out an equally brilliant but considerably more hurried move to the rear. As, however, this strategy on their part had not been unforeseen, a very considerable force of their relations had been massed in the vicinity as a reserve, and these gentlemen promptly received orders to advance. These they received fairly calmly, if without any great enthusiasm, until the point *to* which they were to advance was indicated to them, when the proposal was negatived instantly and unanimously. On being asked the reason why they should *not* advance to that particular spot, they replied, with hysterical laughter: "Of course we couldn't go *there*. Why, that is the very place to which the enemy is advancing!" What kind of a fight can be expected from soldiers ( ?) of this quality?

The days, however, slipped by, and it began to look as if, after all, the impossible might happen and we might be able to hold the town, as we had already received one reinforcement (only a battery, it is true) from Bicherakov's Russians farther up the coast, and more might come in at any moment. I there-for put before the Chief a proposition I had long been maturing, to take a small and very mobile force of six light cars, and ship them as if for return to Enzeli, but, in fact, to land them at a port called Kizil Agoutah, 120 miles down the coast, where there were no telegraphs, and to push across the open steppe there for 150 miles, to reach and blow up the great railway bridge over the Koma River behind the Turks, and so cut their line of communication, ammunition supply, etc.

To my great delight, I received permission to organize and lead this expedition. In the necessary preparations I received the hearty co-operation of the "Minister of War," who undertook to supply me with all particulars of the railway track, as well as with forged orders from the German Commander-in-Chief, bearing his seal and signature, instructing me to carry out a reconnaissance in that district. Of course, my part was to figure as a German staff officer until the job was done, after which the matter would assume a less simple aspect, and we should be free to retreat in whatever direction might offer the best prospect of escape.

This, then, was the general position on August 31st, upon which day a more than usually severe attack upon our defences took place. I was most busily occupied all day in dealing out ammunition to the various dumps I had established behind the lines, and in refusing many hysterical demands for ridiculous quantities of ammunition, as well as in executing lightning repairs upon guns and armament of all kinds.

On the morning of this attack I had a very curious experience, which will be illuminating to those who have been fortunate enough to escape experience of the revolutionary Russian soldier.

Knowing that all my ammunition dumps had been filled up the night before, I was astounded, as soon as the attack began to develop, to receive frantic messages one after the other from a very vital part of the line stating the dumps were empty, the ammunition having been removed during the night by order of the Director-General of Artillery.

A General Officer under my orders immediately dispatched the entire reserve transport ready loaded with ammunition, which I always kept ready in case of emergency, and I proceeded myself to elucidate the mystery, which might easily have led to the loss of the town. I verified the fact that the ammunition for the supply of the forward batteries had been removed by the written order of the General in question, and that the carts removing it were strange to the officers in charge of the dumps, and had afterwards proceeded with their loads in the direction of the enemy's lines! This confirmed certain suspicions which I had entertained for some time, but which had seemed to indicate a position which in my innocence I had hitherto deemed an impossible one, but in coming to that conclusion it was now apparent that I had been wrong.

I therefore mustered the most reliable guard I could get together, and, putting them in a lorry, took my own machine-gun car and proceeded direct to the quarters of the General who was responsible for the removal of the ammunition, telephoning to the Russian Commander-in-Chief at the same time requesting an immediate audience on an affair of the greatest urgency.

Having disembarked and paraded my guard before the General's quarters, I ordered him into my car, and never took my eyes off him till we were ushered together into the private office of the Commander-in-Chief, where I formally accused him of having *sold* the ammunition to the enemy! The Commander-in-Chief, knowing the type of man, to my great astonishment, was not the least surprised, but nevertheless, to my great satisfaction, he there and then deprived him of all authority, and he left the room a prisoner within five minutes, and the incident closed. It will, however, serve to illustrate the general state of affairs, and a small portion of the unheard-of difficulties which we were up against.

Late that evening, at 9 P.M., I went to the hotel for food, as usual, and there saw the Chief, who told me there was a gap some miles wide in the line, which our heroic allies were either unwilling or unable to fill, and that the town lay open to the Turks any moment they wished to march into it.

He also informed me that, under the circumstances, he had notified the Government of his intention to withdraw the troops. This cheerful information, imparted by *him*, in his own inimitable manner, entirely calm and with even a certain humorous reflection upon the quality of the forces whose salvation we had undergone such trials to assure, did not present the same picture which would have resulted from the news imparted by a less striking personality, and in no wise interfered with my enjoyment of my meagre repast. Soon after it was over, however, when he returned from a conference, things assumed a more serious aspect, as he then informed me that the Central Caspians had decided that, should the troops be embarked, the gunboats at the mouth of the harbour would have orders to fire on the ships and prevent their leaving! He therefore did not intend to take such a chance until absolutely obliged.

There was no need for him to explain that, should the Turks come in, this meant a Turkish prison for all of us, and he of course knew that we (the senior officers only were present) all understood very well; but I shall never forget the Chief's very gallant bearing on that occasion, for he had a kind word for all, and carried himself in a way any man might be proud to do, in the face of the disaster which seemed certain to be the result of the whole enterprise entrusted to him, and I must say that at that moment he commanded, more than ever, my deepest respect and sympathy.

Before getting off to my arsenal that night, I told the Chief I could make arrangements to blow up the whole of the ammunition then on the quays, to prevent it falling into the hands of the enemy, and that if he authorized me to do so I would take the necessary steps the next morning, and lay the wires to one of the hulks I had at anchor in the harbour, from whence I would fire the charge at the proper time, without consideration of the damage which was sure to ensue in the town. Afterwards I would do my best to get away in a boat of some kind, as I preferred to take my chance at sea to the certainty of a Turkish prison. He agreed, and gave me permission to do whatever I thought best, and at my request said he would ask the Dictators to send me a Russian naval officer who might be able to procure me some kind of launch to get away with; and on that we parted for the night.

Next day the promised naval officer appeared, and I explained to him that it was my intention to transfer the greater part of the ammunition to hulks which I had at anchor in the harbour, as a measure of safety against the shelling now becoming daily more severe and accurate; and I asked him if he could secure me a launch to tow them to suitable positions and to be at my

## THE "HUSH-HUSH" ARMY 79

orders generally for this purpose. This was eventually agreed to, but such was the nervousness of these Bolsheviks that it was stipulated that their crew of five men should have entire charge of the launch, and that I should never embark with more than two men. To this I agreed at once, as five Bolshevik sailors presented no terrors to me; but I realized at once that we should have to knock them on the head to get away, though this did not appear to be at all beyond our powers; and having had a look at the gentlemen in question, I then felt even more sure of this, and reported to the Chief that the wires would be laid before dark, and I should be standing by to act on my own initiative at any moment.

During this eventful day the Turks, with the town at their mercy, were once more seized with an attack of diffidence. I have known this to happen on several occasions, and it is a national failing of their otherwise courageous and capable troops that when all is clear they often hesitate, not from any want of courage, but from a suspicion of some trap, though in a losing battle they will fight, as a rule, to the last extremity. On this occasion they hesitated to follow up their advantage, and in consequence we were eventually able to fill up the gap, and temporarily to "breathe again."

About this time, as the shelling became more accurate, the streets became more and more unsafe, and our Headquarters at the Hôtel de l'Europe suffered considerably; but these are the ordinary incidents of war, and in no way present the appreciation of any humorous situations which may occur, as the following story will well illustrate. On the transfer of Headquarters from Persia to Baku, the British Consul at Resht, a first-class man and an excellent fellow in every way, was transferred to Baku to establish his Consular Department there, which he did with great success, and was allotted quarters and officers in the same hotel which contained our military Headquarters. He brought with him his staff of stenographers, who were of the female gender, all very skilled in the various languages of the Near East, being mostly themselves Russians, who had evidently been selected, also, with a view that their appearance should in no way "offend the eye," but have rather the contrary effect! It may be easily understood that the presence of this bevy of beauties at meal-times in no way incommoded the military staff, with whom their engaging manners soon rendered them universally popular.

The star amongst them was, I think, of Circassian parentage, with a wealth of golden hair, which, as she explained, owing to the great heat, she was unable to bear coiled round her head, so that she wore it hanging in all its glory down her back and over her shoulders, confined only by a suitable ribbon. This wonderful chevelure reached far below her waist, and formed the most attractive sight to be seen at meal-times, and the lady was the observed of all observers, and would undoubtedly have constituted what is called a "feature" at any beauty show in Europe. Now to the real story.

One night a 6-inch high-explosive shell hit the hotel during the early hours of the morning, and completely wrecked that portion in which were situated the quarters of one of our senior officers, a very popular character with the whole staff. Search was at once made, but, the whole wing being in ruins, no sign could be found of his remains, so that when I arrived for *déjeuner* at midday I was told the news, and many nice things were said about him, and his loss was sincerely mourned. Our friend of the glorious hair was also at *déjeuner* at another table, and as I knew our absent comrade was a great friend of hers, I took a good look at her, and noticed that, apart from trying to catch the conversation at our table, she was otherwise quite unconcerned, and looked, if anything, more attractive than ever.

In the middle of our lunch the door suddenly opened, and who should walk in but our friend himself, whose sad fate we had just been mourning. He advanced quite unconcernedly and took his usual place at our senior officers' table, being instantly greeted by a chorus of congratulations upon his escape. "What escape?" was his surprising answer; and he was immediately told that we had been searching the ruins of his quarters to find some part of him which we could bury with suitable honours. "My quarters!" he said in astonishment, and then relapsed into silence and listened to the whole story without making any further remark. His unexpected action set us all thinking; and glancing up at our friend of the golden hair, and observing the most becoming exhibition of the rosiest of blushes with which she had now become suffused, I made no remark at all, but got up and went about my business, having a shrewd suspicion that the report, subsequently made, "that our friend's escape was due entirely to the good fortune which kept him absent from his quarters that night" was a description of the incident which it would be truly difficult to surpass.

I now began to find that the open ruins and waste ground which surrounded the arsenal, where I slept each night, were not at all an unmixed blessing, as I was invariably fired at there each time I returned after dark, though I never did so at night except in my car. I also noticed every night a considerable amount of desultory firing took place on the ground in question, and each morning there was more or less ghastly evidence of murders of various sorts done there during the night. I therefore applied to the Minister of War of the Republic for permission to requisition a flat in a large, strong building overlooking both the open space and the arsenal. This flat had belonged to a German, and, though now closed, looked as if it would suit me much better to sleep in than my office in the arsenal. The Minister immediately granted my request and signed my requisition, so, taking my driver and another pretty tough British soldier with me, I proceeded to take possession.

When, however, I got on to the landing on to which my desirable flat opened, I found the great doors securely fastened; and whilst I was standing deliberating how to get in, the door of the other flat on the same landing opened, and an immaculately dressed gentleman of obvious Armenian extraction presented himself and inquired my business. This was soon explained and my requisition shown, upon which he retorted that he was the owner of the building, that the flat was closed, and he could not allow me to go in. However, I was little inclined to stand talk of that kind from any Armenian at that time, and I told him very briefly but quite plainly that he could go at once to the very hot place for which he was quite certainly eventually bound; and at the same time I ordered my men to fetch their entrenching pickaxes from the car and to break the door in. This gave them intense satisfaction, and in a moment the whole building was echoing to the smashing blows of their pickaxes and the sound of splintering wood!

The noise was, in fact, considerable, and rang through the empty house, to our entire satisfaction; but the effect on the

Armenian was as excellent an illustration of that race's peculiar nervous organization as one could ever wish to see. The sight of *force* being used has the same effect on Armenians as on rabbits, and this man crouched down just *like* a rabbit and turned as white as a sheet, apparently suffering from some kind of heart attack—of which we, of course, took not the least notice —till at last he crawled across the landing and, grasping my knees, assured me that if I would only stop my terrifying actions and the dreadful noise, which his nerves could not endure, *he* would go round and get in by the back door, of which he had the key in his pocket all the time, and would then open the front door for us. In this manner we obtained possession of a very fine flat, looking out over the arsenal on one side and the Caspian Sea on the other, its only drawback being that at night it was advisable not to stand at a lighted window, as the gentleman who frequented the ruins opposite acquired an unpleasant habit of shooting at any of my windows which showed a light.

In the meanwhile the situation in the lines was going from bad to worse, and it was becoming daily more clearly evident that we could not hope to hold the town much longer with the limited forces at our disposal.

# CHAPTER V

### EVACUATION: THE STEAMER "ARMENIAN"

Enemy shelling—Work of the *Armenian*—Preparations for raid on enemy communications—Turk deserter's information—The final attack—Preparations for evacuation—State of the quays—Guarding the arsenal pier—I traverse the quays to obtain reinforcements—Our H.Q. sentries—Permission to shift for myself—Arrangement of signal—The Commissaire—His treatment—Getting the breech-blocks—Massacre by Tartars—Withdrawal of our last pickets—The Turks in the town—Withdraw my guard from pier—Another Commissaire—The *Armenian* casts off—The hospital ship passes—The anchor is lost—Find and speak the *Kruger* at last—Follow her out—Trouble on board—Challenged by the guardships—They open fire—Trouble with the captain—Trouble with the crew—At sea—Triumphal entry into port—The Chief's congratulations.

During the early days of September the Turks' shelling of the city became much more severe, and as the lines were drawn in nearer the city, they were able to search out our Headquarters and ships with greater ease and accuracy. My ammunition dumps became liable to be hit and blown up at any moment, and it was evident that hour was close at hand when further defence would become impossible.

Under these circumstances I took great pains to embark as much ammunition as possible on old hulks which were anchored in the harbour, which we could sink on the fall of the town. My plans had been so made that I had at my disposal a small Russian steamer, curiously enough named the *Armenian,* of about 200 tons, which I made use of daily in shipping the ammunition out to the hulks. Flying the Bolshevik flag, and being manned by Bolshevik sailors, who acted under the orders of the Caspian Government, its movements created little, if any, uneasiness in the minds of the Dictators, and each day on its return to its moorings I saw to it that an ever-increasing stock of selected munitions remained in the hold, instead of being distributed on board the hulks. As its loading was a daily occurrence, no suspicion of my intentions was aroused even in the minds of the captain and crew, and in a few days I succeeded in having it full to the hatches with a selection of the best high-explosive ammunition in the town, which it was my intention to endeavour to save from the Turks.

These were in the nature of precautionary measures, however, and during this period, in the hope that some chance of the arrival of reinforcements, or any of the many unexpected happenings whose occurrence is the only certainty in war, might enable us to continue our apparently impossible defence, the preparations for the carrying out of the raid upon the enemy's communications which I had been authorized to undertake were pushed on with feverish energy.

The party was to be confined to six cars and the personnel was to be limited to sixteen officers and men all told, with one machine-gun to each car. Each man was carefully selected, and to all was explained what it was intended should be done, and what their own duties would be in every possible eventuality. I also gave them elaborate lectures on the possibilities for our escape offered by the surrounding country, in case the only chance of safety we might have, after the event, should prove to be by means of a general dispersal in all directions, in which case some at least, if they knew the country, might have a reasonable chance of reaching some of the friendly Kurdish tribes on the Persian frontier, from 200 to 300 miles distant.

Good maps of the country were put at our disposal by the Minister of War, who most heartily approved of our plans, and the lie of the whole country and the exact position of our objective (the main railway bridge) was carefully explained to the whole party. It was our intention to use nothing but guncotton, and the charges were prepared with a large plan of the bridge in front of us, each man being shown what his particular task would be, and the manner in which it should be carried out, including the placing of the detonators and the leading of the wires.

We had been supplied with a detailed sketch of the defences of the bridge (held by forty second-line Turkish troops with machine-guns), but from these (if under our German uniforms we could once get close up to them) we did not anticipate any very serious resistance. The telegraph-wires were, of course, first to be cut on the Baku side of the river, and as, once the bridge was down, no pursuit could come from the other bank, we had great hopes that we might be successful in getting away to the mountains in the south well ahead of any pursuing force.

Our greatest difficulty lay in the "getting there," as there were two large rivers, the Aras and the Koura, to cross during our 150 miles' dash over the open country which lay between the coast at the point where we were to land and the bridge which we hoped to destroy. Neither of these rivers was anywhere bridged, and as it was too much to reckon on being able to obtain a ferry-boat, we constructed and tested large bags of leather, which we were to carry with us and to inflate with our tyre pumps on the river bank, it being intended to float the cars over by that means.

All these preparations were made with the utmost secrecy, and the closest attention was given to every detail. Throughout we kept in the closest touch with the Minister of War, who provided us with German passes and who obtained for me the cap and coat of a German staff officer. He also detailed to accompany us an Armenian officer, lately deserted from the Turks, who still had his Turkish uniform and had been born and bred on the open plain which we should have to traverse, and so would prove an admirable guide to the party. On the 11th I was at last in a position to report to the Chief that we were ready, and our departure was fixed for daylight on the 13th.

During this time affairs in the town had become much worse, and the shelling had necessitated the changing of our Headquarters, which had suffered considerably; the moorings of our ships were also changed and brought a few hundred yards nearer the arsenal. The streets had also become even more unsafe, and one could read on many faces of the Tartar population their impatience to get to work on the loot and general massacre which they felt to be growing imminent.

On the 12th an Armenian officer deserted from the Turks and came into our lines. This man was personally known to the Minister of War, who was confident we could rely upon the information he gave us to the effect that he had remained with the Turks till their plans for the final attack and the time at which it was to be delivered had definitely been decided on; and as the time fixed was at daylight on the 14th, he had now come in to warn his countrymen.

This was definite and reliable news at last, and the first effect was that the orders for my departure on the 13th were cancelled, as, unless the attack could be satisfactorily repulsed, which was very doubtful, my success, even if achieved, would come too late to be of any service. This was a great disappointment, but one over which there was no time to mourn, as I received the news only at 5 P. M., and was hard at work all night and the next day with my preparations to meet the attack. We observed no signs of the enemy's intentions until, as the sky began to get grey before dawn on the 14th, every gun in his lines suddenly opened fire and his columns advanced to the attack!

In the first wave of their advance the Turks captured a vital post in the centre of our line; every effort we could make was then instantly concentrated on an endeavour to induce our Armenian allies to deliver the counter-attack which was necessary to recover this post—entirely without success, as the levies simply melted away when it was attempted to concentrate them for this purpose, and the Turks, therefore, were able to retain this vital post throughout the day. Our own handful of British troops fought as only they can fight, and both officers and men upheld that day, against overwhelming odds, the very highest traditions of the British Army.

Receiving, as I did, constant information from all parts of the line, mostly accompanied by fantastic requests for ammunition, I came to the conclusion before midday that our position would soon become untenable, and I therefore concentrated my energies on an endeavour to save as much of the munitions under my care as might be possible.

To that end all my men were set to work to load the little steamer *Armenian* with as much as she could carry of those munitions which would be of the greatest value to us and the greatest loss to the enemy. The hold, thanks to my previous precautions, already contained many thousands of rounds of the best of the high-explosive ammunition, and we now proceeded to embark the most valuable of the guns, which happened at that time to be in the arsenal under repair, as well as case after case of gun spare parts, special tools, etc. Many truck-loads of small-arms ammunition were also embarked, so that when, about 4.30 P. M., the British officer commanding the town personally told me evacuation had been decided on, my own preparations were already far advanced.

As dusk began to fall, I sallied forth along the quay to report to the Chief, then on board his ship resisting hysterical and fantastic demands from the Government that our troops should not be withdrawn. The situation on the quays at that time was so remarkable that an attempt must be made to give some idea of it.

The arsenal pier, where my nondescript Ordnance Corps was hard at work loading the *Armenian,* was between a quarter and half a mile from the piers where our other ships lay. The only men upon whom I could really rely (my two drivers and my batman) were busily occupied holding the shore end of the arsenal pier with fixed bayonets against a crowd of terrified refugees who were attempting to rush the pier, with the probable intention of boarding the *Armenian.*

My little car was drawn up in support of the men, with its machine-guns covering the roadway leading from the quay to the pier. The quays along the whole sea-front were black with a frantic crowd, consisting largely of local levies who had bolted from the lines and were now endeavouring to embark on any kind of vessel which they might be able to reach.

This crowd, most of whom carried arms, was in a state of abject terror, and interspersed amongst them were large numbers of the Tartar (Mohammedan) population, whose sympathies were with the Turks, and who were prowling about, licking their lips at the prospect of a real hectic night after their own hearts, in which these runaway heroes and their women-kind were "cast" for the most sensational parts. All was absolute confusion, from which rose a fearsome and indescribable noise, comprising every sound from the shrieking and moaning of the women to the fierce guttural oaths of the Tartars, all punctuated by constant reports of firearms and the occasional "boom" of the bursting shells which were now falling on the houses near-by.

My note says "I did not much like the looks of things," which I should now say was an extremely moderate statement, and also that "I doubted the ability of my three men to hold the pier." So much was that so, that I installed a Russian officer, upon whom I could place a certain amount of reliance, in my car, with orders to use the machine-guns if necessity arose, and I instructed my drivers to rally on the car if necessary, but only to come down the quay towards the other ships as a last resource, as that would mean the loss of the *Armenian* and all her valuable cargo.

Having given these orders, I pulled out my good Colt 450 automatic pistol, and started through the crowd for the Chief's ship, to obtain what reinforcements and orders might be available. As evening strolls on seaside promenades go, this one I should imagine to be unique, and "incidents" were frequent. One of them, with a German officer attended by five or six Bolshevik sailors, was particularly sharp and decisive, and it was a great relief when I finally saw the stalwart forms of our most self-possessed British sentries guarding the palisaded entrance to the other pier where our ships lay. Great fellows they were, who presented arms to me with exactly the same precision as if they had been on the barrack gate at home, in spite of the expression of astonishment on their faces at my appearance from the crowd "alone" at that moment.

The Chief was, as usual, quite calm, but badgered to death by Dictators, Commissaires, and such-like undesirables. In a few words I informed him that I thought I might be able to "get away" independently of the other troops and to save a lot of most valuable munitions if he could give me a picket of some sort and any indication of the course to steer in going out. It was then arranged that as soon as it was dark he should hoist three lights at his mast-head, which signal had already been agreed on to serve our troops as a rallying-point for stragglers, and that the *lowering* of these lights was to be his signal to me that he was under way and going out, and that I was then to follow as best I could. He gave me a picket of four men—all that could then be spared—and with this powerful detachment, having fixed bayonets, I made my way back as fast as possible, the return journey with this party being a very much easier one than had been my arrival unaccompanied.

On our return a certain expression of relief was to be observed on the faces of my men, as they had barely been able to maintain their position, and were surrounded by a shrieking, hysterical mob of the worse description. However, with the welcome reinforcement of four new heroes, we knew our pier would be for a time in safety, and I went off at once myself to attend to more urgent matters.

The most pressing of these was to get hold of the breech-blocks of any guns in the line which could be got at. This was undertaken at once, and an amazing experience it proved. Every approach to the town from the lines was at this time choked with Central Caspian troops in every phase of disorganization and panic, all converging upon the town; and to get through in the other direction was wellnigh impossible, as Turk skirmishers were following up closely and the firing was incessant.

Night was rapidly falling, and we found the higher parts of the town already in possession of the enemy, whilst bands of looting and bloodthirsty Tartars were, in all directions, breaking into Armenian houses, from which heartrending screams immediately issued. However, we concentrated on carrying out our own particular duty, and in about three-quarters of an hour got back to the neighbourhood of the quay, having in the car the breech-blocks of nineteen of the best of the guns of the defences, and especially of the 6-inch Krupp howitzers.

Just before we reached the quays we found the street corners still being held by a few pickets of our troops, the last to fall back, and we stopped a while with them to observe the course things were taking. At this time fires were breaking out in many places, and the Tartars were everywhere busy at their fiendish work; but although our men kept the streets immediately in front of their own posts clear, the rabble obtained entry at the rear of the houses, and horrible tragedies were being enacted all round us, evidence of which was again and again furnished by the descent of some horribly mutilated body into the streets from the upper windows, whilst our men lay at the street corners firing from behind the sandbags, which they carried with them, in their retreat.

The quays were blocked by a mob of terrified inhabitants crowded right down to the water's edge, and every boat that could be found was crammed with people seeking safety on board the hulks lying out in the harbour. Shelling had in the meantime ceased, and the Turks, as they obtained possession of the town, were establishing order at the point of their bayonets. As soon as news was received that our wounded were safe on board, I scribbled a note to our Chief of the Staff, instructed the last pickets to fall back on the ships, and made off to the arsenal pier to see after my own particular task. It was indeed time to do so, as our small cordon could have held the pier for only a very short time longer.

The reappearance of the car, however, eased the position, and shortly after I received a visit from one of the Commissaires (high officials) of the Government. I received him on board the *Armenian*, which I had had pushed out some 10 feet or more from the quay, with which it was now only connected by a somewhat insecure plank which served as a gangway. He related to me with much gusto that the Government had heard we intended putting to sea, but that we were not to be allowed to do so, as the gunboats had received orders to fire upon the *Armenian* should she try to break out—which fire, considering the nature of her cargo, would quite certainly "blow her up."

This piece of news, in no way unexpected by me, gave him such intense satisfaction that he repeated it twice, whilst I kept my attention fixed upon my men at the junction of our pier and the quays, which I could see through the window, where I saw my most reliable man at that moment leaving his post and hurrying towards the ship, evidently with news. As he stepped up onto the bridge, where my cabin was, I turned to the Commissaire, and this time the gusto was all on *my* side, and remarked that what he said about taking the ship out was perfectly correct, and that such was my intention, and that it was more than possible his realistic picture of the ship "blowing up" was equally correct, which grieved me much for his sake, as under no circumstances could I allow him to leave the ship, and that if she *did* blow up, he would quite certainly be blown up with her!

With the same breath I called to my man, whom I could then hear outside. He at once appeared at the door, all rifle and bayonet, with his eyes shining in their eager search for the first object into which he could legitimately thrust that weapon; and I then ordered him to guard the cabin, and on any attempt on the part of the Commissaire to get out or to communicate with any one, to *shoot him at once*. Having got this off my chest, I proceeded down the pier to the shore-end, where my picket was still holding its own, though with difficulty, and where I understood a second Commissaire had now arrived and was clamouring to pass the picket with a message to me from the Dictators.

This man I knew to be a thorough Bolshevik, and suspected of the intention of making me trouble with the Russian crew of the *Armenian,* who already looked quite "nasty" enough; so, although I greeted him politely enough, I told him that if he had any message for me from the Government, I could only receive it on board the ship, which I was willing to do if he would come on board. On his agreeing, I led the way on board over our slender plank, and, opening the cabin door, assisted him to enter in a very decisive manner, my difficulty being to confine my persuasive methods to my hand only, as every nerve in my body was tingling with longing to make use of my foot also. Before he recovered himself, I told my man very curtly: "If there's any trouble with these blighters, *shoot them both,* as I shall now draw the men on board and get under way, if I can."

Returning then to our small picket, through which some of the most venturesome on the quay were now beginning to worm their way on to the pier, I gave orders to the car to back down to the ship, keeping the guns trained on the pier, and to get on board, at the same time announcing we should shoot any man who ventured to follow us. We then commenced our retreat in the direction of the ship.

Such was the respect which our confident attitude, backed by bayonets and a machine-gun, as well as by my Colt automatic, still in my hand (where it had been the greater part of the evening and appeared likely to remain all night), that the mob did not attempt to follow us, but remained where they were, whilst all those who had forced their way through our line found their retreat to the shore cut off, and these we forced on board in front of us literally at the point of our bayonets.

I had foreseen the eventual necessity of this manœuvre for some time, as my one object was to prevent definite news of our departure reaching the Government in time for them to notify the gunboats to get their big guns and searchlights uncased, as with their smaller ordnance only in action, and without searchlights, on a pitch-dark night, I thought we might possibly have a chance, even if only a meagre one, of getting through. Anyway, such chance as we might find we were all prepared to take, whatever it might be, sooner than accept the certainty of a Turkish prison, even if we might have had the good fortune to survive the night ashore.

As soon as the last of our protesting prisoners had been shepherded on board, I placed my most gallant, fearless driver, Morris, on guard on the plank itself, with orders to bayonet any one endeavouring to leave the ship, and then proceeded myself to cut the ropes mooring us to the pier. Whilst so employed, I happened to look up, and was instantly convulsed with laughter, for this is what I saw:

Over the famous plank which had replaced the ordinary gangway hung what is known as a "nest" of electric lights, which are in general use for handing cargo at night, and which cast a bright light on objects immediately under them, in the same way as the "spot" light does on the central figure on the stage at a theatre. In the centre of this brilliant illumination, and at the same time in the centre of the plank, stood our hero, with his bayonet gleaming and his knees bent, his rifle at the "ready," and an expression of "Let 'em all come" on his eager countenance which would alone have been quite sufficient to "hold the bridge" without any arms at all! The whole effect was to me intensely entertaining, and I remember singing out to the others: "He only needs the Union Jack behind him and a band to play 'Rule, Britannia' to make a matchless poster of the British Army!"

This sally for a moment distracted his attention from his plank, and at the same time a Kurd, seizing his one and only opportunity, endeavoured to dash by, and whilst so doing ran right on to the point of our hero's bayonet; this weapon, even if it was not pushed home, at any rate gave way *not at all*—and the Kurd reeled back on to the deck, where he proceeded to writhe about and emit a series of blood-curdling yells and groans. This was the very best thing which could possibly have happened, as the effect produced on the overstrained nerves of the crowd of Bolshevik riff-raff on board the ship was to the last degree gratifying, and in reality had much to do with our eventful success in overawing such a crowd—all armed and openly our enemies, and numbering *ninety-six* to our picket of four men, two drivers, and one batman.

The ropes were soon cut, and having kicked the plank overboard I proceeded to the bridge, with my pistol in my hand, where stood a very sulky Russian captain. For the moment I took no notice of him, but busied myself giving orders as to the training of the machine-guns in the car to command the deck, and for the demolition outfit, consisting of six large cases of dynamite, to be brought up on to the bridge.

It will be necessary to give here some description of the ship on board which we now found ourselves. The *Armenian* was quite a small vessel, not exceeding 200 tons, built for general cargo, with one large hold, now full to the hatches with high explosives, extending from the bows right aft to the engines, which were placed at the extreme stern; with a kind of hurricane-deck aft, over them, in which were quarters of sorts for the crew, and on the top the bridge, with chart-house and one cabin, of which I immediately took possession, letting my now much less truculent prisoners the Commissaires loose, as soon as the ship was clear of the pier.

The deck extended from the bows right aft to the bridge, and was now encumbered with guns and munitions of all sorts, with many cases of high explosives, for which there was no further room in the hold, whilst immediately under the bridge was my car, with its guns commanding the deck forward, upon which were crowded the miscellaneous herd of armed ruffians whom we had driven on board off the pier; and in the centre of the bridge, over the wheel, burned an electric light, which, whilst it lit up the bridge and all on it, only enabled me from there to discern a vague dark mass on the deck, from which an ugly muttering was rising. This appeared a very disadvantageous position, as we on the bridge should be at the mercy of any shots from the deck, which might be expected at any moment.

I therefore had the dynamite-cases brought up, and, letting it be known what they consisted of, had a barricade built of them along the rail of the bridge in front of the wheel, which barricade rose to our chests, but easily permitted us to see over. The captain looked on at this manœuvre with the deepest interest and with the sweat running down his forehead, and I took the trouble to have each case opened and the contents verified before it was placed in position, at the same time placing a small fulminate detonator inside the lid of each case, of which he well understood the object. I then told him to instruct his mate to spread this amongst the crew and their friends, impressing on them all the fact that any bullet hitting any of the cases would, thanks to the detonators, make it quite certain that the whole ship would instantly be blown to eternity! As this news was eagerly passed round the ship, the nasty grumbling from the crowd on deck ceased instantly, and I felt sure that there was no man amongst them who from that time onward would dare to fire a shot at us, and that each would watch his neighbour closely to see and prevent any such dangerous proceeding.

At this time, just after, 11 P. M., the man I had instructed to watch the Chief's mast-head lights reported that they had been lowered, and I called four of my men on to the bridge, the others being in the motor-car, and intimated to the captain that I wanted steam. Very sulkily he spoke down the engine-room speaking-tube, and we began slowly to forge ahead into the crowded anchorage.

It was my intention, on reaching the fairway down the harbour, to anchor and wait for the *Kruger* to pass, and my action in so doing would have been in accordance with the plan that I had announced loudly on leaving the pier, for the information of those ashore, and by that means for the information of the Government—namely, that we were going to anchor out in the harbour in order to insure the safety of our dangerously explosive cargo. As soon, therefore, as we were a short way out, I gave the word to "let go the anchor." Down it went with a great splash, and the chain ran out with a rattle which could be heard all over the harbour. However, things were not to be quite so easy as that, for no notice was taken of my further order, "Enough chain," and the crew having drawn the shackle-bolt at the end, the whole chain ran out and was lost overboard with the anchor, causing thereby a sensational muttering amongst our invisible enemies on deck.

It was mercifully a very dark night, and it was now, of course, necessary to keep way on the ship, to enable us to keep clear of the many vessels at anchor. Almost immediately after the anchor had gone, our hospital-ship, with our wounded, passed us a little farther out. I had no orders as to her, and as she was steering in a direction which seemed to be quite contrary to that in which I conceived the harbour mouth to be, it seemed possible she was not going to risk the fire of the guardships at all, and so we let her go by, and waited for the *Kruger*. As the fairway was full of shoals and the course for the 15 miles which lay between us and the guardships at the entrance was known to be a most difficult piece of navigation, I now experienced a depth of anxiety I have no desire to deny, for I felt sure our captain would put the ship on a sandbank if he had the slightest chance of doing so, and as minute after minute, and finally half an hour, went by with no sign of the *Kruger*, I was as nearly reduced to despair as I have ever been. Finally, although very loath to approach the quays, I decided that it was imperative to do so, in order to ascertain whether the *Kruger* was still there, or whether what I dreaded most had in fact happened—namely, that she had passed us in the dark unobserved. Very cautiously we felt our way to the *Kruger's* berth and, to my horror, found that she was no longer there! In despair I raised what voice I had left, in what, I fear, was a somewhat quavering hail of "*Kruger*, ahoy!" and to our inexpressible relief was answered from another berth on the far side of the pier: "What ship's that?"

Certainly our old English is a delightful language to hear at any time in outlandish parts, but it never has sounded so sweetly musical to me as it did then. I shouted back, "Colonel Rawlinson in the *Armenian*," and the answer came in a sort of muffled cheer from the crowded transport, followed immediately by "We are coming out now; follow us," and I concentrated upon swinging our very unhandy ship round and getting her going slow ahead for the *Kruger* to pass us; this she immediately did, going the best part of 10 knots, and only giving me time for one plaintive prayer as she passed—"Show a light over your stern," to which came a prompt and blessed "Aye, aye, sir," and a light was at once shown, and no doubt need to be entertained that it was followed. In the meanwhile, although "Full speed ahead" was the order, we went slower and slower, and the light got farther and farther away, so that it became evident we were not getting "steam."

I therefore hailed a Mr. Dana, an American engineer employed at the oil-wells in Baku, whom I had providentially been able to get on board at the last moment, and asked him to repair, with his pistol, to the engine-room and see what he could do, at the same time telling him, so that all might hear, not to hesitate to shoot, and that my men would be with him on the first shot. This manœuvre produced good results, and we were able to keep the *Kruger's* stern light in sight till she turned, about 12 miles down the harbour, to lay her course between the guardships for the open sea. After that her light was extinguished, and we saw her no more, though we heard a series of whistle signals and one or two shots, which, to our intense relief, were small guns only, and as no searchlight was shown, for the first time that night I began to realize that there was really a possibility, if our luck held good, that we might get safely out.

But our own trial was to come. As we closed the guardships and made for the short quarter of a mile of open water which was all that lay between them, the captain began to show signs of active hostility, and to say he wouldn't go out, and that the guardships would fire, and that we should be blown up, or at any rate pursued and caught and shot. So obstreperous did he finally become that I called my four men to stand round him with their fixed bayonets and to allow no one to approach. Meanwhile I stood by his side with my pistol drawn, and swore to him by every oath I could think of in Russian that if the ship did not keep a straight course, or if any signal was made, I would myself shoot him on the spot and take the ship out in spite of him.

This was said sufficiently loudly to be heard all over the deck, and so much impressed the crowd that I remember well seeing one of them who attempted to light a cigarette knocked down by his neighbours, who were in an agony of fear. Unfortunately, the sides of the poop and bridge of the *Armenian* were painted white, and so were fairly easily distinguished, whilst providentially the long low-lying hull forward, where the greater part of our high explosives were stowed, was black and more or less invisible, though probably not so much so as the horribly white part would have been if I had had any notion beforehand of what was coming, and had had an hour or two at it with a black paint-pot.

We were therefore soon seen from the guardships, who signalled to us by blowing two sharp blasts of their whistles. I would not trust the captain to touch the whistle-cord, but replied immediately myself with two whistles, not knowing the first thing about what two or any other number of whistles might mean, except that they wanted us to stop, which was the last thing I intended to do. They instantly replied with *three* whistles, and as we were now closing them fast and were within half a mile of them both, I answered with *five* whistles; this, whilst it gained us a few invaluable seconds, must have "upset the apple-cart" completely, for they opened fire at point-blank range at once.

The next thing I remember was an awe-inspiring explosion within about a foot of my head, and more terrifying still, within not more than 2 feet 6 inches of the dynamite, as a shell struck the light deck over my head, which was only just high enough for me to stand up under. It was, however, only a "common" shell—that is, one charged with gun-powder and not high explosive, and except for some smoke and a good many splinters, we were none the worse, although the effect on the captain was instantaneous and electrifying. As the shell burst he made one dive to get away, leaving the wheel to spin which way it might, and the ship also. If he was quick, however, I was quite a little quicker, for I had him by the collar with a grip of iron as he passed, and threw him over on his back, and with my pistol pressed up under his chin I ordered him to stand up and keep the ship on its course.

I have not the slightest doubt that I was pretty rough, and if so it was what I was intending to be, as we were in a tightish place, and not one where it was wise to leave any doubt possible as to one's intentions, and he had none as to mine. My man, who had been in the navy for years before the war, kept the ship straight on her course during this little tussle, which lasted seconds only, and in the meanwhile three more shells got us in the white-painted poop where we were posted behind our dynamite barricade, which no longer formed as desirable or effective a form of defence as it had before. However, nothing blew up, and we still remained alive, and as we actually got between the two gunboats the fire momentarily ceased, for they were then afraid of hitting each other. As we forged ahead they both commenced firing again, and the Russian captain again started struggling in his terror, so much so that I really thought I was going to be obliged to shoot him, in case he might "start up" all his countrymen, who formed the majority on board the *Armenian*. I therefore jammed my pistol at the back of his neck, and quite quietly asked my man, in English, to stand back, as I expected I should *have* to shoot the swine directly, and it would make a nasty mess! On these words the captain, who had hitherto maintained that he knew no English, just went all limp in my hands, and never offered another struggle of any sort.

We were now leaving the guardships astern, and got four or five more shells into us—all in the infernally white painted construction we were standing in, for apparently the remainder of our vessel was invisible from the guardships. However, no harm was done except to the nerves of our involuntary passengers and crew, and the gunboats ceased firing when they could no longer see us, by which time we could not see them either, even if we had wished to, which we certainly did *not*.

Probably of all the sighs of relief which were heaved that night I heaved the biggest one then, as it was hard to conceive how it was possible to come safely through such a fire as that to which we had been subjected, with such a box of fireworks as the ship we were on, without giving a highly sensational pryotechnic display. Indeed, it would never have been believed that shells could burst so close to fulminate without detonating it. The explanation, of course, is that the gunpowder in common shell "explodes," whereas high explosive "detonates," and there is no comparison between the effect of explosion and the concussion caused by detonation. Without doubt, had any one of the seven shells we actually received in our superstructure been a high-explosive one, we should have gone up like a sky-rocket!

Needless to remark, as soon as the firing ceased we plugged as hard as we could for the open sea, and I had little doubt

## THE "HUSH-HUSH" ARMY

we should not be pursued, as there were at least 200 vessels in the harbour behind, and had the guard-vessels moved, all those vessels would have put to sea at once. Also, I was pretty sure that they had not been warned of our coming, thanks to our precautions, and had no idea who we were, or that we were worth pursuing, or they would have had their larger guns and searchlights in action, when our chance would evidently have been nil.

As the firing ceased during the few moments when we were between the guardships, we had another kind of experience, which was not, however, entirely unexpected. It commenced by the appearance on the bridge of a very offensive Bolshevik sailor, who, addressing me in a tone of voice which I was by no means prepared to permit him to use, told me he represented the "committee" of the crew and was commissioned to tell me they did not intend to allow the ship to proceed. My answer, if short, was at any rate extremely to the point, and consisted of the order, "Down him!" The words had hardly left my lips before he was "down" all right, and a good British bayonet was scratching at his chest, waiting to act on the next order, whatever it might be; and there he remained till the firing ceased and there was time to attend to his business. That did not take long, as, by a somewhat primitive but most effective use of an army boot, he was prevailed upon to sit up, and was told that we were determined to take the ship on to Enzeli, and that we had reason to know we should not be pursued (which last was not, perhaps, the exact truth), and that if he could prevail on the crew to obey our orders, each of them would receive 100 roubles (at that time a large sum to them) on our arrival at that port. If, however, they were not prepared to obey our orders, we were prepared to fight them at once. He was then directed to stand up and address his comrades over the top of our dynamite to the above effect, whilst my man kept his bayonet-point tickling his back. It was so evident that *if* there was to be a fight *he* would infallibly be the first casualty that he fairly burst himself with arguments in favour of accepting our proposal; and as his audience were pretty well cowed by the events of the night, they accepted at once, and we had no further trouble.

As a precautionary measure, however, in case of pursuit,

we did not bear away south on our true course for Enzeli, but held on due east for five hours, till we reckoned we were far out in the Caspian Sea, many miles east of the correct course, when we turned and steered due south all the next day and night, till in the grey of the morning of the 16th we saw the Persian mountains rising up ahead of us, and altered our course to make the entrance of the harbour at Enzeli. During all this time I had kept continuous watch on the course of the vessel, to make certain no tricks were played on us, and as soon as there was sufficient light to make sure the coast was clear of enemy gunboats we knew the job, which had appeared so impossible, had really been successfully achieved. The danger of hitting the bar in entering the harbour was one which, after the others we had already come safe through, only made us inclined to laugh, and we held straight on, and made our preparations to come into port in proper style. These consisted, first of all, in removing the detonators from the dynamite-cases; secondly, in hoisting the small British flag, which had flown on my car, at the mast-head *over* the Bolshevik flag; and, thirdly, in parading our party on the much-battered upper bridge.

So in the end we came proudly into port, with our decks covered with guns and material of all kinds, our little vessel much battered and loaded to the utmost she could carry, ten Englishmen all told (eight of whom only were soldiers), assisted by one American citizen, with ninety-six armed Bolsheviks obeying *our* orders in *their own* ship!

Day was breaking as we came over the bar, and the troops on shore were mostly bivouacking along the banks of the entrance channel. As they saw the ship they had all given up for lost coming in, and saw her cargo, her battered condition, and last, but not least, the little Union Jack flying proudly over all, they rose up with one accord and gave us a truly British reception. It was such a hearty and spontaneous one that the recollection of that moment will always remain to me as the proudest memory of a somewhat adventurous career.

Coming abreast of the General's ship, we hailed them, asking for a boat, an anchor, and some British sailors, to enable us to bring the ship to anchor out in the fairway. On their

## THE BOLSHEVIK STEAMER "ARMENIAN"

On coming alongside the Quay at Enzeli with seven direct hits in the upper bridge

The deck crammed with high explosives. Col. R. in shirt-sleeves by the mast

Unloading—the line of cases of high explosives disembarked extends beyond the ship

coming on board, I jumped into their boat and proceeded to the *Kruger* to report, being met at the gangway by the "Chief" himself, still in his pyjamas, but with his face wreathed in smiles. He took me by both hands and repeated again and again, "You have done very well," which more than repaid me for all our past anxieties.

He took me straight to his cabin, where I even now remember the whisky-and-soda which was immediately supplied to me. It was a "corker," and went down like the nectar of the gods. Immediately after, the Chief of the Staff took me into his cabin and gave me his bed, upon which I was asleep in a moment, after forty-eight consecutive hours the most strenuous it has ever been my lot to go through, and so crammed throughout with sensations and incidents of every kind that I much fear I can never expect to see their like again.

# CHAPTER VI

### HOMEWARD BOUND—THE ARMISTICE

The cargo of the *Armenian*—Kasvin—Journey to Bagdad—The order of the day—Journey to Bussrah—To Suez—To Taranto—Paris on Armistice Day—Fourth Army Headquarters—London.

After about twenty-four hours of well-earned sleep and rest, the first thing to do was to count the cargo of the *Armenian* and to dispose of the prisoners. The latter was soon done, as they were accommodated in the refugee-camps which had by then been formed on shore; and after the Bolshevik crew had received their promised gratuity, all hands turned-to to make an inventory of our cargo.

All papers relating to this which I retained were subsequently taken from me by the Turks; I therefore quote from memory the principal items only, as follows:

1 battery of 4 French Creusot guns, 1916, calibre 105 mm., Q.F., sighted to 14,000 metres.
2 Russian field-guns, calibre 76 mm., Q.F.
22 machine-guns in parts ready for erection.
20 large cases of gun spare parts and special tools from the arsenal workshop.
9,000 rounds of gun ammunition, mostly high explosive.
9,000,000 rounds of small-arms ammunition.
6 cases, 100 pounds each, of dynamite and gun-cotton.
Detonators, electric exploders, fuses, etc.
And last, but not least, 19 *breech-blocks* of the best guns left in the line, which, in consequence, were rendered unserviceable to the enemy, as well as many other items of ordnance stores, including vast quantities of small-arms (rifles).

This was, as may be imagined, a very valuable "haul"—not only to our own troops in such an unget-at-able spot, but also because it deprived the Turks of much material at that moment quite invaluable to them, which would otherwise have been at their disposal.

The work of unloading all this material, even with the help

of the officers and men of our R.F.A. battery, who worked like Trojans in spite of the great heat, took several days, and a considerable portion was dispatched at once by sea to our expeditions operating in Lenkoran, on the west coast of the Caspian, and to Krasnovosk, in the Turcoman country, on the eastern coast, as well as to our Russian ally, General Bicherakov, who was fighting the Bolshevik forces on the western coast of Darbend, north of Baku, at each of which places it proved of the greatest service.

The day after our arrival I received an invitation to dine with the Chief on his ship the *Kruger*—a sad farewell dinner, as he was leaving next morning for Bagdad.

To give an idea of the state of our commissariat, the main items of the menu were one bottle of pre-war vodka and one pot of jam, both of which had constituted his "reserve" during his many wanderings, and which he desired should be enjoyed by his friends before he left—as, indeed, they *were*.

Everyone was remarkably kind to me, and I remember well the pride with which I received a copy of the dispatch which was then sent to G.H.Q. to the effect that the saving of the material was entirely due to the "enterprise and daring of Colonel Rawlinson," which copy I retained as a treasured momento till it was eventually taken from me by the Turks in 1920.

On the evening of the Chief's departure, Major-General Thompson arrived to take over the command, and the Hush-Hush Army (officially known as Dunsterforce) thereupon ceased to exist, the division in future being known as the North Persian Force, with headquarters at this time at Kasvin—to which place I made my way as soon as I had finished handing over the material we had brought away from Baku. At this time peace had been signed with the Jungalis, and my party therefore had a very enjoyable drive through the beautiful hills we had last come through with our fingers on our triggers. We halted only to mine the bridge at Menjil with dynamite, and made a bold bid to drive through the 150 miles to Kasvin in one day; but night caught us in the upper pass, where we were obliged to bivouac, with only the most evil-smelling, stagnant irrigation water to drink, our only supplies of any sort being one small tin of cocoa—a poor enough dinner for four men.

A rotten night we had, as we did not halt till 11 P. M., having started at 5.30 A. M., and all night long the Persian mule convoys coming down the pass (they all travel at night to avoid the heat) kept poking their noses, both man and beast, into my car, to see what they could steal, until the waking snarl of the occupant put the fear of death into them.

Next day, when nearing the final rise of the upper pass, a horrible "knock" developed in our faithful engine, telling us at once that one of the "big end" bearings had gone, and it was only very slowly and with the greatest care that we were able to get the car to Kasvin, my already vicious state of temper being made worse throughout the latter part of our tedious and trying drive by an infernal young Persian "knut" on a really beautiful horse, who amused himself cantering past our car with disdain at every small rise in the ground, till we felt murderously inclined to have a shot at him. However, Kasvin at last, and permission to pitch my tent in General Thompson's garden and to mess with him.

The next morning I heard the Major-General Chief of the General Staff to Sir William Marshall, the Commander-in-Chief at Bagdad, was expected within the next few days, and that I was therefore to wait at Kasvin to take his orders—a most fortunate chance for me, as I got my engine immediately under repair, and went sick myself with a nasty "go" of fever the same day, being pretty well worn out and sadly needing a rest. The General turned up in a few days, by which time both my car and myself were more or less fit for action again. He told me to get on at once to Bagdad, but that he did not think there would be any job for me just then in Mesopotamia. The most valuable information he gave me was that a ship was leaving the mouth of the Euphrates for Suez on October 13th. It was then the 4th, leaving me nine days to do the 1,200 miles which lay between Kasvin and the mouth of the river. This no one thought it possible I could do, except myself, who so well knew the capabilities of my light car over that rough country.

I left at daylight on the 5th, and, seeing that my car had been on this occasion properly "messed about" during its repair, it took us till long after dark to do the first 110 miles, for every part of the engine required readjustment on the road. About midday we halted for this purpose, near the summit of the Sultan Bulak Pass, and seeing a very antiquated ruin there, I went to explore it and to obtain water, if possible.

When I got there I found an interesting relic indeed, apparently the remains of what had once been a Greek or Roman bath, dating, quite possibly, from the time of Alexander the Great. A spring of boiling water impregnated with sulphur here gushed out from the rock and was conducted in a stone channel a short distance to a bath about 10 feet by 4 feet, excavated in the rock, which had once been lined with the old tiles for which in ancient days this country was renowned. Round the bath a brick erection had once existed, which was now in ruins, but what was most interesting was that the length of the open channel by which the water was conducted to the bath had been originally so nicely calculated to reduce the temperature of the water in its passage from the spring to the bath that a hot bath at the temperature most suited to the human body had been always ready there during some thousands of years for any passer-by at any moment.

Needless to say, we—that is, my driver Morris and myself—took instant advantage of such a luxury, and two very clean and newly shaved gentlemen then continued their journey, after having had a great draught of another of nature's luxuries—namely, a spring of aerated water which flowed from an old fountain outside the bath building. We bivouacked that night where we finally stopped at the roadside, at 10.30 P. M., and were off again at daylight, passing through Hamadan about 12 noon.

I neither saw nor reported to any one there, but stopped only to "raid" the General's mess and take whatever I could find in the way of provisions, and also a case of Japanese *beer*, which was an exceptional luxury for us. That night we kept going till past 11 o'clock, having crossed the Asadabad Pass in the early afternoon, as we knew there was an A.S.C. convoy on the road ahead, and wanted to hit their bivouac, knowing we should have trouble to start our rather dilapidated engine and be glad of assistance.

We found the bivouac at last on a pitch-dark night, and, having had some sleep, got assistance to push us off at daylight, as starting-handles had no effect on our engine just then. We passed through Kirmanshah about 4 P. M., and carried on for hours in the dark, finally reaching A.S.C. standing camp at Karind, about 40 miles short of the Tek-i-Gehri Pass, just before midnight on the 7th. Here we found plenty of assistance and stores, and were away again at the first grey of dawn. We were driving as fast as was possible, but the road surface was very rough. However, we got down the pass without incident, and lunched magnificently, on our Karind stores and beer, by the side of the swift-flowing river in the lower valley below the pass.

Nearing the Persian frontier the road got worse and worse, and to our horror our long-suffering car began at last to show signs of wear, the most sensational incident being the whole back part suddenly falling off. This took place in the very centre of the rugged and uninhabited frontier hills; and a good hour's work was necessary to bind it together with any odd bits of rope or wire we could steal from other parts of the car. However, at 5.30 P.M. we finally reached Khanikin, the original base of Dunsterforce, 94 miles from Bagdad, where was, to our great joy, a full-blown Expeditionary Force Canteen, with food of all kinds, of which we were sadly in need.

It took us a good hour to sample the luxuries to be found here, and we left afterwards for the railhead camp at Ruz, where we found dinner, a tent, and a bed.

A difficult start next morning, having to be towed by other cars to get the engine going, but we reached Bakuba, an A.S.C. post about 50 miles from Bagdad, about 9 A.M., and then spent a very necessary one and a half hours repairing the car, with most satisfactory results, reaching Bagdad eventually before 1 P.M.—a great drive of over 600 miles from the Caspian in four and a half days from Kasvin to Bagdad, which, under the existing conditions, wanted a great deal of doing, at the end of a campaign. On arriving at Bagdad I reported at General Headquarters, asking that if there was no post for me in the advance of our troops, which was then taking place, I might be allowed to try to catch the ship leaving Bussrah on the 13th, and so get back to France, where the "band was still playing!"

I was told the matter would be gone into, and, quarters having been assigned to me, I got off there as soon as possible for a much-needed rest, which prolonged itself until the next morning.

The first news in the morning was a message from the Commander-in-Chief to lunch with him at his house, and the next a copy of the "Order of the Day" of the Mesopotamian Expeditionary Force, as below:

GENERAL HEADQUARTERS, MESOPOTAMIAN
EXPEDITIONARY FORCE.
ORDER OF THE DAY, No. 121, OCTOBER 10TH, 1918.

In pursuance of the authority delegated to me by His Imperial Majesty, the King-Emperor, I make the following award for gallantry and distinguished conduct in the field:

*To be Companion of the Distinguished Service Order:*
TEMP. LIEUT.-COLONEL ALFRED RAWLINSON, C.M.G., R.G.A., for conspicuous gallantry and devotion to duty.

With an escort of four men he brought away a steamer, loaded with munitions, from a port under fire, and in spite of the opposition of the captain and crew, who refused to navigate her. Although fired on heavily from a guardship which hit the steamer several times, he, by his personal energy and resource, succeeded in making the crew work, and eventually conducted the steamer safely to another port. Thus by his enterprise and determination the valuable cargo, which would otherwise have fallen into the hands of the enemy, was saved.

(*Signed*)  W. H. MARSHALL (GENERAL),
*Commander-in-Chief.*

I need hardly say that this last took my breath away, as I was expecting nothing of the kind. However, I was, and shall always be, very proud of this most unexpected honour.

The Chief was, as always, very kind, and also anxious for details of our little "stunt" in Baku, which I gave him to the best of my ability. He told me he had nothing for me at the moment, and agreeing that my best plan was to get back to France as quickly as possible, he had given the orders necessary to enable me to leave by train that night. He also told me, to my great delight, that my recommendation of my two best men had been considered, and that an "immediate award" of the Military Medal had been made to them, and that I could inform them they were at liberty to "put them up" (*i. e.*, wear them) at once.

After doing my best to thank the Chief for all his kindness (which I am afraid I did very badly, being rather weak and finding an astonishing difficulty in speaking), I got back to my quarters and found my tough and faithful driver, Morris. I was able, to my great delight, to tell him to go out and get himself a new set of ribbons and a fourth one to put in front of his "Mons," and I there and then wrote the order for them to be supplied to him. We then went and handed over what was left of our faithful car to the Army Service Corps Depôt, and catching the night train that evening, travelled in an excellent cattle-truck, and reached Kut at daylight next morning, October 11th. On arrival at Kut I had some trouble in getting "a move on" to the local Major in charge of the river transport, who suffered from the not uncommon disease which at times attacks Detachment Commanders—namely, a swelled head. He was inclined to, first of all, remain in bed till much later in the morning, and then at his leisure arrange for a boat to leave next day.

However, after I had with some difficulty succeeded in obtaining access to him where he lay in bed, in the privacy and luxury of his sleeping apartment, he became somewhat quickly galvanized into movement, when he became aware that I was obtaining telephone connection with General Headquarters at Bagdad; and a small steamer was then forthcoming in about an hour, and we started, hoping to catch the train which left Amora on the evening of the next day. This was actually done with about an hour to spare, and we reached Bussrah in the early hours of the morning of the 13th. Having lunched with the I.G.C. and cabled home, we went down the last 70 miles of river beyond Bussrah on a light steamer, and, boarding the big transport soon after nightfall, we sailed for Suez before midnight, having done well over 1,000 miles in nine days, including all stops—very good travelling indeed in those parts at that time.

An Indian native infantry regiment was on board the transport, as well as drafts of other native regiments going to Egypt, and I was much relieved not to be O.C. troops, as, though much senior to the Regimental Colonel, the excellent

# MAP OF THE NEAR EAST SHOWING ROUTE IN "RED"

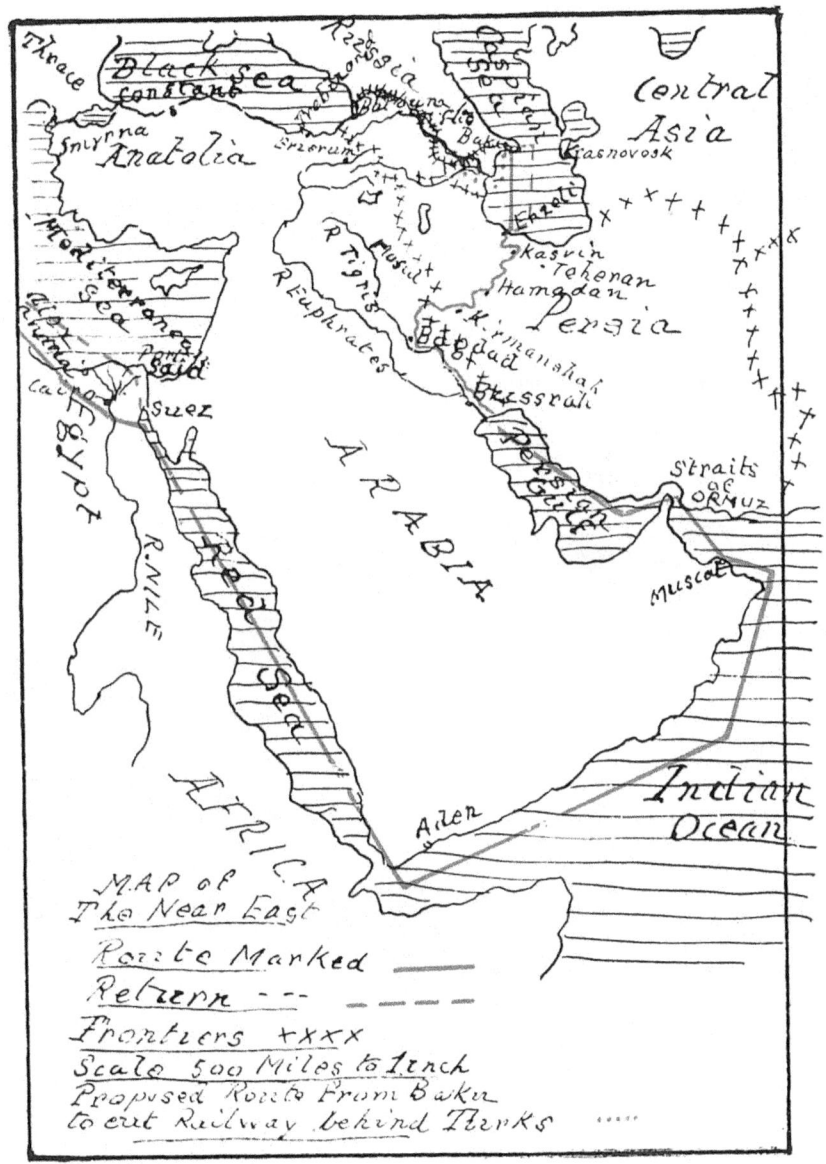

rule is always observed on a transport that the O.C. of a complete unit on board is always O.C. troops.

We had a quite uneventful run to Suez, not half so hot as the outward voyage, and took the train on arrival, reaching Port Said in the small hours of the next morning, where we obtained a tent in a rest camp until a ship should be available. The delay, however, fortunately proved a very short one, as the *Malwa*, a splendid P. and O., was due to sail for Taranto in thirty-six hours after our arrival at Port Said.

When, however, the time came to sail, our sailing was, with much mystery, postponed, and the slow convoy of three slow ships sailed in our place, the two fast ships which made up our fast convoy being detained another twenty-four hours. Part of this, I remember, was very pleasantly spent playing a round of golf in the desert with the captain of the ship; a great match we had, and, if I remember right, finished all square on the last "green," or rather patch of smooth sand, thanks to some phenomenally successful putting.

An amusing incident occurred when we wished to return on board. The sentry on the gangway would on no account let us up the ladder, as neither of us had a pass; and in vain my companion insisted that I was the O.C. troops and he was the captain of the ship. The humorous answer, repeated again and again, was: "Very likely, but my orders 'is' to let no one pass without a pass." So we had to hail the bridge and produce evidence from the guard-room and ship's company of our identity, and on getting on board I remember cordially congratulating the sentry's regimental officer upon the excellent and efficient manner in which his men carried out their orders.

We sailed next morning, and as we went out through the buoyed channel which extends some miles outside the harbour, we understood the reason of our delay in port, for the three slow ships which had gone on the day before in our place had all been torpedoed and were lying with their masts above water, half a mile or so from each other, near the entrance of the channel.

We were bound for Taranto, and on approaching the port got orders to man the ship for a general salute on entering the harbour to the Italian Flag, in honour of the armistice concluded between Italy and Austria whilst we had been at sea. This excellent news made me more than ever anxious to get on, as I was terribly afraid I might even yet be too late to be "in at the death" on the French front. Our entry into Taranto was very impressive. All our troops, over 2,000 British soldiers, were formed up on deck, and as we passed abreast of the fort in the narrow harbour entrance, our flag was dipped, all buglers sounded the general salute, and officers saluted the Italian Flag.

My post was on the bridge with the captain, and the scene from there was very striking. The great ship of 12,000 tons lay below us, whilst, the entrance to the harbour being very deep and narrow, the bridge on which we stood was about level with the streets on either side; these were crammed with cheering crowds, all very obviously employed in "Mafficking," which other nations have also been known to do at other times, with even less excuse.

I caught the *train de luxe* that night, and, stopping only a few hours at Rome, reached Paris in fifty-six hours. Having already wired from Rome to Fourth Army Headquarters to ask that a car might be sent to pick me up in Paris, on arrival at the hotel it was waiting there, and I learned that the Army Headquarters were then in a train at Le Cateau. So I had some breakfast, and then got into a really luxurious bed to enjoy a couple of hours' sleep before starting on the long drive which would land me at the front once more. After having been asleep only a few minutes, I heard the unmistakable sound of gunfire. I opened my eyes and took in where I was, and thought I must be dreaming; but as the firing continued, I thought I'd betted see what was up, and went out into the passage in my pyjamas. There I found all the world gone mad. And from the windows, roofs, and everywhere in the streets, every man, woman, and child was cheering; many were weeping, but all were yelling "*L'Armistice!*" Every available gun of every kind was being fired as fast as it could be loaded; every belfry was rocking as its bells were being rung as never before; and the sirens and hooters of every factory were screeching continuously.

I at once gave up any idea of reaching Army Headquarters that day, and went back to bed and had a good rest, sallying out in the late afternoon to have a look at Paris on Armistice Day. Indeed, it proved a sight worth seeing, and also one to ponder over. I was in London when the news of the Relief of Ladysmith arrived, and well remember the absolutely spontaneous joy which burst out everywhere on that occasion. I also witnessed the hectic scenes which took place all over the town on Mafeking night, which to me appeared to embody quite a different spirit.

Here in Paris, however, on that great historic day things did not, except superficially, in the least resemble either of the above occasions. Of course, the young and rowdy element was much the same in all three cases, but at any rate in Paris, and probably all over France and in England also, on this historic occasion there was a much deeper sentiment to be read on all sides, and tears were as much in evidence as laughter, even on faces which had long been strangers to such weakness. Amongst the hundreds to whom I spoke that day I could see the little twitchings of the muscles and note the little catch in the speech which told of feelings far deeper than any that could be expressed by mere exhibitions of joy and gaiety. The whole atmosphere, in fact, could best be described as filled with a deep and sincere feeling of relief and a thankfulnss far too deep to be expressed by outward signs, but which found its true reflection in the reverent masses who were to be seen kneeling in every church throughout the day and night. All this was most instructive to those who, like myself, looked rather to the attitude of these mute yet speaking crowds of reverent church-goers, than to the thoughtless gaiety of the pleaure-seekers, to give a true indication of the deeper feelings of the French nation.

With regard to the rowdy element, it enjoyed itself, and good-humour was everywhere the outstanding feature. It was early evident that the streets that day were to be for pedestrians only, and every motor-car which appeared was immediately covered with people, who climbed all over it, regardless of expostulation or damage, so that within half an hour of the first firing of guns no vehicle was to be seen, but the streets remained black with people all day, and for the best part of the night, whilst every house and room which had a light lit it, and everyone who had a flag carried it, or hung it out of the window. The contrast of all this "life" to the deserted countries I had so lately left was so startling that I shall always retain the most vivid recollection of the scene in the streets of Paris on that great day.

Next morning I started by car for Fourth Army Headquarters, by the old familiar road I had followed in the 1914 retreat from Mons—through Noyon, Ham, and St. Quentin, to Le Cateau, where the Army Headquarters at that moment was, in a train captured from the Germans during the last advance. It was a truly remarkable coincidence that I should rejoin in 1918 at exactly the same spot, Le Cateau, where I joined the General Headquarters of the Expeditionary Force on August 20th, 1914, just over four years previously, having in the meanwhile travelled half over the world and served on six different fronts.

I found my brother, the Fourth Army Commander, in great form and delighted with his Army's success, as, indeed, he well might be, for their work since I had left them before Amiens seven months before will for ever remain one of the most glorious and successful campaigns in our military history. We talked the greater part of the night, and he told me many of the details of the Allies' advance, and above all of his town troops. No commander could have been prouder than he was of them, nor more convinced that no troops of any nation were capable of stopping them. The Australians and Canadians, at that time forming part of the Fourth Army, would indeed have been pleased to hear the high value their commander set upon their work, and how proud he was of their success in the exceptionally difficult and arduous tasks which he had so confidently entrusted to them.

I slept that night (without giving it a thought) in a newly made dug-out alongside the train, with fresh-fallen snow all round. This was a bit of a trial to my already rather impaired health, having come straight from tropical temperatures, and when I left in the morning it was with a real raging fever. However, I got off all right, and in a covered car, taking the straight road through Cambrai and Arras, and then the old Roman road which passes just north of St. Pol through Therouailles, straight to Boulogne, reaching London at about 8 P. M.—too ill, however, to go and find my wife who did not know I was coming, and afraid that my state would frighten her. So I slept at my club, and sent the faithful Morris to find her in the morning; after which I was in good hands, and, getting the nursing and care which were sadly needed, I was fit for duty again in a very short time.

# PART II

## INTELLIGENCE IN TRANSCAUCASIA
*(February to August, 1919)*

WITH INTRODUCTION BY GENERAL SIR G. MILNE, G.C.M.G., ETC.,
COMMANDER-IN-CHIEF, ARMY OF BLACK SEA.

# INTRODUCTION TO PART II

By GENERAL SIR G. MILNE, G.C.M.G., K.C.B., D.S.O.

Colonel Rawlinson has asked me to write an introduction to the second part of his book, but I feel that there is little I can add to his vividly realistic description of his experiences in Asia Minor and Caucasia.

At that time the political situation was peculiar, and even had its humorous side; unfortunately, it has since changed to a terrible tragedy involving the loss of thousands of Christian lives.

After the signing of the Armistice with Turkey in 1918 it was decided to send troops to Batoum and to safeguard the railway to Tiflis and Baku, in order to open up communication with the British troops which were in occupation of Baku and with those acting in conjunction with the Russians on the eastern side of the Caspian; also, at the same time, to insure the evacuation of the country by both the German Missions and the Turkish Armies.

The whole district south of the Caucasian range was in a state of disorder, fermentation, and incipient revolution; local wars were in progress, and the danger of an outbreak of disease and starvation was imminent. To maintain order in this large area, amongst a population often actively and always latently hostile, there was available only one division of British and Indian troops, rapidly decreasing in numbers by demobilization. It was therefore incumbent on officers to accept responsibility and take decisive action without waiting for reference to higher authority, with whom rapid communication was often impossible. Colonel Rawlinson, one of a family distinguished both in peace and war, naturally took to his new responsibilities as the proverbial duck takes to water. Untiring in his activities and regardless of danger, in which he seemed to revel, he was continuously on the move in the execution of the various missions entrusted to him, and which finally ended in a prolonged imprisonment in a Turkish prison, as described in Part III., when he again revisits Asia Minor.

Little is known in Great Britain of the amount of hard work done by the British troops, in 1919 and the early months of 1920, at a time when the British Flag was held in honour from Merv to Smyrna, when Batoum was a model port, and when it was possible to go by a railway managed by British officers from Constantinople to Egypt; but Colonel Rawlinson paints a very human picture of the situation as he saw it.

His excellent work in arranging for the collection of arms and ammunition in accordance with the terms of the Armistice was stultified by the landing of the Greeks at Smyrna, and the advent of the scene of the now famous Mustapha Kemal, sent to maintain the Sultan's authority in the provinces. From the beginning, however, the Turk showed no great zeal in carrying out his engagements, and played for time.

This book will certainly raise the veil from a part of post-war history of which little has yet become known to the public at home, and as such its value is at once unique and considerable. It cannot also fail to demonstrate to readers who imagine the modern world to be a tame prosaic place, that there are still opportunities to be found for the exercise of that daring and resource of which this book furnishes such striking examples, and that, in short, "adventure is still to the adventurous."

G. M. MILNE (GENERAL).

# CHAPTER I

## "EAST AGAIN"—SALONIKA, CONSTANT, AND BATOUM

Rationing at home—Meet Sir G. Milne—Appointed Special Service "Intelligence" Officer to G.H.Q., Constantinople—Morris left in England—Railway journey during French demobilization—Rome—Rest camp at Taranto—Grecian Archipelago—Mount Athos—Salonika—Kit lost—Journey from Salonika to Constant—Catalja Lines—Constantinople—Palace of Constantine—Old Stamboul—Galata—The Grande Rue of Pera—St. Sophia—Adrian's Roman Wall—Carnival in Pera—Down the Bosphorus—Varna—Samsun—A mine at sea—Batoum.

On reaching home after the Baku campaign, "rationing" was in full swing, but being "emaciated," I was allowed cream, butter, and all manner of good things, and soon began to get my strength back, whilst enjoying a "rest," a form of enjoyment which had been unknown to me since August, 1914.

After a very quiet month so occupied, I had the pleasure one morning of breakfasting with my brother in London, who was then home for a short time before taking charge of the evacuation of our forces from Archangel.

At breakfast it was my good fortune to meet my future chief, Sir. George Milne, Commanding-in-Chief the Salonika Expeditionary Force. This force was then in process of transfer from Salonika to Constantinople, and with it was to be incorporated the North Persian Force, which had crossed the Caspian Sea to Baku, and was then operating with other forces in the Caucasus.

It was evident that strenuous times were ahead of us in those parts, and when Sir George heard that I knew the country pretty well, he to my great delight asked me if I was prepared to go back there; and, on my gladly assenting, he said he would apply for me to be detailed for special service there. A few days later, during December, I learned that I was to be appointed Special Service Officer attached to General Staff Intelligence of the Salonika Expeditionary Force. I did not, however, get my actual "movement" order till February, and left England on the 15th, having been just under three months at home.

My faithful driver and comrade, Morris, of the A.S.C., was to have come with me again, as well as my own well-tried machine-guns. I had all passes, etc., prepared for Morris, but at the last moment learned, to my great grief, that his wife was in the last stages of consumption and not expected to live more than a few weeks, so that under these circumstances I felt I could not take him, as it was his first duty to stand by his poor wife and to look after their child, then four or five years of age only. He accompanied me to the station, and after a hearty handshake and a last salute, which he mournfully gave me as the train steamed out of Victoria Station, I left him very disconsolate, and, much to my regret, have not seen him since, although I have repeatedly endeavoured to ascertain his whereabouts. I therefore started alone on this new venture, with only the guns to remind me of my many queer experiences in the wild countries to which I was once more on my way.

Having slept the night of the 15th in Paris, and seen many friends there the next day, I caught the Rome express in the evening, and then experienced peculiar disadvantages attached to railway travelling in France at the height of the Army demobilization. In the first place, there was no chance, even after long notice, of obtaining a *wagon-lit*, and, indeed, I do not think any were running; but after much trouble, having given ten days' notice, I did obtain a place in what they call a *coupé-lit*, where two upper berths let down so that all four passengers in the compartment can at any rate lie down. We were four in our compartment—a French medical officer, a Transylvanian Bishop, a Russian General, and myself.

Having ample provisions with me, I made tea for them all before we lay down for the night, pushing my "grub-box," with all my cooking-gear in it, out into the corridor after we had finished our supper, to give us more room.

The Russian and I had the two lower berths and the Bishop and the doctor were "upstairs," and we were soon all asleep. . . . About daylight the train stopped at some junction in the mountains, where a branch line comes in from Grenoble, and a few moments afterwards we were awakened by a crash and a bang which sounded rather familiar to my ears and very much like the start of a row. I therefore leapt up at once, and was just in time to meet a terrible-looking scoundrel with a hearty

THE BOSPHORUS AT CONSTANTINOPLE

View from the hill at Pera: Dolma Batchké is the palace with the two white minarets at the head of the bay

## INTELLIGENCE IN TRANSCAUCASIA

push as he was trying to force his way into our compartment. The Russian instantly leapt up and "bucked up" like a man in my support, and together we were able to hold them all back till we could get the door shut and locked, as our first friend was closely followed by a crowd of demobilized soldiers who had broken down the outside door of the carriage and now filled the corridor, forcing their way into the compartments wherever they could. They never succeeded in getting into ours, for, though the doctor and the Bishop were not of much account, the ruffians didn't much like the look of the Russian General and myself—both of us in uniform and every bit as ready for a row as they were themselves. The width of the corridor only allowed them to come at us one at a time; they therefore soon gave up trying to force their way in and left us in undisputed possession.

It was a great nuisance, however, for, of course, my box outside immediately disappeared, and we were confined to our compartment for the remaining four or five hours of the journey to the frontier at Modane, where they all got out and we changed trains.

Once through the Mt. Cenis tunnel and we were in the snow, but with a bright sun and air like champagne, so that it was an enjoyable journey, though the train went very slowly, and did not reach Turin till 8 P.M. There we had a two hours' wait and got some food, which had to last us to Rome, which we did not reach till 2 P.M. next day. Though we were very hungry by that time, yet at any rate we were not cold, as the weather in the plain already showed signs of the advent of spring; and after a restful day in Rome, I started in the evening for Taranto.

The Campagna (the open plain round Rome) was looking beautiful, but as soon as we got through the Apennine Mountains the country got bare and very stony, till at last the great harbour of Taranto came in sight; and after going three-parts of the way round it, we reached the terminus at 5 P.M., having left Rome twenty-two hours earlier. This latter portion was the worst of what was, all the way at this time, an extremely uncomfortable journey, the accommodation provided for three first-class passengers being only half a compartment, the whole ordinary compartment having been boarded down the middle, barely allowing room to sit upright, and rendering it impossible to attain any degree of that comfort which becomes so necessary during a protracted journey.

Crowds of officers were streaming through Taranto at this time on their way home for demobilization, going off daily in troop-trains which then took fourteen days to reach Havre; but no one thought of grumbling, as they were all on the way *home*.

The rest camp where it was necessary to wait till a ship was available was well placed on the cliff, looking over the great lagoon which forms the harbour; but being entirely laid out to be habitable in the summer heat, it was most unsuitable for the cold of the winter season.

I was lucky, therefore, to get a ship going to Salonika on the 22nd, and so to get away from Taranto on the fourth day, on board what had once been a German-Austrian Lloyd passenger-ship, but which was then being used, as were many other similar ships, as a transport for British troops.

We reached Salonika on the morning of the 25th, after a very pleasant journey through the Grecian Archipelago, where we passed many large islands, all mountainous and all pretty, rather like parts of the west coast of Scotland, only the mountains here are much higher and bolder. The weather was lovely—no wind at all, and a sky and sea of the deepest blue: sunny and hot like a midsummer's day in England, and warm at night so that one could walk the deck in pyjamas, though there was still snow on the higher mountains.

We did not see Athens, but passed close to Mount Athos, where are situated many monasteries of the Greek Church, inhabited by many thousand priests, mostly of Russian extraction. It is difficult to visit this very interesting place, but some of our officers went from Salonika, and I have heard descriptions of it from them, from which it appears that it is well worth seeing. The mountain was all snow when we passed, and we could see the large monasteries high up on its rocky sides. The isthmus joining the mountain to the mainland is only $1\frac{1}{2}$ miles across, and here Xerxes, the great Persian King, during his second invasion of Greece, made a canal, so that his ships should not be obliged to go round the cape, where many had been lost at sea on a previous occasion. Traces of this canal can still be seen there, though it was constructed over 2,000 years ago.

## INTELLIGENCE IN TRANSCAUCASIA

The anchorage at Salonika, 40 miles north of Mount Athos, is a magnificent stretch of water, 5 miles across and 20 miles long. High mountains, snow-capped in winter, come close down to the water on the south-east, and rise again to the west, about 10 miles inland, the amphitheatre of snow so formed being 50 miles across, the distant peaks shining brightly in the sun and making a most beautiful picture. The town appears just a line of wharves, warehouses, docks, and piers, for several miles along the south-east shore of the bay, no houses being visible behind them when seen from the ship.

At this time most of the British troops had left, some having moved farther up country, some on to Constant and Batoum, and many home to England for demobilization.

On landing, I got orders to go straight on to Constant (no one in the East ever says Constantinople) by the night train, and as I heard it was likely to be a rough journey, I was anxious to make my preparations accordingly, and therefore had a busy time shopping in the town.

Salonika was interesting. Although nearly half the town was then in ruins, having been burnt some time before, no attempt had yet been made at reconstruction. The parts that were still standing seemed to have a mosque every hundred yards, and their minarets, of course, made a show of a kind, but the streets were in dreadful condition—a mass of holes, no foot pavement, and the whole a sea of mud which every passing lorry scattered liberally in every direction. However, being out to shop, not to admire the scenery, I was glad to get so good an opportunity of effecting purchases, as it was necessary to replace my lost "grub-box" before boarding a war-zone train. I was lucky to get a primus from an officer going home, my other purchases consisting of the supplies necessary for what was likely to be at least a five days' journey, through devastated country where nothing at all would be obtainable.

The population of the town was both remarkable and interesting, as it appeared to consist of every kind of scoundrel of every nation, and formed a collection of blackguards who belonged to no country or race, but who resembled each other only by reason of their universal predatory instincts.

I was to have left Salonika on Tuesday night, the 25th, but on landing found that my machine-guns and valise, which had gone ashore in another boat, had entirely disappeared before my arrival on the quay. It therefore became necessary to give up the train and to spend the night, with the assistance of a patrol of military police, in trying to recover my lost property. I obtained a car and chased all over the stations, camps, resthouses, piers, and lorry parks, till at last, at 3 A.M., my guns were discovered locked up in a naval store, a patrol of naval police having found them lying on the quay. My valise was not recovered till 3 P.M. next day, when it turned up amongst some Red Cross luggage which had been landed from our ship and sent to a camp about 3 miles out; and when it was at last found it had been opened, and of three pairs of boots, some expert had succeeded in extracting the right boot of two pairs, leaving me two left boots only. It was obvious from this that he had done his work in the dark, as on account of the high heel which is now necessary for my left leg, he had concluded that the two high heels of the left boots formed a pair. For my part, I would much sooner have told him of his mistake, had I been able, and given him one complete pair, rather than that he should have spoilt two pairs; however, it was well matters were no worse, as there were a lot of things he had *not* taken.

We got off that evening, Wednesday, the 26th, and a terrible journey it turned out to be. The railway at that time was in charge of the French, and one compartment was reserved for the British Army, three British officers being authorized to take advantage of this accommodation on that auspicious occasion. Our little party was Colonel Grubbe, commanding our army "Signals," Lieut.-Colonel Raikes, R.E., of the Railway Staff, and myself, and our compartment was not a compartment at all, but *half* only, being divided by a boarded partition in the same way as on the Italian train from Rome to Taranto. In this box we travelled from Wednesday night till Saturday morning, getting out, of course, whenever the train stopped, which, luckily for us, it often did. However, the worst part was the cold, which was very severe, with snow and wind for the first part and a cold rain during the latter half of the journey.

There being no glass in any window, we were, especially at night, very cold indeed; however, I had come armed with a loose waterproof sheet, called in army parlance a "ground sheet," and our first operation was to nail that where the windows ought

## INTELLIGENCE IN TRANSCAUCASIA 125

to have been. This kept the greater part of the snow out, but not, of course, either the wind or the cold. An acetylene lamp purchased at Salonika proved the greatest success, as thanks to it we were able at any rate to see what we were doing at night, which few others on the train could do; and as I had also purchased a canvas bucket, we were able to get water when any was available at our stops. The whole train was crammed, people being packed in the corridors like sardines in a tin, every inch of space being filled; so that, as all were cold and hungry, our primus stove and the hot cocoa we were able to make on it must have appeared a banquet to our fellow-passengers.

The country at first was very interesting. We went a long way along what had been the "No Man's Land" of the Salonika front, and then over the mountains beyond Lake Doiran, in deep snow, into Bulgaria, the mountains running up to about 10,000 feet, the highest of them with fine snow scenery, and then went on across a vast uncultivated plain down to the sea again. The country was badly knocked about, with hardly any inhabitants left in it, but the line itself and the bridges were in quite fair condition, all locomotives and rolling-stock, including the train we were in, being German, with the German notices and *Verbotens* (the German for "it is forbidden") stuck up all over the place.

We saw very few Bulgarian troops, but there were parties of both British and French troops at each regular halt, and we began to see Turks after passing over the Maritza River. The country there seemed to be richer than during the earlier part of the journey, and at last we passed through the famous Catalja Lines of defence, about 25 miles out of Constantinople.

We were indeed glad to see them, as they meant that the end of our very tedious journey was approaching. The defensive value of the lie of the country there is easily realized, but the actual defences and forts which we saw did not impress us at all. However, everything comes to an end if one only waits long enough, and we got down to the coast of the Sea of Marmora at last. Then, skirting round between Old Stamboul and the entrance to the Bosphorus, we finally reached the Constantinople station on Seraglio Point at 8.30 A. M., Saturday, March 1st, after sixty-one hours—that is, three nights and two days—of that terrible train. Only one incident stands out in my recollection (besides the cold), and that is that Colonel Grubbe, the Signals officer, who had brought a tin of sweetened milk with him (horribly sticky stuff it is), having opened it, elected to place it in the remains of the railway parcels net, *over my head*, from whence it leaked its beastly contents over me all one night whilst I was asleep, or rather as near sleep as was practicable. This, for me, most unpleasant incident led to a somewhat animated conversation between us in the morning.

My letter from Constantinople about the journey says that it was the worst one I remembered; but not having ever been a Turkish prisoner at that time, my experience was sadly incomplete, and *now* there doesn't seem to me to have been much the matter with it.

On arrival at the station a car was awaiting me, sent by the "Intelligence" Branch of the Headquarters Staff to which I was now attached, and we proceeded to the house in Pera then used as the "I" (Intelligence) mess.

The "I" mess was a fine house belonging to a Greek, in the best part of Pera—that is, the fashionable quarter—on the top of the hill, the back of the house looking out over the junction of the Bosphorus and the Golden Horn, Old Stamboul (the purely Turkish town) being on the hill on the opposite side of the waters of the Golden Horn. From this position a really fine view is obtained, which would be hard to equal anywhere, but which was then spoilt by the houses in the foreground, on the slope of about half a mile down to the water, having been burnt before our troops arrived, and all still lying in ruins.

We were a small party of six only in the mess, quite comfortable, but all very busy. Next day I reported to the Chief, and got orders to go on, as soon as a ship could be found, to Batoum, *en route* to Tiflis, where our advanced Headquarters then were, and where I was to act under the orders of General Beach, who was then in charge of Intelligence in the Caucasus.

The Chief had himself just returned from a tour of inspection, in the course of which he had been right through to Baku and over the Caspian Sea to Krasnovosk, and from him I learned much about what had been going on in those parts. I was, he told me, to have two cars and to mount my guns on them, so as to be in a position to go to any part of that wild Caucasian country to report what might be going on there—to me a most

## INTELLIGENCE IN TRANSCAUCASIA 127

congenial task. He expressed surprise that the War Office had been so long in sending me out, as he had expected me a month before. The delay had really been due to lack of transport, which at this time was very limited. The Commander-in-Chief was, as always, charming in his manner, and inspired the greatest confidence at a time when the situation was a very difficult one, in which the Government at home appeared unable to indicate what their policy was, or to settle on any definite line of action.

The next day, having obtained a car, I went to have a good look round Constantinople, to which city this was my first visit, and I will try to give the reader some idea of my first impressions of that city, which since that time I have come to know so well.

Constantinople to-day consists of two quite separate cities on the European shore of the Bosphorus, an important suburb also existing on the Asiatic side. The Sea of Marmora gradually narrows down at its north-eastern end till finally, between Seraglio Point in Old Stamboul and Haider Pasha on the Asiatic shore, the water is only about 4 miles across and becomes the mouth of the Bosphorus. The old city itself stands on high ground on the promontory which lies between the Sea of Marmora and the Golden Horn. On a high rock at the point stands the Seraglio Palace, originally built and inhabited by the Roman Emperor Constantine, and afterwards used to house the Turkish Sultans and their seraglios or harems.

The old palace is a fine building occupying a spacious and truly magnificent site, dominating the waters both of the Bosphorus and of the Golden Horn, and commanding the modern suburbs of Pera and Galata, which lie opposite it on the northern side of the Golden Horn. It is now used, I understand, as a museum, but I have never yet succeeded in obtaining access to it. Immediately behind it stands the great Mosque of St. Sophia, with many other mosques of nearly equal interest in close proximity, the remainder of the promontory being covered by purely Turkish houses, the majority of ancient date and built of wood only. Large tracts of the city now lie in ruins, the result of fires during the war, and the whole is enclosed by the old Roman Wall, which stretches a distance of from 4 to 5 miles from the coast of the Sea of Marmora to the headwaters of the Golden Horn. Such is the site of Old Stamboul, the Christian city of the Roman Emperors, which was for centuries the pride of the Orient, and has always, as to-day, proved an irresistible attraction to draw the Turks to Europe from Asia, the continent to which they more properly belong.

Siege after siege Constantinople has withstood, having only been taken twice in days gone by, first by the Crusaders in 1204, and secondly by the Turks in 1453, since which last date the Turk has reigned supreme there till the occupation by the Allies after the Great War.

The situation of the city is certainly unique throughout the world, and, approaching from the Sea of Marmora, it offers a spectacle of unrivalled splendour, as, in addition to its truly beautiful site and situation, it appears, when the rays of the setting sun strike its countless gilded mosques and minarets, to be a veritable city of palaces.

On landing, however, the disillusionment is both sudden and complete. Filth and squalor are to be seen everywhere, and the city of palaces of an hour ago becomes a collection of hovels and ruins, cropping up out of a sea of mud, with here and there a more pretentious building which, by the evidence it offers of its original splendour, only serves to emphasize the many signs of decline and decay.

Such was the impression I received on my first visit to Old Stamboul. But on crossing the really fine Galata Bridge over the Golden Horn, here about twice the width of the Thames at Westminster, to the modern city which gives its name to the bridge, one feels that one has left Asia and is once more in Europe. Here are fine, though steep, streets, pavements, electric light and trams, fine buildings, and all the evidences of prosperity and enterprise which distinguish a modern European capital.

Continuing up the hill, within a mile, we find ourselves in the "Grande Rue" of Pera—the European residential suburb—and here things recall Paris irresistibly, as the shop-windows in many instances would not disgrace the Rue de la Paix, and, incidentally, the prices charged would also at least equal the Paris ones.

The most striking part of this most interesting modern suburb is the "crowd" always to be found there, for the Grande Rue is invariably crowded at any hour of the day, as well as during the greater part of the night; and the crowd in early 1919 was a truly remarkable one. In late afternoon or early evening the crush was so great that it was a slow and difficult matter to get along the pavement of the Grande Rue, whilst the trams were so crowded it was a hopeless mattter to board one, and an unceasing stream of motors flowed continuously in both directions.

Here were uniforms of all descriptions, the Allied armies and fleets being all strongly represented. The civilians were for the most part Greeks, or Levantines of one sort or another, whilst about the rarest apparition was a genuine Turk, at any rate of the humbler class, the majority of such Turks as might be met there having more the appearance of European noblemen, which impression would in no way be weakened if one was privileged to enjoy their polite and refined conversation.

There were a number of cinemas and shows of various sorts, and the general impression created was one of prosperity and gaiety, though this was largely on the surface, and there was much misery and privation, especially amongst the many Russian refugees who had found their way there from the Russian Black Sea ports.

Next day I visited St. Sophia and Adrian's old city wall, and the following is an extract from my letter written at the time:

"It (St. Sophia) is a most wonderful place, and I could write for hours about it and then not give an adequate description of it. First of all, it is of enormous size—not as large or as high as St. Peter's at Rome, but the dome is probably just as great in diameter, though very much flatter, which form is infinitely more difficult to build, as the outward thrust, caused by the great weight, is colossal. Although the dome is constructed of specially made hollow and therefore light bricks, and the buttresses have been many times strengthened, ominous cracks are to be seen, and it would never be surprising to hear the walls had been unable to bear the strain and that the whole roof had fallen in.

"I paced the width of the dome, and found it 180 feet across, and the length of the central hall is twice this, so you have a great 'hall,' 360 feet by 180 feet, without a single pillar, with a sort of chancel built out at each end, and side-chapels each side, all of them 90 feet wide, opening into the central hall. Twenty-five thousand people are said to kneel and pray there at the same time on the occasions of the big festivals—and they probably could do so, for it is the largest single hall I have ever seen. The floor is covered with fine old prayer-carpets, all about the same size, literally hundreds of them, and the whole vast place is lit by a multitude of small lamps, just little open cups with a wick in them, that are hung in clusters by long wires from the roof and ranged along ledges all round the walls, the effect of which must be truly wonderful when they are all lit, as they are on great occasions.

"The most curious part is that, as St. Sophia was first built as a Christian church, it faces, of course, east, but as the followers of the prophet (Mohammedans) must always pray towards his holy city, Mecca, and as Mecca lies nearly south-east from Constant, the altar has now been made to face skew-ways across the church, and all the rows of prayer-carpets, etc., are woefully out of line with the church in consequence, which gives the whole arrangement a most curious 'temporary' appearance. There is little of any oramentation inside, or indeed outside, the building, which depends for the remarkable impression it creates upon its vast size alone.

"To show how truly 'Turkish' it all is to-day, it looks, from the outside, a most mean and miserable-looking place; it is painted, or coloured, a dirty yellow—just stucco over the bricks, with many portions now falling off. It stands in an open square, at present more like a bog, and is surrounded by a broken-down railing, inside which the ground is more like a farmyard than anything else, with odd chickens and other animals running about, up to and even *into* the mosque, although all human visitors have to put on slippers or take their boots off to go in, and there are also at the moment Turkish troops bivouacking in the outer chapels—hardly our idea of a great cathedral.

"After seeing St. Sophia, I went on to look at Adrian's old wall, which stretches from the Sea of Marmora to the Golden Horn, and quite encloses the old city. It is now pretty well in ruins in many parts, but what are left are extremely interesting, as it certainly is on a colossal scale. The top of the wall (which is of brick and stone about 60 feet high) is sufficiently broad to carry four lines of railway abreast if desired, and a second wall rises on the top of the first one, the whole being somewhere near 100 feet high, with towers rising higher still, at frequent intervals. To realize the gigantic undertaking its construction was, it must be remembered that this huge wall stretches for a distance of over 4 miles, each flank reaching to the water's edge. No wonder the city in those days proved impregnable!

"At this time in Pera there were many attempts at holding 'carnival,' and many idiots were to be seen parading the streets in fancy dress, all of them masked, but forming processions behind a man who carries a street piano-organ on his back, a great load to a European, but nothing to a Turk, who would be capable of carrying even a house on his back if he thought he could 'get away' with it. All the jovial followers in the procession go up and turn the handle when they please, and they all dance along the streets, waving their hands and looking too foolish for words, but appear, nevertheless, to enjoy themselves immensely."

So much says my letter written at the time.

During the five days which I spent this time at Constant, it was cold and some snow fell, which is quite unusual. Almost every day the mornings were lovely, with a bright sun and the keen air which is so invigorating. However, our ship came in on the 4th, and on the morning of the 5th we sailed, bound first of all for the Bulgarian port of Varna, then across the Black Sea to Samsun, on the Anatolian coast, and on to Batoum, the Russian port in the Caucasus.

On leaving Constant I went down the Bosphorus for the first time, and felt that all I had read about it—and that was much—had not done it justice, for it certainly is a wonderfully beautiful place, even in winter, and I will quote the little I say about it from my letter at that time, and wait to give a better account when I was there in the late summer, when the Allied fleets were all anchored there. The letter is as follows:

"Going down the Bosphorus was a wonderful sight. I have seen no place in the world like that. The sun came out, and it all looked too beautiful, and must be still more so in summer. It is a narrow strait, varying from 4 miles to 1 mile in width, and it winds in and out the mountains on either side for 25 miles from the Sea of Marmora to the Black Sea. Leaving Constant, the European shore is a line of palaces and fine houses built right on the water's edge, with others on the slopes behind them which rise steeply from the water, itself of the deepest blue. All the houses *look* from the water like fairy palaces, though, like most things Turkish, they are probably very much less pleasing when seen from near-by.

"The Sultan's old palace of Dolma Batchke, on the water's edge, is about the first on leaving the city, followed by the Yildiz Kiosk (where he now lives) a little farther on, lying farther back up the hill, surrounded by a fine-looking park and woods; these are very handsome buildings in Oriental style, and *look* as if they were of white marble, which they probably are not. And there are many others nearly as fine scattered about as one goes on, with queer old forts and fortified villages also, relics of times long past, but interesting to see. About 10 miles or more from Constant is Therapia, a lovely spot in a deep bay on the European side, with the hills rising steeply behind it. Here are the summer quarters of the Embassies and of many of the prominent residents in Constantinople, who have the advantage of enjoying there as beautiful a summer retreat as can be found in any country.

"On leaving Therapia the hills become wider and more rugged, with much more rock showing, and at last two old forts appear, one on the European and one on the Asiatic side of the water, and, the land falling away on either hand, we find ourselves quite suddenly on the open waters of the Black Sea."

On this occasion there was a bright sun and an exceptionally clear atmosphere, so that all the details of the mountains showed up with striking clearness, making a memorable picture, but one it was not possible to enjoy for long, as an icy north wind was blowing, which no furs could keep out. Even writing in my cabin I was obliged to keep my overcoat on and wrap a rug round my legs, and then found my fingers so cold I could only write with difficulty.

Next morning, the 7th, we arrived at the Bulgarian port of Varna, famous as the site of the British hospitals during the Crimean War, and for little else except the existence there of the terminus of a most indifferent railway. The harbour is good, but had hardly any shipping in it at that time, and here we landed 700 British troops and got away the same day for Samsun, where we were to land 200 more.

Samsun, on the Anatolian coast of the Black Sea, about 400 miles east of the Bosphorus, and 300 miles west of Batoum, is, or was, a prosperous place, for although it has no harbour, but

## INTELLIGENCE IN TRANSCAUCASIA 133

only an open roadstead, yet, situated at the end of the main road which runs through Sivas to the Mesopotamian plain, whatever trade there is in that part of the country uses it as a port.

The road into the interior from Samsun is a good one, and there is only one other road passable for wheels which comes down to the coast in the 300 miles which lie between Samsun and Batoum. That one, which reaches the coast at Trebizond, about halfway between Samsun and Batoum, is generally blocked by snow in winter, whilst the Samsun road is very rarely closed, and therefore carries all winter traffic of merchandise.

The population of this coast, which is known as the "Pontine" coast, consisted, previous to the deportations which have resulted from the war between Greece and Turkey, largely of Greeks, whose occupation of this coast and its valleys dates back to 500 B. C., many centuries before the Turks first came west from their original home in Central Asia. The valleys are rich and were well cultivated, producing many good crops, notably tobacco, the best qualities of Turkish tobacco coming exclusively from the Pontine coast valleys.

We anchored off Samsun on the 9th and landed 200 men. The troops were received with every sign of rejoicing by the Greek population, who were in great fear of the Turks, some portions of the Turkish armies being in course of demobilization and considerably out of hand, so that the presence even of a small number of British troops was a great relief to the Christian population. Leaving Samsun in the afternoon, the coast, as we went farther east, showed high mountains coming right down to the water's edge, with many deep valleys, and over all vast masses of snow which crown the hills the whole way, until the main chain of the Caucasus is reached, 400 miles farther on.

On approaching Batoum Harbour next day, our guns suddenly opened fire, which brought me very quickly on deck. However, the cause was only a derelict Turkish mine, which was promptly destroyed, and we then approached the grand but most uninviting coast of the Transcaucasian Russia. The weather was bright but very cold indeed. On approaching Batoum, the high snow-covered mountains can be seen rising well over 10,000 feet and coming down close to the shore as far as the eye can reach on either hand.

The harbour is well protected by a "mole," but is not of any great extent, and the town is mean and presents no architecture worthy of the name, the houses rarely being of more than two stories. The quays were busy at this time, for Batoum was the base for the British forces, amounting to two divisions, then in the Caucasus; but in normal times the main industry of the place is oil, which is transported from the Baku oil-fields by a "pipeline," and here shipped in tank steamers to all parts of the world. Here also is the terminus of the great Russian Imperial Railway, communicating via Baku with Moscow, and through Tiflis with the Persian and Turkish frontiers.

On landing I experienced quite exceptional good fortune, as the Chief of the General Staff at Constant, General Cory, had arrived in a destroyer a few hours before us and was going straight on that night to Tiflis, Baku, and then over the Caspian Sea to Krasnovosk and on to Merv, on a tour of inspection. He had the late Czar's private train at his disposal and offered me a place in it, which was accepted with great thankfulness, and we left Batoum for Tiflis the same evening.

# CHAPTER II

### THE CAUCASUS—AFTER THE ARMISTICE

The Czar's Imperial train—Party on board—Journey to Tiflis—Georgia and its capital—British Advanced Headquarters—My duties and establishment—The Azerbaijan frontier—Tartar brigands—Conditions in Tiflis—The main chain of the Caucasus—The Georgian Road—Queen Tamara's summer palace—The Russo-Georgian frontier—Russian brigands—The Ingoush tribe—Orders to equip a train and go to Kars—Snowed up—Conditions at Kars—Escape from Kars—Report to Commander-in-Chief at Batoum—Further orders.

We left Batoum for Tiflis at sundown on March 10th. The Imperial train itself in which we travelled is worth description, as it would have been a most luxurious and comfortable way of travelling in any country at any time, and in this out-of-the-way part of the world, at the end of the war and revolution, it was indeed a pleasant surprise.

The car we occupied ran on two six-wheeled "bogies," and consisted of a small open observation-platform at the end, with a roof over it, opening into the saloon, very nicely but in no way extravagantly built, a sofa being fixed at one end and a table large enough to dine eight people running down the centre. Large plate-glass windows and electric light were fitted throughout the carriage, which contained five separate single-berth state-rooms opening into the corridor, and at the end a bathroom with the great luxury of a shower-bath. Immediately in rear and communicating with the main carriage was the kitchen-coach, with good cooking-stove and accommodation for servants, whilst both in front and in rear of these two coaches were others for the escort, consisting on this occasion of 100 British infantry. This was very necessary at that time, as only the previous day a train had been stopped and robbed, and the country was infested by bands of Bolshevik and other classes of brigands capable of any atrocity.

On this occasion our escort was much too strong for these gentlemen, and we ran through to Tiflis in fourteen hours without incident, instead of two, or even three, days which the journey might otherwise have taken, although the actual distance is very little over 200 miles. Our small party, in addition to the General's staff, included Sir Hubert Gough, late Commander of the Fifth Army in France, then on some cilivian mission to Baku, and the conversation was most interesting. Everywhere was the same uncertainty as to our Government's intentions, than which no condition could be less encouraging in the face of the many diametrically opposite political aspirations which were then existent among the various races inhabiting the Caucasus.

The railway was in fairly good order, and after running north for about 40 miles between the mountains and the sea, turned east up the valley of the Rion River, which runs into the Black Sea at Poti. This valley is at first a good 20 miles wide, and consists of rich cultivated land; it is bounded by high snow-covered mountains to the north and south; these close gradually in until the watershed between the Black Sea and the Caspian is reached at the Suram Tunnel—120 and 350 miles respectively from those seas. After passing through the tunnel we followed the valley of the Koura River to Tiflis; the valley is narrow, enclosed by high mountains, the land, though under cultivation, being nothing like so rich as on the Black Sea slope. We were now, of course, in Georgia, and reached Tiflis, the capital, about 9 A. M.

Georgia, for over 1,000 years an independent kingdom, with its own Czar, until merged in Imperial Russia in 1800, did not take kindly at first to the Bolshevik revolutionary principles, and is at heart always desirous of re-establishing its independence. The people, however, are imbued with Socialiastic ideas, with the result that they manufactured a revolution of their own and established a Georgian Republic. The outstanding feature of this movement was the nationalization of property, whereby, in theory, the nation was to own everything for the people's advantage; whereas, in practice, it seemed to result in everyone who owned anything losing it, without those who previously owned nothing becoming any better off. And it seems needless to remark that that state of affairs pleased nobody, except certain officials who alone profited thereby. This was the extremely unsatisfactory state of affairs in the early part of 1919, and it cannot be said that they have much improved up to the present (October, 1922).

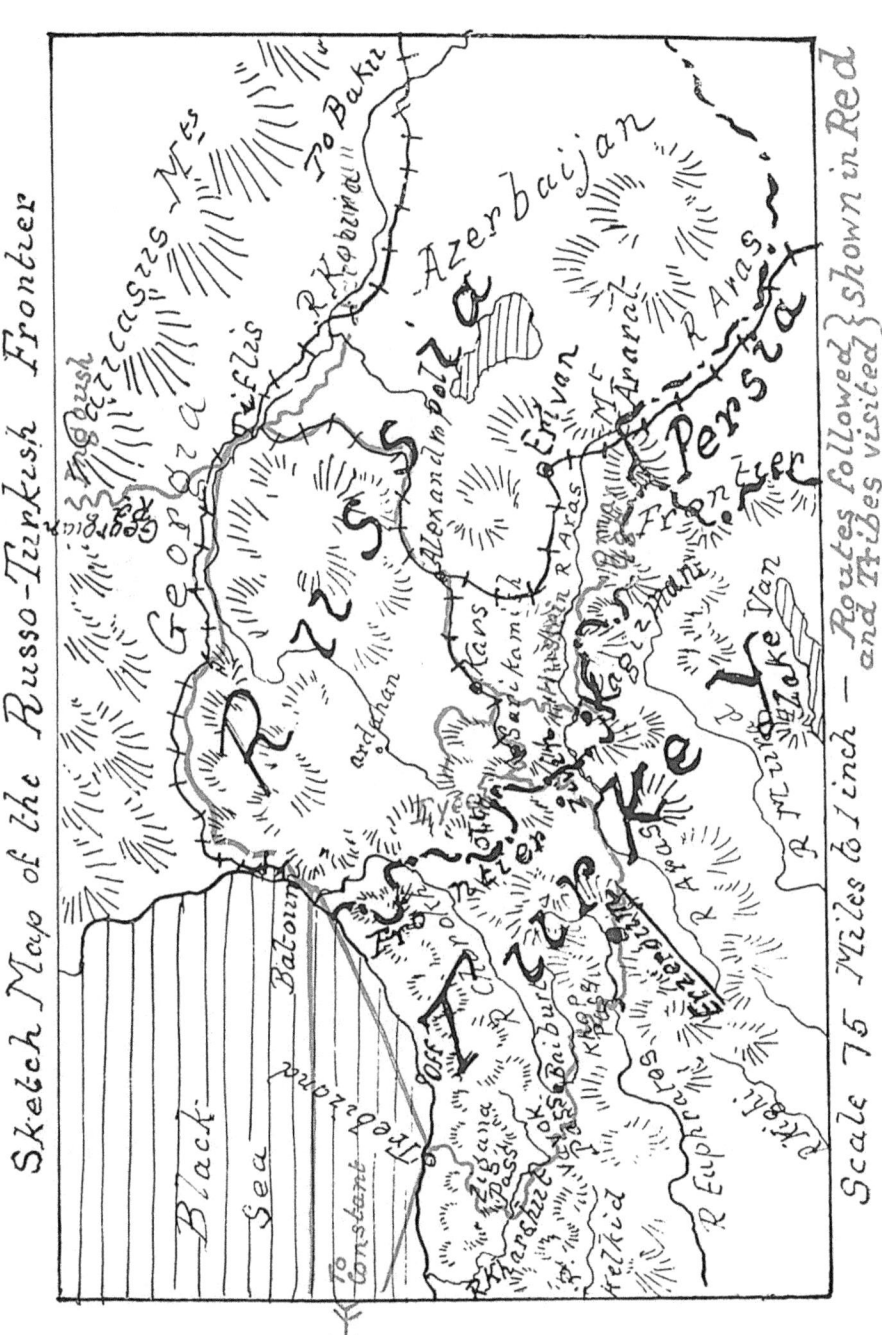

Tiflis itself is a most interesting city, and even at the time with which we are dealing it was hard to imagine, when there, that one was in the Caucasus. The town is finely sited astride of the Koura River, which, rising on the old Russo-Turkish frontier, flows through Georgia and its eastern neighbour, the old Russian province of Baku (now the Republic of Azerbaijan), and falls eventually into the Caspian Sea, about 100 miles south of the town of Baku. The valley, rising by an easy slope to the north of the river, is well cultivated on that side; but to the south rises more abruptly till, within 2 miles of the river, almost precipitous heights are reached at 2,000 feet above the river level. The main public buildings and the better part of the city are situated between the river and the steep hillside on the south; the streets are well laid out, with electric light and trams, fine hotels, an opera-house, the old Royal palaces, and all the marks of Western civilization.

The Advanced Headquarters of the British forces was at this time in Tiflis, and the Intelligence Branch occupied a good house in the upper and residential quarter of the town. Here I was allotted a room and reported to my immediate Chief, General Beach, who was in charge of the Intelligence Branch, and whom I had previously known in Persia when he occupied an identical position on the Headquarters staff of the Mesopotamian Expeditionary Force at Bagdad. From him I quickly learned the general situation, of which the most vital part was that much was going on all round us with regard to which our information was by no means as ample or reliable as we could wish, and it was therefore very desirable that we should augment it by every means in our power.

During the few hours I was at Batoum I had applied for and obtained two Ford cars, and had had my pick of some of the best and most experienced drivers and campaigners whom I had ever seen, they having come on to the Caucasus from Salonika after the Armistice, and having been through the Macedonian campaign as well as the original most arduous retreat through Serbia. My two cars and the men having come up to Tiflis by train, I quickly got my guns prepared, and in a few days we were ready to go anywhere.

It appeared that my immediate duty would be to go to whatever districts were most interesting, and of which we had but meagre information, to have a good look round and to report what was going on. Nothing could have suited me better, nor could any more congenial task have been allotted to me. In the meanwhile I was told that in a short time I should probably have to go farther afield, and that I was therefore to get together and train a party which would be capable of going right away into the wild frontier countries and of remaining for a considerable time in disturbed districts, to form a centre for reports, etc.

For this purpose "authority" was given me to draw upon the troops for a certain "establishment," who were described with the subtle and entirely unconscious humour which is to be found in many military documents, as follows:

"*Colonel R——'s Establishment, to consist of*—1 personal officer (!), 1 interpreter, 1 clerk, 1 N.C.O., 3 cars and drivers, 2 horses, 1 groom, 1 cook, 1 mess waiter, 2 batmen—14 in all."

This being the *number* authorized, it followed that I was entitled to draw pay and rations for fourteen and to select my own men. I set to work at once, knowing well what was wanted, and in a few days I had them in training. Of course, fourteen really tough fellows were required who could go anywhere and do anything without expecting three meals a day and a bed at night, which were about the only things they could be quite certain they would not get.

I fancy that even in Tiflis, at that time, the more enterprising element, which is never lacking amongst our troops, had heard some tales as to previous "stunts" of the same sort connected with myself, as when volunteers were called for it became a question of selecting the fittest men for the job from among the many that offered themselves, and a better lot than those we at last got together it would be impossible to find. The interpreter, however, was the only one who corresponded in any sense to his official description. The others, instead of being cooks, or waiters, or farriers, or anything else, were just bright fellows with plenty of devil in them, who were ready to take on any job; and if they didn't know anything about it, they were ready to learn. So they were put to work at once to learn their duties, in order that our party might be ready to start off "on our own" at any moment, whilst I took on some preliminary intelligence work, which was badly wanted and proved very interesting.

## INTELLIGENCE IN TRANSCAUCASIA

The first point upon which it was desired to acquire reliable information was the actual state of affairs existing on the frontier between the new Sosialistic Republic of Georgia and its neighbour on the east, the new Tartar Republic of Azerbaijan. Although we had representatives in the Azerbaijan capital of Baku, they did not appear to be any too comfortable there. It was evident, also, that all these old countries were "in the melting-pot," and that new combinations were springing up all over this part of the world. It was therefore important to know what was going on under the surface, in order to arrive at an intelligent forecast of what policy these new Governments might be expected to pursue in the face of various possible decisions, as to peace conditions, at which the Allies might eventually arrive. My instructions in this case were to start in the early morning and to cross the Georgian frontier into Azerbaijan, and drive as far as I could on the road to Baku, and to return the same night and report. I therefore started next morning with one car only and a very light load, taking only one driver and my interpreter.

The first 15 miles were easy going and, though all the bridges had been destroyed by the Turks in their retreat from Baku after the Armistice, we had no great difficulty in getting round them all in one way or another, till the road led into a mountainous district where things were much more difficult. We spent three hours doing the 5 miles through the mountains, having to turn back time after time at broken bridges in that difficult country, till we finally were forced to leave the road altogether, and to strike out by instinct across country, picking up the trail again in the open plain beyond the hills.

After being twice bogged, and also getting the engine under water in crossing a deepish river, we eventually reached the Azerbaijan frontier. Here was a bridge over the frontier river and a frontier post of Azerbaijan Tartars. These gentlemen promptly surrounded us, and were proceeding to loot the car, when they found themselves looking down the muzzle of my automatic pistol, whilst the interpreter yelled that I was an "English Pasha from Tiflis." Then, laughing at their astonishment (which appeared the best, and in fact the only, thing to do), we distributed some cigarettes amongst them, and, taking one of them in the car, proceeded to try to find their officer, who was said to be in a village 2 miles farther on. When we got there the officer was "out"; however, we persuaded our passenger to get out himself, and drove on ourselves, hoping we might be able to find another way for our return journey.

The road then became much better, and we kept up a good pace, with no incidents, till about 20 miles farther on, where we saw a man on a hillside who looked suspiciously like a "lookout sentry, and we therefore made ready for any eventuality, and kept on over the shoulder of the hill on which he stood, where, sure enough, we found three terrible-looking ruffians awaiting us, kneeling in the road, with their rifles to their shoulders, whilst about ten more were racing down from their camp on the hill to intercept us.

In a moment they were all round the car, "on the loot," and I came very near beginning to shoot, as no notice was taken of the interpreter's yells. However, in a few moments a venerable-looking old man, with a long white beard, appeared on the scene, and when he heard we were English he gave these ruffians a proper dressing-down, and made them disgorge what little they had succeeded in taking from us. After which, with many polite thanks to him, we started on again.

A few miles farther on a large town came in sight on the far side of a big river, which I knew at once to be Kazak, 60 miles from Tiflis, and the first place of any importance east of the Azerbaijan frontier. In view of the uncertainty of our return journey I decided not to go farther, but halted in the middle of a large open plain where we could see anyone long before they could come near us, and then proceeded to have lunch, whilst I made notes as to the town, the river, and the military possibilities of the position. That done, we made for home, getting a friendly salute this time from the "look-out" on the hill; and then all was plain-sailing till the frontier bridge, where we were again surrounded by the frontier post, which had been largely reinforced.

There were now about twenty-five armed ruffians, all Tartars, and an N.C.O. of sorts in command, and they insisted that we should go back with the N.C.O. to the big town we had left behind. This I definitely refused to do, and we stopped there over an hour arguing, during which time things looked very queer indeed. It appeared there had been a wedding in the village that day, and the majority of these ruffians were more than half drunk, and crowded round the car all the time, so that at one time I was afraid we should have to go back, as they had blocked the bridge with a tree-trunk and it was impossible to rush it. What added considerably to the interest was that the revellers still in the village close by, in true Oriental fashion, kept up a constant fusillade, and we could hear the bullets whistling over our heads all the time, of which, of course, we took not the slightest notice, though it was pleasant to think that, in event of a lower shot than usual, our friends round the car would get the benefit of it before we did. I think, in the end, that had much to do with their letting us go, which they finally did, to our infinite relief, and we then made the best of our way back to Tiflis.

On our way back we got bogged once and had to jack the car up to get it out, and also had a very close shave in the deep river, which we were obliged to charge at full speed, the car even then having only just sufficient "way" on to carry it through the deepest part before the engine stopped in the shallower water, and we were obliged to dry it before we could start it up again. Coming to the mountains, it was dark, and I determined to follow the road to the bridge, where we had been obliged to turn back in the morning. Arrived there, we took a great chance—that is, we faced the car down the almost precipitous slope alongside the bridge, and *slid* gracefully down, and so along the open country below, till we could get on the road again, finally reaching Tiflis safely at 11.30 P.M., after sixteen and a half hours on the road. The next few days were devoted to training the men, in which task the three regular machine-gunners there were amongst them proved most useful. The state of affairs in Tiflis at this time was really interesting. The people were the usual mixed crowd with which I had become familiar in Mesopotamia, but there was in the Caucasus a much higher percentage of Central Asian Tartars and, of course, many more Russians, whilst superimposed on all these we now had Georgians, Ossitines, Ingoushes, Avars, and many more of the tribes from the wild hill-countries lying to the north of the great Caucasus Mountains.

The Georgians are a type quite by themselves, They had at this time what they were pleased to call an army. This consisted of very small and indifferent bodies of cavalry, artillery, and infantry, the officers of which swaggered about the town in magnificent uniforms, covered with cartridge-cases, inlaid daggers and pistols, very tight waists, and long skirts to their coats, finished off with Persian lamb (astrakhan caps, collars, and cuffs. There had been, before the revolution in Georgia, a fine aristocracy of landowners, wealthy and well educated, many of them Russian Princes, and a refined and hospitable people. But their fate had been tragic, for the old owners of the land had no money left at all, and lived by selling their personal belongings, whilst Princesses went out as housemaids, or accepted gladly any post where they could earn enough to keep their parents or children alive. It was a repetition of what happened in France at the time of the French Revolution, though in Georgia the aristocrats were not killed (at least, not often), but the people were content just to let them starve. These poor Georgian nobles, however, were so proud that they would not accept any help at all from us, nor even let us give them wood for firing.

One most pathetic story came to my knowledge which well illustrates the sad state of these cultured families, upon whom, through no fault of their own, fell the cruellest effects of the revolution. One night, some of our officers told me, they had "asked themselves" to dinner with a charming Georgian family whom they knew to be actually starving in their own great house, without food, light, fire, or money to buy any of these things. Our men said they would bring their own food and fuel, if they might have the use of the big kitchen of the house to cook it in. So they collected provisions from everyone, and took care to take with them a supply which would leave over sufficient to keep the whole family for a week, until they could offer to come again without hurting the feelings of their hosts. A true and, I think, pretty story of the spirit which distinguishes the British Army, and which makes them welcomed the world over.

It was here that I first had an opportunity of judging of the glorious work in the relief of suffering which was being carried out by the great American organization of Near East relief. Ships arrived at the port of Batoum with supplies of food which were subsequently distributed throughout the country, reaching eastwards as far as Batoum and southwards from Tiflis to the famine-stricken districts of Kars and Erivan.

The work of those responsible for this distribution was most

## INTELLIGENCE IN TRANSCAUCASIA

arduous, but was in all cases most conscientiously and capably carried out under conditions of extreme difficulty.

A host of people who would otherwise most certainly have been lost, were saved, and an immensity of suffering relieved by the efforts of this most practical of all philanthropical organizations. It cannot fail to be a source of satisfaction to those who from their far distant homes in the United States contributed their share to this glorious work, to know how deeply their efforts were appreciated by all who were in a position to judge. Personally I rejoice that I am able here to find an opportunity of joining in the universal chorus of thanks which still resounds throughout those countries where the fame of American philanthropy is now immortal and where the generosity of the citizens of the United States will for ever remain the one bright spot against a dark background of misery, suffering and death.

My next expedition was more interesting than the last, as rumours had been reaching us of the actions of some of General Deniken's volunteer Russian Army, portions of which were at this time operating on the northern slopes of the Caucasus, far from their headquarters, and were reported as not being under effective control. I was instructed to cross the main Caucasus range and to get in touch with these Russians if possible, and to report as to the conditions then obtaining in those parts, of which no definite information was forthcoming.

In order to make clear what this order meant, it will be necessary to give a short description of what the main chain of the Caucasus Mountains is like, for, although the name of the great range is well known, few people have ever heard much about that most interesting country, and fewer still have ever been into its remoter valleys or seen the many tribes of widely varying races who inhabit them.

The main range of the Caucasus Mountains can be taken as about 600 miles long, and is in many places 100 miles in breadth, stretching practically the whole distance from the Black Sea to the Caspian. Throughout the whole range it is traversed by only one road passable by wheeled vehicles. This pass is known as the Georgian Road, and reaches a height at the summit of upwards of 8,000 feet. There are a few mule-paths which cross in other places, but for over 100 miles there is no path under

10,000 feet, and for 400 miles there are but very few, the only easy communication from north to south being along the shore of the Caspian Sea, where the railway now passes north from Baku to the Steppes of Southern Russia. The main peaks of the Caucasus Mountains are Mount Kazbeck, 16,500 feet, under which passes the Georgian Road about the centre of the range, and Mount Elburz, slightly the higher of the two, about 120 miles to the northwest. The average height of the range for many miles is nearly 14,000 feet, and nowhere else in the world can be found such a formidable and continuous mountain barrier, extending from sea to sea.

This is the explanation of the extraordinary diversity of races and languages which is to be found amongst the peoples inhabiting its remote valleys, between which there is little, if any, intercommunication. In every migration which has taken place of conquering or conquered races from Asia to Europe, the varied hordes of Medes, Persians, Greeks, Romans, and Arabs, from the south, and of Mongols, Scythians, Turks, Tartars, and Slavs from the north, have surged up against the vast barrier of the Caucasus like angry waves against a rocky coast, and each and all of them have left their representatives in the isolated valleys, where they retain to-day the salient physical characteristics and language of their race.

It is even said that there is a valley in the western portion of the southern slopes where is to be found to-day an isolated tribe whose language is the Gaelic of Scotland, and amongst whom the bagpipes and the kilt have come down from their ancestors of long ago, who are said to have been a party of Scottish Crusaders who lost themselves in these mountains in their endeavour to find their way back to Europe from Palestine by land.

The whole range is, of course, capped by perpetual snow, and although every effort is made, by means of snow tunnels and constant labour, to keep the Georgian Road open in winter, yet it is frequently impassable, and at the time I received orders to cross it was months since any vehicle had achieved the passage. Under these circumstances we set out from Tiflis in the early morning of March 18th in a very chastened spirit, with great doubts as to our competence to get over the pass at all, and still greater doubts as to the possibility of our being back in Tiflis on the night of the next day, which formed the two salient features

# INTELLIGENCE IN TRANSCAUCASIA 145

of my official instructions. Of course, no question of what our reception the other side might be, entered into the official picture at all, and though I had my own doubts about that also, I kept them strictly to myself.

Having made sure the car was sound all over and petrol plentiful, and having borrowed all the furs which we could raise, I left Tiflis at daybreak, accompanied by my driver and interpreter only, in a Ford van, less its hood, and all the weight it was possible to dispense with. For the first ten miles we followed the river and railway of the west, and then, crossing both, made north for the towering mass of snow, the interminable line of which stretched as far as we could see on either hand, its upper slopes everywhere lost in the clouds above. As soon as the river was crossed the road began to rise, and we had several minor passes to cross before we reached the valley of the stream which we were to ascend to its source in the very heart of the great range.

Our valley was narrow, the road following a roaring mountain torrent, between steep hillsides covered with thick, low woods, rather like the Exmoor combes; the tops of the hills, however, were everywhere hidden in cloud. We followed this road, of which the surface was fair, except where it had been washed away by tributary torrents, for at least 40 miles until we found ourselves at a bridge spanning our torrent, on the other side of which rose a sheer precipice of rock, in which zigzags were cut ever rising till they were lost in the clouds overhead. Over the bridge we then went, to start the real climb to the snow-fields far above us.

The zigzags were well traced and well made, with a severe but uniform slope, the road being cut out of the solid rock, and built in many places with walls and buttresses of good masonry. The climb appeared endless, and actually is, I believe, nearly 3,000 feet, until, all at once, a sharp turn, and we were facing a great snow-field extending for miles on either hand, whilst immediately above us, appearing, in fact, almost over our heads, towered a great snow-peak, many thousands of feet (actually over 9,000 feet) above the snow-slope upon which we then found ourselves. This was the great peak of Mount Kazbeck, with the exception of its neighbour, Mount Elburz, and Mount Demavend above Teheran, the highest peak between the Himalayas in

India and the Andes in South America—higher by 1,500 feet than any peak in Europe.

Night had now fallen and a brilliant moon lit up the whole snow landscape, the vast sea of cloud which had been above our heads all day being now behind and far below us. The bright moon on the snow made it as light as day, and we paused a moment to admire this truly magnificent scene, and also for a more practical purpose—namely, to put on all the furs we could lay our hands on. It was freezing hard, and the frost not only made the snow shine and sparkle with wonderfully beautiful effect in the moonlight, but also froze our breath, till I found my moustache a solid block of ice.

In the front of us lay our road, a narrow track, rising steeply, cut across the great solitude of the snow. The snow was everywhere as hard as concrete, and we had little or no trouble in following the track, which had been laboriously dug through the deep snow. However, once between its snowy walls nothing else could be seen; even standing up in the car one could not see over the snow on either side, reaching as it did far above our heads. After another hour's climbing in the bitterest cold, we at last reached the summit of the pass, marked by a stone building covered entirely by the snow. We did not stop here, however, but, as our motor was pulling well, kept on in the hope of reaching a less arctic climate in which to pass the night.

The descent on the northern side proved even more interesting than the ascent, and we were able once more to appreciate the endless resources of Imperial Russia. In the places where the snow was thickest there were "tunnels" built, over which the snow had drifted and slid from above till it had reached incredible depths and lay as deep as 40 feet and more in many places. These tunnels were built many years back, and so solidly are they constructed that they will last for as many more, the entrances being of brick and the roof consisting throughout of planks laid on enormous wooden beams which are single baulks of sound timber, sawn square, each 18 inches thick and more than 20 feet in length. These tunnels are erected at the most exposed points, and some of them are several hundred yards in length.

We descended rapidly, soon reaching a valley where there was much less snow, and we were then able to push on at a higher speed, finally reaching a small village at 11 P. M. Here we found a hovel into which we could creep with all our belongings and our lamps and primus stove for a cup of hot tea, after which we enjoyed a well-earned sleep on the cushions we had kept unfrozen, if not warm, all day by the very practical means of sitting on them.

Whilst boiling our humble kettle, to my intense surprise we received a visit from a Georgian General, who was making a round of the frontier posts, and lodging for the night in a similiar hovel to ourselves, not many yards away. He expressed himself delighted to see our party, and having shown him our credentials, he gave us the various reports he had received from the country over the frontier, and at the same time promised to detail an officer to go with us to the Georgian frontier post next morning, 10 miles farther on down the pass, for which we tendered him our sincere thanks, and a good day's work was at last finished.

Next morning we were astir at daylight, and the Georgian officer having duly appeared, we set off down the pass at a fine speed, the road being quite good and the gradient very favourable. Within a mile or so of Kazbeck village, where we had spent the night, we entered the famous Dariel Gorge, a truly remarkable spot. The Terek River, which eventually falls into the Caspian Sea, and whose upper waters we were then following, here runs for 3 miles through a narrow gorge, not more than 50 yards in width at its narrowest point. The sides are perpendicular cliffs rising sheer for 1,500 to 2,000 feet, and about the centre, where the gorge is widest, rises a most extraordinary isolated rock with perpendicular sides. In ancient days a twisted road, traces of which still remain, climbed in zigzags to the summit, where are still to be seen the ruins of a palace, 500 feet above the level of the gorge below. This was built, and occupied as a summer residence, by the great Georgian Queen Tamara, who in the twelfth century first extended the Georgian kingdom from the Black Sea to the Caspian.

A more unique site for a summer palace can, I think, hardly exist anywhere, as in the great heats of summer not only is the gorge entirely sheltered from the sun by the height of its encircling cliffs, but a cool and gentle breeze blows always through it, of which the lofty site of the palace insures its occupants reaping the full advantage. There is also, towards the lower end of the gorge, an old fort, now unoccupied and in ruins, but in bygone days the site of many fierce fights between the mountaineers and the wild Tartar tribes of the northern Steppes. Immediately beyond the fort the river takes a sharp "S" turn, and the cliffs approach so close as to hardly leave room for the river and the road as they pass out side by side on the same level. Here is the Georgian frontier post, and here our officer left us, with many injunctions to keep a sharp look-out, as things were "queer" down below.

From this point the cliffs receded and the valley widened out, whilst many tributary streams came in and our river grew fast. To our astonishment, however, we saw no sign of a Russian post, nor of any frontier patrol, although on reaching a village called Lars, some 15 miles after crossing the frontier, certain suspicious-looking objects hanging from the trees, affording a much appreciated repast to many carrion crows, brought home to us the fact that there were indeed queer characters about. Shortly afterwards, on halting in the village street we were approached by some villainous-looking specimens of humanity, who announced themselves as an "outpost" of Deniken's volunteer army. It only needed a glance to "size them up," as we had been prepared for some time, by the absence of any guards or patrols, for the kind of thing we were likely to find—namely, just a rabble, without any pretence of discipline, living on the country by extortion and crime, and entirely out of touch with the military chiefs in whose name they purported to be acting.

We therefore continued our way without taking any notice of them as they all spoke at once, and there appeared no one of them with any authority, from whom could be obtained an explanation of the objects decorating the trees in the village street, a matter as to which it was clearly our duty to obtain information. A mile or so farther on we saw an inhabited village across the river, where there seemed to be some kind of guard kept, and I therefore crossed the river and approached, announcing that I was a British officer come from Tiflis to inquire into the state of the country.

The village was one of those of the Ingoush tribe, whose country lies to the east of the pass, the tribe of the Ossitines lying to the west, and the head-men of the Ingoushis immediately assembled and greeted me with great cordiality. They told me the

## INTELLIGENCE IN TRANSCAUCASIA    149

ruffians we had seen in Lars had been there about a month, and had not only looted the entire village, but had hung the principal inhabitants on the trees in their own village street, after they had surrendered all the property they possessed. The speakers themselves had thus far escaped only by calling in all the armed tribesmen from the surrounding country and putting up a good fight in defence of the passage of the river, a form of reception these particular Russians had no use for.

Having assured them the matter should be reported in the proper quarter, and having also taken a photograph of these village heroes, and enjoyed some fresh milk and eggs with which they insisted upon supplying us, we started on our return journey as quickly as possible, realizing that it was then past midday, that it was a far cry to Tiflis, where we were due that night, and that the high pass had to be recrossed on the way.

Returning through Lars, we were prepared to meet any kind of trouble, and, seeing the road clear, drove fast, pistol in hand. The Russians, however, were possibly either drunk or frightened, or more probably both, as none of them showed themselves in the street. We therefore kept on at our best speed over the frontier and up the gorge over the pass. Night overtook us long before we were clear of the mountains, but we finally reached Tiflis safely shortly after midnight, both to our own great satisfaction and to that of our comrades who were anxiously awaiting us.

Next morning, the 20th, I received a cable from Commander-in-Chief at Constant, instructing me to proceed at once to Kars, on the Turco-Russian frontier, about 170 miles south-west of Tiflis, to examine and report by wire as to the situation there, as the Turks were thought to be about to give trouble; and although we had a battalion of the Rifle Brigade there already, more troops could be sent if really needed. We therefore set to work at once to prepare a train, and got a locomotive, a closed cattle-truck for the men, and what had been a private four-wheeled railway-carriage for myself, with a float, or open truck, for our cars. Having obtained an ample and very necessary stock of provisions, we left Tiflis on March 22nd, on what was my first independent railway trip in those parts in my own train.

My party on this occasion consisted of two cars and drivers, two machine-gunners, one interpreter, one batman (soldier servant), one N.C.O. (corporal), and myself—eight in all—with our arms, my two machine-guns, and a good supply of ammunition, the whole covered by our British flag, which flew proudly on my little railway-carriage.

We got through the pass, on the line which goes from Tiflis to Tabriz (in Persia), during the night, and reached Alexandropol (known to the Turks as Gumri) about 9 A. M. on the 23rd. Here is the junction of the line passing through Erivan to Persia, with the military strategical line which goes through Kars to Sarikamish, the old Russian military camp on the Turco-Russian frontier.

The Russian town of Alexandropol lies in a loop of the river, forming the boundary between Georgia and the province of Kars. The river winds round three sides of the town and is from 3 to 4 miles distant from it. The town itself is unpretentious but is of considerable extent, having had a pre-war population of about 40,000, more than half of whom were Armenians, the balance being made up of Russians and Tartars. Between the town and river lies a flat plain where at this time were encamped many thousands of destitute Armenian refugees who had fled from their villages in the surrounding country to seek the aid given by the liberality of the great American public and which was so effectively carried out by their most efficient and self-sacrificing representatives on the spot.

Just beyond Alexandropol we crossed the river which divides the old Russian provinces of Erivan (Armenia) and Kars, and in order that the events which followed may be understood, it will be necessary here to give a short account both of the general geographical features of the country and of the political situation existing there at that time.

One hundred miles south of Alexandropol is Mount Ararat, the culminating-point of the vast system of high mountains which form the boundaries of Persia, Turkey, and Russia, the frontiers of which three countries actually meet on the summit of the great mountain. Immediately north of Mount Ararat lies the old Russian province of Erivan, at that time known as the New Armenian Republic, which is bounded on the south by Persia, and on the east, north, and west, by Azerbaijan, Georgia, and Kars, all three old Russian provinces, of which the two first

# THE GEORGIAN ROAD
The only pass for wheeled vehicles over the main Caucasus Mountains.

The entrance to a snow-tunnel

The Northern "Gate" of the Pass

# THE GEORGIAN ROAD (continued)

The Dariel Gorge

The headmen of the Ingoush tribe

declared themselves to be independent republics after the Bolshevik revolution in Russia.

The province of Kars, which had during the war been occupied by the Turks, and was evacuated by them in accordance with the Armistice terms, contained a considerable proportion of Armenians, although the majority of its population has always consisted of Tartars, of the same Mohammedan sect as the Turks and Azerbaijanis. Much political unrest had been fostered and encouraged there by the Turks on their retirement, with the object of bringing about the declaration, by the Tartar inhabitants, of Kars as an independent Moslem republic, as the province would then become Turkish rather than Russian in its future political tendencies.

Things being in this condition, our rulers at home, in their wisdom, advocated, at the Supreme Council in Europe, that Kars Province should be handed over to the New Armenian Christian Republic, and certain British troops were sent there to see to the carrying out of this operation. This was the first of the many errors of policy committed by that same Supreme Council, whose decisions with regard to these countries were such as could only have been carried into effect by the permanent occupation of the districts dealt with by considerable forces of European troops; and although at the moment such troops were within reach, yet it had even then been decided that they should be entirely withdrawn in the near future.

In Kars Province itself the immediate result of the announcement of its proposed "Armenian" future was the organization of all the Tartar population throughout the district into more or less military bands, supported and armed by the Turks, now officially considered to have retired behind their pre-war Russian frontier. In every Tartar village throughout Kars Province, at this time, drill and machine-gun practice were daily carried out under the general supervision of both Turkish and German officers, whilst at the same time no Armenian's life was safe out of reach of the protection of the British troops. The Tartar population also proposed to set up a local Parliament, or "Shura," entirely Moslem in its constitution, in Kars City, to control the country, under President Wilson's brilliant idea of "self-determination."

It is, I think, impossible not to understand and even to sympathize with the attitude of these Moslems in the face of the decision to give their country to the Armenian Christians, whom they cordially despise and who are physically incapable of ever dominating or controlling the Turk and Tartar Moslem element under any circumstances, without the support of European troops. However, orders are orders, and such was the policy which had to be carried out, so that it will be readily understood that the position in Kars at this time had become somewhat difficult.

On leaving Alexandropol and crossing the Kars frontier, we therefore expected to meet with every kind of trouble and difficulty, and in fact did meet them at once, though not at all in the shape we were expecting. During the very first morning the snow got deeper and deeper, till we finally stuck fast in a great snow-drift about 30 miles beyond Alexandropol and 25 miles short of Kars, with 15 miles more of it in front of us and the snow over the roofs of our poor little train.

We were very lucky in that, where we struck the beginning of this great drift, we were within a quarter of a mile of a dump of ammunition and stores which the Turks had been obliged to leave behind in their retreat, and which was now guarded by a party of Our Rifle Brigade, with two officers, who occupied a small hut with snow nearly up to the roof. The officers came to see me in my snow-bound train, and we did a "swap" of twenty-five Egyptian cigarettes, of which they had just received a supply from home, for some revolver cartridges, of which I had plenty and they hadn't, and I afterwards shared their tea and bacon in the "ice-house" which formed their quarters.

At Alexandropol we had been fortunate enough to pick up a railway officer and twenty men, who now were worth their weight in gold, and got to work in proper fashion in clearing the snow, and at the same time in "gingering up" an old Russian snow-plough, so that as we had two locomotives and a plentiful supply of crude oil ("mazoot" they call it) as fuel, we had every hope of getting through eventually. There was a stove in my carriage and plenty of wood and rations, and so we knew we should be all right for a time; but it was very cold, and if our fuel ran out before we could clear the line we knew we should have to go back, as it was impossible to go on on foot

## INTELLIGENCE IN TRANSCAUCASIA   153

over the new-fallen snow until it became frozen hard enough to bear our weight, and it was quite likely we should ourselves freeze first.

We heard here that General Thompson, whom I had met in Persia after the evacuation of Baku, and who was now in military command in these parts, was coming up twenty-four hours behind us, also hoping to get to Kars, and I wired at once to him from the military post to stop him, if possible at Alexandropol. However, just at nightfall on our second night in the drift we could see his train coming over the snow behind us, and he joined us with his men in the cutting we were doing our best to clear. He had fifty Gurkhas with him, whom our party was right glad to see, and whom we knew the small party which was in a tight place ahead of us in Kars would heartily welcome, as they also would the two trucks of provisions we had on our train, as both were very badly needed at that moment by the troops ahead. Both train-parties therefore turned to and worked with a will both day and night, and progress was good, but we did not get clear of the drift till the 26th, our fifth day after leaving Tiflis.

After the General's arrival I spent part of my time in his car, which had an arrangement of pipes so that it was water-heated, and I had dinner with him one night, but mostly I stopped in my own carriage after dark, as the cold was terrible outside and it was a very difficult matter to get from one train to the other. The dump produced some excellent sheepskins, which served to stop up the windows of my carriage and to cover the floor, in both of which were many gaping holes which let the arctic air in, so that I lived in my great fur coat under a pile of sheepskins; these, however, though certainly *warm*, had many drawbacks easily to be imagined.

On reaching Kars on the 26th, we found things in a very queer state, and the General, having taken stock of the position, left the next day, as he was due to meet the Commander-in-Chief at Batoum on April 1st.

The situation of Armenian refugees at Alexandropol was reproduced at Kars and, though their number was not so great as at Alexandropol, their misery and destitution was even greater. Here again we found the American Near East relief organization saving countless lives and administering the funds provided by the liberality of their countrymen with a practical common sense and a competent management which were beyond all praise.

I remained at Kars, gathering every kind of information, and sent off a long cipher cable on the 28th to catch the Commander-in-Chief at Batoum, with details as to what was going on, and saying that I proposed to go on another 70 miles to the Turkish frontier beyond Sarikamish, where I thought I could learn still more.

About midday on the 30th, when I was just starting to go on to the frontier, I acquired documentary evidence of great importance as to the Turkish military support of the Tartars at Kars; and whilst considering these, I also observed certain facts myself which caused me (instead of going forward as the railway people expected) to go over to the "points" when our train was coming off the siding where it had been standing, and, having then run the train right across on to the main line, to get off back the way we had come, as hard as we could go, to try and catch the Commander-in-Chief at Batoum before he left on the 2nd. For this I had very good reasons, and luckily acted instantly, without giving any sign of my intentions.

The first indication I got of trouble was that I saw through the window of my carriage some very Turkish-looking Tartars take a locomotive off a siding and run it down to the "points" where a short branch ran to the boiler-filling pump, the only place where "running," and therefore unfrozen, water could be obtained for the locomotives. These men looked to me so suspicious that I watched them carefully, and saw them, as soon as the front wheels of the locomotive had passed the "points," deliberately force the lever over, and by so doing derail the locomotive, blocking the access of all other locomotives to the water-supply. They then moved to another locomotive on another siding, with the obvious intention of carrying out a similar manœuvre at the main line points, and so blocking the main line to Alexandropol and Tiflis, which was, of course, a single track only, and formed our only means of communication with our base.

It was the merest chance that I happened to notice them at all, as the whole thing was done quite quietly, and, had I not been of a suspicious turn of mind, I should never have watched them nor immediately have grasped their intentions. However, by the time they reached the second locomotive our train was already on the move, and I was standing over the points, with my pistol drawn and very much in the mood to use it. They had evidently had their orders to let our train go on towards the Turkish frontier, which was known to be our intention, for they made no attempt to interfere with the train passing on to the main line; but as the engine passed the points, going backwards pushing the train, I leapt on to the footplate and kept the throttle open and the reversing-gear in action, so that we did *not* stop and reverse, as they expected, to go on to the frontier, but continued to go backwards all the way to Alexandropol. Here the engine-driver disappeared and was seen no more, having suffered a severe nervous shock from the contemplation of my automatic pistol all through the journey. I should imagine the Turks' disgust at the failure of their scheme must have been great, but it was nothing at all in comparison with my satisfaction at defeating their plans, for I had no doubt, under the circumstances, that my cable had no chance of getting through, and that the only chance of communicating with the Commander-in-Chief was to go myself, and go quickly, before it became too late.

Every sign on our return journey through Kars Province confirmed my convictions, as bodies of Tartars were everywhere on the march towards the Armenian frontier outside Alexandropol, where the many thousands of Christian Armenian refugees were collected in a loop of the frontier river outside the city for the purpose of taking advantage of the life-saving ministrations of the American Near East Relief Organization. Here they were already, as we passed, being "sniped" at by the Moslems rapidly mustering on the high ground on the western bank, who were obviously bent on their annihilation.

We made a stop of half an hour only at Alexandropol, where we were lucky to obtain an engine-driver, in the person of an Armenian, any of whom could be trusted to make their way as rapidly as possible out of the neighbourhood. We then carried on successfully to Tiflis, where we arrived about 1 P. M. on April 1st, it being necessary at every halt on the road to guard our train by force from the thousands of refugees who struggled to board it. A few hours at Tiflis, to report to Advanced Headquarters, and having left my men and train there, I went on by myself and reached Batoum at 1 P. M. on the 2nd, arriving only just in time to catch the Commander-in-Chief, to make a personal report and to show him the documents in my possession, before he sailed at 3 P. M. that day.

Having taken much responsibility in leaving my post, the kindness of his reception was the greatest possible relief to me. But it was a far greater satisfaction to see the grasp of the entire situation which he already had, and the instant action which he unhesitatingly took. General Thompson, who left Kars three days before I did, had already placed him in possession of the apparent state of affairs existing in the Kars Province, of which my news and documents I brought provided both amplification and verification. Within ten minutes of my reporting to him telegraphic orders were on their way to Tiflis for the immediate dispatch to Kars of the reinforcements necessary to control the situation and for the action which should be taken to that end, which precautions proved immediately effective.

After a roughish three weeks it was a pleasure indeed to lunch with the Chief on his ship and to hear all the news, and before he left, at 3 P. M., for Constant, I received his orders to go back and pick up my party at Tiflis, and then, if possible, to reach the frontier through some *other* line of country this time, but in any case to meet him at Kars on April 27th (only three weeks later), by which time the situation could not fail to have developed further throughout all the Turkish frontier country.

## CHAPTER III

### EASTERN ANATOLIA—TREBIZOND AND ERZEROUM

Orders—Appointment with Commander-in-Chief at Kars—Leave Tiflis—The Advent of "George"—The Rion Valley—Batoum again—Landing at Trebizond—The Zigana Pass—The Kharshut Valley—The Vavok Pass—Baiburt—The Khop Pass—Bivouac in snow—The Upper Euphrates—Erzeroum—The Kars Road—The Russo-Turkish frontier—The Saganli Mountains—Kars again—Return to Erzeroum—The fortress town—Kiazim Karabekir—Difficulties—"George" and the camel—Reinforcement reaches Trebizond.

Immediately on the Commander-in-Chief's departure from Batoum I returned direct to Tiflis, to rejoin my party and to take orders from Advanced Headquarters as to the best method of carrying out the Chief's general instructions.

It was decided that I should take my party to Batoum, and, having embarked them there, land at Trebizond, about 100 miles farther west on the Pontine (Black Sea) coast of Asiatic Turkey. From Trebizond I was to make my way, if possible, inland 200 miles to the Headquarters of the Turkish IXth Army at Erzeroum, and, having presented my credentials to the army commander and taken stock of the situation there, then get on as best I could another 200 miles east over the old Turco-Russian frontier to report to the Commander-in-Chief at Kars on his arrival there from Tiflis on April 27th. As it was April 3rd when I received these orders, and we had 200 miles to go to the coast, and then obtain a ship and travel another hundred by sea to Trebizond before starting to tackle a further 500 miles of country of which our only information was that "it was ex-extremely difficult, with many high passes all under deep snow," no one will be surprised to learn that I much doubted our competence to cover these 800 miles in time to keep my appointment with the Commander-in-Chief at Kars on April 27th, in three weeks' time.

The decision was taken at 3 P.M. and without wasting one moment I got my men together and we steamed out of Tiflis in our own little train before dark that same evening. Our progress was very slow, for our locomotive was an indifferent one and we were sadly short of fuel, and it was late the next afternoon before we reached the mouth of the Suram Tunnel, about 100 miles west of Tiflis, where we were for the third or fourth time obliged to stop to obtain fuel.

This tunnel is near the head of the Borzom Defile, through which runs the Koura River, and in these parts the Russian Grand Dukes, Viceroys of the Caucasian provinces of Imperial Russia in the days before the Bolshevik revolution, had for many years occupied a magnificent summer palace. This palace had now long lain in ruins, as had also the village surrounding it. During our halt there I observed with much interest a great black shape wandering amongst the ruins, which, though a skeleton only and in the last extremities of starvation, I could see at a glance was in reality a magnificent hound, evidently one of the Imperial breed of bear-hounds, which have for generations been exclusively bred for the Imperial family in the Caucasus.

This magnificent animal, more resembling a Great Dane than anything else, but showing more quality than the finest of that breed, was very shy indeed, and it took a good half-hour, after we had obtained our fuel, to entice him on to the observation platform of my carriage, with the assistance of my one and only sirloin of beef. Even then we were unable to induce him to enter the carriage, until I went there, leaving the meat on the floor, and went out again by the farther door; when, after a while, he entered, and having in the meanwhile gone round outside the train myself, the door was quickly closed and the train started, not stopping again except for fuel till we reached Batoum about midday next day, April 5th. By this time the splendid though starving animal had become completely at home, having consumed the greater part of my small stock of provisions. From that time, with the exception of my short visit to London in August of that year and the six months which he spent in quarantine in 1922, he has never left me, and lies beside me whilst I write here, at home in England, to-day.

We called him "George," as he is a Georgian born and bred, and he has since then become well known to the Army of the Black Sea, the Turkish XVth Corps, the greater part of the Mediterranean Fleet, and even to the British public, his portrait having appeared in the *Daily Mail* and many other papers.

## INTELLIGENCE IN TRANSCAUCASIA 159

A more faithful and intelligent friend and companion no one can ever hope to find. He has only this one shortcoming, that, being "only a dog," he cannot speak, though he comes terribly near doing so at times, and it is never the least difficult to understand anything he desires to convey. It is, in fact, on record that on one occasion he actually *did* make a remark, so excessively *à propos* at the time that even the Turkish guards who also heard him were duly impressed. That incident can, however, be better described when we come to its occurrence during our captivity.

The last of our journey through the Province of Kutais, by the valley of the Upper Rion River, before reaching Batoum Province, was beautiful. I had never seen that bit of country before, having always passed there during the night; but this time we were fortunate, not only in passing it by daylight, but also during the spring-time, when, of course, the valley is seen at its best.

The river, then a rushing torrent from the snows melting above, ran here through rich pasture-land, with the trees all freshly green in spring, and apple-blossom was everywhere. Lovely little wooden cottages, covered with flowering creepers, each with its little paddock and orchard in full bloom, crowned the high, steep banks of the river, and behind them rolling slopes of green reached upwards to the magnificent beech forests which clothe the lower slopes. Above these, again, were belts of fir-woods thinning gradually out into the snow-fields above, range after range of which framed the picture on either side as far as the eye could reach.

This valley was certainly a dream of beauty and peace, nice and warm without being hot, with a bright sun lighting up the whole scene, which included everything that Nature can produce that is lovely, all at their best and all in sight at the same time. Even my British soldiers were impressed, and were hanging out of their carriage, passing remarks on the scenery—about the very last thing I was expecting them to do.

Reaching Batoum on the 5th, there was much to be done, in drawing all our stores and cars, as we found it would be necessary to take six Ford vans, our party now consisting of sixteen in all, and it being necessary to take everything with us which we might require, including spares for the cars and tents for ourselves. Also, it was necessary to modify the Ford vans to enable us to sleep in them, which it would certainly in the future be frequently necessary to do.

This work and the preparation of the necessary "authorities," including a "Firman," or official authority signed and sealed by the Sultan, took nearly a week, and it was not till the 11th that we were able to embark all our gear on board the small "drifter" which had been placed at our disposal and to start on our sea-passage to Trebizond.

Our "drifter" was of the very smallest size, certainly less than 100 tons, so it may be imagined it was a work of art to stow six cars on board. This, however, was done by the help of the steam crane; the tops of the cars being taken off, and three having been found room for, the others were then lowered on the top of them, and, thanks to a calm sea, arrived safely. The puzzle that presented itself for a solution on our arrival at Trebizond was how to get the cars ashore, there being no harbour where one could bring the ship alongside a pier, and the drifter having no crane or derrick by which they could be lifted. After an examination of the material available, the solution was eventually achieved in the following manner:

There was drawn up on the beach an old derelict iron barge, originally used to pump oil into from Batoum steamers, and this, though far from water-tight, was calculated to float for an uncertain space of time, which we hoped might prove to be sufficient for our purpose. At anchor in the roadstead was a small Turkish steamer which had a diminutive hand-crane; so, having launched the barge, we took it in tow astern of our drifter and proceeded alongside the steamer, where we unfolded our plan to the Turkish captain, which, having been agreed to, we then proceeded to lift one car from the deck of the drifter by means of the hand-crane, and then, leaving it hanging in mid-air, we moved the drifter ahead, bringing the barge under the crane in its place; on to this we then lowered the car, repeating the process until the whole six cars were artistically balanced on this very insecure support.

By that time the barge was on the point of sinking, and barely remained afloat long enough to allow us to "beach" it near a pile of Decauville railway rails, which happened to have been left on the beach, and with which we easily built a

## THE ZIGANA PASS
Over the coast range of Eastern Anatolia on the southern shore of the Black Sea

Camp at Khamsi Keui, north side (3,600 feet)

Looking south into the interior from the summit (6,600 feet)

temporary gangway, and so ran the cars ashore on the beach. This proceeding was watched by the greater part of the population of Trebizond with the greatest interest and astonishment, and is a good instance of what may be done if only people will *try,* for on our arrival the landing of the vehicles from our drifter without a crane or pier was on all sides considered an impossibility.

In order that the objects of my mission can be properly understood, it will be necessary here again to give an idea of the political situation at this time in the eastern Turkish provinces for which I was now bound.

By the terms of the Armistice granted by the Allies to the Turks, the latter agreed to demobilize their armies and to surrender their armaments, until both were within certain maximum limits laid down by the Armistice conditions. In order, however, to insure these conditions being carried out, it was, of course, necessary to inspect and, in fact, to supervise the measures taken by the Turks for the purpose, and this was the duty now officially allotted to me.

I carried as my credentials the "Firman" from the Sultan in Constantinople, authorizing me to visit the Headquarters of his armies in the eastern provinces, at the same time instructing the Army Commanders to furnish me with full information and to afford me every facility in carrying out my inspection. I also was provided with an official military communication from the Turkish War Office at Constantinople to the Army Commanders, notifying them of my duties. On arrival, therefore, at Trebizond I immediately announced the official purpose of my visit to the officer commanding the garrison there, asking him to communicate with his Army Commander at Erzeroum, and to notify him of my intention of proceeding into the interior forthwith, at the same time requesting that the Turkish military posts along the road should be at once instructed to afford me every assistance.

Pending the arrival of an authorization to proceed, I commenced the official enumeration of the armaments in the Trebizond District, an inspection of all demobilization orders which had been issued, and the progress which had been made in their execution. This work took me to all parts of the town and the surrounding districts, and I was thus once more able to judge of the good work being done by the American Near East Relief Organization whose headquarters for this part of Anatolia were established at Trebizond. The relief staff at this time at Trebizond consisted, I believe, of six persons including several ladies—who had come all the way from the United States to devote their energies to the relief of suffering, and who were working under the experienced direction of Mr. Albert L. Christiansen. The Armenian element in the Trebizond was less numerous than it had been in the Alexandropol and Kars districts, but it was nevertheless considerable, and in addition there was much destitution amongst the Christian Greek population who have inhabited and cultivated the difficult valleys of this (Pontine) coast of the Black Sea for over 2,000 years. Ample opportunity was therefore afforded for the exercise of that careful relief of suffering and misery for which that great American organization has now become so justly renowned throughout the civilized world.

From the first it was evident that, although we had been received with great civility, it would be a difficult matter to ascertain exactly what was going on. Under these circumstances I gave explicit instructions to the excellent British Intelligence Officer, Captain Crawford, who was permanently quartered at Trebizond, and who had been placed under my orders, as to the course he was to pursue in my absence; and as soon as I received authorization from the Army Commander at Erzeroum to proceed, we started on the 200 miles of arduous travelling which lay between Trebizond and the Army Headquarters at Erzeroum, leaving the coast in the early morning of April 18th. During our stay at Trebizond I had been daily exercising my party in the duties which they would be called upon to perform on the march, until I had every reason to be satisfied that they would be equal to the particularly rough time which I anticipated lay before us.

The steep and rugged southern coast of the Black Sea contains no harbour at all in the 700 or more miles which lie between the entrance to the Bosphorus and the port of Batoum, and during the last 300 miles of this distance the coast range becomes higher and higher, until in the neighbourhood of Trebizond the mountains rise abruptly from the sea and culminate in a continuous line of snow-covered peaks, which attain an

# INTELLIGENCE IN TRANSCAUCASIA 163

altitude of from 10,000 to 11,000 feet within 50 miles of the coast.

The only road passable for vehicles, which crosses this range for at least 200 miles, is one that rises from Trebizond and crosses the Zigana Pass, at 6,500 feet above the sea about 50 miles inland. In our innocence we supposed that we should easily cross this pass the first day, as much of the snow had melted, and, our cars being in good condition, we anticipated no difficulty. Night was, however, coming on when we arrived at a Greek village, Hamsikeui by name, still 2,500 feet below, and 15 miles distant from, the summit.

As we were just on the edge of the snow, we there pitched the first of the many mountain camps and bivouacs we were destined to occupy in this wild mountain country. Our delay on this occasion proceeded from no defects on the part of our cars, but from the fact that the gradients were stiff and our loads heavy. However, the men were all well trained and full of "go," and we had the tent pitched and our meal prepared in less than half an hour, and after a very comfortable if somewhat cold night, were away again half an hour after daylight next day, to enter the forest belt which lies just below the snow, and after three hours' hard climb we reached the summit before ten o'clock.

Here, on the summit of the Zigana, looking south, we had our first view of the interior of Anatolia, and a very marvellous and beautiful one it was. In the bright morning sun, range after range of snow-capped mountains appeared on every side, except on the north, in which direction the great mountains on either side of the narrow valley we had been following obstructed our view. The impression produced by this remarkable scene was of an incredibly rocky and rugged country, of precipices and narrow, deep valleys, with absolutely no flat country in any direction, and the clearness of the atmosphere was also so deceptive that distances were impossible to estimate.

On many occasions since that first morning I have studied that view at my leisure, when, having become thoroughly familiar with the country for many miles, I have been able to pick out and identify prominent peaks of 11,000 feet and upwards, which I knew then to be over 100 miles away, but which on this first occasion, in our ignorance, we took to be not more than 30 or 40 miles distant.

The descent was steep at first, but after about 5 miles the road rose again, being there cut out of a sheer rocky cliff with a mountain of 11,000 feet rising perpendicularly on the left, and a deep, narrow valley on the right, at the bottom of which ran a roaring torrent at least 2,000 feet below the road. The rise continued for a mile or more, till a steep zigzag descent commenced which continued to the Kharshut River, 15 miles from the summit of the pass and 3,000 feet below it. Here we halted, took our midday meal, and, having closed up the column, continued on our way, ascending the narrow valley of the river to the eastwards.

This river, which is considerably the largest stream rnnning into the Black Sea in the 300 miles which lie between the mouth of the Chorokh River, near Batoum, and that of the Kelkid Irmak (the Halys of ancient history), near Samsun, was at this time in full flood from the melting of the snows. During the last 30 miles of its course, below the point where the road enters the valley, the Kharshut runs through narrow gorges between perpendicular cliffs, where not even a mule-track is able to follow its course, though there would be no insuperable difficulty in constructing a railway from this point to its mouth at Tireboli. Above its junction with the road the valley becomes wider and receives three large tributaries in the next 20 miles.

Here, before entering the town of Gumush Khaneh (the Silver House), we halted and closed up our column again, as we heard the late Army Commander from Erzeroum was in the town, on his way to Constantinople, whither he had been called by order of the Sultan. We passed him in the main street with a polite salute, about five P. M., and made the best of our way up the valley beyond, without making any halt at all in the town.

The Kharshut Valley round Gumush Khaneh is far from spacious, being not more than a mile across at the widest point, with steep mountains everywhere rising to the snow on either side. The valley itself, however, is here well cultivated and the land rich and sheltered, there being many

## INTELLIGENCE IN TRANSCAUCASIA 165

orchards which produce apples and cherries famous throughout all the upland country—a beautiful sight at this time in April, when the whole valley was a mass of apple-blossom. We kept on till dark, rising all the time, and were finally forced to bivouac at the roadside in the darkness, just under 100 miles from Trebizond, with the defile leading to the Vavok Pass just before us. Our bivouac was only 500 feet higher than our camp of the previous night, but was infinitely warmer, as, although the snow was all round us, yet the roadside where we had halted was well sheltered by the steep sides of the gorge.

Next morning at daylight we were quickly on the move, as we hoped we might be able to cross *two* passes during the day. Immediately on leaving, the gorge became so narrow as to barely leave room for a car beside the roaring torrent, but after not more than a quarter of a mile we came suddenly out on to the snow-field, with the ridge of the Vavok Pass (6,500 feet) 2 miles in front of us. Once over the ridge, on the southern slope the snow was less and the gradient favourable, and so we made good progress, passing through the outskirts of the town of Baiburt at 5,300 feet, 125 miles from Trebizond, before midday.

Baiburt, an ancient city, stands on the edge of an extensive and once well-cultivated plain on the banks of the Chorokh River. It was at this time the headquarters of a Turkish brigade of regular troops, and I instructed the Turkish Transport officer, who had been detailed at Trebizond to accompany us, to inquire at the military post outside the town what arrangements had been made by the Brigade Headquarters to help us over the dreaded Khop Pass, which lay some 25 miles ahead of us, and which we knew to be deeply covered with snow. The reply was "that a company of infantry had been sent out some days previously to endeavour to clear a passage for us, but no news of their success had yet come in." We therefore carried on in the hope that we might find the pass open.

Amongst the many difficult passes of Eastern Anatolia, very few can be passed by wheeled vehicles. The Khop is certainly the most difficult of these, as, although the road is well traced and constructed, not only is the actual upper pass unusually long (about 15 miles), but half of it is at over 8,000 feet, the road there is also much exposed, the wind being frequently very high and so cold as to have an absolutely paralysing effect on any one exposed to its full force.

The summit rises to 8,250 feet, and forms the actual watershed between the Black Sea and the Persian Gulf, the nearest point of which is 1,000 miles distant as the crow flies. No winter season ever passes without many lives being lost on this pass from exposure, as travellers who are caught on the upper pass in the dreaded *tépis,* or storms of snow and wind, which are frequent there, have very little chance in the deep drifts which rapidly form in the freshly fallen snow, and it is little wonder that the summit is often impassable for months on end. On this occasion fresh snow had fallen within the previous two days, and the troops who should have had a post at the commencement of the upper pass were, on our arrival there, nowhere to be seen, so that, in view of my appointment at Kars, still over 300 miles distant, it was hard to know what course to pursue, for more snow might fall at any moment and block the pass hopelessly for weeks. In the end, however, we decided to go on as far as we could before dark, and succeeded in getting more than 1,500 feet up the zigzag as night was coming on, before we reached fresh snow, where no sign of any road at all could be seen, and there we halted for the night.

Two tents were pitched in the snow, one for myself with two men and our machine-guns, and the other for the Turkish Transport officer and any men who might wish to join him there. The majority of the men, however, preferred to remain in the cars, which were fairly sheltered by the deep snow. I took the greatest care in pitching my own tent, as I was very doubtful of its ability to resist the icy gusts which were then increasing both in frequency and severity, and I went round every tent-peg myself before finally lying down, with my snow-boots and all my furs on, in the snow. It was indeed well that I did so, as during a more heavy squall than usual, about 2 A. M., we heard an outburst of yells which told us the other tent had "gone." It was impossible to give any assistance, as the men and myself had all our work cut out to save our own tent, and we could hear that the occupants of the

## INTELLIGENCE IN TRANSCAUCASIA 167

other tent eventually reached the cars, where they got some kind of shelter till daylight.

Soon after daybreak some Turkish troops came into sight, coming in single file through the fresh-fallen snow. It appeared that they had sheltered the night before in a stone *khan*, or hovel, 3 or 4 miles farther on. They gave us a poor account of the state of the pass, as it appeared that the road on the slopes immediately above us had been entirely carried away by an avalanche within the last few days, and that higher up fresh snow lay deep, so that they had had oxen brought up from the other side of the pass to endeavour to get our cars over the summit if we could reach the place where the road still existed.

We therefore at once proceeded to carry out a survey of the ground immediately above us, and found that by keeping on up the extreme point of the spur on which we had halted we could get "up" on solid ground, from which the force of the wind had largely cleared the snow during the night. The slope, however, proved terribly steep, and it was necessary to unload the cars entirely, and then, having attached long ropes with cross-poles at intervals, we manned them with as many Turkish soldiers as possible, and with the greatest difficulty hauled the empty cars up, one by one, by main force. On reaching the road again, we found the Turks had collected about forty oxen, with their yokes and ropes, ready to tow the cars, and a start was promptly made with three pairs of oxen to each car. At frequent intervals it was necessary to double the oxen, putting twelve or more to one car, to get through some exceptional morass, and going back afterwards to bring on the others by the same means.

Some of these roads during the melting of the snows appear absolutely impassable, and it is only by the use of a long line of oxen that a passage can be effected. In places the mud and slush appear to be unfathomable, and two or even three yoke of oxen will at times absolutely disappear in the half-frozen mud. If, however, a start is made in the early morning, on the thin coating of ice which has formed during the night, the leading yokes who pass safely over may then succeed in dragging the following pairs, who break through the ice, safely across the morass, and last of all the cars may be made to slide over, with their floor-boards forming sleighs on the surface of the frozen slush and mud, into which, however, they must on no account be allowed time to sink.

It may be imagined that the rate of progress under these circumstances is not great. However, on this occasion, starting at daylight, we were able to cross the summit, about $3\frac{1}{2}$ miles distant from our camp, by midday, and here enjoyed a view which is unsurpassable in any country. From the summit of the Khop, at 8,250 feet, the ground falls away steeply to the south and the main Euphrates Valley lies spread out far below, the foot-hills on either side of the river being about 25 miles apart, the crests of the main ranges beyond being from 30 to 35 miles distant. In every direction the scene is bounded by snow, with countless volcanic peaks and precipitous ridges rising everywhere to 12,000 feet or more.

In spite of the wild grandeur of this prospect, it is not advisable to waste any time in admiring it, for in winter the force of the wind on this exposed watershed is so great as to be dangerous, and the temperature falls so low that on several occasions the whole of my party have lost the skin off their faces from exposure to this truly "icy blast," not to mention other even more distressing effects resulting from the glare of sun on the snow which we have also experienced there.

On this occasion we were able to slide down off the main ridge without delay, as the force of the wind had done much to clear it of fresh snow. It was, however, long past nightfall ere we reached the last zigzags of the main pass, which we were able to descend in comparative shelter, and finally camped at 11 P. M., amongst deserted ruins, in a small village named Pirnikapan, which lies only 1,000 feet above the level of the great Euphrates River, 45 miles west of Erzeroum.

The sight afforded by our party of six cars descending the endless zigzags on the face of the perpendicular cliffs in the dark was truly remarkable, for looking back up the almost precipitous mountain the effect of the brilliant headlights of the cars on the rocks in all directions, as they followed each other, about 100 yards apart, down all the twists and turns on the face of the cliff was most effective, and was, in fact, the most striking incident of an eventful day.

## INTELLIGENCE IN TRANSCAUCASIA 169

Next morning all the party were suffering pretty severely from their exposure on the pass, and camp was not struck till 12 noon, when we started up the plain for Erzeroum. The road being good and fairly clear of snow, we reached the ramparts of the great Turkish fortress before 5 P. M., and were met at the carefully guarded gate by an officer sent by the military Headquarters to conduct us to the house placed at our disposal by the authorities. This proved to be a spacious mansion, originally an American school, and an officer and guard of twenty-five Turkish soldiers were quartered there, to assist us generally, or rather, as we well understood, to keep in touch with our operations. We reached Erzeroum on the 22nd, having taken five days to cover the 200 miles from Trebizond—not at all bad travelling, over that now familiar road, at that time of year, particularly as its peculiar difficulties were then all unknown to us.

Next day I called upon the Turkish civil Governor and on the temporary Commander of the Army Headquarters, as the late Army Commander (whom I had passed at Gumush Khaneh) had not yet been replaced. Presenting my credentials and the Sultan's "Firman," I was duly authorized to inspect all armament and military stores, as well as to examine the army muster-rolls and pay-sheets. The next two days were spent in a rapid survey of the arsenals and fortifications and an inspection of the army books, in order to obtain a rough idea of the progress of demobilization, and on the 26th, at daylight, I was able to start again, this time with only two lightly loaded cars, to cross still two more high ranges of snow-mountains and the old Russo-Turkish frontier, to report to the Commander-in-Chief at Kars, 130 miles away, on the 27th, as ordered.

Immediately on leaving Erzeroum the main road to the east crosses at over 7,000 feet the high Deveboyun Ridge, which here divides the valley of the Euphrates from that of the Aras, and so forms the main watershed between the Persian Gulf and the Caspian Sea. However, as the road was good and the snow hard in the early morning, we were soon over this comparatively easy pass, and descended into the wide valley of the Upper Aras River, known here as the Passim Plain. After travelling 25 miles across this plain, we reached Hassan Kalé, an old fortress now in ruins, but the site of many important battles dating back to the earliest times of which any historical records exist. The permanent Turkish barracks which stood here before the Great War were destroyed by the Russians under the Grand Duke Nicholas in their victorious advance on Erzeroum. Their ruins, however, still remain, and other signs are not wanting of the Russian occupation, especially the road over which we now travelled and the small Decauville Railway, extending to the frontier, which follows the same route and was constructed in six months, during the Russian advance to Erzeroum in 1916-17.

Beyond Hassan Kalé the great plain contained nothing of interest except its state of desolation, which, in view of its great natural fertility, was most remarkable. About 40 miles east of Erzeroum our road turned a little to the north and commenced to climb the foot-hills of the great Saganli Mountains, till 20 miles farther on we reached the Turkish military frontier position at Zivin, at the foot of the upper frontier pass. The latter part of the road was bad, as all roads become, in these parts of the country, when the snow first begins to melt, and we were bogged several times; so that night was coming on as we reached Zivin and bivouacked at the roadside for the night. The Turkish frontier post had been warned of our coming and were very friendly. We were able, therefore, to pass a good night, and early next morning we reached the actual frontier, and crossed the "No Man's Land" then existing between the last Turkish post and the first post of the new Armenian Republic, which the Allies were supporting in their occupation of Kars Province.

The road through the upper pass was good, but the pass itself was both long and difficult, as it extended for 30 miles with much deep snow, the summit being at an altitude of 7,500 feet. At Sarikamish, the old Russian miltiary camp beyond the pass, 33 miles from Zivin, the snow had nearly gone; we were therefore able to average a good rate of speed across the plain, and to reach the fortress of Kars, 130 miles from Erzeroum, before 4 P. M. The Commander-in-Chief's train was in the siding there, where my own had been on the occasion of my previous visit, and though he himself had not yet returned from inspecting the Kars defences, we learned that he was not due to start back till late that night; there would therefore be all the time necessary to make my report. So we went

# THE KHOP PASS

Camp in the snow; the road has been swept away

Up a wind-swept spur by man-power

## THE KHOP PASS (*continued*)

The road picked up again—ox-power

View from the summit, 8,300 feet, looking south over the
Upper Euphrates valley

## INTELLIGENCE IN TRANSCAUCASIA

straight on to the military Headquarters to arrange for a bed that night.

We received a very pleasant reception from the staff, and a good room with a fire and all the comforts of an English mess were duly appreciated; as also was an invitation to dine with the Chief on his train, which reached me whilst I was enjoying the unusual luxury of a good hot bath. The Chief was very kind at dinner, and I learned from him all the news, and in addition he gave me some invaluable English newspapers, to which I had long been a stranger.

My own orders were to return to Erzeroum to enumerate all the armaments in the hands of the Turkish IXth Army, and to take note of the measures being taken for demobilization, reporting the results of my inquiries to Constantinople by cable. I was told officers would be sent to assist me in the work, and was instructed to examine and report on any means which might be available for getting out of the country all armament in excess of the limited amount which was allowed by the Armistice conditions. Ever thoughtful for our welfare and comfort, I found the Chief had even given instructions for two bottles of whisky to be put in my car, from his small private store on the train; these, of course, would have been otherwise unobtainable and would be worth their weight in gold in our freezing mountain camps after long days in the snow; and I feel sure that no man's health has ever been drunk with more enthusiasm than was his by my men when I served out this most welcome present to them from "Uncle George," under which familiar designation our Commander was universally known and loved throughout his army.

The Chief left for Batoum that night, and I was indeed fortunate to have reached such good quarters and a British doctor, as next day I had a bad "go" of fever, which, though it was nothing at all where I then found myself, would have been a very different experience had it caught me in camp in the snow. After the luxury of a long day in a good bed, with a blazing fire and English newspapers to read, I was all right next morning, the 29th, and we got away early on our return journey to Erzeroum, camping again at Zivin that night, and reaching our quarters before dark on the 30th.

The snow was now getting less daily, but the roads got worse, as the country becomes sodden at this time of year, and mud, of the depth it is found in those mountains, is an even worse obstacle to travelling on wheels than snow is, however deep the latter may be. The month of May in Erzeroum is always the most unhealthy of the year, as in May and June the snows are melting and all the evil smells and germs, which the arctic winter has hidden under its blanket of snow, begin then to come to light, causing us all to suffer from both malaria and dysentery. Our house was the only one still standing in the Armenian quarter, having been American property and therefore left untouched when the Armenian houses were destroyed. The ruins all round it, however, were to the last degree insanitary, so that even without reference to the peculiarly poisonous and persistent form of malaria which distinguishes the great marsh of Erzeroum, we soon found ourselves sadly in need of the medical stores and advice which we had been told were to be sent us from Constant on the first opportunity.

At Erzeroum both the fortress and town are full of interest, even though the former is quite out of date and the latter largely in ruins. The actual permanent fortifications round the city are elaborately constructed, with bastions, ravelins, curtains, sally-ports, etc., according to the old French system, and all these are well made and in fair repair, though quite out of date. The town, however, now depends for its military value on the defensive system of works which have been of late years constructed on the hills covering the fortress. The whole position is designed to cover the main road from the east, and is very elaborate, extending to a distance of 50 miles from flank to flank; the lines would thus require a force of 50,000 men to adequately garrison them, which is a greater force than the Turks would probably ever be in a position to produce for this purpose to resist an advance from the east (the Russian frontier). The works also have now little real military value, as the whole position is capable of being turned and passed on either flank. The fortress itself has always been the great military centre of the Turkish power in Eastern Anatolia, and the taking stock of its ancient and very miscellaneous military contents was therefore a somewhat arduous undertaking.

The town contains several most interesting old buildings, now mosques, which, however, before the advent of the Turks, were

Christian churches, and previously were the seats of various much more ancient religions, some of them still bearing the device of the Sun-god fructifying the palm-tree, the sign of ancient Nineveh, which is easily decipherable on several of them to-day. The great plain of Erzeroum, which lies north of the city, is 25 miles broad at that spot, and is roughly 50 miles long, the greater portion of that large tract being occupied by the marsh which forms the true source of the great Euphrates River, although a mountain stream, one of several which feed the marsh from 50 miles or more beyond, is usually indicated as the parent stream. The town itself stands on the slope of the great Palenduken Mountains, at an altitude of just under 7,000 feet at its upper or southern ramparts, the hills immediately above the town reaching to 12,000 feet, and the marsh itself being 6,250 feet.

It is sufficient to remember that the great rivers of this part of Asia, which run to the Black Sea, the Persian Gulf, and the Caspian Sea, all rise within a few miles of this city, to realize at once that even in that bare and arctic country the city of Erzeroum, by reason of its great altitude and most exposed position, is a particularly uninviting spot, which no one who was familiar with that country would ever voluntarily select as his residence. The winds there blow with terrific force, and a piercing cold defies all furs, as it also does adequate description in conventional language. No tree or shrub of any sort can be found within over 50 miles, either to afford fuel when cut or shelter of any kind, and the words "dismal," "dreary," "desolate," and "damnable," suggest themselves irresistibly as a concise description of the whole locality. Our work in this delectable retreat was important, as on its result depended the estimate to be formed of the future intentions of the Turks. Though every facility was afforded to me in my inspections, I early understood and reported that no real progress towards disarmament was being made, or was, indeed, intended.

Shortly after our arrival the new Army Commander, Kiazim Karabekir Pasha, appeared on the scene, and as a formality to propitiate the Allies, the old IXth Army was reduced to the status of an Army Corps only, and numbered XV. Needless to remark, this made no practical difference at all to the military position. Kiazim Pasha, a native of Eastern Anatolia, is the most genuine example of a first-class Turkish officer that it has ever been my good fortune to meet. He has had much experience of war, and was Chief of the Staff to the German Marshal von der Goltz, who Commanded-in-Chief the Turkish armies which defended Bagdad against the British advance. Any army he has under his command may always be relied upon to be thoroughly well commanded. Not only has he the advantage of a naturally quick and bright intelligence, but he is master of every branch of his profession, and extremely conscientious in the exercise of his multifarious duties. I am anxious to add, first, that, having had much to do with him in many extremely delicate positions, I have always found him as straightforward as his orders would permit him to be; and, secondly, that although it was my fate to be his prisoner for a long time, and to suffer great hardships at the hands of some of his subordinates, yet he himself has never ceased to command my respect as an individual, and my appreciation as a thoroughly competent Commander.

For some time past he has commanded the Eastern front of the Nationalist armies, and much of their success in the west must be attributed to his enlightened handling of the complicated position in the east. It is easy, therefore, to realize how great must be his influence in the critical days which now lie before the new Empire of Nationalist Turkey, and particularly upon the future relations of his country with Soviet Russia, on which his well-proved loyalty and patriotism must continue to have the most important bearing.

During May the work of the enumeration of the armament of the Turkish Eastern armies proceeded apace, as far as the contents of the Erzeroum arsenals were concerned; but with regard to the divisions quartered on the Eastern frontier it was impossible to obtain reliable information, the passes being all blocked by snow. I was therefore obliged in respect of those divisions to report only the figures furnished me by the Turks themselves, with the explanation that until the passes should be clear of snow it would be impossible to verify those figures in the outlying districts.

However, in Erzeroum alone I found upwards of 500 guns, mostly of antiquated pattern, and over 200,000 rounds of gun ammunition. This was mostly useless, and in many cases in an

## INTELLIGENCE IN TRANSCAUCASIA

absolutely dangerous condition. My instructions were to render the guns unserviceable, with the exception of a very limited number, and to correspondingly reduce the ammunition and machine-guns; the small arms (rifles) were also to be reduced from a total of upwards of 100,000 to 3,300 per division, or about 15,000 in all. I was likewise instructed to devise and organize some practical method by which this very arbitrary proceeding could be successfully carried out.

It was evident that the utmost which could be hoped for was to obtain the breech-blocks of the guns and the breech-bolts of the rifles, above the Armistice minimum, and to then endeavour to get these vital parts out of the country. The only hope of effecting even this, lay in the efficient repairing of the small Decauville Railway which had been built by the Russians during the war, connecting Erzeroum with the Russian main line beyond the Eastern frontier at Sarikamish, for it would have taken years to remove the quantities with which we had to deal by means of any other transport which was then available. During the month of May I prepared, and reported by cable to Constant, a full statement of the position, making certain propositions and asking that, if my suggestions were approved, I should be sent an adequate staff to carry them out, and I was duly advised this would be done forthwith.

In the meanwhile my party was entirely cut off from our own bases except by telegraph, for after we had, by great good-fortune, succeeded in getting over the damaged road on the Khop Pass, no other wheeled vehicles had succeeded in passing it, much fresh snow having fallen there in May, and a still greater portion of the road, over which we had then passed with such difficulty, having been subsequently washed away. This meant that we suffered what, in our innocence and ignorance of Erzeroum and its possibilities, we then looked upon as considerable hardships, for we were without stores of any kind, or letters or news. Also, being obliged to subsist on eggs and black bread only, without any form of vegetables, we suffered from scurvy in addition to the particularly noxious form of fever and dysentery which is universal there in the spring, and has obtained for the fortress of Erzeroum its evil reputation even amongst the hardy natives of that most desolate district.

Our one joy was our dog—"George." The miserable skeleton whom we had rescued from the ruins in Georgia had now developed into a truly magnificent animal. Of gigantic size and the greatest possible enterprise and activity, he became the idol of the men. He conceived a particular antipathy to all things Turkish—man, woman, camel, horse, donkey, or dog, and he was always prepared on the least encouragement to "go for" them all, the peculiar "baggy" seats of the country Turks' trousers having for him a particularly irresistible attraction.

The great rough Tartar dogs, who all have their ears clipped as a precaution against frostbite, were his special prey, and many, acknowledged champions amongst them, arrived in their pride to rob our apparent affluence, only to retire howling as the result of short and decisive interviews with "George." On one famous occasion a particularly vicious old bull camel paid us a predatory visit, only to be instantly charged by our canine hero, who pulled out enough of his mane to stuff a mattress with, until finally, after having entertained us to a concert, containing every grunt, groan, and squeal in the camel vocabulary, all "crescendo," with a "finale" of an ear-splitting shriek "fortissimo," the huge and vicious animal made off at his lumbering gallop, kicking and biting in all directions, whilst "George" remained wagging his tail, licking his lips, and shaking hands, one after another, with every man present, to their huge delight and diversion.

During this time, however, trouble was brewing in many directions, and it was with much relief that we heard rumours through the Turks, about the end of May, of the landing of what they described as a troop of British cavalry at Trebizond. These we took to be our promised reinforcement from Constant, but as I had no word from them nor from my Intelligence officer at Trebizond, I concluded I had better go down the coast myself and see what was happening there at the very first moment I could leave Erzeroum.

# CHAPTER IV

### THE RUSSO-TURKISH FRONTIER—TROUBLE BREWING

Visit from General Beach—Interview with Kiazim Karabekir Pasha—Plans for repair of railway—Our supplies looted—Start for Trebizond—Beautiful camp—Our reinforcements—Hidden guns discovered—Return to Erzeroum "sick"—Our party augmented—Plans for removing armament—Arrival of Mustapha Kemal—Reports of trouble on frontier—Joined by Russian officers, also American naval officer and others—Leave for the frontier—Railway blocked—Night journey on a trolley—Armenian Generals at Kars—Leave for the South—Hussein, the Kurdish Mountain Chief—The race down the pass.

On June 1st I went again to the Russian frontier on the road to Kars to meet General Beach, Chief of Intelligence at Tiflis, under whose direct orders I was acting. There had been, as is usual in the spring, some bad landslides in the upper pass, above the frontier, on the Armenian side, and the railway was reported impassable on both sides of the frontier. The country had now at last begun to dry, and we had no trouble in covering the 100 miles from Erzeroum in the day, camping 10 miles beyond the frontier, opposite the landslip, three-parts of the way up the pass, before dark.

Here General Beach met me the next morning, coming from Tiflis via Kars, and after inspecting the damage and discussing the possibilities, he came back to Erzeroum with me, reaching there on the night of the 3rd. Next day we went together to visit Kiazim Karabekir Pasha, and discussed the methods to be pursued in the actual disarmament. The Pasha proved very affable and appeared quite prepared to carry out any proposals we put forward, with the result that General Beach returned to Tiflis next day, leaving one Engineer and one Intelligence officer to assist me, and undertook himself to see to the repair of the railway on the Armenian side of the frontier, and to send me from Tiflis a railway officer to assist me on the Turkish side.

It was the greatest possible pleasure to see him, as I had known him a long time, having first met him in Bagdad. He was, as usual, a mine of information, and being an extremely able man, as well as a most experienced one, his deductions with respect to the general situation in this most disturbed and unsatisfactory part of the world were full of interest to me. After being so long alone, it was indeed a welcome change to be able to discuss the position from our own point of view, and to get news of the outside world again. I now also discovered the reason of our having received none of the supplies which it had been agreed should be forwarded to us from Tiflis.

It appeared that, although I had specially stipulated that our supplies should always be sent "under escort," the gentleman at Tiflis, being imbued with entirely European ideas, did not consider this necessary, and had therefore sent off several lots without a British guard. The result was as I expected, and the supplies had all duly disappeared whilst passing over the portion of the line then in Armenian hands, so that nothing had ever reached the frontier, where I had already twice sent cars to meet and fetch in our long-expected and sadly-needed stores. However, as the General had brought a certain amount with him from Tiflis, we had a very enjoyable dinner together on his arrival, and, after remaining two nights at Erzeroum, he returned to Tiflis.

On the 7th, at daybreak, I started for Trebizond, with two cars and three men only, hoping, with these very lights loads and a road which I expected now to find dry, to do the 200 miles in two days. Crossing the Erzeroum Plain the road was dry and good, but the foot-hills of the Khop were deep in mud, though the pass itself was dry and fairly clear of snow; so, in spite of deep mud again in the Baiburt Plain, we were able to camp for the night in a beautiful orchard on the banks of the Kharshut River, 8 miles east of Gumush Khaneh and 120 miles west of Erzeroum. This camp was in such a really beautiful spot that it has lived in my memory ever since, and it was pure chance that enabled us to find it.

The evenings were now lengthening out, and as we had made good progress, about 5.30 P. M. I decided to halt for tea, and to go on afterwards in the late summer evening; we therefore selected a spot where the road ran actually on the river-bank and water was easy to obtain, and there halted. Whilst our primus stoves were doing their work, I strolled along the water's edge, below the steep bank at the top of which the cars had halted, and there came across a most curious and very ancient bridge over

## THE COAST COUNTRY ROUND TREBIZOND

The bay at Platana

Hidden guns discovered

## THE RUSSO-TURKISH FRONTIER

Our frontier camp at Zivin

View looking south from the edge of Kars plain over the Aras valley to the frontier range; Mount Ararat is 50 miles east

the torrent. A single span of stone crossed the river, and on the far side a tributary stream came in from the north, between them being a small orchard, with fresh long grass and every tree a mass of apple-blossom, the whole absolutely secluded and quite out of sight from the road above.

The old bridge itself was evidently built to take an *araba*, or small native cart, the model of which to-day is exactly as it was 2,000 years ago, and I much doubted if there was breadth sufficient to allow a car to pass over; ascent and descent also were so steep, and the arch pointed at the top, that the crossing in any case would be one of the greatest difficulty. However, the spot beyond looked so delightful that I hailed the men, and, all having had a look, we decided to try. So, bringing the cars one by one up the goat-track which led to the bridge, one of us drove and the other three pushed, and so we finally got our cars over, and then, having camped, we spent a most delightful evening amongst the flowers and grass, the air heavy with scent of apple-blossom and the two torrents roaring one on either side of us.

I fancy anyone would have appreciated the beauty of this spot, but to us, after so many months of snow and ice, without ever a shrub or tree, or even a green blade of grass, to gladden our eyes, the contrast here was restful beyond expression, and we dreamed we were in England far away, and woke next morning with the same idea. That one lovely summer evening still remains in my recollection as just one beautiful dream amidst a long succession of nightmares.

Next day we met with a certain amount of bad road and mud in ascending the Zigana Pass, which caused us some delay; but the summit was clear of snow and, driving very fast down the steep gradient, we reached Trebizond by 4 P.M., receiving a hearty welcome from our reinforcements, who were there awaiting us. This party had come from Constant, and consisted of two Intelligence officers, two interpreters, eight horses, two mules (for the interpreters), a perfectly invaluable Medical Officer (with a hospital orderly and outfit of medical stores), two N.C.O.s, and twenty men—the whole under command of Captain Fletcher, R.F.A.—and with them they brought stores of many kinds to which we had long been strangers.

Having checked the lists of the Trebizond armament prepared

during my absence, I took a drive round the coast country on the day after our arrival, having a shrewd suspicion that there were many guns about, which were not included in the lists which had been presented to us, although the number already acknowledged as in the Trebizond area was over 300.

I was also anxious to observe the general condition of the surrounding districts, and it was as always a real satisfaction and pleasure to me to observe the excellent results of the work of the American Relief Organization, of which evidence was here again available on every hand. In many of the villages in the valleys of the coast range the inhabitants consisted entirely of Christian Greeks, and these people to the extent of many thousands depended entirely for their support upon supplies furnished by the American organization at Trebizond, without which assistance they would infallibly have died, as indeed they eventually did when that generous assistance was withdrawn.

Our haphazard search was not so hopeless as at first sight it appears, for on a precipitous coast such as this is there are not many spots to which guns *can* be moved, and we were well rewarded by coming upon a nice artillery park in a secluded valley some miles out, which contained over forty most excellent guns of modern design and much ammunition. These the Turks assured me had been "overlooked" by *them,* but, thanks to our enterprise, they were *not* overlooked by *us,* and the fact of their having been found naturally discounted the value of other returns which we had received, and of which we had not been in a position to verify the accuracy.

Having made all arrangements for the subsequent march of the reinforcing party to Erzeroum, we got off on our return journey at daylight on the 11th, but, hard as we drove, were unable to reach our ideal orchard camp before dark, for there is a difference of many miles between a day's drive *up* a steep gradient and the same drive in the opposite direction, and we were eventually obliged to camp 14 miles short of our lovely orchard, although we kept going till long after dark in the hope of reaching it. This left us 136 miles next day to Erzeroum— a very arduous undertaking indeed, and I eventually arrived there with one car only, at 3 A. M. on the 13th, worn completely out and with a bad attack of fever, which, indeed, we all had,

## INTELLIGENCE IN TRANSCAUCASIA

as the result of crossing the marsh after nightfall in spring. The other car broke a front spring on the Khop, which necessitated a delay, to fit the yoke of an ox-cart as a substitute, after which my car rapidly left the crippled one behind, and it arrived sixteen hours after us, with both its occupants also badly sick with fever.

I now began to receive constant complaints from the Pasha as to attacks being made upon Moslems by the Armenians all along the frontier, and it became evident that I should have to go and see and report what was really going on amongst the frontier Kurds and Tartars. In the meanwhile a railway officer joined us from Tiflis and others from Constant, so that our little mess rapidly grew, and we soon arrived at a total of ten British officers. Our work went forward at good speed, and we began to get properly verified lists of the surprising stocks of arms and munitions, then stored in Erzeroum, forwarded to Constant with great regularity.

Great quantities of gun breech-blocks, machine-guns, and rifle-bolts were collected and packed; some were sent by camel caravan to be shipped at Trebizond, and others were loaded into trains to be ready to be sent to the frontier as soon as the railway could be repaired, which work was pushed on with all speed under the supervision of our railway officer.

There now arrived at Erzeroum the Inspector-General of the Turkish Eastern armies, who has since become famous as Mustapha Kemal Pasha, a great Turk, the remarkable nature of whose striking personality never fails to impress itself on all who are brought into contact with him.

European rather than Asiatic in type, with fair hair and blue eyes, Kemal is more Teutonic than Turkish in appearance. He has read much and travelled widely, and is thoroughly competent to give a considered opinion on all subjects of general interest either at the present day or in the history of the past. A man of great strength of character and very definite and practical views as to the rightful position of his race in the comity of nations, he is no seeker after personal fame or advancement, but is imbued with a deep sense of duty, which causes him to place his country's interest before all others, and to labour unceasingly towards those ends which he considers to be most to her advantage.

This is the secret of his remarkable success in the creation of the Turkish National Party, of which he himself is the moving and controlling spirit. It is by means of the undoubted earnestness and loyalty of his patriotism that he has been able to weld together the many divergent interests of his countrymen, and to lay the foundations of a Turkish democratic power which cannot fail to dominate the field of Eastern politics in the near future.

His military training is of German origin, but it is more than doubtful whether his sympathies to-day have any inclination towards either Germany or Russia, except in so far as the support of those countries may be made to serve in the forwarding of Turkish interests. Many scurrilous reports have been circulated from time to time with regard to his private life, but I have never observed the slightest foundation for them, though I have had every opportunity of doing so had any such existed. His general bearing, though invariably courteous, is not such as to encourage social intercourse, but it is impossible to doubt either the sincerity of his convictions or the tenacity with which he is prepared to support what he considers to be the legitimate aims of his country.

During the month of June, when at Erzeroum occupying the post of Inspector-General, Kemal Pasha was recalled to Constant by the Sultan (I concluded at the request of the Allies), and, on his refusing to go, he was deprived of his military rank, thus being left free to devote his activities to politics, in which, although a lifelong enemy of Enver, he was already deeply committed to the support of what had previously been known as the Young Turk Party. I frequently saw and had long talks with him at this time, and was well aware of his political aspirations and also of the difficulties he was meeting with in their prosecution, and of the objects of the Conference which he was then arranging to hold at Erzeroum in July.

As time went on I became less and less satisfied with our progress towards the disarmament of the Turkish troops which was the main object of my mission. It appeared to me that the railway suffered a suspiciously large number of "accidents," and being in regular communication with G.H.Q., Constant, I therefore notified them that I proposed to proceed up the railway to the frontier, and would from there report further by the more certain route via Tiflis. On July 3rd I started for the frontier yet once more, but by the Decauville train this time, in order to see for myself what was happening on the actual railway-line in the Turks' country, before going on to the frontier districts, ordering three cars and a picked party of men to proceed by road and to meet us at Zivin, the Turkish Eastern frontier post.

During the last fortnight previous to our departure for the frontier our party had been augmented by a Russian Colonel and his orderly officer, who were anti-Bolshevik, and most useful to us, as the Colonel had himself commanded the right wing of the Grand Duke's army during the Russian advance on Erzeroum in 1916-17, and had carried out the wonderful flank march through the winter snow, by way of Olti, which brought about the eventual evacuation of the fortress by the Turks; his accurate knowledge of the difficult frontier country was therefore invaluable to me. He also proved of equal value in locating hidden armament, as he was able to indicate many spots where the Russian arms and munitions had been buried by the loyal Russian officers when it was seen that the revolution would involve their troops. These hidden stores were well known to the Turks, though they did not appear on their returns and no attempt had been made to dig them up.

We also received a visit from an American naval officer, Lieutenant Dunn, of the American Intelligence Staff, attached to Admiral Bristol, the United States High Commissioner at Constant. Our naval friend and ally was both bright and cheery, and excellent company, finally leaving us for Sivas, a good 300 miles to the westward, on his way to Samsun, mounted on a native pony, with a Kurdish saddle, accompanied only by a native cart and several Turkish soldiers, and, to my great surprise, wearing his blue cloth naval uniform and trousers(!), than which it would be hard to conceive a more unsuitable costume for such an arduous journey. Neither this, nor the fact that he had no stores at all, and only a most elementary knowledge of the language, seemed, however, to cause him the slightest concern—a great contrast to the attitude adopted by a senior French officer who visited us about the same time, and who wanted everything from a motor-car to an aeroplane.

Kiazim Pasha having placed a small Decauville train at our

disposal for our journey, I foresaw it would have to become our headquarters for a considerable time, and therefore went to some trouble to make it habitable. We had a most peculiar little locomotive, originally built in America for the Russian Government, adapted to burn either wood or oil; one covered truck as men's quarters; one similar, which I fitted up for myself and a railway officer; and also a truck to carry wood, three cars being the utmost our small engine could pull. With this small outfit we started, rumours of all kinds reaching us before our departure indicating that the whole situation was rapidly coming to a head, it being evident that the Turks were becoming more and more restive in the face of the inexplicable delay of the Allies in reaching any definite decision with regard to the future.

Travelling on this little "war-time" railway was indeed an experience, and it was necessary to carry a "gauge," and to test the rails with it frequently, for in many places, owing to the sinking of the embankments and the washing away of the ballast, the rails required rectification before we were able to get our train over, even at a foot pace; each bridge also required elaborate examination before adventuring the train upon it, and eventually we were obliged to carry large baulks of timber to temporarily shore up many of the bridges and culverts whilst we passed over them.

Under these circumstances it may be imagined that our progress was by no means rapid, and as we had frequently to halt also to replenish our supply of wood fuel, we considered we had achieved wonders when, on the evening of the second day, 60 hours and 70 miles out from Erzeroum, we finally entered the gorge of the mountains where we understood our worst troubles to lie. This is the same gorge into which the road from Erzeroum to Kars descends from the foot-hills to cross the frontier; the railway, however, follows the main Aras River valley till the frontier gorge enters it, whilst the road cuts off the corner and joins the rail again at the frontier post of Zivin, some 15 miles from the main valley.

Soon after entering the gorge, we were confronted by the first serious fall of rock—about 2,000 tons having fallen from the cliff face and entirely obliterated the railway track. Here, therefore, we halted, and, sending our engine back, prepared to make our headquarters in the train for a considerable time. Next morning we dragged a small trolley over the mass of débris and launched it on the line beyond, but after 3 miles came upon another equally severe fall; this was crossed in the same manner, and we found three such falls in the 12 miles which lay between our train and the Turkish frontier post at Zivin.

It was evident that it would take months, even if an adequate supply of labour had been available, to open the line, and that, therefore, any munitions or armament which had to be transported by rail would have to be unloaded at the spot where we had left our train and carried to another train farther up the valley, if we could succeed in bringing one down the pass to Zivin. I therefore wrote to Kiazim Pasha at Erzeroum advising him of the situation, and asking him to forward the trains already loaded with armament, and to provide troops to execute the "portage," whilst I continued on over the frontier to examine into the many complaints he had brought to my notice of the persecution of Moslems beyond the frontier, and at the same time asked him to take steps to have trains ready at Zivin to receive the armament, as and when it arrived there.

I entertained great hopes that by these means we should be able to bring about the position, so difficult to achieve and so much to be desired, where the Turks would be obliged either to surrender their armament or to formally refuse to do so, which latter course I was by this time convinced it was their intention eventually to adopt, though they were evidently desirous of postponing such a far-reaching decision till the last possible moment. Having forwarded my letter to Kiazim, I left my railway officer in charge of our train, with orders to superintend the work and to take charge of the armament trains when they arrived, and moved up myself to the Turkish post at Zivin, to see how matters progressed in the upper pass across the frontier, pitching my camp close to the last Turkish post in the valley by the side of the railway.

The work on the railway beyond the frontier was, of course, in Armenian hands, superintended by a British railway officer from Tiflis who had been placed under my orders. I found the progress which had been made was very unsatisfactory, chiefly on account of difficulty in obtaining Armenian labour,

our engineer having had the misfortune to "lose" a train of workmen when bringing them down the pass without having first properly tested the line, as one line of rails had suddenly slipped under the weight, and the whole train had rolled over and over down some hundred feet of steep slopes, with somewhat disastrous results—for not only was one man killed outright, but fifteen others were pretty seriously injured. The remainder, being fairly scared to death, had bolted to their homes, and spread terrible reports of the dangers any of our workmen would be required to face, which, very naturally, had caused our work to be somewhat less popular for the moment. It therefore became necessary to go on at once to the Armenian headquarters, now at Kars, to induce the Armenian General there to detail some of his troops to carry out the necessary work. The condition of the Armenian Christian population in Kars city and district was at this time one of extreme privation, the majority relying for their support entirely on the supply furnished by the American Organization of Near East Relief. Glorious work was being done by the representatives of that great organization in Kars, their supplies being drawn via Tiflis from Batoum and the distribution carried out under conditions of great difficulty and hardship. It cannot fail to be of great satisfaction to the generous subscribers that seldom if ever throughout all history has money been spent in a better cause, nor brought relief to so many suffering souls. It must be of far greater value to them to know that their liberality has been the means of saving so many innocent lives which otherwise would have been lost by that most painful of all deaths which results from the excruciating agonies of slow starvation.

On returning to our camp at Zivin, after inspecting the line in the upper pass, we had the misfortune to break a wheel of our car. This caused delay, and necessitated telegraphing to our Headquarters at Erzeroum for another car and a spare wheel; the delay, however, was compensated for by the wonderful experience it procured for us, under the following circumstances.

Our wheel broke in the worst part of the pass, about 25 miles above the frontier, late in the evening, and it appeared impossible to reach our camp below that night. However, whilst seeking a spot to bivouac, we came across a small four-wheeled hand-trolley, used by the men working on the railway, and I determined to endeavour to "coast" down the railway on that. We were well aware that the gradient was both severe and continuous, but we, of course, paid no heed to the terror of the Armenians, who endeavoured to dissuade us from essaying the trip, saying that we should certainly be killed (which in itself really did not worry them at all), and that *they* would certainly be accused afterwards of having made away with us. This last possibility, however, reduced them to a state of abject terror. Having first cut poles and fitted them to the trolley as brakes on the wheels, we started soon after midnight upon what proved to be a really glorious and wonderful trip, with just that amount of uncertainty about its successful achievement which was required to lend it the best "thrill" of the many it was destined to afford us.

Our altitude at starting was 6,700 feet, and we knew we had to descend 3,000 feet in about 30 miles or less. There were four of us on the trolley, and none of us had been down the line before, nor had any of us previously undertaken any trip of the kind. We, however, knew the line had been certified by the engineers as unsafe for the little train to go over carrying the labour-parties, and we were profoundly ignorant as to the actual efficiency of the pole-brakes which we had improvised. However, at the same time, in case it be thought that the whole affair was a foolhardy undertaking, we also knew, first, that a truck loaded with wood had got away by itself the day before and had reached the bottom safely, though at a terrifying speed, although its brakes had been fixed "hard on" all the time; and, secondly, that the worst construction would certainly be put on our absence by the Turks, and a very awkward situation would most likely be created between the Turkish and Armenian posts on the frontier in the event of our not turning up by daybreak.

The scene was one of entrancing beauty. A beautiful warm summer's night, with the wildest of rugged mountains and rocky precipices on all sides of us; foaming waterfalls descending from the slopes above, and a boiling torrent ever roaring far below; whilst over all hung a bright full moon, causing each rock to stand out in bold relief, and showing clearly every detail of what seemed to be a fairy valley lying far beneath us in the peaceful silvery moonlight.

As may be imagined, we started very slowly, amidst the audible prayers of the Armenians; but finding our brakes seemed very efficient, we soon "let her go" a little, and on checking the speed got our first emotion, as our wooden brakes promptly took fire and commenced to burn up—a most unpleasant situation, especially for the two men sitting immediately over them, for whom the scenery instantly lost all attraction. This necessitated a compulsory stop at the first waterfall. In spite, however, of all our efforts, it was at the second stream, about a mile and a half farther on, that we at last succeeded in bringing our "vehicle" to a stand-still. Then followed a very animated discussion, for we found that our two poles, which had originally been about 15 feet long, were now burnt down to about 6 feet, and it would evidently be necessary to carry a stock of spare poles with us. By great good-fortune, in the valley of the little stream where we had at last stopped, some small trees were growing, and of these we proceeded to lay in an ample supply, arranging now to apply them to all four wheels instead of two only, and soaking them all well in the stream before starting.

Profiting by our previous experience, we then used them alternately, and, having no further trouble, were able to enjoy the beauty of our novel form of locomotion amongst surroundings the beauty of which it would be impossible to describe. We finally arrived safely at our camp as the first grey of dawn was showing in the eastern sky, to find all in commotion there, and the Turk Commander mustering his men, whilst awaiting orders from the Pasha at Erzeroum, to whom he had already telegraphed as to our having been detained by the Armenians. For this action I expressed our thanks in suitable terms, and, being well aware of the urgent desire of the Turks to take advantage of any excuse for launching an attack upon the Armenian posts, arranged to strike camp forthwith and proceed to the Armenian headquarters at Kars.

The road, through the pass and beyond, was in excellent condition, and travelling light, with two cars only, we reached Kars, 75 miles distant, before dark, where we found a British Intelligence officer, who obtained an interview for me with the Armenian Army Commander the next morning. At this interview were present the three Armenian Generals who were in command of the Armenian troops both in Kars Province and

## INTELLIGENCE IN TRANSCAUCASIA 189

along the Turkish frontier, and I laid before them in detail all the complaints made by the Turks as to the treatment the Moslems were receiving at the hands of the Armenian soldiery.

As I expected, many of the facts they found it impossible to deny, and confined themselves to making counter-charges against the Turks, doubtless equally well founded. Their main argument, which they insisted on all through, was that the Allies had authorized them to take possession of the country, and in order to obtain control it was an absolute necessity that they should disarm the Tartar Moslem population; as this could only be done by force, it obviously led to fighting; and fighting, as between Moslem and Armenian, of necessity led to massacre and atrocities of all kinds.

This was all very evident, but the best method of proceeding under the circumstances, in the face of the Allies' decision as to the fate of the country, was very much less evident. I therefore announced that I would travel along the frontier districts myself and judge what the real state of affairs was by personal investigation before making any official report, provided that they would in the meanwhile give our railway engineer all possible assistance in completing the repair of the railway. This proposal, having for its object, as they well knew, the immediate reduction of the Turkish armament, they very readily agreed to, and we were thus able to leave Kars again by midday, now following a new Russian strategical military road which led south into the Aras Valley, through a district from which many reports of trouble had been lately received.

Crossing Kars Plain towards the south, about 30 miles of open and now deserted country is traversed, rising gradually all the way, till suddenly the edge of the plain is reached at nearly 8,000 feet, and from that point the ground descends steeply for about 15 miles to the Aras Valley, some 3,000 feet below. A beautiful view is obtained from this ridge, terminated only by the summit of the great mountain range of the Ak Dagh, which forms the frontier-line between Russia and Turkey, some 70 miles distant to the south. This high range, under snow even in late July, commences at its western extremity, at a peculiar conical isolated peak, known as the Keusse Dagh, 14,000 feet high, and continues due east, with but few practical passes, for 170 miles till it culminates in the historic peak of Mount Ararat, just visible on the eastern horizon from where we left the plain. This massive giant rises to a total height of 18,000 feet, is capped by 5,000 feet of everlasting snow, and dominates the whole of this rugged and intricate mountain system, from whence flow all the great rivers of which the patriarchs of early Biblical days had any accurate knowledge.

Our road, descending through the foot-hills which lay spread out as a map below us, was visible from the edge of the plateau for at least 10 miles, twisting and winding in all directions in its descent. Although night was fast coming on, we had no thought of camping where we were, but made haste to descend and seek shelter from the icy wind, then blowing over the plain, by camping in one of the sheltered valleys far below, where we might expect to be much warmer and more comfortable.

We had descended only 2 miles, and not more than 500 feet in altitude, when we suddenly found ourselves in the presence of a strong detachment of several companies of Armenian infantry, drawn up on parade, evidently awaiting our arrival, having apparently been warned of our departure and intended route by telephone from Kars. The commanding officer intercepted us in the road and informed me that he had quarters and a good dinner prepared for us, and counted upon our stopping for the night at his post, as he declared the hills below to be entirely unsafe for us to camp in.

This, however, was exactly what we were there to find out, and I was in no way desirous of appearing to be more friendly with one side than with the other, which would have been the impression infallibly produced among the Kurds by our remaining for the night at an Armenian post. I therefore thanked him civilly, and told him that our orders did not permit of our accepting his invitation, but that we should camp below and take our chance; and we forthwith kept on another 6 or 8 miles, finally camping on a beautiful carpet of wild flowers, in a valley by the side of a roaring torrent, by moonlight some time after night had fallen.

Next morning, at daybreak, I sent our interpreter in a car down the pass to a Kurdish village, to say I wished to see, and talk to, the Chief of those parts, and to ask if he would come up the pass in the car. I received a reply, within an hour, that the Chief was in the higher mountains, about 10 miles away,

## INTELLIGENCE IN TRANSCAUCASIA 191

but that a mounted messenger had been dispatched to him, and if I would send the car in the afternoon he would doubtless come up in it to see me. We had a quiet morning, and had our camp most imposingly arranged, the grass having been cut in front of my tent and our machine-guns set out there, and also some good carpets which I had brought to give a "tone" to the outfit; so that, with a car on each side of the tent and the little British flag flying over all, we undoubtedly presented an effective contrast to any small travelling party which had ever been seen in those wild mountains before.

It will not be out of place here to give a short description of the kind of people these true mountain Kurds are, as, though their name is well known, yet few people have any intimate acquaintance with them, and they are constantly being confused with the Turks, whom they do not in the least resemble, and whom in their hearts they hate, although they have long been nominally under Turkish rule.

As a race the true Kurds of the Anatolian Mountains are physically the finest men it has ever been my privilege to meet. They are to this ancient and inaccessible country what the Bedouin Arab is to the desert—that is to say, they have been in occupation of the land since prehistoric times. They are divided into various distinct tribes, which have for many centuries each occupied certain well-defined districts in the mountains. These tribes were already ancient in their occupation long before the first Turks appeared on their gradual migration westward from their original home in Central Asia. The Kurdish chiefs, who rule their tribesmen with the absolute authority of the patriarchs of old, trace back their descent unbroken to the days when England was still a wild country of forest and marsh, the home of barbarians of whom the first facts that were known centuries later, were that they had fair hair, worshipped the sun, mined tin, painted their naked bodies with woad, and fought like the devil.

These Kurds both look and behave as one might expect such men to do, for, though they are brigands by descent as well as by inclination and training, once their confidence is gained their word can be relied on with absolute confidence. They are, however, both wary and suspicious, and it is to be feared that the policy, or rather the want of it, which distinguished the Allies' actions subsequent to the Armistice has tended to destroy what little confidence the Kurds might previously have acquired in the justice and reliability of the Western Powers.

Under these circumstances I was well aware that I was taking a great chance in presenting myself, with a small party, uninvited in the very heart of their wildest fastnesses, and should have been in no way surprised if trouble had arisen, the least of which would have been our being "run" quickly out of the country.

The Kurd, on the other hand, fearing nothing on earth himself, might, I considered, possibly appreciate the confidence shown in his hospitality by the visit of a small party in quite a different spirit from that with which he would have viewed the arrival of any considerable force; and especially was I certain that they would have been instantly informed of our refusal the night before to camp with the Armenians. From this they would certainly deduce two things: first that we were no allies of their enemies, the Armenians; and secondly that we came into their country with confidence, relying on their traditional hospitality to give us a friendly reception. Also, be it not forgotten, I was well aware that they knew there were then large bodies of British troops *not very far off!*

About 3 P.M. we observed a great cloud of dust in the pass below us, and finally the car arrived with Hussein Bey, the principal Chief of those parts, seated in it in great state, with a dozen or so of his principal supporters riding as escort. He was, as are all the Kurdish chiefs, a splendid man, and presented a truly magnificent appearance. Although it was a hot summer's day, he wore splendid furs, and was hung all over with silver-mounted pistols, purses, and boxes, as well as many ivory daggers, gold chains, and other ornaments, and was altogether horribly reminiscent to me of the general appearance of a pawn-broker's shop-window in London. However, he was excessively affable, and "tickled to death" (as they would say in America) at his first ride in a motor-car; also he had been intensely entertained by the efforts of his kinsmen on horseback to keep up with the car, so that he was in a specially good temper; and having presented me in turn to each of his escort, we sat down on the best carpet and had a long and most interesting talk.

It appeared he owned thirty-eight villages in the mountains

between the Aras River and Kars Plain, and held the sole right to the *yailas,* or upland pastures, all through these mountains north of the Aras River, a tract about 40 miles by 15. It being summer-time, all his people had left the villages, which lie in the deep valleys and are only inhabited in winter, and were now camped with their flocks and herds on the upper slopes, or *yailas,* where the pasture is excellent as soon as the snow has melted there. He told me he could muster 1,200 mounted men, all well armed, within two days, and had latterly been obliged to do so, as the Armenians had advanced into his country with the intention of carrying out a general disarmament of his people, against which he and all his tribe were prepared to fight to the last man; and that, in the face of his attitude, the Armenians (at whose name he spat) had, as usual, found discretion more in their line than valour, and had cleared off, having only succeeded in catching the few old Kurdish men and women remaining in the villages, who had been too infirm to reach the upper *yailas.* These, of course, had been subjected to the usual horrors, which, although they appear ghastly to Europeans, did not appear to Hussein to be worth talking about, and I rather thought he seemed to imply that his tribe was well rid of the "old uns," who were of no further service, he considered, but had become a general charge on the community!

He announced that his people would be quite prepared to submit to the government of any European Power, preferably the English; but if it was decided to endeavour to put them under Armenian government, and if European troops were to support the Armenians, they would evacuate their country with all their goods and herds, and go bodily over to their kinsmen beyond the Turkish frontier. For the moment, however, he had no complaint to make, and was quite confident of his ability to hold his country against all the Armenians in the world for ever.

I thought this Hussein a fine fellow, perfectly fearless, surprisingly well-informed, and very intelligent, and I did not doubt for a moment his and his fellow-chiefs' ability to look after themselves. This ability the Turks have long ago discovered, for, as in the case of all these Kurdish frontier tribes, the Turks, after many ineffectual efforts to rule them, have definitely given up that idea, and are content to allow them to rule themselves, exacting only a nominal allegiance, which in reality amounts to leaving them to all intents and purposes independent.

After about an hour's most interesting conversation, I told him his views should be reported in the proper quarter, and that I now intended going on to Khagizman, across the Aras River, which town had lately been occupied by Armenian troops, as to whose position and behaviour I was anxious to obtain information, and I concluded by an invitation to him to come down the pass with me in the car as far as the last of his villages 5 miles below. At this he was delighted, and we struck camp forthwith and started.

It is impossible, I think, for an Englishman not to feel a certain sympathy with these high-class Kurds when they are met with in their own country; for, though robbers all, yet they are real "sports," and ready at any moment for any kind of game which has a spice of danger in it, and the greater the danger the better they like it. Of course, they love a real good "fight" best of all, though the only fight that appears to them to be a really serious one is an intertribal battle with a neighbouring tribe. This may seem strange to us at first, but is not really hard to understand, for, being all robbers, and there being rarely anyone else to rob, each tribe has robbed its neighbour for generations; therefore, when a tribal fight does eventually come off, it becomes a serious affair, as there are many old scores to settle, and it really does then entail a genuine fight to a finish, when few are ever left on either side to carry on the race.

On this occasion Hussein, who had never been in a car before in his life, confided to me that he wanted to go "fast," as he had taunted his mounted relations by telling them they were no horsemen and would never be able to keep up with the car and that *he* would certainly reach the valley before them. The pass in front looked to me a pretty bad place for a race, especially as I did not know the road at all, and there was every kind of zigzag down precipices with many hairpin turns, all to be done on a very steep down gradient and on an absolutely strange road. I have had the good fortune to enjoy a good deal of road motor-racing in the past twenty years, since the days of the early Gordon-Bennett races, and have raced over many of the most difficult courses in Europe, but they were

## HUSSEIN BEY'S COUNTRY—UPPER ARAS VALLEY

Hussein Bey visits our camp with his Kurdish chiefs

Hussein's "Yailas"—the race down the Pass started here; the road dips over the edge of the cliff on the left and descends some 3,000 feet by zigzags

all of them child's play to this proposition; and I could not help thinking that many more experienced friends of mine in England, France, and the United States, would have hesitated considerably before urging me to excessive speed on such a road in the way this unsophisticated "hero" did.

Anyway, we drew up in line, one Ford motor-car and six picked Kurdish horsemen, that being already about three times as many as there was room for on the road, and then away we went. All the world knows, I imagine, that the Kurd is a born horseman and lives his life in the saddle and in the mountains; also, these fellows knew every rock and pebble of the road and were full of confidence, so that it was not the one-sided competition which at first sight it might appear to us, and, in addition, they, as horsemen always can, were able to get away a few yards quicker than the car, and so got an excellent start.

The first 200 yards of the race took place in the more open part of the valley, and then came a sharp turn to the right, under a steep wall of rock, the road then descending steeply, following a ledge cut in the face of the perpendicular cliff, with the river roaring through its rocky gorge in the valley far below. Luckily for us, the road did not go quite straight, and our friends left it to take a short cut, which allowed the car to get up its speed unhampered by the galloping horses, so that it then became a race as to who should reach the entrance to the ledge first. *They* did, but, as I expected, they were by that time going too fast to be able to take the turn safely, and two of them bumped into the face of the rocky cliff, with what result I do not know, but at any rate we saw them no more, and I was then committed to trying to *pass* these wild riders on the ledge of rock; this I did not intend to adventure, as I was confident the next turn would be sure to be in the opposite direction, so that I could imagine them, if they kept up the rate of speed at which they were then going, shooting clear off the road into space at the turn and hitting the river-bed some hundreds of feet below with a sickening squelch. I therefore kept behind them, and so enjoyed a wonderful exhibition of hair-raising horsemanship which I wouldn't have missed for worlds.

All this time *we* were doing some pretty "tall skids" round the bends ourselves, and Hussein had to hold on with both hands to keep his seat. One would have expected him under these circumstances, being an absolute novice, to keep pretty quiet; but not at all! I stole a glance at him, for one moment only, between the turns, and saw he was yelling with sheer delight, and screaming at his pals by name, letting out a shriek of joy every time a horse slipped (which was pretty often), till at last one of them took a real beauty, clean heels over head. At that Hussein as nearly as possible fell out of the car, for he let go his hold in order to clap his hands with delight, and as at that moment we had to swerve to avoid the fallen horse still rolling in the road, he was thrown clean out of his seat and only saved from going overboard by my having the luck to catch a firm hold of the tail of his long coat, and, holding on to it like grim death, being just able to pull him back into his seat. I think this really only increased his enjoyment, and he kept crying "Faster! faster!" whilst the slope got "steeper" and "steeper," and the turns "sharper" and "sharper," till suddenly there were only *two* horses left in front, instead of *three*, though I never saw the other one disappear, having enough to do to mind my own job.

The road got worse and the surface became loose and bad as we got lower down, and although the horses in front were getting pretty well beat, yet we were unable to catch them, and eventually, when the village appeared in sight, at the bottom of the last zigzag, they were still 10 yards ahead. We therefore did the last turn a little "extra," and with a loud "bang" away went one back tyre, clean off the rim, with the other following it a moment later, and we did the last 50 yards on the rims only; for any attempt to put on a brake at that pace, without tyres, would have skidded us over the edge in a moment—so we all arrived pretty well together, amidst an indescribable ovation from the whole population of the surrounding country, who had all come down from the upper *yailas* to the village for the occasion, and had been watching us in great excitement all the way down the face of the cliff.

My first action, when we finally stopped, was to jump out of the car and to go and congratulate the two now dismounted and somewhat exhausted heroes on their magnificent and most daring horsemanship, which commanded my most hearty and cordial admiration; and I next congratulated Hussein also on both his men and horses. After that, the latter were attended to, as they always are amongst the Kurds, with the very greatest care, and, the other car shortly afterwards arriving, with news that no one had been seriously hurt, Hussein then dragged me into a hovel to give me the best entertainment he could, which consisted of fine curdled milk, the true mountain drink, the same being provided outside for my men, who were then busy putting on new tyres and a new wheel, some of our spokes having been badly sprung in our last effort.

This over, we bid good-bye to Hussein and his wild mountain sportsmen, in the midst of great cheering, with the certainty that we should all of us at any time be safe in his country, if we got into any trouble farther on—a state of affairs which seemed to be far from improbable.

## CHAPTER V

### THE RUSSO-TURKISH FRONTIER—KURDS AND ARMENIANS

Cross the Aras—Reception at Khagizman—The town—The general situation—Omar Aga, the Kurdish brigand—Interview—We run out of petrol—Return to Zivin—Position in Olti District—Camp in the Olti Hills—Eyeeb Pasha—His troops—Moslem refugees—Robbers' punishment—Machine-gun practice—Kurdish national game—Kurds going into action—Our car attacked and corporal shot—Return again to Zivin.

On leaving our friend Hussein Bey's last village, we had still 10 miles of the wildest of passes to descend before reaching the main Aras River. Our road was good, and on reaching the river, followed the bank to the west for about 10 miles, when it crossed a very modern-looking bridge of iron, showing once more how much trouble and expense had been incurred by the Russians in preparing their strategical roads, so as to permit of a rapid concentration of their troops on the Turkish frontier.

Once across the bridge, we were confronted by an Armenian cavalry regiment, or what was meant for one, drawn up on the river-bank to receive us, and having halted I got down and shook hands with the commander, afterwards, at his special request, inspecting his men. The Armenians were very civil, and told us we had now to climb 4 miles, up the steep valley to the south, to reach Khagizman, the principal town in that part of the Aras Valley, where their headquarters were, and where the town authorities had prepared an official reception for us.

A mounted party were told off to escort us, and we started upon a stiff climb through lovely scenery. The valley on which Khagizman stands is a peculiar one, more like an American canyon than anything else. The torrent has cut its course deep into the plain, leaving steep cliffs on either side, at whose base grow many beautiful trees and the richest of grass, as well as many flowers, which, in contrast to the barren plain above, present a wonderfully cool and restful picture. We were much entertained during the ascent by the efforts of our Armenian cavalry escort to keep pace with us, particularly by contrast with the

## INTELLIGENCE IN TRANSCAUCASIA 199

class of horsemanship of which we had lately been such interested spectators; in fact, it is hard to imagine a greater contrast than that presented by the Kurdish horsemen racing full speed downhill and Armenian cavalry painfully creeping uphill.

The town of Khagizman is purely Russian, and is built on the plain along the edge of the canyon. The houses are plain but pretty, each standing in fairly spacious gardens with many fruit-trees, at the time all loaded with fruit, a great contrast to anything we had see since leaving the coast. The streets are broad and trees are everywhere, the centre of the town being a large square surrounded by fine trees, from which the principal streets radiate, and here we found an astonishing concourse assembled to greet us.

Of the pre-war population, which numbered from 7,000 to 10,000, barely 1,000 now remained, but every one of these had assembled to greet us in the square, where the garrison of about 400 Armenian infantry had also been paraded. In the centre a space had been kept clear, and to this we were directed on our arrival. Here we found a large table covered with a white linen cloth, on which was set out a large loaf of bread and some salt, of which we were expected to partake. Here also were the Governor of the town and the chief priest waiting to deliver addresses, the former attired in what he evidently considered to be the absolutely correct official European costume, and the latter in ancient and magnificent priestly vestments.

In order that the reason and object of all this ceremony may be understood, it must be borne in mind that Khagizman has for long been a Russian town, and, being remotely situated on the frontier, has been the centre of Russian activity in the road-making and other developments undertaken by the Imperial Government in those districts. When, therefore, the Allies announced that Kars Province was to be handed to the Armenians, the latter flocked to Khagizman and took possession of the town itself, many houses, and much other property which had previously belonged to the Russian inhabitants and officials who had returned to the north on the outbreak of the Bolshevik revolution.

It is doubtful whether the Armenian population would have been able to carry out the occupation of this district had they not profited by the relief work of the American organization in

Kars. This fact, whilst it reflects the greatest credit upon the American charity and provides most practical evidence of its success, at the same time undoubtedly added considerably to the general difficulties of the situation. The Moslem population, whose plight was far from enviable, not unnaturally looked upon the assistance given to the Christians with feelings of extreme jealousy, and regarded it as a sign that the strife between the cross and the crescent was still as strong as ever in the Western Countries. The effect of this feeling was to considerably aggravate the animosity already existing between the races at that time, with the result that when the assistance of the Western philanthropists was eventually withdrawn, the miserable remnant of the Christian population undoubtedly suffered even more severely on that account than would otherwise have been the case.

As we were the first party of the Allies' forces to visit the place since the Armenian occupation, the population were anxious to give us an official reception, and to deliver addresses of welcome to us, and of thanks to the Allies, to whose decision as to the future ownership of the whole province their own occupation of the city was due. On reaching the centre of the square we halted, and I descended and shook hands all round, accepting at the same time the bread and salt, the tendering of which is the immemorial custom of the country. Our hosts were certainly people of astonishing appearance, and were all in the highest state of excitement, so that it took a considerable time to clear a space and to obtain some degree of silence to permit of the Governor audibly delivering his address. During this time we were gradually reduced to a state of hysterical laughter by the amazing appearance of the crowd around us, whose garments were quite beyond description.

In order to convey some rough idea of what we may call the "incompleteness" of their attire, it will be sufficient to say that if a gentleman found himself with *one* entire leg to his trousers he was quite exceptionally well dressed. Few, indeed, could boast a costume of such pretensions to completeness, and some fell very far short of that ideal. We were, above all, anxious to be in no way uncivil, and to behave ourselves as became the representatives of the Western Powers, but we had a hard struggle to maintain composure, and on the appearance of the

## EYEEB PASHA'S OLTI COUNTRY

The "road" into the hill country proves somewhat difficult. The bucket swinging from the lamp bracket indicates the perpendicular —the rope prevents the car overturning

Our camp—note the machine-guns, the flag, and our breakfast— still feeding

## EYEEB PASHA'S COUNTRY (continued)

Our visitors. From left to right: a cousin—an uncle—Eyeeb Pasha—Col. R.—Bekir Bey (the eldest uncle)—a German drill-instructor. Note—Col. R.'s height is 6 feet

Eyeeb Pasha's Kurdish cavalry. Col. R. mounted in centre

Kurds dancing in camp. Eyeeb Pasha third from the left

Governor we incontinently succumbed one and all, and were convulsed with uncontrollable laughter.

I shall retain to my dying day a vivid recollection of the official in question, and I experienced a distinct feeling that it was unfair of him not to have shown himself until the last moment, when we were all of us already exhausted by our previous efforts to keep up an outward appearance of that gravity which was suitable to the occasion, and also until I was stuck out by myself, for the purpose of being addressed, in full view of the assembled multitude. The result was that my stock of solemnity proved inadequate to the demand made upon it, and the tears rained down my cheeks in my endeavours to contain myself during his doubtless very emotional address, which lasted about half an hour, and of which neither I nor any of my party understood one word.

His Excellency the Governor, for the occasion, had donned a pair of flannel trousers which in the dim and distant past had once been white, but were so no longer. There were other remarkable shortcomings about these trousers besides their uninviting colour, a comparatively unimportant one being an entire absence of buttons; but they were mercifully worn under what had once been a frock-coat, and these two garments constituted, apparently, the entire official full-dress of his department, as he wore no other garments of any description, with the exception of a hat, which, however, was the gem of the whole collection.

In days gone by it had once been a "billycock," and though the crown still retained vestiges of its original form, the brim had not been so fortunate, only a very small portion remaining at one side, by which His Excellency, at the most affecting portions of his speech, was able to lift it from his head in solemn and polite salute. He, of course, could not realize how irresistibly his appearance and gestures recalled the immortal Charlie Chaplin, but each salute caused us fearful spasms of hilarity; these, in conjunction with our streaming eyes, were providentially received by all as evidence of our deep appreciation of the unknown but doubtless harrowing tale which was being unfolded for our benefit.

When at last His Excellency concluded his impressive but incomprehensible address, he was followed by the head priest—

a "beaver" of the first magnitude, who, with great consideration, "let us off" with a short twenty minutes' discourse, and we finally were able to retire to very excellent quarters, provided for us in an old Russian house. Here, after manfully resisting many pressing invitations to a banquet prepared in our honour, we were at last able to get some sadly-needed rest, in spite of the echoes of the joviality of the banquet, which lasted deep into the night and reverberated through the whole town.

Next morning we were early afoot, and, borrowing a horse, I rode round with my interpreter to gather information, long before the heroes of the banquet had sufficiently recovered to permit of them appearing on the scene. The result of my inquiries revealed a rather peculiar position then existing in that part of the country; for whilst the Armenians, with a force of not more than 400 men, had taken possession of the town itself, they were unable to go outside its precincts except as an armed force, the open country round the town being watched by parties of Kurds from a tribe farther down the river, who saw to it that any Armenian who ventured forth alone never returned. Evidence of the fate of such as had left the town singly or in small parties was easily to be found in various directions even within a mile of the centre of the city.

It appeared that the tribe in question occupied all the mountain country on the south side of the Aras River, between the river and the Turkish frontier, which latter follows the crest of the range to the westward until the Persian frontier is met on the summit of Mount Ararat, 75 miles distant. These Kurds, under their Chief, Omar Aga, had cleared the whole country of live-stock, and driven all the animals to one of the higher valleys, where their own summer camp was established, close under the snow, and from which they were able to pass their loot over the frontier and dispose of it to the Turks.

In the face of this very unsatisfactory state of affairs, I decided to visit the great Omar Aga in his mountain retreat, and to judge on the spot what steps it might be advisable to recommend in my report with regard to the local position generally. We got off soon after midday, and, having descended to the Aras Valley, followed the military road south of that river for about 20 miles, till we reached another military road leading directly south into the mountains in the direction of the frontier. This road had evidently been constructed either immediately previous to or during the war, as there had been no trace of it on any map I had ever seen, and it was doubtless one more means for a rapid concentration of their troops on their frontier which the Russians had provided.

Proceeding due south for 10 miles through the foot-hills, we came to a purely Russian village at the mouth of a gorge leading into the heart of the great range. Here we halted and made inquiries as to the road and as to Omar Aga's whereabouts. The road had been made some years before, but had never been used for military purposes, and the timber of the bridges had now been removed and used as firewood by the Kurds, whose camp we were told we should find on an upper *yaila* about 15 miles farther on, close under the snow. I therefore determined to try to get up the gorge, to see whether there was any prospect of our being able to get through to the upper hills.

Just as we were starting a truly magnificent Kurd appeared on the scene, who told us he was Omar Aga's nephew, living temporarily in this village, and had heard from Hussein that I was in the country, and would probably visit his uncle. He was quite friendly, and told us he thought we might get up the gorge, but that it would be difficult. We then started, and finally did get up the pass, though only with the greatest difficulty, owing to the loose surface and the many big boulders. About 5 miles above the village we arrived on the *yaila*, a beautiful rolling upland plateau, where the grass was of exceptional quality. This plateau gradually sloped for some 10 miles upwards to the snow, and extended far away to the westward, where we could see still higher peaks rising from it.

The *yaila* itself was impassable for our cars on account of bogs and mud; and though we could see many large flocks of sheep and herds of cattle and horses grazing on the upper slopes, yet we could see no Kurdish camp, that being doubtless hidden in some fold in the ground. We therefore turned and made the best of our way down the pass again, stopping at the village to notify Omar Aga's nephew that I was anxious to meet his uncle, and that I would come to the foot of the valley on the banks of the Aras the next day at 2 P. M., in the hope that Omar

Aga himself would ride down and meet me there. He agreed to take this message to him, and we reached Khagizman again just after nightfall.

Next day, on arriving at the mouth of the valley, an imposing array of mounted Kurds was awaiting us—fifty at least, all apparently leading men, magnificently mounted, and armed with efficient modern weapons. They were apparently rather nervous, and did not move to meet us, but remained mounted and drawn up under some trees in rather an ominous-looking line. I therefore halted about 50 yards from them, and having brought two cars with me, and six reliable men in addition to my interpreter, I drew the cars up broadside to the Kurds, so that they could see their armoured appearance, and had the gun-ports open and the guns trained in their direction. Having completed this manœuvre, I then advanced towards them, when my friend of the night before came to meet me and presented me to his uncle.

The latter needs a description, as he was a most unprepossessing-looking ruffian. About sixty-five years of age, his features wore an evil expression, and he evidently possessed a fiery temper, of which the other Kurds were obviously terrified. He received me with just the barest civility, and we sat down on bundles of osiers which had been cut for the purpose on the river bank, and commenced our conversation. He began by asking me what the devil I was doing in his country, and what the Allies meant by announcing to the Armenians that in future his country was to become theirs. Without allowing me time to reply, he said then that, though he was prepared to submit to a mandate being granted to any of the Great Powers, yet he would never submit to any Armenian authority, but would cut the throat of every Armenian who came within his reach, and intended, if they did not leave Khagizman, to attack them there and kill them all. This was a pretty good start, I thought, and as he was working himself into a rage which made him appear more of a murderer than ever, I took the precaution of glancing at my men before answering.

I saw them standing steadily to their guns, ready to "let fly" on the first sign of trouble; and I felt a comforting certainty that they held the life of every Kurd present in their hands; so I turned to this ferocious villain with considerably more con-

## INTELLIGENCE IN TRANSCAUCASIA 205

fidence than would otherwise have been possible, and told him that I noted his views, and the spirit in which he put them forward, and that I came to his country to see what was the real state of things existing there, so that a proper report might be rendered, in order to enable the Great Powers to arrive at a correct decision in the face of the many conflicting reports hitherto received from other sources, and, further, that a decision would certainly be come to as soon as reliable reports were forthcoming.

This he took in good part, but I then went on to say that if in the meanwhile he continued his practices of wholesale murder and robbery all over the countryside, the only real certainty, amongst many uncertainties, was that, whatever European Power might undertake a mandate for that part of the world, their first action would be to round him up and shoot him! This caused general uproar, and Omar Aga half rose from his seat, at which my N.C.O. leapt from his car and stood well out in front, ready to give the order to fire. This action was observed and immediately understood by the Kurds, and had a steadying effect on them all. So, pointing to the cars and machine-guns, I went on to explain that they were "covered" by the guns, and that my men had orders to fire without further instructions from me if they judged me to be in danger.

That kind of attitude was appreciated at once, and things then quieted down and became much easier. A little while afterwards the old fire-eater became quite friendly, and eventually consented to come and stand with a selection of his supporters by one of the cars to be photographed with me under the British Flag. So all ended peaceably, and we went our several ways, each, no doubt, having learned more of the other's ways in one short hour that afternoon than years could have achieved by any other means.

We left Khagizman next morning to return to our railway camp at Zivin, about 150 miles distant; but the double journey to Omar Aga's valley had used up our reserve of petrol, and we found we had only enough to take *one* car as far as the Armenian post in the mountains, beyond Hussein's country, from whence we should be able to telephone to Kars for a fresh supply. Actually, however, our supply in the one car gave out in the pass, some miles below the Armenian post, which we finally only reached by the help of a horse, who towed the car up. We then camped there for the night, sending petrol back to Khagizman for the other car as soon as it arrived from Kars the next day, and all reached our camp at Zivin the next night, without further incident. Here we found the railway on the Armenian side of the frontier now open, and I at once telegraphed to Erzeroum to have the breech-blocks of the Turkish guns and the other armament dispatched to the frontier to be ready for transhipment to the Armenian trains, which were at the same time ordered to be brought down the pass for the purpose.

On my arrival at our camp at Zivin I found many reports that a state of open war between the Kurds and Armenians existed along the frontier to the north, and I also received further complaints from Kiazim Pasha as to the treatment Moslems were then receiving at the hands of the Armenians throughout the northern portion of Kars Province. I therefore arranged to proceed into the higher mountains in the north at once, and, for that purpose, had to recross the main pass, the only access for vehicles to the northern portion of the wild frontier district being from Kars Plain.

The northern half of the Province of Kars consists of a mountainous frontier country known as the Olti District, which has an exclusively Kurdish population. In the plain below, however, the majority of the inhabitants are Tartars, although many purely Armenian villages are to be found scattered over the plain. The Tartars are Moslems of the same "Sunni" sect as the Kurds and Turks, but differ from them both, as they belong to no definite tribes, but have gradually dribbled into the country from the East in comparatively modern times.

These are the people whom we have seen in the earlier chapters, incited by the Turks and drilled by German instructors, massing to attack Armenian refugees at Alexandropol. Their plans were then defeated by the dispatch of a British brigade from Tiflis to Kars and the arrest of the Moslem Parliament, or "Shura," which the Tartar population had set up there, with the object of establishing a new and independent Moslem Republic. The arrival of this British brigade was followed by the announcement that Kars Province had been allotted by the Supreme Council of the Allies to the Armenians, and that an-

## INTELLIGENCE IN TRANSCAUCASIA 207

nouncement having been made, the British troops were then completely withdrawn, and Armenian occupation commenced. Hence all the trouble; for the Armenians at once commenced the wholesale robbery and persecution of the Moslem population on the pretext that it was necessary to forcibly deprive them of their arms. In the portion of the province which lies in the plains they were able to carry out their purpose, and the manner in which this was done will be referred to in due course; but on approaching the Olti District, which lies in the mountains, they found themselvés face to face with the true Kurds of the Olti and Ardahan Mountains, under their Chief Eyeeb Pasha, who at once occupied the frontier of their own territory in force, and brought the advance of the Armenian armed rabble—soldiers only in name—to a sudden and very definite halt.

Such was the position when we started for Eyeeb's country, and it was quite evident that the trip was going to be extremely instructive and interesting. At that time I had not the pleasure of Eyeeb's personal acquaintance, but I knew much about him, and had little doubt that if I could once get into his country, without having any trouble whilst passing through his line, I should probably be well received by him, and should learn much upon which to base an opinion as to the possibilities of the future.

We therefore left Zivin about midday, and, going through the pass, proceeded out on to the plain as if bound for Kars. About 10 miles from the mountains, however, we left the main road in the dusk and turned north across country, swinging back towards the mountains so as to strike them about 20 miles north of the pass, at a place where I knew large *yailas* existed on the upland plateaux upon which all the Kurdish tribes would surely be encamped at this season. The boundary of Eyeeb's Olti country is a ridge of hills which rises out of the plain and forms the edge of the upland country; this ridge rises steeply about 1,200 feet above the plain, and we ascended it by moonlight, following an insignificant goat-track, which, after infinite difficulty, we succeeded at last in successfully negotiating.

This particular ascent remains in my memory as the most difficult I have ever successfully undertaken with motor-cars under their own power. The track was in places so much inclined on the hillside that it was necessary in order to keep the cars upright on their wheels to attach a rope to the upper part of the car bodies; this, held by men higher up the slope, served to prevent the vehicles turning over sideways and rolling down the hill. This method was adopted as I could not allow the men to endanger their lives by attempting to support the cars from the lower side. The ropes, however, proved very successful, and having finally reached the *yaila,* we soon found a spring, and camped in the open close to it, just as dawn was breaking. Having then carefully hoisted our British flag at the top of the tent-pole, all hands were soon fast asleep, having perfect confidence that "George" would give us instant notice of the approach of any stranger.

The sun had been up some hours when I awoke and sallied forth, to find the rest of the camp all peacefully sleeping, whilst about a quarter of a mile away was a party of mounted Kurds, driving some sheep and evidently watching for the first sign of movement in our camp. On my appearance they at once advanced, saying they came from Eyeeb Pasha, who, having heard of our arrival, bid us welcome to his country and sent us six sheep as a present, asking, at the same time, at what time it would be convenient to me for him to call and pay his respects. This was a most welcome and much appreciated civility on his part, and, it then being past ten o'clock, I sent back a message that I should be very pleased to receive him at any time convenient to him after 4 P.M. I then woke the men, and all went busily to work to render our camp presentable.

Our good carpets were spread, and some chairs, which we had this time brought from our train, were got out, and, our arms and cars having been cleaned, by afternoon the camp presented quite an imposing appearance. The site, which we had chosen the night before, turned out in daylight to be a magnificent one, with the rolling green uplands at the back and the plain spread out below, visible for many miles; whilst beyond, in the blue haze of the far distance to the east, was dimly traced the faint outline of the great snow-covered peaks of Georgia. Towards 4 P.M. we observed a body of cavalry approaching, in line and in good order, over the hills to the north-west of us; they numbered about 250, and in advance of them rode four Chiefs. On their approach I went to meet them, and knew Eyeeb at once from the many descriptions I had received of him.

## INTELLIGENCE IN TRANSCAUCASIA 209

Among the many fine Kurds I have met, this Chief is the finest specimen of all. Not more than thirty years of age, he stands 6 feet 8 inches in his bare feet, is extremely active, and very intelligent, and the better I got to know him the more I appreciated the good-fortune of his tribe in having at their head a man so capable of safeguarding their interests in the extremely difficult times through which they must have to pass in the immediate future. The Pasha was very civil, and introduced me to his two uncles and a cousin, who, though none of them quite so tall as he was himself, were yet all cast in the same mould.

We then all sat down and had a most interesting conversation, from which I learned that he had upwards of 2,000 men then actually under arms, and was holding the frontier of his upland districts against the Armenian troops, who, having pillaged and destroyed all the Moslem villages in the plain, had announced their intention of acting in a similar manner with respect to his hill-country, which was to be included in the territory placed under Armenian control by the Allies. Eyeeb declared that he and his people were prepared to defend their country with their lives, and that volunteers were daily joining them from other Kurdish tribes, who were ready to lend all the assistance in their power, foreseeing that their own fate would be dependent upon the success of his defence. Caravans of refugees were in the meanwhile constantly arriving from the plain, from which the whole Moslem population was fleeing with as much of their personal property as they could transport, seeking to obtain security and protection within his lines.

He further told me that in those Moslem villages in the plain below which had been searched for arms by the Armenians everything had been taken under the cloak of such search, and not only had many Moslems been killed, but horrible tortures had been inflicted in the endeavour to obtain information as to where valuables had been hidden, of which the Armenians were aware of the existence, although they had been unable to find them. He then strongly urged me to go myself to certain named villages recently attacked to verify his statements and to obtain evidence of the horrors which had been committed there. This was straight talking indeed, bearing out exactly the reports I was receiving from Kiazim Pasha, and I therefore determined to go down into the plain and to see for myself what was the position there at the earliest opportunity, and told Eyeeb Pasha at once that such was my intention.

He next begged me to come out and inspect the detachment of his men which he had brought with him, and to watch them manœuvre in their native hills. Horses were then brought, and I was offered a splendid liver-coloured chestnut mare of the very highest true Arab breed from Diabekir; she was furnished with a general service military saddle of unmistakable British manufacture, and had her lovely foal at foot, as is the custom in the East.

I then proceeded to review the regiment, which was drawn up in single rank, with their leaders one horse's length in front of the line. I was much impressed by the condition of both the men and the horses, and do not know which I admired the most, both being equally full of quality and courage and showing their breeding unmistakably. Their saddlery and equipment, however, was of very poor description, though their rifles, which were, as usual, carried slung over their shoulders, were all modern and fitted with magazines. I noted English, French, Italian, Russian, German, and Turkish rifles amongst them, so that there was no uniformity, a matter of less importance there than it would be elsewhere, as ammunition-trains are unknown in the mountains, and each man carries 300, and sometimes even 500, rounds in bandoliers slung over his shoulders and in belts round his waist. In fact, a Kurd's financial position can approximately be judged by the number of bandoliers he carries, the cartridges themselves being frequently used as money amongst all these tribes, where coins or notes are few and far between.

After the inspection Eyeeb asked me if I would like to see the regiment "on the move," and, if so, what form of exercise I would suggest. At that moment we were standing on a very good defensive position on a ridge commanding the ground for several miles; I therefore intimated that I should much like to see them treat us as an enemy, and attack the position we were then occupying. To this he at once assented, and, having spoken to his two uncles, the regiment then divided, one uncle going to the right with one party and the other leading the remainder

## INTELLIGENCE IN TRANSCAUCASIA

to the left, all moving off at a hand-canter and being quickly lost to sight on the undulating surface of the *yaila*.

A very short time afterwards small parties appearing momentarily on the sky-line in various directions announced that the advance had begun. Evidently these Kurds were well trained and thoroughly at home in their work, for they took advantage of every piece of favourable ground and of all cover, so that at no time during their advance would they have been exposed to any damaging fire; and finally, a shot having been fired at a signal, the whole body came over the last ridge about 300 yards from us in line, as hard as ever their horses could gallop, and charged home on our position with much cheering, firing their rifles in the air in true Eastern style, and at the same time yelling like madmen. Having expressed my hearty approval of their methods and training and thus made friends with these interesting people, we adjourned to my camp, where their sheep were by this time roasting.

The whole party bivouacked round us that night, and the Pasha's two uncles expressed a wish to sleep in my tent—as a guarantee of my safety, they said. I, of course, accepted their offer with every appearance of gratitude, though it was a courtesy with which I could have very well dispensed. Eyeeb himself gave the old Scriptural excuse that he "had just married a new wife," and returned to his own house, about 10 miles off, saying he would ride over next morning, as in the afternoon we were to have an exhibition of their national game of "Djerrid."

Next morning I had a long talk with Bekir Bey, the eldest uncle, and learned from him the different localities in which it would be advisable to search for evidence of the atrocities lately committed in the plain, after which we had out my own machine-guns, and I gave them an exhibition of what my men could do with them. This created an astonishing impression on the whole band, both on account of the accuracy and rate of fire which were achieved, and many were the quaint grunts and snorts uttered as a rock on the hillside, 600 yards away, at which we fired, rapidly disintegrated under the heavy and accurate shower of our bullets.

Soon after midday, whilst we were resting preparatory to the afternoon's excitement, Bekir appeared in a great state of excitement, saying a caravan of Moslem refugees was just coming up the hill from the plain, seeking refuge in Eyeeb's lines, having been warned that an Armenian force had started from Kars with the object of "disarming" their villages. I should therefore be able to look and judge for myself of their condition.

Shortly afterwards the head of the miserable column appeared. There were in all about 200 persons, mostly old men and women and children, with a few ox-carts, ponies, and donkeys, carrying all their worldly possessions, except a few sheep that they were driving before them. Their leader interviewed Bekir Bey, and was told to keep farther on into the hills, where he would be able to cross the frontier into Turkey unmolested by his enemies.

Whilst listening to their conversation, there occurred an incident which strikingly illustrates the absolute authority wielded by the Chiefs of these old Kurdish tribes.

Bekir, without a word of warning, suddenly dashed away from my side and ran toward a spot where a group of his men had suddenly collected, calling at the same time to his younger nephew and yelling out orders. He then returned and apologized for leaving me so suddenly, saying that he had seen some of his men catch a sheep belonging to the refugees and cut its throat, and that it was necessary for him to hurry, or it would have been all cut up and distributed before he could have stopped it. "You will see now," he said, "how we treat a robber who robs amongst his own tribe, for these refugees are our guests whilst passing through our country, and are therefore sacred."

A procession then appeared of three parties, each consisting of four men. Each party carried a pair of rifles lashed close together, whilst between each pair of rifles protruded the naked feet of one of the robbers who had been caught in the act, and who were thus dragged forward on their backs with their feet in the air. Bekir Bey then himself took a heavy stick nearly as thick as his wrist, and each pair of feet was lifted shoulder-high by its bearers, the Chief laid into the soles of each of the robber's feet just as hard as ever he could hit, whilst the rest looked on in silence, saying only "Khirsizlar" (thieves). When the old Chief was tired he gave the order to cast them loose, and then began a torrent of language from the robbers of which I was only able to understand a part. It appeared that

## INTELLIGENCE IN TRANSCAUCASIA  213

these men did not belong to Eyeeb's own tribe, but to a neighbouring one, and were in the nature of volunteers come to help Eyeeb's men in the defence of their country; they therefore considered their treatment shameful. Bekir, however, "went for" them like a tiger-cat, and cursed them in a hill vocabulary quite new to me, telling them that they had broken the law of hospitality common to all Kurds, and had got off much lighter than would have been the case had Eyeeb himself been present.

Two of the culprits took this very quietly, and had nothing to say; but the third, a very burly-looking ruffian, said he would not remain, but should go off and call his tribe to arms to avenge him. This sally was received with jeers, and, somewhat to my surprise, he was told to go if he wished. On hearing this he made off on his hands and knees over the grass up the steep hill behind the tent, his feet being for the moment "out of action." When he had succeeded in painfully climbing up about 100 yards, Bekir called four of his men by name and gave them an order, on which they promptly lay down and commenced firing at the man, hitting the ground close to and all round him, whilst Bekir called out to know if it still was his intention to try and go and raise his tribe against them, or whether he was prepared to come back. On which he at once turned round and crawled back. This incident, so illuminating as to the methods by which discipline is enforced amongst these wild tribes, then closed and was promptly forgotten.

In the afternoon Eyeeb arrived, and all was made ready for the national game of "Djerrid." This I had already seen played at Erzeroum by the Turks, as every Friday, which is, of course, the Moslem "Sabah" or Sunday, all the "knuts" amongst the Turks, who fancy their horses or horsemanship, ride to a great open space within the fortifications. There the game is played, and invariably attracts a crowd of onlookers, and forms, in fact, the chief and most fashionable entertainment on Sunday evenings in summer.

The game is a kind of "Prisoners' Base" played on horseback, with any number on either side. No points are scored and there is no "winning side," but any inefficiency in horsemanship or any lack of enterprise on the part of the players is invariably greeted by derisive jeers from the crowd. The great peculiarity of the game is that, instead of a player being merely "touched," as in "Prisoners' Base," he has in this game to be "hit with a stick." All players are provided with about half a dozen sticks, called *djerrid*, as strong as heavy walking-sticks and of about the same length. A line, or "base," is marked out at each end of the ground, and any player leaving his base is at once pursued by one or more players from the other side, who gallop after him and endeavour to hit him with their sticks. The usual method adopted is to throw the sticks like javelins; but, should a player be fortunate enough to get within reach of an opponent, he will belabour him with real good-will, which invariably delights the crowd. As these manœuvres are all carried out at full gallop, and there are often many separate pursuits going on at the same time, there are frequent collisions and sensational falls, which afford the greatest delight to the onlookers, and form the principal attraction of the entertainment.

Having played polo regularly in many countries for over twenty years, the game appealed immensely to me, and though in my official capacity in Erzeroum I had not considered it advisable to take part in it with the Turks, yet here in the wild mountains, when Bekir Bey offered me again his beautiful Arab mare, I was only too delighted to accept his offer, and, having very considerably the best mount, I feel quite confident that I was, by that means, enabled to hold my own, to the great delight of the owner of the mare, the only complication being the presence of her foal, who followed her closely throughout, and although a perfect marvel of activity, yet got knocked over on several occasions.

We were all in the very middle of this most exciting pastime, when, quite suddenly, all riders stopped dead, as if turned to stone, every face at once becoming wreathed in smiles—a wonderful sight, absolutely characteristic of these tribes, and one which could only be produced by the prospect of a fight. The cause in this case was the sound of gunfire which suddenly echoed through the hills, indicating that a battery was in action somewhere within a mile or so of our playground.

Instantly every man flew to his arms, and within five minutes the troops were away up the hill, every man's face lit up with joy at the imminence of a fight, all singing their war-song, which to be justly appreciated must be heard as sung by those fighting robbers amongst their own wild echoing hills as they go into battle.

In the meanwhile our position became somewhat difficult, for it was evident that the Armenians from the plain were attacking the Kurdish line with artillery, with probably a large force in support. And therefore, much as we should have wished to join in, I decided to strike camp at once and make the best of our way back to the railway camp, trusting on the way we should meet our other car returning, which we had that morning sent in to bring out supplies.

Reaching Sarikamish, the Armenian frontier headquarters, about 35 miles from our late camp in the Kurd country, just before nightfall, we found our other car there, and were furious to hear, from the driver, that Armenian troops had attacked them and shot the corporal, afterwards proceeding to loot the car, which, as was evident from the many bullet-holes in it, had been subjected to a severe fire at short range. The driver had, as soon as he could find an Armenian officer, requested to be taken to their headquarters, and the wounded corporal had at once been dispatched from Sarikamish by train to hospital at Kars.

As he was there in good hands, I dispatched a telegram to the Armenian Commander-in-Chief, to the effect that he would be held responsible for the undisciplined and barbarous action of his troops, and made all haste to get back to Zivin, where I feared we should find the whole situation had now reached its climax, and that "all the fat was in the fire."

# CHAPTER VI

### THE TURKISH ARMISTICE A FIASCO—FOUNDATION OF THE NATIONALIST PARTY

Arrangements for evacuation of Turkish armament—Rumours of Erzeroum Conference—Turks refuse consent—Proceed to Erzeroum—Cable Commander-in-Chief, Constant—Cable Tiflis *re* Armenian atrocities on Moslems—Meet Commission appointed to investigate—Taken prisoner by Kurds—The armament is stolen—Commander-in-Chief's cable order to evacuate my men from Turkey—Proceed to Erzeroum—Interview with Kiazim and Mustapha Kemal—Result of Conference—The Nationalist Pact—Halt at Sarikamish—Ordered to Constant—Tiflis and Batoum—An American destroyer—Report to Commander-in-Chief—Orders for home—Dinner at Therapia—The Turkish train—Roumania and Bucarest—Journey to Trieste, Paris, and London.

We reached our camp at Zivin in the evening of July 24th, and next morning the railway officers whom I had left to superintend the reconstruction of the railway on each side of the frontier came in to report.

On the Armenian side, trains had been brought down to the frontier, and were only waiting for Turkish authorization to cross to receive the armament. This would have to be carried to them from the Turkish trains, which had already reached our railway camp on the southern side of the main fall of rock which blocked the line. I therefore telegraphed to Kiazim Pasha at Erzeroum, requesting that the transfer of the armament over the frontier should be authorized, and military working parties supplied for the purpose. I was very confident that this move would bring matters to a head, by forcing the Turks definitely to declare their attitude with respect to the fulfilment of the Armistice conditions, on their compliance with which it was my duty to insist.

In the meanwhile rumours were rife amongst the Turks as to the progress of the Conference then proceeding at Erzeroum, where had assembled representatives of the Young Turkish Party from all the Eastern vilayets( provinces), who were, it was said, organizing a revolution with the eventual object of establishing a Turkish Republic on the ruins of the old Ottoman Empire. Under there circumstances I was by no means surprised to receive, in the late evening of the 25th, a telegram from Kiazim Pasha. This was very carefully and ambiguously worded in Turkish, but the effect of it was to state that he was not authorized to permit the munitions to cross the frontier, and was therefore not in a position to comply with my request. Here, then, at last, was a definite refusal on a vital point, and I therefore replied at once that his action was "directly contrary to the terms of the Armistice granted to the Turkish Government at their own request, and, if persisted in, must bring the Armistice to an end." I concluded this very definite announcement by stating that I was leaving at once for Erzeroum, and would call upon him on my arrival. Our camp was therefore at once struck, and we reached Erzeroum in the evening of the 26th.

The next morning I had my interview with Kiazim. He was, as usual, very polite, but assured me he was not in a position to comply with my request, and, amongst other excuses, said that the Conference was now sitting and the whole country in a very disturbed state, so much so that he doubted if the population would allow the armament to cross the frontier into the Armenian country, even if he had been in a position to give the necessary orders. I thanked him, also politely, and intimated that it would be necessary for me to forward by cable an official dispatch to my Government, at the same time asking if he would have it sent for me over the Turkish wires. To this request he at once acceded, and I returned to my quarters, and drafted a cipher dispatch directly to Commander-in-Chief, Constantinople, its special urgency being emphasized by the magic words "Clear the line." This formula is very rarely resorted to, and then only in instances of extreme importance, for the effect is to give, the message so headed, precedence over all other telegrams of every description.

My message was to the effect that at the last moment I had met with a definite refusal to allow the armament to leave the country, and that I had in consequence declared that such action must automatically bring the Armistice to an end, and concluded by asking for instructions. Having handed this, in cipher, to Kiazim personally and obtained his receipt, I asked and obtained permission to telephone orders over the Turkish military line to my officers still on the frontier to rejoin my headquarters at once.

As soon as I got into communication with my officer on the frontier, I very carefully spelt out my cipher dispatch to him over the phone, and instructed him to get it sent to our Army Headquarters at Tiflis by the Armenians, to be forwarded from there to Constantinople via Batoum, and afterwards to return to Tiflis himself and to send the other railway officer, who was on the frontier in charge of the armament trains on the Turkish line, to rejoin my headquarters at Erzeroum. The next day I had a long and most interesting interview with Mustapha Kemal with respect to the Conference then proceeding, and he undertook to furnish me with any formal decision which might eventually be arrived at. This was quite satisfactory as far as it went, and left me free to return to the frontier, where events were now moving apace.

Before leaving Zivin on receipt of Kiazim's telegram *re* armament, I had received further very definite information of horrors that had been committed by the Armenian soldiery in Kars Plain, and as I had been able to judge of their want of discipline by their treatment of my own detached parties, I had wired to Tiflis from Zivin that "in the interests of humanity the Armenians should not be left in independent command of the Moslem population, as, their troops being without discipline and not under effective control, atrocities were constantly being committed, for which we should with justice eventually be held to be morally responsible."

The result of this report was that on the 28th I received a wire from Tiflis, to the effect that a commission under a Lieut.-Colonel with a small body of British troops was being sent from Tiflis to inspect the district, and to gather evidence of the conditions obtaining there, at the same time instructing me to meet the commission at Sarikamish, the terminus of the Tiflis railway in the mountains, for the purpose of furnishing them with information. On the 29th, therefore, I once more returned to the frontier hills, and, having met the commission at Sarikamish, gave them all information as to where to seek for evidence of atrocities, which, I subsequently learned, they were only too successful in obtaining.

FRONTIER SCENES

A halt for lunch. The corporal, in shirt-sleeves on the right, was shot that afternoon and the car pierced by thirteen bullets

Prisoners again, in spite of the white flag—a bath-towel

The descent to Zivin

# RETURN TO CONSTANTINOPLE

Leaving our headquarters at Erzeroum

The entrance to the Bosphorus from the Black Sea, taken from the American destroyer

The Bosphorus at Therapia

## INTELLIGENCE IN TRANSCAUCASIA

Before returning to Erzeroum, it seemed advisable to see how the fight had progressed in the mountains since our hurried departure from Eyeeb's camp. Instead, therefore, of returning directly through the pass, we struck out to the north by an old ox-cart track which followed the main line of the hills high up on their now grassy slopes, and, passing through the Armenain lines, camped for the night on a high *yaila* between the Armenian and Kurdish lines.

Next day we proceeded to enter Eyeeb's country from the south, by a very difficult track, which very soon got us into trouble through the breaking of a radius rod on one of the cars. This brought us to a halt for repairs, in some marshy ground infested with every kind of bug and fly, and we soon became aware also of a very considerable, although irregular, fire, which was being carried on from the ridge of the slope we were about to ascend. I took no notice of this, as such incidents, of course, come "all in the day's work" in those parts; but after a while one of the men remarked to me: "Do you know, sir, those d——d Kurds are firing at *us?*" I said that I did *not* know it, as, though I could very well hear the thud of a bullet hitting the rising ground behind us every now and again, yet there was nothing to be seen, and the firing, whatever its object, was a good way off as yet; also they were possibly, at that distance, unable to see my one and only bath-towel, which flew as a big white flag from a pole on the leading car.

I then proceeded to point out to the men the peak of Mount Ararat, just visible in the extreme south-east as the sun shone on the snow, and I started telling them about Noah and his ark, which was supposed to have rested there after the Flood, into which he took with him a pair of every kind of animal, to which action we owed all the animals we now had. This story, of course, was told to distract their attention from the firing, which was getting closer, but my tale had no success at all compared with that of a remark of one of the men, who came from "Zummerzet" and was an acknowledged wit. He said old Noah was all right, but he wished the old beggar had forgotten to take a pair of these blankety-blank *flies* with him! This sally was greeted with a genuine roar of laughter, for, as our halt had taken place in a marshy bit of ground, we were at the time all being literally *eaten* by every kind of insect.

In the meanwhile the firing was getting brisker, and, as they were evidently now getting within more accurate range, it became necessary to take steps of some sort to either put an end to it or to return it before any one was hit, which might now happen at any moment. I therefore ordered the men to lie down, and went and stood out on the grass beside the road, waving my empty hands, at the same time ordering the interpreter to wave our improvised white flag. It was for a time a somewhat unpleasant position, and I began to think it would soon become necessary to bring our machine-guns into action if it continued. Fortunately, however, the fire then ceased altogether, and the interpreter, a Russian named Marr, a very brave man, who had seen much fighting, volunteered to advance towards the rocks from whence the heaviest fire had proceeded, and to parley with the Kurds. This he very gallantly did, and after a while I joined him, and it was agreed that we should go on and see a Chief who was to be found over the ridge in front of us.

Thither we went, and found the party who had been firing at us were some of Eyeeb's Kurds, though they had not been amongst those we had met before. On reaching their bivouac I received a nasty shock, as I found the Commander to be the German officer who was responsible for all their training, and whom I had seen in camp with Eyeeb, though he had then been very surly and had refused to talk. He told me we must consider ourselves prisoners as an advance was about to begin, but that I might pitch my tent by the side of his bivouac, and he would send in to Eyeeb's camp for orders. I then begged him to send a note to the Pasha from me, which he consented to do. He then moved off to proceed with what appeared to be an attack on the Armenian position on a front of 4 or 5 miles in very hilly and difficult country.

We could see nothing of the fight except shells bursting on the hill-tops all round, but the sound of much firing, and occasional cheering, rose out of the deep valleys below, so we concluded the Kurds were enjoying themselves. We saw no more of the German till next day, when he turned up about midday an ordered our release, telling me they had driven the Armenians back about 5 miles, and were now threatening Sarikamish and the main pass, of which they hoped to get possession within the next few days.

As soon as we were released, we set off by another route to our camp at Zivin, which we reached the same night, to find unpleasant news. It appeared that, soon after our departure, the armament train, in charge of our railway officer and two men, had been surrounded by what he described as "brigands," and he and his men had been placed under guard in a railway-carriage, whilst these apparent brigands produced a caravan of general service waggons drawn by *mules*, and carted all the armament off into the mountains; after which he and his men were released and told to get over the frontier out of the country as quickly as they could. This they had expressed themselves very ready to do, and had come at once to report to me.

I also received a message from Kiazim to the effect that this incident had already been reported to him, and that he believed that the population had now taken the matter into their own hands and had made off with the armament, sooner than allow it to cross the frontier. This was, no doubt, very plausible and difficult to disprove. I had been long enough in the country, however, to know that there were no general service waggons to be found in it, other than those attached to the army, and no mules at all except amongst the army transport. I therefore kept my own counsel and accepted his expressions of regret, as I saw no object to be gained by making accusations which I was not in a position to prove.

On August 5th arrived the long-expected answer from the Commander-in-Chief at Constant; this arrived in cipher via Tiflis, and was brought by an Armenian officer as far as the frontier post. It was in answer to my telephone dispatch, which had gone safely through via Tiflis, no news at all having been received through the Turks. It gave me definite orders to get all my men out of the country at once, and to subsequently watch the situation from Kars District. I therefore rang up Erzeroum on the military telephone, and ordered my headquarters to move at once to Sarikamish, as many as possible by train, and the horses by road, with just sufficient guard for their safety. I also sent a message to Kiazim, asking him to afford us the necessary facilities for the move by rail, and advising him that I would come to Erzeroum myself, the next day, to take leave of him.

On the morning of the 6th our camp at Zivin was finally struck, and the party proceeded over the frontier and up the pass for the last time, with orders to camp in the Sarikamish Valley alongside the Armenian headquarters, whilst I proceeded, with one car and driver only, to make what was to be my last entry into Erzeroum from the east. The ground now being dry, we travelled fast, and had done the 75 miles by 2 P. M., and I had my interview with Kiazim Pasha, the Turkish Army Commander, at 3.30. This passed off civilly and quietly, and we parted good friends. From him I learned that the Conference was to conclude that night, and that it would rise at 5 P. M.

On leaving him, therefore, I obtained an interview with Mustapha Kemal on the rising of the Conference. This was of extreme interest, and lasted three hours and a half. It took place in his private house, Réouf Bey, the late Minister of Marine, who was then living in the same house with Mustapha Kemal, being present part of the time. We discussed all the possibilities of the future, and the eventual aspirations of the new Nationalist Party. Kemal told me of the National "Pact," which had been adopted that day. This "Pact" had been then put forward for the first time, and it has ever since formed the main object of the Nationalists, and the end to which all their efforts and diplomacy have been, and are still, directed. He promised me that he would have the final text telegraphed for me to the frontier next day, which undertaking was scrupulously carried out. We then parted, with every civility, both appreciating the gravity of the developments which the future certainly held in store.

On the morning of the 7th, having seen the party in charge of the horses all ready to start on their four days' march by road, the remainder having left by rail on the previous day, I got away myself with my single car soon after 8 A. M., and reached Sarikamish, over 90 miles distant, before 3 P. M., where I found the party from Zivin quartered in a very fair Russian barrack building allotted to them by the Armenian Commander. The next day was spent in inspecting Sarikamish, which had been the great central camp of the Imperial Russian frontier forces in this district, where the country much resembles some parts of Switzerland, the mountains being heavily wooded and the valleys green and fertile.

The Sarikamish Valley itself, when the Russians first made a camp of it, some forty years ago, was a bad swamp, and one of the most fever-stricken spots in those mountains; but thanks to their excellent system of drainage it is all now dry and firm, and has become about the healthiest place in the whole province. The buildings also are excellent, and although almost entirely constructed of timber, they are well designed and both original and picturesque, so that we looked forward at last to both comfortable and healthy quarters.

However, at about 6.30 P. M. on the 8th, having been there one night only, these fine dreams were all knocked on the head, for I received a wire from Constant, via Tiflis, instructing me to come there at once to report. This meant, pretty certainly, that I should be for London direct, and within ten minutes I had obtained a train from the Armenian Commander, and an hour after was in it, saying good-bye to my invaluable men, whom it was sad indeed to leave behind, but whom I was able to assure that they would now soon follow me.

My train, consisting only of an engine and one cattle-truck, travelled fast, and we reached Tiflis about 1 P. M. next day. On arrival I reported to General Beach, and having written a rapid report on the whole situation for local information, and also translated Mustapha Kemal's copy of the National Pact, which was afterwards to become so famous, I caught the night train from Tiflis, and reached Batoum once more early on August 10th, having been absent about four months.

It was necessary to wait two nights only at Batoum, as I was fortunate enough on the third day to get a passage on an American destroyer which was proceeding to Constant. Leaving at midday on the 12th, the entrance to the Bosphorus was in sight soon after daylight on the 14th, and anything more beautiful than our run up that unique waterway in the early hours of an August morning it would be impossible to imagine.

The American destroyer had brought us most comfortably, running at an easy cruising speed of 18 knots, the internal combustion engines not causing the slightest vibration, and the Commander and all on board being most pleasant and hospitable. The only possible "fly in the ointment" was the fact that she was a "dry" ship, which was no fault of our hosts, but the result of the decision of their electorate at home, who are no doubt most particularly well situated to understand the conditions their vessels encounter abroad. Those conditions, however, did not disturb me, as I had long since become accustomed to dispensing with the ordinary luxuries of civilization.

We anchored off Top Khaneh (the gun-house), which lies in Galata, at the entrance to the Golden Horn, and had then become the headquarters of the Ordnance Department of the British forces, soon after 10 A. M., and I at once got a car and reported at G.H.Q. in Pera. After a long and most interesting conversation with the Commander-in-Chief, in the course of which he told me that he had received a cable from the War Office to the effect that my brother, who was then acting as Commander-in-Chief in charge of the evacuation of our troops from Archangel, had applied for me to be attached to his expedition, and that I was to be sent there if and when convenient. This subject having then been put aside for the moment, I proceeded to make a full report of the state of affairs in the Eastern vilayets and the frontier generally. I produced the text I had obtained from Mustapha Kemal of the Nationalist "Pact," which he had explained to me would form the platform of their party, and would be presented to, and certainly confirmed by, conferences to be subsequently held in other parts of the country, the first of which was fixed to take place during the month of September at Sivas, a large city about 300 miles west of Erzeroum, on the road to Angora.

I was, of course, unable to vouch for the accuracy of Mustapha's record of the actual decisions arrived at, nor as to their being the *only* ones settled or discussed at the Erzeroum Conference. The only real fact which I was able to emphasize and guarantee was that here, at first hand, was the text of the "Pact" in the form in which Mustapha, as President of the Conference, desired me to transmit it to my Government. This, of course, was much, and the Chief at once decided that I should proceed home immediately by the quickest route, and report to the War Office, and probably to the Foreign Office also.

He gave me a much-appreciated invitation to dine with him

at his country quarters at Therapia the same night, and also told me he was very well satisfied with the work done, and had recommended me for a suitable recognition of service. This, of course, was good hearing for me, as I had been very anxious lest I might not have been able to give him satisfaction, in the face of the unexpectedly difficult political situation with which I had found myself confronted. The remainder of the day was spent in seeing my friends, and in ascertaining which was the quickest method of reaching London, the first step being to ascertain whether any ship, naval or otherwise, was sailing in the next few days, as the railway was not yet open through Serbia, and a transcontinental trip would therefore mean a circuitous journey of uncertain duration.

During my absence in the Caucasus and Anatolia the old Salonika Expeditionary Force had blossomed out into the Army of the Black Sea, and was in process of rapid reduction in strength by demobilization, so that I found many of my friends had left, and only one officer of the intelligence mess who had been there when I left still remained on my return. However, I was accommodated with a good room at the old "I" mess, and was provided with a car to take me to dinner with the Chief at Therapia in the evening.

The drive from Constant to Therapia is about 12 miles, and is by no means beautiful at most times of the year, as the road runs high up amongst rounded hills of no particular interest, the magnificent waters of the Bosphorus remaining entirely hidden from view in the winding valley through which they flow. On this lovely August evening, however, all seemed wonderful, and when, after descending the steep and narrow valley through which the road finally reaches the Bosphorus at Therapia, more green trees and fields, and eventually the blue water itself, came into sight, the scene formed indeed a striking contrast to the bleak mountains to which I had lately become so accustomed.

The Commander-in-Chief occupied a fine and spacious house, standing on a terrace actually overlooking the water. This house is much like a really good English country-house, with a large galleried hall in the centre. It was built as his summer residence by the representative in Turkey of Messers. Krupp, the great German manufacturing firm, who had provided the

Turkish Army with its armaments, and is fitted in the same way as any first-class residence in Europe would be whose owner enjoyed the same practically unlimited financial resources to draw upon.

We sat, before dinner, upon the terrace overlooking the Bosphorus, which on this peaceful summer evening was looking its very best. The water was quite calm and of the deepest blue, and the hills on both sides were clothed with shrubs and trees in full flower and leaf, all blending most harmoniously together in the twilight glow as the sun sank behind the hills, the whole scene producing a most striking impression of restful peace and exceptional beauty.

At dinner I reported to the Chief that no ships would be sailing for some time, but that I had ascertained that a King's Messenger would be leaving within two days, travelling overland, and that if he saw no objection I proposed to go with him. To this he agreed at once, saying he would give instructions for the necessary letters to be prepared for me to take to the War Office.

During dinner many subjects were discussed, the Chief showing himself to be in as perfect touch with the actual political situation in every part of the Near East as he was in hesitating doubt as to what might be the eventual, but as yet undeclared, policy of the diplomats at home. I drove back afterwards to Constant in the moonlight with feelings of the greatest loyalty to him, but of irrepressible dissatisfaction and wonder at the unaccountable delay which was occurring in the adoption of any definite line of policy on the part of the Allies which must always be an indispensable preliminary to the conclusion of any permanent peace. This delay was even then causing untold suffering and misery to many thousands of innocent people, dislocating all commerce in what should naturally be the greatest trading centre in the East, and heavily discounting the value of those successes which had been so dearly purchased during the Great War.

Next day I obtained my letters for the War Office, the necessary passes and passports, and also full information as to the route to be followed, from which I learned that, the bridges not yet having been repaired, the direct railway route, via Sophia and Belgrade, to Trieste was not yet open, and it would

## INTELLIGENCE IN TRANSCAUCASIA 227

be necessary to take a line branching from the main line north of Adrianople, and reaching the Danube at Rustchuk. Here the river would be crossed by boat, and a motor-car from Bucarest would meet us on landing and convey us to that city, whence we could take a train running north through the Roumanian oil district and crossing the Transylvanian Alps, afterwards traversing the great plain of Hungary via Zegedin. Recrossing the Danube, we could then proceed via Agram and so reach Trieste, from whence the Simplon Express would take us to Paris.

This was estimated to take eight days, though this estimate was admitted to be rather optimistic. The journey, in fact, took ten, but, though rough, it was full of interest, for the conditions existing in most of the countries traversed were at that time somewhat "unsettled," and considerable uncertainty existed as to our rate of progress, and also even as to our eventual safe arrival.

I joined the King's Messenger, who was to be my companion on the journey, next morning at the station. He had lately been a Lieut.-Colonel in the army, and, though only temporarily acting as King's Messenger, had already done the overland journey several times under similar conditions. He confided to me at the station that he had come provided with certain special and indispensable supplies, the necessity of which he had learned by experience, and we then together examined the compartment reserved for us in the little train which was to take us to the Danube.

The carriage and compartment appeared to me to be most luxurious, after the cattle-trucks in which I had long been accustomed to travel, the upholstery being of a soft material having the appearance of tapestry, and the seats provided with spring cushions covered with the same material. On entering, he produced, before sitting down, a bag containing quantity of tins of Mr. Keating's invaluable preparation of powder, and with these he commenced to thoroughly dress the walls, seats, and carpets, using many tins, and telling me that, though he had purchased the entire supply available, yet he much doubted whether it would prove sufficient, as this carriage was in a very bad state. This he demonstrated by holding up one of the cushions, of which I had so much admired the luxurious appearance, at arm's length for my inspection, when I realized at once that it was literally "moving" with vermin.

After this gratifying demonstration, I should vastly have preferred travelling in a bare cattle-truck, which one could at least have washed out with some buckets of water in the usual manner, but, as no other accommodation was available, we had to make the best we could of this already thickly populated compartment.

The first step was to purchase a quantity of newspapers, which we spread everywhere, upon which we took our seats, hoping that "Mr. Keating" was carrying out his good work successfully underneath, as if he should succeed in gaining for us the immunity he claimed to ensure from the attentions of our noxious fellow-passengers, the unpleasant smell of his preparation would be an insignificant price to pay for his services.

We then started, at 8 A. M., and spent a very dreary and tedious forty-three hours in that carriage, although our defensive measures proved entirely successful, and Mr. Keating entirely justified his wide reputation for efficiency. The journey was carried out through Thrace at an exasperatingly slow speed, with long and frequent halts in that desolate country, but after the first twenty-four hours, as we began to approach the Balkan Mountains, the country presented a more fertile and cultivated appearance. The ascent of the pass over the Balkans was effected at a foot's pace, but the scenery was grand, and the great engineering difficulties which had been successfully surmounted by the original constructors of the railway were appreciated by us to the full.

Once over the summit, our speed improved, and in the northern foot-hills the views we obtained were frequently of great beauty, whilst the large farms and residences scattered about in prominent sites as we descended into the Danube Valley bore evidence to the natural richness of that part of Bulgaria, which, in the plain, appeared to be everywhere under some degree of cultivation, although it was mostly of a somewhat elementary description.

We reached the town of Rustchuk between 3 and 4 A. M. on the third day, and after a few hours' rest boarded the steamer which was to take us across the great river. The Danube here is three or four times the width of the Euphrates at Bussrah, and as our landing-place was some miles farther down the stream, our passage took us forty-five minutes at least, for the current, in view of the width of the river, ran with surprising strength. Arrived on the northern bank, we found, to my surprise, the Roumanian town where we had landed had been much knocked about by artillery-fire during Mackensen's successful Roumanian campaign.

An open motor-car was awaiting us on the quay, and we quickly started on our drive of something under 100 miles to Bucarest, across the richest agricultural district of Roumania. From the very start our driver drove as if we were starting in a race, with the result that shortly after the start, when only about 12 miles from the river, a loud report signified a back tyre had burst from the heat, and we were in for a long halt and repair.

This was interesting, as it enabled us to get a look at the Roumanian peasantry amongst their native surroundings.

The most salient point about them was that they appeared well nourished and clothed, and generally of a quite "affluent" appearance, a most remarkable fact in view of the late occupation of their country by the army of their German invaders.

The land on this plain is undoubtedly as rich as any in Europe, and we found it everywhere well cultivated with an intensive cultivation of a kind of which few countries can boast. Seventy-five per cent. of the crops were of maize, which had grown to a great height and appeared to be a heavier crop than any I had ever seen elsewhere. Of course, therein lay the affluence of the inhabitants, as the maize furnishes all their requirements, constituting the staple food of both man and beast, and commanding a rich and ready market in every part of the world. The villages were well built and in good repair, having here, in this part of Roumania, suffered little, if at all, from the curse of war which had brought desolation in its train to every other country over which it had passed.

After a good half-hour's delay we continued our journey at a more reasonable speed, and had therefore more time to observe the farms and villages, and occasionally large country-houses, which everywhere presented the same aspect of calm prosperity, and finally we reached the town of Bucarest and proceeded to the headquarters of the British Mission in that city.

I here learned that it would be necessary for me to personally attend at no less than five Embassies to get my passport *viséd*, and that upon my being able to do that before 5 P. M., when the offices would close, depended the possibility of getting away the next day by the one train which went daily, through Trieste, and which left at 8 A. M.

Having with great difficulty, as the town was full to overflowing, obtained a room at an hotel rejoicing in the name of "Excelsior," where the food, furniture, and attendance were suggestive of the Ritz in Paris or London, I instructed a car to meet me there at 3 o'clock, with an Embassy dragoman who knew the formalities which were necessary.

During the afternoon the *visa* business was only just completed in time, as I was obliged to drive to many different parts of the city, but I thereby obtained an opportunity of seeing a good deal of it. My first impression was one of surprise to find such a handsomely built and prosperous town, very much more attractive than anything I had previously heard of it had led me to expect. Fine streets were everywhere and handsome buildings, more in the French style than in any other; imposing open spaces and gardens, and many shops in the more fashionable thoroughfares, which would have been worthy of any capital city. The streets were busy and full of well dressed and apparently prosperous people, and many carriages and motors were to be seen, which would in no way have been out of place in Hyde Park during the London season.

The female portion of the population, however, commanded my most cordial and spontaneous admiration, for, possibly as the result of my long residence in strictly Mohammedan districts where no woman is ever seen except as a spectre shrouded from head to foot in veils, the ladies of Bucarest seemed to me to be remarkably well turned out as well as of naturally handsome and attractive appearance.

My business done, I took a drive in the park on the outskirts of the fashionable quarter of the city, and found much to admire there, as it closely resembles the Bois de Boulogne of Paris, the principal difference being that in Bucarest the trees are much older and therefore larger and finer than in Paris, where they were all cut down during the German siege in 1872.

In this wooded park were several excellent restaurants where one could dine under the trees and enjoy first-class music, and as the weather was very hot I reserved a table at the very best of these for dinner, my fellow-traveller, the King's Messenger, having promised to be my guest that night. There in the cool of the evening we enjoyed a first-class repast and listened to beautiful music, whilst watching some most graceful and interesting dancing on the part of the élite of Bucarest society.

Next morning we caught our train at 8 A. M., and found it so packed that, but for the fact of a compartment having been officially reserved for the King's Messenger, there would have been no chance of our travelling by that train at all. The Express consisted of international "wagon-lits," with a restaurant-car attached, and we were told it would take us right through to Trieste in, it was hoped, three days' time, although there were rumours of trouble on the Hungarian plain, where Roumanian troops were then occupying the country in their advance on Buda-Pesth.

Our route at first lay to the north, to a place most aptly named Brasso, situated in the centre of the Roumanian oil country, where many derricks were to be seen over oil-wells, reminding me much of the oil-fields at Baku. On leaving Brasso we began to climb the Transylvanian Alps, where the wooded mountain scenery was magnificent, and after several hours amongst the mountains emerged on to the open plain of Transylvania; this gradually descends from an open upland plateau till it is merged in the great plain of Hungary. The upper plateau is extensive and is a rich grazing country, full of large homesteads and farm-buildings, as well as many imposing and ancient residences, which have for generations been the homes of the great landed proprietors.

I was also much interested in observing, with such accuracy as may be possible from a train, the traces, in several strategic positions, of much older constructions, pointing to this country having been a battleground in the days of the Roman Empire, or even earlier, as various unmistakable mounds and ridges are to be seen in commanding positions, indicating that ancient defences existed there in times long past. When the long and gradual descent is completed and the great plain reached, the character of the country changes to a purely agricultural one, and here, before reaching the Hungarian town of Zegedin, we met with our first, and fortunately our only, adventure.

Our train stopped at a wayside station, and much jabbering in many tongues commenced, accompanied by loud and vehement protests from the passengers. It turned out that this was due to the locomotive staff refusing to continue the journey, unless and until they had levied a toll of an unheard-of number of florins from the passengers, which they immediately began to collect. On entering our carriage, however, they observed our British uniforms, and as that time the British Army enjoyed a prestige which, alas! has since sadly depreciated, they thought it better to pass us by without making any attempt at extortion, and the train shortly after moved on again.

The next incident was the recrossing of the Danube by a magnificent bridge, for the river there is still a great one, though very considerably smaller than at Rustchuk, where we had crossed it for the first time. From there we ran on to Agram, and over the lovely Istrian Alps to Trieste, where we arrived in the early afternoon of the seventh day after leaving Constant, and were fortunate in finding a compartment reserved for us in the Simplon Express leaving next day. We stayed the night at an excellent hotel on the sea-front at Trieste, and left next morning via Venice, Milan, and the Simplon Tunnel, which journey, being to the last degree civilized, and familiar to so many, needs no description here.

Arriving in Paris in twenty-four hours, the King's Messenger was obliged to continue his journey the same morning to London, but, as I had been suffering from my persistent persecutor the Erzeroum fever during the latter part of the journey, I took advantage of the invitation of some kind friends in Paris, the Robert Rothschilds, who had invariably shown me the greatest kindness all through the war, and remained at their charming house in Paris for the night, continuing my journey next day, and reaching London on the evening of the tenth day after leaving Constant, having been absent from England this time for about seven months.

# PART III

## IN KEMALIST TURKEY

(*November*, 1919, *to November*, 1921)

WITH INTRODUCTION BY LIEUT.-GEN. SIR CHARLES HARINGTON,
G.B.E., K.C.B., Etc.,
COMMANDER-IN-CHIEF, ALLIED FORCES IN THE NEAR EAST

# INTRODUCTION TO PART III

### By LIEUT.-GEN. SIR CHARLES HARINGTON, G.B.E., K.C.B.,
#### COMMANDER-IN-CHIEF, ALLIED FORCES IN THE NEAR EAST

Colonel Rawlinson has asked me to write an introduction to his Part III., which is called "In Kemalist Turkey."

He has chosen a title that perhaps caused me more anxiety than anything else during the interesting period which I have spent in Constantinople. I came here knowing that we had many prisoners like Colonel Rawlinson "in Kemalist Turkey," and it was almost impossible to get any news of them. Such news as we got was unreliable. They were completely cut off from us, and yet they had belonged—at any rate the majority—to the Army of the Black Sea. Weeks and months passed by. All efforts of the Foreign Office to secure their release failed. The Kemalists took no notice of representation made through the Constantinople Government. Some of their leaders were in our custody at Malta during this period, and they intended to keep ours. It was a heartrending time. The anxiety of the prisoners' relations unable to get any news was very great. At last I got some news. It was to the effect that Colonel Rawlinson and his men were suffering much in prison, and, unless released, there would be little chance of Colonel Rawlinson or many of them getting through another winter. The Foreign Office then gave me permission to use any means I liked to secure their release. I therefore got into direct touch with Mustapha Kemal, and, in fact, very nearly had a meeting with him. My object was solely to secure the release of the prisoners. Other motives were, however, ascribed to the proposed meeting, which was never held. Negotiations continued, and I think we owe a debt of gratitude to General Rafet Pasha, with whom I have had many dealings since. He was, I believe, the Kemalist authority who prevailed on the Grand National Assembly to negotiate for the exchange of prisoners, which happily ended their troubles. Alas! I am sorry to say, the numbers we hoped for were not forthcoming, but I am convinced that all who had survived were released and that there are none now in Kemalist hands with the exception of two airmen recently captured, whose release it is hoped soon to effect.

Colonel Rawlinson and his brave men arrived at Constantinople shortly after their release, accompanied by their faithful companion "George"—the most human animal that I have ever seen. It was just a glimpse of life which one can never forget: the devotion of Colonel Rawlinson for his men, the devotion of the men for Colonel Rawlinson, and the devotion of "George" for them all. They had all suffered together. They had been through more than we could ever know.

When he left us, Colonel Rawlinson had one fixed resolve which impressed me very much, and that was that he was going to personally deliver each of his men back to his home and family. I have often pictured the scene. I know no better example of an officer's care for his men.

I have a souvenir of this gallant contingent which I shall ever value—namely, a signed photograph of them all and "George," with a tribute of their appreciation of our humble efforts to secure their release from "Kemalist Turkey."

As I write, we are anxiously awaiting the result of meetings being held at Angora. Is it to be peace or war? One prays sincerely for the former. We hoped, after Moudania, that we were within sight of peace. We hoped the same throughout the Lausanne Conference. I went to bed on February 4th thinking I should wake up next day to find peace had been signed and our troubles over. What a disappointment! We are passing through critical days. Will Mustapha Kemal and Ismet Pasha, both of whom desire peace, carry the Assembly? Let us hope so! England wants peace. Turkey wants peace. The world wants peace. Let us hope that we shall get it and that we shall see Turkey settle down to peace and prosperity. We shall then be able to take away with us happy memories of our time here and of the kindness which we have received on every side. The relations between the Allies, the help and friendship which I have received from my French and Italian colleagues—Generals Charpy and Mombelli—the firm friendship and close work of the British Naval, Military and Air Forces, are matters never to be forgotten.

(*Signed*) C. H. HARINGTON.

*March*, 1923.

# CHAPTER I

### LONDON AND CONSTANTINOPLE

Interview with Sir Henry Wilson—Interview with Lord Curzon—Reception of my reports—My instructions—Journey via Paris and Rome to Taranto—Embark on a hospital ship—Call at Salonika—Passage of the Dardanelles—Orders to fit out a new party at Constant—"A" mess—Organization of my Mission—Their training—Adrian's Aqueduct—The Forest of Belgrade—General Sir Tom Bridges—General Sir Henry Wilson—Admiral Webb—Admiral de Robeck—Dinner on the *Iron Duke*—Fox-hunting—Golf—A fire-ship in the Bosphorus—Loading mules on the transport—Sail for Trebizond—Landing in Anatolia.

Reaching London on August 28th, after a record journey of twenty-one days from Erzeroum, I reported at the War Office next morning, and had the honour of having a long and extremely interesting interview with the Chief of the Imperial General Staff (Sir Henry Wilson).

I reported to him the details of the Turkish Nationalist Movement and its progress up to the time of the Erzeroum Conference, which had concluded on August 7th, and handed him a summary of the National "Pact," then agreed upon, the details of which had been supplied to me by Mustapha Kemal himself.

I pointed out to him that the definite refusal of the Eastern Turks to submit to disarmament and demobilization, according to the terms of the Armistice, was no sudden decision on their part, but was rather the result of the deliberately patriotic attitude adopted by the delegates at the Erzeroum Conference, and formed an important and integral part of the future policy of the whole Nationalist Party throughout the Turkish Dominions.

At that time the intention of the British Government to retire their troops completely from the Caucasus and to evacuate the port of Batoum had already been decided upon, and this decision, having been published, no doubt had much to do with the choice by the Nationalists of that particular moment for the throwing-off of all disguise, and the adoption of a policy of open defiance of the Supreme Council of the Allies.

The outcome of my report as to present conditions in the interior was that eventually the Chief of the Imperial General Staff agreed to reconsider the date upon which Batoum was to be evacuated by our troops, and the garrison there, then under orders to leave the port during October, received instructions that the evacuation would be postponed for a time at any rate, pending the further development of the political situation.

I was then instructed to report to Lord Curzon at the Foreign Office, whom I had the honour of seeing in person the following day. This interview, of which I retain the most vivid recollection, was, of course, chiefly devoted to the political aspect of the situation, and particularly to the personality of Mustapha Kemal, his influence and aspirations, his prospects of organizing a successful revolution against the Sultan's Government and the Constantinople Party, and the ultimate aims and objects to which such a revolution, in the event of its success, would be directed. With respect to these very elaborate and difficult questions it was only possible for me to offer the opinions that I had formed on the spot, from personal acquaintance and discussion with the principal members of the Nationalist Party, and the result of my observations as to the spirit and general attitude of the civilian population, as well as those of the military element.

With suitable emphasis and, I trust, due reference, I rendered my report, and answered many searching questions. In the course of the interview I was repeatedly astonished to find the diversity and depth of the knowledge possessed by Lord Curzon of the whole situation in the interior, down to even small details, his familiarity with which impressed me more than anything else. The conviction was irresistible that our Government were fortunate indeed in having at their disposal, in the person of their Foreign Minister, a degree of knowledge and a variety of experience of the character and views of our diplomatic adversaries in the East, in all probability unrivalled by any of his predecessors in that great and responsible position.

The impression with which I left the Foreign Office on that occasion, however, was that, although my reports were listened to with considerable interest, particularly as containing certain elements of novelty in the picture I presented of the possibility of a great future Moslem Republic, yet they were by no means taken as furnishing reliable information as to the aspirations of the new Turkish Party; nor was it considered that, even if the forecast put forward should prove to be correct as to the objects of the Nationalist Movement, there was the least likelihood of the Turkish Revolutionaries having either the enterprise or the resources at their command which would be necessary to enable them to carry out the unexpectedly ambitious program which I ascribed to them. It can hardly be disputed to-day that the subsequent policy of our Governnment and the course of events since that date have tended to confirm the above conclusions as to the British official attitude towards the Kemalist Revolution at that time.

Having rendered my reports to both the War Office and the Foreign Office, it was intimated to me by the Military Authorities that instead of proceeding, as had been proposed, to Archangel, it would be preferred that I should, if I was prepared to continue in the Service, return to Constantinople as a Special Service Officer, in the same position as before; and on my stating my readiness to remain in the army as long as I could be of any service, I was instructed to call again at the Foreign Office, and then to proceed once more to Constantinople.

I therefore had the honour of a further interview with Lord Curzon, on which occasion I again repeated what I had gathered Mustapha Kemal's objects and intentions to be, and what possibilities there appeared to be of his being in a position to carry them out. I then received instructions from Lord Curzon that I should, if possible, see Mustapha Kemal again and endeavour to ascertain as definitely as might be possible from him what Peace terms his party were expecting to obtain, and what conditions (short of the terms of their "Pact," which was looked upon as impossible) they would be prepared to accept. At the same time it was to be officially understood that I was returning to Anatolia on purely military duty, for the purpose of reporting as to the fulfilment by the Turks of the military conditions of the Armistice, and that any interviews I might succeed in obtaining with Mustapha Kemal would be of a quite informal and unofficial character, and that I was in no way to be considered as other than an officer employed on ordinary military duty.

Armed with these somewhat vague and purely verbal instructions, I left London on October 20th, to report once more for special service at General Headquarters of the Army of the Black Sea at Constant. The journey, via Paris and Rome, to Taranto offered no special incidents of interest, but the trains were still very crowded, although a little less so than on the last occasion of my following this route. I found, however, that travelling had become considerably more expensive; not only was it no longer possible for a soldier in uniform to take a certain meagre amount of kit with him without payment, but prices had gone up in every direction; especially was this the case in Rome, where the hotels were crowded to overflowing, and a decent meal not only cost a small fortune, but was actually difficult to obtain. All trains were also many hours late and we were seventeen hours between Rome and Taranto, with no chance of obtaining a meal.

On arrival at Taranto, it was again necessary to wait some days for a ship, during which time I once more experienced the amenities of the rest-camp, and suffered even more from the cold and damp than on my previous visit to that delectable retreat. I was, however, able eventually to embark, on October 27th, on the *Gloucester Castle*, a hospital ship doing temporary duty as a transport, and then bound for Salonika and Constant. On going on board I found myself again O.C. Troops, with 198 officers and between 500 and 600 men under my orders.

The doctor who was in charge of the ship was an old friend of mine, whom I had known in London before the war, and whom I was very glad to see again. The officers were a very nice lot, a considerable portion of whom were going to join Denikin's Army in South Russia, to see to the equipments furnished to that force by us and to the training of the men. We had a pleasant journey as far as Salonika, where we had to take on board a number of Bulgarian and Turkish "sick" prisoners, not pleasant shipmates at any time. The weather was good, quite hot, and a calm sea, and, this being my first trip through the Dardanelles, I was deeply interested. We passed close up to Cape Hellas, where the first landing on the Gallipoli Peninsula took place. My note made at the time says:

"I gazed with horror and astonishment, unable to conceive how anyone could order men to land at such a spot, in the face of a strong resistance, as, above the low mud cliffs, a gentle

# IN KEMALIST TURKEY

slope, without cover of any kind, rises up for several miles to the heights which command it absolutely. No one can have any hope of crossing this slope to storm the heights above, unless the works there had first been reduced by artillery-fire. Those who tried to were heroes, every one; and there they lie to-day in the many, many cemeteries which, together with the wrecks of the ships on the beach, serve now to mark the spot."

That was written when seeing the place from the sea, and for the first time, but on the next occasion of my passing there I was able to land and go over the whole ground, including the Turkish positions on the heights of Achi Baba, with reference to which there will be more to tell later on.

The Dardanelles is much the same class of waterway as the Bosphorus, but bears no comparison to the latter with respect to natural beauty, as the hills on the Gallipoli shore, though high, are bare of all but low scrub, and on the Asiatic side the country is much flatter and offers no interesting points except at the "Narrows" below Chanak, a small and insignificant town, near which the waterway narrows to about one mile, and some higher ground on the Asiatic side comes nearly to the water's edge.

This is the site where Xerxes, the great Persian King of ancient days, threw across his bridge of boats for the passage of his army to Europe. Here, also, in the days of Ancient Greece, Leander swam across the Hellespont, as it was then called, to court Hero, as many a man has swum since, without the same attraction; and here in the late war was an old Turkish big-gun battery at the water's edge, commanding the Straits and the entrance to them from the open sea.

The Straits in all, from the open sea to the Sea of Marmora, cover a distance of 40 miles, and have a maximum width of about 4 miles, the land on the European shore (the Gallipoli Peninsula) dominating the ground on the Asiatic shore generally throughout, although, to render the water-passage perfectly safe for shipping in the face of an enemy on the Asiatic side, it would no doubt be necessary, in addition to the peninsula, to hold the ground on the Asiatic shore also. After a pleasant voyage across the Sea of Marmora, past the island of Prinkipo (where General Townshend spent his time as a prisoner) off the mouth of the Bosphorus, we anchored off Constant on November 2nd. On reporting at General Headquarters next day, I had the pleasure of once more meeting my old Chief, General Sir George Milne, then Commander-in-Chief of the Army of the Black Sea. I learned from him that I was to return as soon as possible to Anatolia, in the same capacity as before, but that, in the meanwhile, as my previous party had been demobilized, I was to organize a new party of volunteers from the troops in Constant, and that orders would be at once given to facilitate my fitting them out in a suitable manner, as I should this time have to cross the mountains in mid-winter, which was understood to be an arduous and somewhat precarious undertaking.

I found myself quartered on this occasion in "A" (that is the Senior Officers') mess. This mess occupied the townhouse in Pera of the representative in Turkey before the war of Krupps, the great German munition firm, the same gentleman whose country-house at Therapia was occupied by the Commander-in-Chief. I found my quarters most comfortable, and the establishment of the same class as the country-house, already described, at Therapia. The mansion in Pera occupied a really splendid site, commanding the anchorage of the Allied Fleets in the Bosphorus, and the view obtained from there on the bright sunny mornings which distinguish the winter in Constant would be hard to equal anywhere. On a moonlight night, also, the effect was even more beautiful, the only disadvantage being that the approach was through a quarter of the town still in ruins, as the result of one of the many fires which occurred in Constantinople during the war, no attempts having yet been made at rebuilding.

The occupants of the mess on this occasion were all delightful company, under the genial presidency of General Sir William Rycroft, then in charge of Administration, and as Mr. Krupp, or his representative, had with true German thoroughness seen that nothing was wanting to make his house comfortable, or his cellar without a rival in the East, the busy time passed in preparations for my journey formed a most pleasant contrast to my previous experiences of the East.

The party I was to get together was to consist of twelve men all told, including myself and an interpreter, as well as four cars, with my own two machine-guns and two others, so that each car might be armed. I was also given a pretty free hand to draw clothing, in the shape of fur coats, gum-boots, etc., for

## IN KEMALIST TURKEY

the snow, and also to fit out the cars so that we could cover them in with sail-cloth and sleep in them in the snow, as we were sure to be frequently obliged to do. I was authorized to ask for volunteers, on the understanding that they were not expected to be away more than three months, a somewhat optimistic estimate it seemed to me at the time, but about which it was well to make no remarks.

The men were to be made up as follows:

Four Army Service Corps drivers and four machine-gunners, with one non-commissioned officer from the Machine-Gun Corps, as well as my own batman, Leadbeater by name, who had been with me on the last trip, and was both a skilled machine-gunner and also a motor-driver, and was therefore capable of replacing any man in either category who might be incapacitated.

With regard to the machine-gunners, so many volunteered that it was necessary to parade them all and select the most likely-looking ones, which I did. With respect to the Army Service Corps drivers, however, the proposition was much more difficult, as, although I was fortunate indeed in obtaining one really first-class man at once, yet in order to obtain the remainder I had to be content with whomsoever I could get. A suitable interpreter was even more difficult, as, although there were any quantity of "Armenians" fully qualified for the post at the disposal of the Intelligence Corps, yet I was determined, in view of my past experiences in that direction, to take no "Armenian" with me into the interior. I was therefore delighted when one evening I was accosted in the streets by a miserable-looking specimen of humanity in civilian clothes, who addressed me by name, and whom I at once recognized as a Russian who had been with me as interpreter on my last trip from Tiflis to Kars and Erzeroum, whom I was very pleased to take on again in the same capacity.

The "personnel" being now complete, the preparations of the cars and the drawing of kits was pushed on, so as to permit of my giving them some training before starting on our travels, and this I was soon able to undertake. The training took the form of expeditions through the surrounding country, packing and unpacking the cars, bivouacking, and also forcing our way through difficult country where there were no roads worthy of the name, a state of affairs in no way difficult to find in the neighbourhood of Constantinople. It was also necessary to exercise them in the use of their arms from the cars, and for this purpose I had to obtain permission to take them into the forest of Belgrade, a large and beautiful natural forest, lying about 12 miles to the north-west of Pera. This forest is said to be infested with brigands of sorts, and our officers were not supposed to go into it; but upon my representing that, if we should be fortunate enough to meet the real article, it would be by far the best form of training for my men, I obtained the necessary permission to visit this most promising training-ground.

We started for the forest very early one morning, and after about 10 miles passed under the ancient Roman Aqueduct constructed by the Roman Emperor Adrian, at the beginning of the second century A. D., to bring water to Constant. A wonderful monument this remains to-day to the engineering skill of the Roman Empire. Where we passed under it, it spans a valley possibly 100 feet deep and a quarter of a mile wide, and has in places as many as four tiers of arches, superimposed one above the other, all of excellent masonry, still in quite good condition.

After passing the aqueduct, the road we were following simply "faded away," and we found ourselves on the outskirts of the great forest with no road to follow. This was what I had been expecting, and, as there was no undergrowth to speak of, we boldly set out through the trees, and very soon had all the trouble I was looking for in the shape of bogged cars and streams without bridges, etc. All these, however, were duly overcome, and after about 4 or 5 miles we struck a large open glade leading down to a lake some hundreds of yards broad and over a mile long, an ideal place for our purpose, and here we bivouacked and prepared our midday meal. During our passage through the forest a bright look-out had been kept for any sign of the native brigands, of whom, however, we had seen no trace, the only traces of any interest which we observed being those of deer and wild-boar, both of which were fairly frequent.

After lunch we commenced practice with our machine-guns over the lake, where we were able to observe the accuracy of the firing by the splashes of the bullets on the water. The practice was, on the whole, good, but the most interesting effect of the firing was to "rise" countless wild-fowl from the water, though none of them came within shot of us, and after further efforts with their revolvers, which the men used extremely badly, we packed up and, following our tracks back through the forest, arrived at our barracks at 9.30 P. M., in good order, having gained much invaluable experience of the capacities both of our cars and our comrades, as well as considerable confidence with which to tackle the rough conditions which lay before us in the interior.

At this time I had the pleasure of dining out on several occasions with various kind friends then in Constantinople; amongst them was General Sir Tom Bridges, whom I had known in the retreat from Mons, when he saved the lives of many exhausted men by raising a band, with instruments consisting of petrol-tins and penny whistles, and playing thereon "The British Grenadiers," "Tipperary," and other tunes of so inspiriting a nature as to induce the exhausted men to make one more effort, and so succeeded finally in marching them into safety. He afterwards was with the Headquarters of the Fourth Corps both on the retreat from Antwerp and during the first battle of Ypres, when I saw much of him. I had not seen him since that time, and now found he had had the misfortune to lose a leg in one of the later campaigns, although it would take much more than that disaster to interfere with his vitality and enterprise, and I still found him as cheery as ever.

I also had the pleasure of dining with General Sir Henry Wilson, the then Governor of Constant (not the Chief of the Imperial General Staff), and also with Admiral Webb, then acting as Deputy High Commissioner, of whose lavish hospitality at the Embassy I retain the most pleasing recollections; and finally I had the honour of an invitation to dine on the *Iron Duke*, the flagship of the Mediterranean Fleet, with the High Commissioner, Admiral Sir John de Robeck, one of the most illustrious representatives of the British Navy, whose personality is as charming as his record is distinguished. I have before me a letter, written on the day after the dinner, which may be of interest to many who have not had the advantage of partaking of the hospitality of an Admiral Commanding-in-Chief on his own flagship. The letter runs as follows:

"I dined last night with Admiral de Robeck, on his flagship, the *Iron Duke*. His barge took myself and several other guests on board from the landing-stage at Dolma Batchké, one of the Sultan's palaces. It was so rough in the Bosphorus that, whilst waiting alongside the landing-stage for one of the guests who was late, another of the guests, already on board the barge, was sea-sick. I am not quite sure what effect that may have had on his capacity as a dinner-eater, but quite possibly it did him good, and certainly the boat danced about in a manner which quite justified his emotion.

"We dined on board the flagship in the most spacious and palatial apartment, the ship being about 100 feet broad and the dining-room in proportion, and much the largest room (a cabin hardly describes it) that I had ever seen on a ship, other than the dining-saloon on a big liner. The ship's band of first-class musicians played during dinner, and afterwards we went up on deck to see a variety entertainment, given by a most excellent company, all members of the 83rd Brigade, who had come off from their camp ashore to give the flagship a 'show.'

"They must, I think, have been in 'the profession' before joining the army and pretty good performers even at home, as one would see many worse shows, and none better, in London. The company consisted of six men and two 'ladies'; the latter, who were splendidly got up, sang in falsetto and danced to perfection, causing all the sailors to roar with delight. As there were about 1,200 men on the ship, and they were all there to the very last boy, you may understand that they made some noise! I know that I enjoyed it immensely, and so, I think, did everyone else, the Admiral included."

The weather up to the middle of November had been excellent, bright and sunny, and neither too hot nor too cold, with that pleasant nip in the air in the morning which is such a distinguishing feature of autumn in Constant. After the middle of the month, however, storms came on, and most unfortunately held up the transport for which we were waiting, as she was kept in the Dardanelles, being unable to discharge her cargo there, except in calm weather, so that our departure was delayed till December 3rd. In the meantime, not only did we complete our training, but an opportunity was afforded for enjoying the various forms of amusement which the British Army is in the habit of organizing at any place where its stay may be a prolonged one. Having been a stranger to any form of amusement since 1914, this opportunity was much appre-

## THE ALLIED FLEETS IN THE BOSPHORUS
## SEEN FROM GALATA HILL

The anchorage by moonlight

The "Iron Duke" turning

## LANDING AT TREBIZOND

Approaching the town from the sea

Lowering the Ford vans into Turkish lighters

## IN KEMALIST TURKEY 247

ciated, and I enjoyed several days hunting with the army hounds, and several rounds of golf on the links which had been established on the hills to the north-west of Pera.

With regard to the hunting, this was carried out with an English pack of hounds and a professional huntsman, in the scrubby hills to the north and west, where jackals abounded; but the country there does not lend itself to sport of this description, and I have had far better fun hunting similar animals in India.

The golf was, however, quite good of its kind, and the course, if not up to English standards of perfection, was at any rate interesting, and full of a variety of obstacles in the shape of nullahs and old fortifications, which are unknown at home. The surroundings, also, were both varied and beautiful, and, above all, the air on the high rounded hills where the course is situated, about 4 miles north of Pera, is fresh and invigorating in the extreme, and a great change after the far from sanitary conditions which exist in the town and amongst the ruins there.

One night, just before leaving Constant, I determined to obtain a photograph of the Bosphorus, with the Allied Fleets at anchor by moonlight, in the endeavour to obtain a record of a sight the beauty of which I considered could not fail to appeal to many who might never have the opportunity of seeing it. I therefore arranged my camera for a long exposure on the topmost balcony of Mr. Krupp's residence from which coign of vantage the whole anchorage was clearly visible, glittering in the moonlight.

Quite unexpectedly, just at this moment, the crews of all the ships at anchor seemed suddenly to become wild with excitement. Sirens commenced to hoot in all directions, and every warship commenced signalling with her signal lights, whilst the beams of many searchlights shot up from all parts of the anchorage. These, gradually sinking and concentrating on one spot, revealed at last the cause of the commotion.

A large ship, burning fiercely, was floating down the current from the direction of the Black Sea, straight for the crowded anchorage, where over one hundred ships were lying at their moorings. It was a most remarkable sight: bright moonlight and a silver sea alive with lights, the crew of every vessel becoming suddenly as busy as bees, whilst little launches converged from all directions upon the burning vessel. The whole scene produced the effect of a gigantic illuminated regatta, suddenly startled into the extreme of activity.

From the care with which the launches approached the burning ship it was evident that they momentarily expected her to "blow up," but, as her sides commenced to show red from the heat without the expected explosion taking place, a chain was finally got on board, and she was towed across the current and allowed to float harmlessly past the crowded anchorage, close under the Asiatic shore, out into the open waters of the Sea of Marmora. Having enjoyed this almost unique spectacle, I was able to get my photograph, which turned out more successful than I had dared to hope.

At the end of the month our transport at last arrived, and, having discharged her cargo, commenced to load with many mules and horses, as well as munitions of all kinds, which were to cross the Black Sea and be placed at the disposal of the Russian forces then operating under General Denikin in Southern Russia.

On going down to the Galata Wharf, at the entrance to the Golden Horn, where the transport was moored ready to load, I found an extraordinary state of chaos, which was chiefly due the unruliness of the animals which were to be embarked. These horses and mules were no longer in charge of the British military transport men, who had been, of course, thoroughly familiar with their idiosyncrasies and quite competent to control their vagaries, but had been collected in a depôt, where they were under the care of a variety of "scallywags," consisting of Russians, Armenians, Maltese, and all the heterogeneous riff-raff who are always to be found in the East when any chance exists of obtaining rations without any too strenuous effort. These heroes turned up on the quay, each in charge of at least four unruly animals, the result being that, when I reached the wharf, I found the approaches blocked by a crowd of animals quite uncontrolled and in absolute disorder, among which those quite unrivalled agitators, the transport mules, who were present in force, were specially prominent.

As these animals had all been drafted from our transport lines, to be now got rid of once and for all, it may easily be imagined that all the most vicious and unpleasant characters among our menagerie were there, and the result was a pandemonium of kicking, squealing, biting, and generally refractory brutes, all mixed up in hopeless confusion.

My own party and their gear would have to be disembarked *first*, and therefore would have to be loaded *last* so that it was "up to" me to do anything I could to assist in restoring order and getting on with the work, and the result was that I spent a very busy but excessively entertaining morning, during which many incidents occurred which raised shouts of the heartiest laughter, and reminded me constantly of a picture I had seen somewhere or other, and which I had never forgotten.

The picture I refer to, most beautifully drawn, represents one of those brave members of the British Army whose duty it is to look after the transport mules. This gentleman is depicted at the moment when he has, in dismay, let go the heads of two very vicious mules which were under his charge, and which, whilst violently kicking at everything within reach, had at the same time just "bared their teeth" with the evident intention of "eating" him. He is at that moment accosted by a very superior staff officer, mounted himself, and in a position of comparative security. This gentleman shouts: "Why the devil don't you hang on to their *heads*, my man, and then they can't *kick* you?" To which the man returns the crushing reply, unsurpassable in its delightful sarcasm: "Yus, and if I catch hold of their *tails*, I suppose they can't *bite* me?"

Fortunately, on this occasion the quay was provided with a really good gangway for horses, boarded up to a good 8 feet high on each side, and this led straight from the level of the quay to the head of the slope, or ramp, built on the ship to give access for the animals to the hold where they were to travel. Having had lots of experience in loading horses, we soon got things into proper shape, and with strong hawsers, each manned at both ends by fifteen or twenty men, we very soon came to terms with even the most refractory of the mules. The moment any hesitation was shown, the hawser was dropped round the stubborn animal's quarters, and, all the men putting their weight on to it together, it was run "neck and crop" by main force on to the gangway, up which the procession was kept moving. The amusing part of the show was the succession of extraordinary antics these wild mules indulged in in their endeavour to resist being made to do something which they had made up their minds they would *not* do. Quite a number, when tired of biting and kicking, sat up like dogs, which on previous occasions they had doubtless found was a most effective form of resistance. It availed them nothing at all here, however, for no sooner were the hawsers dropped behind them than they were slid along on their hams, loudly squealing and protesting, and tumbled heels over head into the gangway, to the huge delight of everyone present, but more particularly of the men who had lately been in charge of them, and who now "got some of their own back." By these means we had the job finished by the early afternoon without any casualty to either man or beast, and to the great entertainment of all concerned.

I had the honour of dining once more, before leaving, with the Commander-in-Chief at Therapia, and of taking his final instructions, the official portion of which was in writing, with reference to my military duties. The unofficial portion was conveyed in a personal conversation of which I took private notes, which I subsequently submitted to the Chief for his approval and then committed to memory and destroyed. After a farewell interview with the High Commissioner (Admiral de Robeck), who told me that if I was in trouble he would send a ship to take my party "off" from any Black Sea port at any time, we finally embarked on His Majesty's transport *Huntscastle*, on December 3rd, bound for Trebizond.

This vessel, originally an Austrian-Lloyd liner, had been for some time in use as a transport, and was very uncomfortable, especially in the cold which at this time of the year in the Black Sea is very severe, and we were glad indeed to disembark at Trebizond on December 6th, after a very cold and uneventful passage. Thanks to the steam derricks on the ship, we were this time easily able to lower our cars into native boats, and we also obtained the use of a hand-crane on a small wooden jetty near the custom-house to hoist them ashore, so that our landing compared most favourably with our last effort at the same spot, this being about the only point where any comparison between the two missions is possible. Our trip this time, which was estimated to last three months as a maximum, actually lasted two years, and each of those two years seemed to us to be ten.

# CHAPTER II

### ANATOLIA IN WINTER

Trebizond in winter—Camp at Hamsikeui—The Zigana Pass—Our house at Gumush Khaner—Visit of Greek Bishop—The Vavok Pass—Persian Travellers—My men exhausted—Bivouac in the snow—Reach Baiburt—Start for the Khop—Our Turk mountaineers—Their Chief and their oxen—The Climb—Ankers' good work—Bivouac on the summit—Christmas night—Sunrise amongst the peaks—Casualties on the road—Reach Erzeroum.

Our first duty on landing in Anatolia, on December 6th, was to advise the Turkish Army Commander of our arrival, and to request facilities for reaching his headquarters at Erzeroum. Therefore, the day after landing at Trebizond, I visited the Military Commander of the district and handed him a copy of my military orders from the Commander-in-Chief of the army of the Black Sea, requesting him to communicate the same to General Kiazim Karabekir Pasha, and at the same time to ask that our journey might be duly authorized and assisted by the Military Authorities.

This duty performed, it was necessary to await a reply, and in order to profit by the delay the men were daily exercised in travelling under the conditions obtaining in the country at the time, so that they might be thoroughly familiar with their jobs before reaching the snow-line, after which every task would, of course, have to be carried out under much more difficult conditions than those existing on the coast. Although, in December, all the upland districts of Anatolia are under snow, the coast districts then enjoyed a nearly perfect climate. The extreme low temperature in the upper air produces a peculiar clearness in the atmosphere and an absence of all humidity. This makes the weather particularly invigorating and healthy, and at the same time offers no resistance to the sun's rays, which, without having the fierceness of summer, yet serve to supply a genial warmth in daytime, and to render the months of early winter in these districts the most agreeable of the whole year. Our daily training marches through the foot-hills of the coast districts therefore became more like pleasure-picnics than hard training, and as the country in the lower hills round Trebizond is of the greatest natural beauty, the week we spent there awaiting authorization to proceed was undoubtedly by far the most pleasant of the many we were destined to spend in other parts of that elsewhere most desolate country.

On this occasion also I again met the representatives of the American Near East organization who were as ever carrying out their glorious work of relief of suffering humanity. Too little I feel sure is known in America and Europe of the terribly arduous conditions under which this work was done, and of the amount of suffering which this organization was successful in relieving, as well as the enormous number of lives which were undoubtedly, for a time at any rate, saved by the liberality of the great American public. The subject is such a large one that it would require a volume to describe the work which was done, the difficulties under which it was carried out, and the success which was achieved, will join with me in gladly testifying that no more glorious undertaking in the cause of humanity has ever organized or carried out with the same success.

The thanks of the whole civilized world are due to the originators, the contributors, and the representatives of that great charity, for the object lesson they have afforded of the possibilities which exist for each and all of us to help our fellow creatures wherever they may be suffering and dying even in the uttermost ends of the earth.

Our most pressing need was, of course, to acquire information as to the state of the road before us. Owing to the long delay in Constantinople, which had been forced upon us by the lack of transport, it was now very late in the season to undertake the passage of the passes; and even if they were not already blocked by snow, which was most probably the case, heavy falls might now be expected at any moment, in which event a long delay would be caused before the snow became hard enough to enable the journey to be continued on sledges. The cars and some of the party would in that case have to be left behind till such time as they might be able to rejoin us. There was, however, no doubt that we should be able to cross the Zigna Pass, which rises to 6,600 feet and crosses the coast range, as that pass

## THE COAST RANGE

Camp on the northern slope (3,600 feet)

The Kharshut valley on the southern slope (4,300 feet)

# THE ROAD INLAND

Entering the snow on leaving our house at Gumush Khaneh

The town of Baiburt with ancient ruined fortress on the hill above

## IN KEMALIST TURKEY

is neither so high nor so exposed as those which have to be crossed farther inland, and I therefore applied for, and obtained, the use of a small but decently built native house in the Kharshut Valley, near the town of Gumush Khaneh, about 70 miles from the coast, so that on receiving the authorization for our journey we might proceed first of all to that house, and there wait a favourable opportunity to try the higher passes which lay beyond.

On the 14th our authority arrived; and at the same time we were informed that the house at Gumush Khaneh was at our disposal, and that another house was ready for us at Baiburt, a town some 50 miles farther on, on the far side of the Vavok Pass, which rises to 6,500 feet, in a very exposed situation. We were also informed that snow now lay deep both on the Vavok Pass and in the plain of Baiburt beyond, and the next pass, the dreaded Khop, 8,300 feet high, had already been for some time impassable, but that arrangements were being made to give us assistance in our endeavour to force our way over it. This news, though by no means encouraging, was in no way a surprise, and, in fact, it was a relief to me to find that it was no worse. On December 15th, the day after the authorization arrived, we started on our really arduous journey.

Leaving Trebizond at 8 A. M., the first 6 or 7 miles are fairly level, but after that the climbing begins, and is both long and severe, the rise in under 25 miles being 3,500 feet. Owing partly to the bad state of the road, but more still to the inexperience of three out of four drivers, night was coming on before we reached the head of the last valley, at the foot of the upper pass, only 30 miles from Trebizond. Here we pitched our first camp, in which operation the men had now far more experience than they had of the difficult driving which these terrible roads necessitate. Many times during the day did I long for my old experienced drivers who had been with me over this road before; but though three of the new ones needed constant assistance, I was fortunate indeed in the fourth, who was at least as good as any that I had had before. This man, Ankers by name, had volunteered first of them all, although he was at that time on his way home for demobilization, having previously been through all the campaigns of the Salonika Expeditionary

Force, including the first retreat through Serbia, and had therefore already had an unrivalled experience of rough tracks and difficult conditions.

Ankers, whom I had promoted corporal before leaving Constant, had been brought up by his father as a butcher, so in that line also his experience was most valuable to us; but far more valuable still was the stout heart in his rather diminutive body, which never failed him in the face of any adversities, and again and again later on cheered and encouraged his comrades at moments when such encouragement was invaluable, and many times his unfailing courage earned my deepest gratitude.

Knowing the temperature to which we should be exposed at these high altitudes at this time of the year, I had made special preparations to render our camps as well equipped as possible to resist the cold, and for this purpose we carried a large sail-cloth of thick canvas. On reaching the site of a camp our cars were drawn up in pairs, the back of one pair facing the back of the other pair, and the sail-cloth then spread over all four, the edges reaching the ground all round, and the centre supported by a pole between the cars. By this means the resistance to the cold afforded by the covers of the cars themselves was doubled, and at the same time a covered space was provided, outside the cars, for cooking or for the storage of kit, so as to afford more room for the men to sleep on the dry floors of the cars. This answered very well, and by practice the men had become used to the arrangement, of which on this first night in the snow they appreciated the full value.

We were afoot at daylight the next day, and on tackling the upper pass the men got their first experience of snow at high altitudes. Although they had been frequently told what to expect, I am sure the facts exceeded all their expectations, when they finally found themselves really face to face with these vast frozen solitudes, where no outside assistance is to be expected, and where all have to rely entirely upon their own efforts. On leaving camp, we had a sheer climb of 3,000 feet to the summit, entering the snow immediately on breaking camp. On this occasion I travelled last myself, to be in a position to render help to those that needed it, and to see that no one fell behind by the way. This was a very necessary precaution, and we travelled much faster in consequence, but it was ten o'clock that night before I brought the last cars into our resting-place, only 42 miles distant from our camp of the previous night. Our halt was at the house which I had obtained the use of, just west of the town of Gumush Khaneh, on the banks of the Kharshut River, at an altitude of only 3,300 feet, 72 miles from Trebizond, close to the beautiful orchard which had made us such an ideal camp in the summer-time.

On this occasion even the low-lying valley was under snow, though of no appreciable depth compared with that on the Zigana Pass at 6,600 feet which we had crossed on our way. Our house was a small one, consisting of four small rooms only (of which one was sealed up), built above a kind of basement used for storing fuel. Camp was therefore pitched alongside the house and our kit brought indoors, the men preferring this arrangement, as the cold was not severe. I also was glad to adopt it as a means of accustoming them to the conditions, which I knew well would become much more arduous farther on. We remained at this camp three days, doing slight but very necessary repairs to our cars, and collecting all available information as to the state of the country immediately in front of us. During this time snow fell intermittently, and I felt that, as heavy falls might now be expected at any moment, it was necessary to push on with the least possible delay.

The day after our arrival I received a visit from the Greek Bishop of the country, who at once began to complain of the general treatment of his neighbours by the Turks in that part of the world, though he could advance no definite statement of specific cases of oppression and injustice. This most reverend and "highly seasoned" pillar of his Church succeeded eventually in very nearly reaching the end of my patience, for not only was his society highly unpleasant in the very small but, up to his arrival, scrupulously clean and sanitary retreat in which I was ensconced, but he appeared from the very outset to take an entirely erroneous view of his own position and that of his countrymen, and spoke rather as if he considered the region to be Greek and the Turks to be intruders, instead of appreciating that the position was absolutely the reverse. He appeared to assume that, because the philanthrophy and the charitable liberality of the American nation was supporting many thousands of his fellow countrymen who would have died but for the relief so obtained, his nation was therefore to be supported in all their demands whether reasonable or otherwise. It appeared hopeless to convince him of his true position and I therefore finally dismissed him rather peremptorily, pointing out to him that his people were in the Turk's country and subjects of the Turkish Government, and that as the nation of which they claimed to be members was at that time actively at war with the Turks, I could not but be surprised at his attitude, for, if the precedents of the Great War were followed, it appeared to me that the least that he and his fellow-countrymen could expect would be to find themselves confined in detention-camps, in the same manner as the Germans had been confined in England.

This very straight and unexpected rebuff made his "aromatic" holiness "sit up," and I heard afterwards that I had been held up in the Greek Press along the coast as a most unsuitable representative of my country, and one who should be immediately, if not crucified, at any rate degraded. This exhibition of spite, however, in no way affected either my own opinions as to the position of the Greeks, or those of my Chiefs as to my qualificatons to act as their representative.

On the third night the snow ceased, and as it froze hard we made all our arrangements to start next morning at the first peep of day, before the sun's rays had a chance to soften the upper crust of the snow on the lower ground. We knew that, as we had to rise to nearly 7,000 feet at the summit of the Vavok Pass, we should there, at any rate, be sure to find the snow hard enough to bear the weight of the cars, even at midday, although at the lower levels the surface would soften as the sun gained in power. We therefore got off in good time, and, the climb being long and gradual, the first 25 miles were done fairly easily, during which we climbed 2,500 feet in a constant ascent through snow which was hard, but gradually getting deeper.

At this point the road enters a narrow rocky defile, and becomes for a quarter of a mile excessively steep; and here we were held up unable to advance, although we assembled our entire party in the endeavour to push one car at a time up the steep defile. The wind through the gorge was so cold and strong that I saw my young men's noses getting bluer and bluer every moment, and their courage likewise was suffering. I now began to feel anxious, knowing that things were likely to be far worse on the slopes of the actual pass, not more than 2 miles in front. It was therefore with the greatest relief that I saw an enormous covered waggon coming down the gorge, drawn by four horses abreast, and sliding like a sledge, its wheels locked by chains and the crowd of travellers, who had been riding in it, now guiding it by hand, by this means only, and with great difficulty, keeping it on the road down the very steep incline. The gorge here is so narrow that there is only just room for the torrent and the road between the perpendicular cliffs, and it was evident that this huge waggon had no chance of passing our cars on the narrow part of the ascent where we had been brought to a halt. I therefore hurried to meet them to stop them higher up, where the road was broader, as well as to enlist their assistance in getting our cars "up," which I was assured of obtaining, as otherwise they themselves would be unable to get "down" the gorge.

I found the party consisted of about twenty Persians on their way from Persia to Constantinople via Trebizond, this being the old regular caravan route, and the only one available, with any degree of safety, since the withdrawal of the British troops from Baku. The Persians readily gave their help, and, after attaching ropes to our leading cars, we soon had our new friends all in harness. As thirty men on a rope, even if twenty of them are only Persians, are vastly more effective than ten, we got all six cars up without any further difficulty, leaving the gorge free for the Persians to descend, which they immediately proceeded to do, after receiving our thanks, as well as more solid tokens of our gratitude.

We were now confronted by the open snow-slopes of the rounded hill-tops which form the Vavok Pass, the summit being about 500 feet above us and 2 miles distant. Here we were well over 6,000 feet high (the summit being actually 6,560), and were in deep snow, exposed to the full fury of a really icy wind, and so for the first time my new volunteers found themselves really "up against it."

While nothing could have been better than the behaviour of three or four of the men, I was sadly disappointed in the others, who were inclined to be hopeless, and whom it was difficult to induce to struggle. Each car, of course, had to be "manhandled" one at a time through the snow these two terrible miles to the summit, and it was only by the greatest effort on the part of the whole party of twelve that we were able to achieve this very arduous task, it being long past nightfall before the last car finally reached the summit, the whole party by that time being blue with cold and physically exhausted. There then still remained over 20 miles to negotiate before we should reach the town of Baiburt, on the plain below, where we were expected, and where I hoped to obtain assistance next day, in the case of our being unable to reach its shelter that night.

In the meanwhile it would have been madness to have stayed on the exposed summit as long as there remained any chance of reaching lower ground. We therefore started the engines and undertook the descent, my orders being for the leading car to go on as far as it could before halting, and that I would bring up the rear. There were many minor casualties and mechanical troubles on the way down, all of which were successfully surmounted, but after about 10 more miles had been covered the occupants of the leading car came back on foot and met me at 11 P. M., to announce that they could go no farther, as they had lost the road, and their car could not climb the slope then in front of them, the snow having there drifted to a depth of many feet. By the lie of the ground I knew that we must be within not more than 10 miles of our destination, but it was evident to me that our bolt was shot, and that my men were at last "cleanbeat"; and, much as I should have liked to have got over the slope ahead, from whence it would be all downhill, and so have got them into shelter for the night, it was evident that they were most of them "all in," and that we must therefore stop where we were for the night. I therefore at once gave orders to stop the engines and empty the water from the radiators, which is, of course, under such circumstances, the first and most important precaution, any neglect of which will certainly result in cracked cylinders and hopeless engine breakdown.

In the meanwhile, with infinite difficulty, I worked my car through the deep snow from the rear to the head of the column, and, instructing the invaluable Ankers (whose spirit, although he was at least as tired as the rest and had done far more work all day, was still as high as when he started in the morning) to keep the water in the radiator of our car, and run his engine at intervals to keep it from freezing, I then made a circuit of the cars, to see what sort of weather my inexperienced "children" were going to make of it, to lend a hand, and out of my long experience to assist them in making the best of a situation that was proving an "eye-opener" for them.

In spite of many protests, I had got them all into their high india-rubber "gum-boots" before starting in the morning, so that we had no wet feet to contend with, and therefore less chance of frost-bite; I now personally saw that in each car a primus stove was lit and a kettle put on, the sail-cloth covers being well pulled over the cars, the edges being then heaped up with snow to keep as much wind out as might be possible. I then stopped at each car till they had all had a boiling cup of strong cocoa, and left them with the strictest orders to lie as close together as was possible, and to put as much *under* them as they did *over* them, using coverings of every sort of description for the purpose; after which, I waded back to my own car and got in, where I found my faithful batman, Leadbeater, with Ankers' assistance, had our own lamp lighted and primus going, so that I had a real good cup of boiling cocoa myself, which I felt to have been pretty well earned.

We three spent the night in my car, running our engine at intervals, to keep the water from freezing, for we knew that we should want the water at daylight, and it is a terribly long and tedious job to thaw snow enough for an engine over a primus, as each kettleful is apt to freeze again before the next is thawed. It was my intention to endeavour to get on to the town at daylight, and to send back oxen from there to bring in the remainder of the party.

That night was hardly a pleasure-party, but I have known many worse, and although we were all pretty well worn out, yet the two gallant fellows with me would have scorned to admit it, and their officer was certainly not going to do so. We passed the night sitting as close together as possible, dozing and talking, and starting our engine every ten minutes, keeping it then running for at least two minutes on each occasion, till the sky at last began to grow grey before the dawn. Then we all three got down with spades, and turned to with a will to clear a way for our car through the drift ahead, so that we could get on into the town and send back assistance. After about an hour's hard work we dug a ramp (slope) out of the cutting where the drift was, on to the higher ground at the side, where the weight of the wind had partially cleared the snow, and, going back, got the car and started on our voyage of discovery before the "children" in the other cars had commenced to move, and long before there was any sign of the sun, which would surely later on melt the frozen crust and so make any movement of cars under their own power very difficult if not quite impossible. After many difficulties we reached the military outposts of the town by 11 A. M., and carried straight on to the offices of the Military Governor. He, we found, had had everything prepared for our reception the night before, but, as we had not appeared, he had concluded that we had been unable to get over the pass, and that we had remained in the Kharshut Valley. He now undertook to send cavalry to the assistance of the remaining cars and to bring them in, after which we proceeded at once to the house reserved for us, where we found fires and food, both of which were most acceptable. After that, we were soon asleep, so that we got an hour or two much-needed rest before the other cars turned up in the late afternoon, towed by oxen, their occupants being in the last stages of exhaustion and discouragement. They both needed, and received, a good deal of attention from us, and a general rather forceful "bucking-up" also, before they were capable of presenting a proper appearance, as British soldiers, before the Turks, who are pretty keen judges, and unbelievably hard and tough themselves.

We remained in the town of Baiburt, which is situated at an altitude of 5,300 feet, for three days, very comfortable in the good house provided for us. Here I received a cipher cable from the Commander-in-Chief at Constant, instructing me not to go beyond Erzeroum without further orders. This was the first indication I received of any serious trouble being expected. We also received daily news of the condition of the dreaded Khop Pass, which lay about 28 miles ahead of us, the summit at an altitude of 8,300 feet. The information we obtained as to our chance of forcing our way over before the pass became finally blocked was far from encouraging. We, however, decided to make the attempt, and, having notified the Military Authorities on the previous day of our intentions, we left Baiburt at **daylight on Christmas Day**, all determined to do our best to **achieve success.**

The first 12 miles out of Baiburt were fairly easy travelling, as the road follows the valley of the large river, the Chorokh, upon which the town is built. This river issues from the great Khop range, about 2 miles east of the town, and it was not till we crossed it, 10 miles up the valley, that our troubles began. The crossing was by a good bridge, and the road afterwards followed the bed of a small stream flowing down a deep and narrow valley for the next 8 miles. The gradient here was much steeper in many places than it had previously been that day, though the total rise is only 1,000 feet in the 8 miles; also, the snow was much deeper generally and lay in frequent drifts, causing us much trouble and labour; so that it was past 1 P. M. when we were once more forced to stop, unable to get on without assistance, being then still 2 miles short of the commencement of the upper pass, where a strong force of men and oxen had been instructed to meet us.

I at once sent on some Turkish soldiers, whom we had brought with us from Baiburt, to the foot of the upper pass, to bring back the oxen to the drift where we were then badly held up, and seized the opportunity to feed the men, who were by no means as bright and as gay as I could have wished in view of the kind of entertainment which, as I knew, lay immediately before them. However, hot cocoa and food did them heaps of good, and an hour later about fifty oxen turned up, accompanied by the same number of real tough mountain villagers, who were immediately put to work clearing a passage through the drift. We then had rather a curious incident, which may seem strange to our English ideas, but which is typical of the country, and particularly of the Turk, and of the only treatment which he understands and respects.

Having put the diggers to work. I came back to the oxen, in order to divide them among the cars, and found them peacefully eating, and the men in charge of them already nicely "snuggled down" in the snow, having evidently no intention of moving again that day. They assured me that those were the orders of their Chief, who on arrival had himself immediately disappeared into a hovel, where he had promptly lit a fire, and was making himself at home for the night.

This was altogether too much for my patience, as I knew that, although it was now fine, snow might begin to fall again at any moment, and I could imagine that quite probably our only chance of forcing the pass was in danger of disappearing, without any effort being made in the few hours during which the ascent might be successfully undertaken. I therefore sent two Turkish soldiers with strict orders to bring the great man to me, by main force if necessary, saying that the English Pasha commanded his presence. Presently he turned up, and casually told me that "he could not think of allowing his oxen to ascend the pass that day, as it was then too late, and that we should have to wait till next morning."

He had entirely mistaken his man, and before he had finished speaking I had him by the throat, and there, before all his own men, I cursed him with all the Turkish oaths I could think of, and shook him again and again till his teeth rattled. The moral effect of this manœuvre was excellent, for though he was stuck all over with knives, daggers, pistols, etc., he dared to touch none of them. The atmosphere instantly and entirely changed, and not only were my orders from that time on instantly obeyed by the mountaineers, but my own men were considerable heartened up also, a still more desirable result.

We now got going immediately, and soon covered the two remaining miles to the foot of the zig-zags of the upper pass. Here we were confronted by about the most serious climb I know of on any road which has any pretensions as such. The rise is 2,000 feet and the total distance 3¾ miles, long portions of which average 1 in 12; of these, many stretches are too steep for an empty Ford van to climb even when the road is dry and free from snow, without at least three men pushing to help the motor.

On this occasion the snow lay very deep on the zig-zags, and although a track had been dug, yet the surface of rammed snow in this track was as bad as it could be, and the walls of snow on either side reached far above the roofs of the cars. The only favourable point was that, as we should be tackling the ascent in an icy wind and during the night, we could count on the surface everywhere being frozen as hard as iron, with no danger of meeting the soft surface which results from the sun's rays in daytime, and which would have certainly rendered our task impossible.

We hitched twelve oxen to the first car, and ten to each of

the last three, as the first has generally the most difficult task. I, as usual, travelled in the last car, to be ready to assist in case of trouble, and also to keep them moving, as night was already falling before we started on the climb. Many were the troubles that we met with, but all were surmounted in the end, the worst being a badly damaged steering on the last car, caused by a very deep drift, after two-thirds of the distance had been covered. The leading cars had here worn through the frozen crust of the drift, and the last car nearly disappeared altogether in the icy slush, its steering being damaged during the lengthy and difficult process of its extraction. This occurred about 10 P. M., and, of course, at about the most exposed corner of the whole ascent.

Here Corporal Ankers showed once more the indomitable courage which was in him, and commanded the admiration of even the hardy Turk mountaineers, who themselves were shivering with cold and, for the most part, sheltering from the icy wind against the oxen. It was found to be necessary to take down the steering, and to then straighten the rods, which operation could not be carried out whilst they were in their regular position. Ankers lay in the snow, exposed to the full fury of the paralysing wind, for over an hour, sticking to his work like a true hero, long after he had lost all sense of feeling in his hands and feet. Here he got a wound in his right hand which, though he made no mention of it at the time, eventually necessitated the amputation of his thumb.

With the assistance of Leadbeater, who also did his duty that night like a man, we supplied Ankers with hot cocoa from our primus, and did all we could to shelter him from the wind, as it was impossible for more than one to work at the same time, and he would not give way to anyone else, saying, quite rightly, that he was best able to effect the repair, as he knew exactly, having just taken the pieces down, which way it was necessary to replace them. At last we were able to start again, and we reached the summit at midnight, finding that the others had already been there some time, and had all sought refuge in a kind of underground hovel, which I had told them existed there, with an earthen roof heaped up high to carry the snow. In this they had lit a fire, and were packed tight together fast asleep long before we arrived. We therefore backed our car against the back of one of the other cars, and, having lowered the tail-board of each, covered both the cars entirely with our large sail-cloth sheet, and so prepared to spend our Christmas night, as best we could, in the open.

Our first step was to light our little oil-lamp, and then our primus, on which we made some cocoa and fried some bacon, the fumes of the latter, cooking in this confined space, making us cough incessantly, though no one had any idea of lifting even the smallest corner of the canvas cover, as the wind was now blowing sharply, and was of a temperature quite beyond description. We were, however, quite cheery, though grimly contrasting our Christmas cheer with the experience our comrades were having in other less exposed positions; and although thoughts of home were uppermost in all our minds, yet no one dreamt for a moment of referring to a subject which could only serve to make the already difficult task of keeping up our spirits infinitely harder still. That night was certainly the coldest it has ever been my lot to experience, and I trust that I am not fated to go through any in future that will in any way compare with it. We lay down on the floor of the car, as close together as possible, for the sake of the warmth, each having round him every sort and kind of covering upon which he could lay his hands. My letter, written a few days later, says "I had on my British warm, my big waterproof, and over all those my big fur coat, with my fur gloves and fur cap on, as well as my snow-boots, the whole being enveloped in a large fur rug, inside all of which I felt as if I was standing in an icy wind with only a silk vest on." I do not know if that gives a realistic impression, but it really was exceedingly cold—too cold, in fact, to sleep for more than a few moments, as under such circumstances it becomes necessary constantly to move one's limbs, and to make quite sure that there is no numbness creeping on.

When at last daylight appeared, the wind dropped, and the snow having ceased to drift and cut one's skin, we therefore sallied forth, to meet, to our surprise, the most glorious sight I have ever witnessed—that is, the sun rising on an absolute fairyland of rose-coloured snow. The "col" which forms the summit of the pass is 8,300 feet in altitude, surrounded by a succession of peaks (all extinct volcanoes), which were close

## THE KHOP PASS

Site of our bivouac in the open, on Christmas night, 1919, at the summit of the pass (8,300 feet)

to us in the range we were then crossing, whilst below, to the south, snow-ranges extended in interminable succession to the far horizon. All these snowy giants, which average in the neighbourhood of 14,000 feet in height, become, as the sun first touches them a rosy-pink colour, as delicate in shade as it is beautiful in effect, and everywhere the snow shines and twinkles in the hard frost as if scattered all over with brilliant diamonds.

Most wonderful of all, the moment the wind dropped and the sun shone out, its rays passed so easily through the dry air that the cold was no longer felt; but in its place came an extraordinary feeling of exhilaration, making us inclined to dance, or sing, or jump about, from pure joy at being alive. All the troubles and cares and the tedious years of our misspent lives then fell from our shoulders like a discarded cloak, leaving us free and eager to do with all our might whatever task might lie nearest to our hands, to justify our existence in the beautifully bright and spotless world we saw spread out in all its shining glory around and beneath us.

After enjoying for a few all too short minutes this magnificent demonstration of an Oriental mountain sunrise, and running up and down vigorously to bring back the circulation after our not altogether luxurious Christmas night, Ankers and Leadbeater started to prepare, one the cars, and the other some breakfast, whilst I braved the truly stifling atmosphere of the underground retreat occupied by the remainder of our party. These sleepy-heads were soon roused up, and came blinking out into the brillant sunlight like a lot of moulting owls, but the magnificent air outside put new life into them, and we were soon away, hoping to get the worst part of the descent over before the sun's rays had time to melt the crust of the snow. We made good progress, behind our oxen as before, till the afternoon, when, as the snow was no longer so deep on the lower slopes and the gradients there were all favourable, we finally dismissed our Turks and their oxen, with substantial rewards, and continued our journey under our own power.

There is a small village, rejoicing in the name of Pirnikapan, at the foot of the pass, at 5,700 feet, 46 miles from Erzeroum, and, arriving here in the late afternoon, I was obliged to leave two cars, as they were both in need of repair. Their crews were also badly in need of rest, neither cars nor men being in fit condition to continue the journey. I, however, continued myself, with two cars only, having every intention of reaching Erzeroum that night if possible. One car, however, developed bad trouble on the way in the big end-bearings of the engine, and I was obliged to leave it at Ilija, a village only 8 miles short of the great fortress-city, where I eventually arrived myself with one car only, accompanied by Ankers, Leadbeater, and my interpreter, the Russian, Polakoff by name, at 10.30 p.m. As may easily be imagined, we were all pretty well tired out, though still cheery and going strong, after two successive days, each of which had necessitated over seventeen consecutive hours of strenuous effort.

I had telephoned to the Army Commander from Ashkala, the first military post east of the Khop, 35 miles from Erzeroum, to say I expected to reach the town that night, with the result that we were met at the entrance to the fortress by some of his Headquarters Staff, who escorted us to the house allotted to us, of which we took possession, and, finding some food already prepared by the Turkish guards who had been appointed to attend us, we enjoyed a much-needed repast and a well-earned rest in our new quarters, where we were destined afterwards to remain so long and to suffer so severely.

# CHAPTER III

### ERZEROUM IN 1920

Our house—The Army Commander—His orphan military school—The climate—The food—The wolves—I send some of my party in sledges to the coast—Our arrest—Destroy my papers—Surrounded by a mob—Play chess—Turk preparation for a military offensive—Kiazim Pasha leaves for the front—He is succeeded by Kiazim Bey—Teach the men Morse signalling—Make and plant a garden—Peace terms are announced—Our cars are taken—Our officer is withdrawn—Our guards steal our food—We become ill and weak—Our Irish driver joins the Turks—Our Christmas festivities—We receive a box from the Americans at Trebizond—We are removed to the prison.

It was on the night of December 26th that we reached Erzeroum, and within the next few days we got our stragglers in who had been left on the road. The house allotted to us was not at all bad. It had been before the war the "Ajemistani" (Persian) Consulate, and, except for being short of windows and woodwork generally, it was in fair condition—at any rate in winter, when the snow was down and there was 6 feet of it on the earthen roof. The stairs were always rather a difficulty, as the banisters—and all other easily removable woodwork—had long ago been burnt for fuel. There was, of course, no furniture, but in a kind of outhouse on the ground floor was a chimney, under which we at once proceeded to build a fireplace and construct an oven, luxuries unknown in those parts, where cooking is done over an open fire, very rarely of wood, and generally of *tezek* (dried cow-dung), which not only gives very little heat, but also imparts its own peculiar and very unpleasant smell to any food cooked on it.

General Kiazim Karabekir Pasha, the Army Commander, received me very well. I think he was really pleased to see me again, and we had many long talks, he telling me of happenings in his part of the world during my absence at home, which I reciprocated by giving him the news of Europe. After having presented to him my official military orders, and explained to him my duties, I told him privately that I was anxious to get in touch with Mustapha Kemal, who, he informed me, had left Erzeroum immediately after the Conference and gone to preside at another Conference at Sivas, 275 miles farther west, after which he had continued to Angora, about the same distance farther on, where he was establishing the headquarters of the Nationalist Revolutionary Government. He, Kiazim, promised to let Kemal know that I wished to have an interview with him when opportunity offered, but it was agreed that a journey to Angora from Erzeroum was out of the question at that time of the year.

Kiazim Pasha is very pleasant company, and an extremely intelligent man, exceptionally well informed on all international questions, so that his views with regard to the future which lay before his own country, and the effects which would be produced throughout the East by the Nationalist Revolution, were of the greatest interest. I had no doubt that the conclusions he had arrived at were correct, and they were, in fact, the same as those which had formed the basis of the reports which I had rendered in London. He was, however, much afraid that the decisions which the Allies might come to with regard to the terms of peace which were to be offered to his country would be dictated by men whose sympathies were alienated from his people, and who were either entirely ignorant of, or desired to ignore, the vast strides his countrymen had latterly made, and the attitude now adopted universally by the Turks in Asia with respect to the Sultan's Government at Constantinople. Although, of course, I was careful not to say so, I certainly shared his views, and was surprised to find how accurately he read the position in Europe, and the probable eventual trend of the long-delayed "Peace Terms."

We had at this time many discussions with reference to Russia and her future, and although it was evident that, in case of trouble with Europe, the Turkish revolutionaries would of necessity be thrown into the arms of the Bolsheviks, he did not disguise from me that they would greatly prefer to establish friendly relations with the Allies, and especially with the British Empire, as any *lasting* agreement between Turk and Russian, whether Bolshevik or not, has always been, and always will be, an impossibility.

Kiazim invited me to visit a training-college he had just established for the training of orphans whose fathers had been

## IN CONFINEMENT IN OUR HOUSE

The back yard—potatoes growing

Outside the guards' room—the windows are wired. Left to right:
Pte. Carter, a Turkish guard, Col. R., Corpl. Ankers, Interpr. Polakoff

# ERZEROUM

The approach across the plain; the town 8 miles distant, at 6,350 feet. This is the only road to North-Western Persia from the West

The fortress town

killed in the war, saying that he was anxious to have my opinion with regard to it, and I willingly seized the earliest opportunity of inspecting this entirely novel and extremely interesting institution, established in the very last place where one would have previously expected to find such evidence of effort for future development. I was more particularly anxious to study this institution, as I was informed that he was organizing similar establishments in every town of any consequence throughout Eastern Anatolia. The result of my visit surprised me beyond measure. I found over 1,100 boys, from little fellows of five and six, to lads of fifteen and sixteen, well clothed and cared for, all receiving a good elementary education, and also, one and all, being taught many useful trades. Workshops of all kinds had been established, where the boys turned out good work of various kinds, such as tailoring, boot-making, building, and many other useful occupations, which would render each of them invaluable members of the communities in their various local towns and villages in the future.

They were also being brought up under the strictest military discipline, in thorough familiarity with all soldierly duties and the use of modern arms and defences, so that they will all be highly trained modern soldiers from their youth up. It is not difficult to appreciate that, if this is going on throughout the whole country, the Turk of the future, with his natural gifts of courage and endurance, will become a power in the East, if not in the West also, that will presently have to be reckoned with in a very different spirit from that adopted by the European Powers at their post-war conferences hitherto. After my inspection I congratulated the Pasha most heartily on his enlightened policy for the future advantage of his country, which, I gathered, greatly pleased him. The organization of these schools, if not entirely due to his own initiative (which I rather doubt, as it is more suggestive of the aspirations and foresight of Kemal himself), at any rate owes its development to Kiazim's constant personal care and effective supervision.

Erzeroum at this time of the year (midwinter) is arctic in its climate, and subject to sudden storms, which in America would be termed blizzards, but are here called *tépis*. The wind during these storms is of a force and quality which render it as much as a man's life is worth to be caught in them when out of reach of shelter. In consequence, as soon as a storm commences, all houses are shut up, and no one moves out of doors till it is over. Sometimes two, or even three, days may elapse before the wind drops and the driven snow finally settles down; all then come out smiling, and begin cheerfully to dig out the entrances to their homes, often covered by many feet of snow. The calm after such storms is delightful, with a bright sun ever shining; the only precaution which it is necessary then to take is to smear the nose and cheek-bones with soot or some dark substance (the natives mostly use mud for this purpose), as, in the absence of sun-glasses or the above precautions, the effect of the glare is to cause a splitting headache, and eventually snow-blindness, a really terrible affliction.

It is remarkable also how in this clear, dry atmosphere the skin becomes burnt by the sun as quickly even as on the hottest day in summer; but the effect is infinitely more painful in winter, for the cold causes the skin to crack, with results that are frequently serious. The best preventive is to grease the skin, wherever it may be exposed, with soap or oil or any lubricant. This precaution, though it produces rather a comical effect, is extremely effective, and is universally adopted.

Soon after our arrival we all began to suffer in our digestions from the black bread, made from flour which is full of impurities, as, much grit, mostly from the millstones, is absorbed with the bread, causing intense internal irritation and consequent suffering and weakness. Within three weeks we were all of us so suffering, and my young heroes soon began to lose flesh a great deal faster than they liked or expected. We were, however, pretty well off for stores, as I had brought all that our cars could carry, and at this time, though some of them thought they were undergoing great privations, the conditions of our life were by no means really hard. The men's spirits nevertheless needed a lot of "bucking up"; for being shut up in the snow and cut off from all communication with their countrymen seemed to some of them to be a very great hardship. The only entertainment it was possible to obtain for them was to let them go out to shoot wolves at night. These animals exist in great quantities in the mountains close to the town, and roam about the ruins after sundown, so that in moon-

## IN KEMALIST TURKEY

light they can easily be shot, and in winter their skins carry a heavy fur and are well worth obtaining.

I was at this time in regular communication by cipher-wire with Constant, and although I received no official warnings, yet I had no difficulty in "sensing" an atmosphere of approaching trouble. The elections to the new Turkish Parliament having now been held (at the request of the Allies), the new members (all Nationalists) had all gone West, and were now in session at Angora, instead of at Constantinople, as had previously been the established custom. This new departure did not at all meet with the approval of the Allies, who intimated that the Parliament should meet at Constant, and be opened there with the usual ceremony of the Sultan's speech, as they were not prepared to recognize the new assembly at Angora. After considerable hesitation, a proportion of the newly elected members had agreed to go to Constant, under the leadership of Réouf Bey, and to take their seats there, and they were already, during February, actually on their journey to the capital.

Knowing Réouf Bey's opinions, and also his character and fearless patriotism, I felt sure that the position would become critical on their arrival in Constantinople, and I therefore decided to reduce the strength of my party at once to the smallest possible dimensions, retaining only two drivers and one machine-gunner in addition to my batman and interpreter. This left us four men only in addition to myself and the interpreter, to get away our four cars if it became necessary to do so, but I considered I had selected the best of the men, and felt confident I could do better with a smaller number upon every one of whom I thought I could thoroughly rely, than with a larger number many of whom would probably in an emergency be more trouble than assistance. On March 2nd, with the Turkish authorities' consent and assistance, I dispatched two drivers, two machine-gunners, and one non-commissioned officer, in sleighs to the coast, at which decision these men themselves were much relieved, but I doubt greatly whether their relief in going was as great as mine in seeing them go! Immediately on their departure I made every preparation myself to be ready to get off with the remainder, at half an hour's notice, immediately on receipt of a warning hint of any kind from Constant, which I believed was now to be expected at any moment.

This was the state of affairs when, on the night of March 16th, I had just finished working at an up-to-date map of the country, which I was drawing to show the new roads, railways, and other communications constructed during the war, and had written the opening lines of a letter to my wife in England, when I heard the tread of many men outside and the rattle of arms, followed immediately by my door being flung open and the entry into my room of the Governor of the fortress. As he stood in the doorway I could see in the gloom that the hall and the staircase behind him were filled with soldiers with fixed bayonets, and I could also hear words of command being given outside, so that it was evident that the Turkish Army was present in force.

I, however, rose at once and, with, I trust, proper politeness, invited the Colonel commanding the fortress, whom I knew by name and repute only, to take a seat by the stove (then, as I thankfully noticed, burning brightly), and offered him a cup of coffee, at the same time inquiring to what circumstances I was indebted for the honour of his visit so late at night.

To this very courteous reception he replied, I was glad to observe, by taking both a seat and the coffee, telling me at the same time that he was sent by Kiazim Pasha to express his Chief's regret that he was unable to come himself in person, and also that the Pasha had that evening received important and disquieting news from Angora to the effect that, on the meeting of the New Parliament at Constant, on Réouf Bey, the Nationalist leader, officially declaring, as was his duty, the policy of the party he had been elected specially to represent, he and his principal supporters in the House had been arrested by the Allies, and were to be sent as prisoners to Malta forthwith! The city of Constant had also, it appeared, been occupied in formal military manner by the Allied troops, and under these circumstances he was requested by the Pasha to inform me that it was believed that as soon as this news became generally known in the town my party would not be safe, and troops had therefore been detailed for our protection!

To assist in the pacification of the population, he told me he was instructed to request that I should order my men to surrender their arms, and to haul down the British flag which floated so proudly over our quarters, in order to avoid the aggravation of the feelings of the public which would result, under existing circumstances, from its continued display and our immunity from any form of reprisal. This intimation, as may be imagined, in no way lost in gravity from the extremely courteous manner in which it was communicated, and I at once expressed my regret at the deplorable course which events had taken in Constant, of which up to that moment I had been in entire ignorance.

Whilst expressing my warm appreciation of the concern of the Pasha for the safety of my party, and acknowledging the insecurity of our position in the quarters we then occupied, I at once took exception to the suggestion that we should surrender our arms and haul down our flag, putting forward the alternative proposal that we should move immediately to the citadel with all our belongings, where, in the centre of the Army Headquarters, we should be quite safe from any exhibition of popular feeling. I expressed my readiness to carry out that move during the night, so that at daylight our present quarters would be found to be unoccupied.

To this I received a still courteous reply to the effect that my visitor, being a soldier, could do nothing but carry out his orders, which he had already the honour of communicating to me! On that I drew his attention to the excellent terms upon which I was, as he well knew, with the Pasha, and requested him to be good enough to submit my proposal to his Commander, so that at any rate he should be aware of my opinion before the matter proceeded further. To this end I immediately began to put my suggestion in writing before any more could be said, using for the purpose, in my haste, the very paper I had before me, which bore as a heading the endearing terms in which it was my custom to address my wife, but in which it was by no means my intention to address the Pasha. To my great relief, the Colonel consented to do me the favour of personally handing my note to his Chief, who occupied a house less than 100 yards from my own, and on going out for this purpose I heard his word of command to the troops outside to stand fast to await his return.

I had, of course, not the least doubt as to what would be the result, but I had by my alternative proposal at any rate achieved the vitally desirable object, which at first appeared to me to be so difficult if not impossible, as I had got the man *out of the room* for a few invaluable moments, to my own infinite relief. Hardly had the door closed upon him before I was hard at work collecting all my papers, orders, dispatches, and especially cipher-keys, and was cramming them into the stove, so that when, in ten minutes' time, he returned, a vast amount of priceless destruction had been effected, which fact afforded me the greatest possible gratification all through my long subsequent imprisonment.

On his return he told me that the Pasha could not consent to my proposal, but that he was authorized, if I so desired, to demonstrate to me the fact that the house was surrounded in force, and to beg me, on behalf of the Pasha, to resign myself to the fortune of war, adding at the same time a somewhat complimentary statement, which has no place here. I therefore accompanied him to the window of my room, and afterwards to other windows, commanding all four sides of our isolated house, from whence I was able to convince myself that there were at least two battalions in position all around it—a fact which, as I remarked to the fortress Commander, I took as a great compliment to the *four* British soldiers whom I had the honour to command. Then, with quite indescribably bitter feelings, such as I trust never again to experience, I proceeded myself to haul down the British flag, which I reverently folded and placed in the breast of my coat, where it remained, in the only safety which it was in my power to command for it, until at long last I was eventually hoisted over the side of one of His Majesty's ships of war, after twenty long months of suffering and peril. That flag now forms one of my most valued treasures, and hangs above me in my English home as I write.

This painful ordeal over, I sent for Corporal Ankers, and ordered him to surrender our arms, for which the Commander of the fortress undertook to give me a formal receipt. The latter then left me, saying that he would see to the posting of his troops, and return to take leave of me when he had done so. After about half an hour he returned, saying that he had detailed a strong guard to hold the house and an officer to command, and that the ground-floor windows were then being wired with barbed wire as a defence against any sudden attack. We were told we were to consider ourselves as confined to the house, but that the office was authorized to effect purchases, with our money, of anything we might need, and on that he finally departed, having carried out his most unpleasant duty with courtesy and restraint, upon which I made a point of offering him my congratulations, whilst assuring him that his behaviour was adequately appreciated by me, and, under the circumstances, did him infinite credit.

The next day I wrote formal letters of expostulation as to our detention, which I had no doubt was destined to last for a long time, for the claim that it was for our protection was obviously only an excuse, and I was anxious to put it at once on record that I claimed the protection of the **flag of truce** under which I had been officially received as the representative of the British Army. All these representations, however, produced nothing, though I did receive an official receipt for our arms, including my own two dearly cherished machine-guns, which had done such long and valuable service.

A few days later an incident occurred which largely bore out the Army Commander's statement as to the temper of the population and the feeling existing among all classes in the surrounding country against the Allies. I was at first rather tempted to consider that the demonstration in question was one "got up" for our benefit, with the object of influencing any communications which I might subsequently have the opportunity of making to our Headquarters, but as it developed there were many indications of its genuineness, the most remarkable amongst these being the attitude of our guards. The following is an account of the incident, which I trust may be found of interest, though I am quite confident that under no circumstances can the *reading* of the incident excite even a small proportion of the sensations which it actually afforded *us* at the time.

About 2 P. M., several days after our confinement commenced, I was sitting writing in my room on the first floor, when I became aware of a remarkable muffled roar outside the house, and at the same time of a certain commotion downstairs, where our guards were quartered. On looking up through the window without leaving my seat, I saw that all the flat-covered roofs of the houses round were black with a collection of the most villainous-looking ruffians that I had ever seen, who appeared capable of, and anxious to commit at once, unspeakable atrocities of every description, and also that a crowd of several thousand other "gentlemen," of even more forbidding aspect, were spread over all the open spaces amongst the ruins immediately surrounding our house.

The noise came from all these far from pleasant-looking neighbours, who were hooting, and cursing, and shaking their fists, and altogeher demonstrating a decidedly antagonistic, or rather an actively hostile, attitude towards us. It has never before been my privilege at any time or in any place to hear a more unpleasant sound than that which this very repulsive-looking crowd were then making, for it reminded me most realistically of the commotion in which, during my childhood, I ever took the greatest interest. This may always be observed at the Zoo at any time when their food is brought in to the lions and other similarly pleasantly dispositioned animals. At the Zoo, however, the animals are safely shut up in their cages and their prey is brought to them; whilst in our case it was ourselves who were shut up in the cages all right, but the safety was problematical only, as we seemed destined ourselves to represent the prey, especially as we were without arms of any description, and the attitude adopted by our guards towards the hungry-looking "gentlemen" outside was far from encouraging to us.

However, as there was nothing to be gained by any kind of demonstration on my part, I quietly continued my writing in full view of the excited murderers on the roofs opposite me, as if quite failing to realize that I was myself the succulent joint which they were expecting to be served up to them, or that I was in any way concerned in the proceedings.

Shortly afterwards the officer in charge of our guards burst into my room in a state of considerable excitement, and requested me to come downstairs at once to the guard-room, as he had no confidence in the behaviour of his own men, and was, I was delighted to hear, personally responsible for our safety. He assured me, by way of encouragement, that he had telephoned for further support, and that he had every hope reinforcements would arrive before any disaster occurred. As I entirely shared his sentiments in this respect, I at once followed him downstairs, in a manner which, I trust, appeared entirely unconcerned, and therefore I saw no more of the entertainment provided, though I noticed that the expression on the faces of our guards who were posted at the front door was far from showing that genial spirit towards us, and anxious concern for our safety, which I could have desired to observe at that particular moment.

I found my men also in the guard-room, and was, as I expected to be, entirely satisfied with their attitude of calm self-possession; in fact, I am convinced that far more emotion was shown by our guards than by any member of our party. Soon after this we heard the noise greatly increase, and, to our considerable relief, were told that a large force of Turkish police, armed with revolvers, had arrived to support our guards in their half-hearted defence, and very shortly afterwards the unpleasant mutterings died away and I was escorted back to my room, some months subsequently elapsing before we were again treated to a similar highly sensational entertainment.

During the next few months our life was monotonous in the extreme, but not too arduous, as we had permission to use the back-yard of our house for exercise; and as I had a certain supply of money hidden away, and an officer was then permanently stationed in the house, we were able to purchase food without being robbed in too extortionate a manner. I also had a certain amount of seeds of vegetables, which we planted in the back-yard, after clearing away the ruins there and digging the ground to make a garden, where we might hope to grow our vegetables, and so to prolong the time which our money would last us in the purchase of food. To this object, from the very first moment of our confinement, I devoted my greatest attention, being well aware that our lives would in all probability eventually depend upon our care in husbanding our meagre resources.

My party now consisted of Corporal Ankers; my batman Leadbeater; Private Carter of the Machine-Gun Corps, a worthy representative of that justly famous corps; Driver Mahoney of the A.S.C., of whom more hereafter; and Polakoff, the young Russian interpreter.

My own room was on the first floor, with a small room next to it, where Leadbeater and Polakoff slept, and where we did our cooking, such as it was, on a primus. The other three men were downstairs, in a small room next to the Turks' guard-room. It now became vitally important to keep ourselves constantly occupied, and as at this time we were permitted to move freely about within the house, I devised all kinds of means of occupying ourselves, especially in the evening, the preparation of our garden taking up most of our time during the day.

To this end I taught the men many things, amongst them chess, which we played on a paper board, with chess-men consisting of Oxo cubes as Castles, corks as Knights, large revolver cartridges as Bishops, machine-gun cartridges as Queens, and big Russian cartridges as Kings, small revolver cartridges being the Pawns. With these rather "explosive" chess-men we had many an interesting game, Polakoff, being rather an expert and knowing all the correct openings, affording me often the great entertainment which can always be obtained from a close match at that king of games.

I also taught them signalling by the Morse code, both with flags and by tapping, so that we could communicate by sight, or by sound only, at which I kept them in constant practice, never knowing when it might become of vital service to us, especially in the event, for which I never ceased to hope, of our receiving assistance from outside.

Carter, a very nice, sensible, and most intelligent fellow, was of the greatest assistance with respect to our garden; his father, being a Norfolk farmer, had brought him up to know everything that there was to know about preparing the ground, planting seeds, etc., so that as the spring came on we were able to watch the result of his effort with an ever-increasing interest. As time went on, however, we all began to suffer in health, chiefly from privation, for we reduced our expenditure to the very lowest possible amount and suffered accordingly, all being pretty constantly ill with fever and dysentery, and becoming gradually weaker. Ankers undoubtedly suffered by far the most, though in spite of the great pain which he constantly endured from his wounded hand (of which the thumb was amputated in July), I never at any moment heard a complaint from him, nor ever saw the least sign of any faltering in the steadfast courage with which he faced every adversity.

At this time we still had our cars in the back-yard, and kept them ready for use at any moment; but as the summer came on we learnt from our Turkish officer that there had been a Conference at San Remo, where the enlightened "Supreme"

COL. RAWLINSON

After six months', out of twenty months', confinement

## AT ERZEROUM BEFORE ARREST

Col. Rawlinson

The party

Council of the Allies had decided and announced that certain portions of eastern Anatolia were to be given to the Armenians Of course, to us, who were in a position to know the utter futility of such a proposal, the appalling results which must of necessity follow such an announcement were clearly evident, and from that time onwards there were constant signs of preparations for a military offensive by the Turks.

Recruits constantly arrived at the fortress, having been conscripted from all parts of the country; and at the hospital, which could be seen from the back windows of our house, several hundreds of newly arrived conscripts were medically examined daily. Machine-gun practice and drill of all kinds were at this time carried on in many places outside the fortifications every day from sunrise to sunset. During May many detachments left, with full active service equipment, for the Eastern frontier, and our guards were constantly changed, their discipline and quality deteriorating rapidly as the more efficient and reliable soldiers proceeded to the East.

On May 26th we first heard that the "Peace Terms" had been announced in Europe, and that it was proposed by the Allies that large tracts of country should be handed over by the Turks to the Armenians. On the same day arrived the first Bolshevik Mission, who were received with great demonstrations and a parade of all the troops in their honour, as they passed through the town on their way to Angora, and on the next day I saw from our window, for the first time, a German officer in uniform in the streets of Erzeroum.

In early June we heard that the "Peace Terms" had been published in Anatolia. They were received on all sides in Erzeroum with derisive shouts of laughter, and the activity of the military preparations was immediately much increased, as also were the arrivals of bodies of conscripts, which could be seen crossing the plain towards the fortress in daily-increasing numbers.

About this time General Kiazim Karabekir left Erzeroum, to take command at the front, leaving a Colonel Kiazim Bey in command of the fortress. This officer, who was more German than Turk, I knew before my incarceration, though I never saw him afterwards. His assumption of command initiated a series of events which could never have occurred had the energetic personal supervision of General Kiazim Karabekir not been withdrawn from the Erzeroum garrison, and we soon commenced to experience the deterioration in the military discipline of the garrison resulting from the departure of that enlightened and efficient Commander.

On June 15th I received a visit from an officer of the new Headquarters Staff, who demanded the surrender of our cars, handing me at the same time a letter from the new Commander informing me that they were needed for the use of the Turkish Army. I replied that I was, of course, unable to resist this demand, but that at the same time we yielded only to force; and during that night I took effective steps, as it was, of course, my duty to do, to render them unserviceable, although the Turks were as unable to obtain any evidence of this, as they were incapable of locating, and remedying, the highly technical causes of their unserviceable condition. The following day a party of their transport-drivers arrived, headed by an experienced mechanical transport officer, and we then passed several very agreeable hours watching their ineffectual efforts to start the cars, which eventually were removed in tow, a pair of bullocks being required for each car.

On this occasion I first became aware of the horrifying possibility that there might be found amongst our party any man who could prove capable of disgracing the uniform which we were all so proud to wear, by giving assistance to the enemy; for although I pointed out to the Turkish expert the cause of the trouble in starting the cars was due to the worn-out condition of the electrical ignition devices of the motors, replacements for which I assured him I had ordered from Constant, our one Irish driver Mahoney did his best in every way to assist the Turks in their endeavours at repair, though the other men quite properly refused to afford them any assistance whatever.

I am anxious here to state that under the command of Kiazim Karabekir we had been treated with every consideration, and, an officer being quartered in the house, I had been at liberty to communicate to him any points, with regard to our confinement, to which I might wish to draw the attention of his superiors. I had also been permitted at any time to write to the Army Commander, with the certainty that my complaint would not only reach his hands, but that it would with equal certainty receive all reasonable consideration from him. From this time onwards, however, the treatment accorded to us was entirely different; our resident officer was withdrawn, and our guards consisted subsequently of the lowest class of ignorant Turkish recruits, under the orders of a corporal, at whose mercy we were left, and who was careful to see that none of my complaints reached his superior officers, who ceased either to inspect, or even to visit, our quarters.

The consequence of this neglect of supervision was that the food and necessaries which we were able to purchase were taken from us by our guards, who waxed fat as we starved, and that it became necessary to pay them fantastic sums to obtain a tenth part of their value in food. Our health, therefore gradually began to deteriorate, and we became so weak as to be incapable of the least effort, and also, in the absence of proper nourishment, we suffered severely from fever, dysentery, and general emaciation.

In early August the first Bolshevik troops arrived, and were greeted by more demonstrations, torchlight processions parading the town in their honour; the Turkish officers at the same time adopted the Bolshevik marks of rank on their uniforms in place of their own, and all became (for the time at least )"Tavarish" (the Russian term for Citizen-Comrade). At this time, also, the Turkish officers were all paid in Russian gold, Russian ten-rouble gold pieces becoming more common in Erzeroum than golden sovereigns were in London before the war.

On August 4th Mahoney, the Irish driver, was taken to hospital at his own request, as he had neither the courage nor the desire to make any effort in the face of the conditions we were called upon to endure. At the same time I applied for the issue of rations to my party, alleging that I had no funds remaining upon which to subsist. About mid-August the first rations were issued to us, consisting of terribly inferior black bread and the odd remains of the army commissariat meat, after the Turkish soldiers' rations had been cut up and distributed.

On this we might just have subsisted had the quantity which was issued for our support ever reached us, but our guards saw to it that we obtained only the barest amount which would suffice to keep us alive, and at the same time the oil which was issued for our light and the wood for our fuel provided the maximum of light and warmth for our guards, whilst we were forced to dispense with such luxuries. We now became very considerably weaker, and about this time one of the men secured a photograph showing my own general appearance, which will convey a better idea of our physical deterioration than it is possible to gather from any description in words. The snow now came down again to last for the winter, and our condition became more and more deplorable.

During this time we were being constantly approached by emissaries from the Mechanical Transport Department, who endeavoured to persuade us to render them assistance in the repair of the cars, in consideration of which assistance they promised us everything (up to, and even including, our freedom), which they considered might prove to us an adequate inducement to come to their assistance. In the case of the men now left with me, however, their efforts in that direction never even received a moment's consideration. And in any case we were well able to estimate their promises at their proper value.

Eventually, on October 3rd, our house was again surrounded, and an officer told me that he was empowered to search the house. He subsequently proceeded direct to the spot on the ground floor where certain spare electric coils had been buried, and, having dug them up, took them away, at the same time taking with him the driver Mahoney, who had returned that day from the Turkish hospital, and whom I did not seen again for many months.

As the things they dug up had been the only portion of the hidden parts which were known to Mahoney, it was, of course, quite evident whom we had to thank for our betrayal, and as, the next day, the interpreter Polakoff was also taken by the Bolsheviks as a deserter from the Russian Army, we were left in doubt whether he had not also been concerned in the matter. However, I cannot bring myself to accuse any man of such conduct without definite proof, and that, in his case, was not forthcoming, as we saw him no more, and are still ignorant of his fate.

From this time on we went from bad to worse, till we were hardly able to crawl about the house, and I then considered it highly improbable that I myself should survive the winter, though the younger men might be able to do so. I had, however, kept a small store of money in reserve, and with its assistance we contrived to eke out a truly miserable existence, although frequently without any food at all.

I have a note that on December 18th, in perishing cold weather, "we had then been sixteen days without the smallest particle of meat, and had not had even black bread, or any supply of food at all, for six days," whilst the note continues: "All complaints unnoticed, misery extreme." These last two words strike one now as being rather superfluous.

This was our condition on Christmas Eve, when the cold was intense and I slept in all my great-coats, wearing my snow-boots, and being also wrapped up, including my head, in every blanket that I had. In the first grey of the winter dawn on Christmas Day I suddenly awoke, and, to my infinite surprise, heard a very weak and trembling voice addressing me, saying, "*A Merry Christmas, sir.*" My first thought, of course, was that this was as good a dream as I could expect, but, on the words being repeated, I crawled from my little camp-bed, and found my batman Leadbeater standing in the doorway, supporting himself, in his weakness, by holding on to the post. I thanked him, of course, most "heartily" for his Christmas wishes, and wished him the same in return, but all the while I was gradually taking in his appearance, with the utmost astonishment.

He was dressed in full uniform (it is true that it was in some places in sad need of repair), but everything was scrupulously clean, to the last strap and fold of his puttees, whilst his boots and his brass buttons and badges shone like stars in the dim light of the winter's morning.

As soon as I got over my astonishment I congratulated him upon the appearance of my "Army" (the men always spoke of themselves as such) on Christmas morning. He then said, in rather quavering tones, that the "*Army*" wished to know at what time I would prefer to take my "*Christmas dinner*"! and again I gasped with astonishment, and then begged him, for the Lord's sake, to tell me what it was all about, for, as far as I knew, we had nothing to eat but a piece of two of black bread. He then told me that the "Army" had been preparing a surprise for me, and that each of the three of them had prepared a dish for my Christmas dinner, and, please, what time would I take it?

I then consulted him as to what time would be the most convenient, as it was evident to me that the right place for their delicacies was downstairs, and not in my room, and I was determined that my share of them should be the most infinitesimal which they would allow of, and that their feast, whatever it might be, should get down to these gallant fellows just as soon and in as complete a condition as I could managed to ensure. It was then agreed that dinner should be at twelve o'clock, and that each expert *chef* should bring in his own special masterpiece, and on that he left me.

No sooner had the door closed upon him than I went to my trunk and got out my one good tunic, which I kept always against the long-hoped-for day when we might eventually be released, and which made a brave show of colour, with a brand-new set of ribbons, etc., and I "started in" at once to clean it properly; also my belt and boots, being determined to be in no way behind my comrades in showing our guards how the British Army "turned out" for their great national "Bairam," as the Turks call their feasts.

Twelve o'clock, therefore, found me seated at my little camp-table in my very best attire, which, I trust, did no discredit to the "Army" downstairs or elsewhere. On the sound of the midday gun the door opened, and Ankers appeared, carrying a dish, about which there was a certain suggestion of "eggs," and resplendent himself down to the last buckle and button.

He wished me a "Merry Christmas," which I reciprocated, and I then told him how proud I felt of their pluck, and how I hoped they would allow me to come to see the men's dinner, according to the immemorial custom of the army. He said that they would be delighted, and so I got him away as soon as possible with his wonderful production undisturbed. He was immediately followed by Carter, whose appearance was, if anything, even more resplendent, but who was sadly weak, as he had long suffered, even more severely than the rest of us, from acute dysentery.

His masterpiece was a "plum-pudding" (!), made, as I learnt afterwards, from crumbs which they had swept up from the now very weevilly dust remaining from our tins of army biscuits, long since considered as finished, but at which he had been working for weeks to produce from them some semblance of a pudding. This also was rapidly passed over, though it was insisted on that I should cut off a piece; and he then also left me.

Last of all Leadbeater appeared with a tart, made I know not how, but which he was graciously pleased to allow me to admire without detracting from its magnificent appearance, or interfering with the elaborate motto of "A Merry Xmas" which distinguished its truly wonderful "crust." It was then agreed that I should join them downstairs in five minutes' time, and assist at their festivities, and he then "tottered off" after the others.

I found myself now faced by the most difficult problem of all, which was to get down the stairs myself. However, there being at the moment no Turks about to see me, I made a great effort, and, sticking close to the walls, eventually reached the head of the very dilapidated staircase, where I was at once in apparently hopeless difficulties, owing to the absence of any form of banister or hand-rail. There, having made quite certain that I was unobserved, I got down on my hands and knees, and so descended backwards with great success, regaining my feet against the wall at the foot of the staircase before reaching the men's door, when I knocked, and was at once told to "come in."

The few odd old boards which served as a table were covered with a towel, scrupulously clean, as were also our few dilapidated iron cups and plates, the table being already spread with the "delicacies" which I had passed in review upstairs, the men on my arrival standing to "attention" with marked and rather unexpected success.

The first proceeding was, of course, to sit down as soon as possible, before anyone had time to *fall* down, of which there was very imminent danger. I then addressed them, and asked by what possible means they had managed to provide this repast, in which I saw signs of eggs, raisins, and other unheard-of delicacies which were far beyond our means.

For a long time they would not tell me, but I was very insistent, and at last the secret came out, told in almost a whisper, as they knew well I should never have allowed it had

I known what they proposed to do, for they confessed that they had *sold their socks,* sooner than be unable to keep up the traditions of the British Army, by some attempt, however poor, to celebrate their Christmas Day in their quarters, as is the custom throughout the British Army. I then told them what I wanted to say to them, and *did* say, which cannot have differed much, I expect, from what those who read this story would have wished to say to such glorious men as these, had they been privileged, as I was, to address them at that moment.

During this time our guards, who occupied the next room, had become aware that something unusual was in progress, and each hole in the wall and crack in the door was gradually filled with dirty, Turkish, low-class faces, whilst quite a number were also peering in through the barbed wire which covered the windows. As my discourse proceeded, they finally invaded the room itself, and crowded round our miserable table, furious all of them at our undefeated aspect, and also at the fact that they could not understand a word we were saying.

Finally, I asked the men if they would back me up if I tried to sing "God Save the King." Some very weak voices answered me that "they were willing enough to try, if I so wished, but that they feared it was beyond their powers to do themselves justice." This feeling I perfectly understood, and I therefore stood up, and they with me, and, taking off our caps, we gave, with all the strength we could muster, three very trembling cheers for "The King."

I much fear that they were very weak and quavering cheers, but the hearts that beat behind them were stout and strong and true, and I feel confident that if His Gracious Majesty could have heard them he would have appreciated them as deeply as many far more powerful ones he has heard from the lusty throats of his soldiers, who shout, on Christmas Day at home, with the power that comes from the good roast beef and beer of Old England, enjoyed amidst happy surroundings. Our humble effort came from loyal hearts, indeed, but from men cut off entirely for many weary months from their homes and their comrades, shut up in a wild and desolate country, weak and ill, and "blue" with cold, and with sadly empty stomachs, but still undefeated, and, as such, commanding the respect even of the wild guards around them.

## PHOTOGRAPH OF WOODEN MODEL

The model made out of twenty-eight odd pieces of firewood by Col. R. with a broken pocket-knife from his own designs, which were also made in prison, without india-rubber, on a piece of dirty card-board which had been used to replace the glass of the window

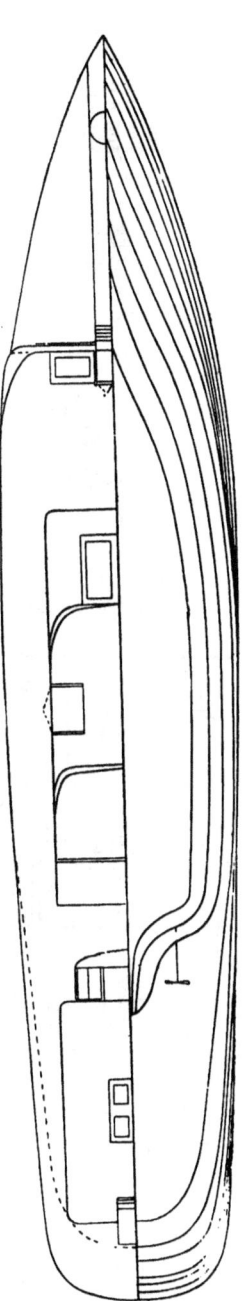

The deck-plan and lines of the hull

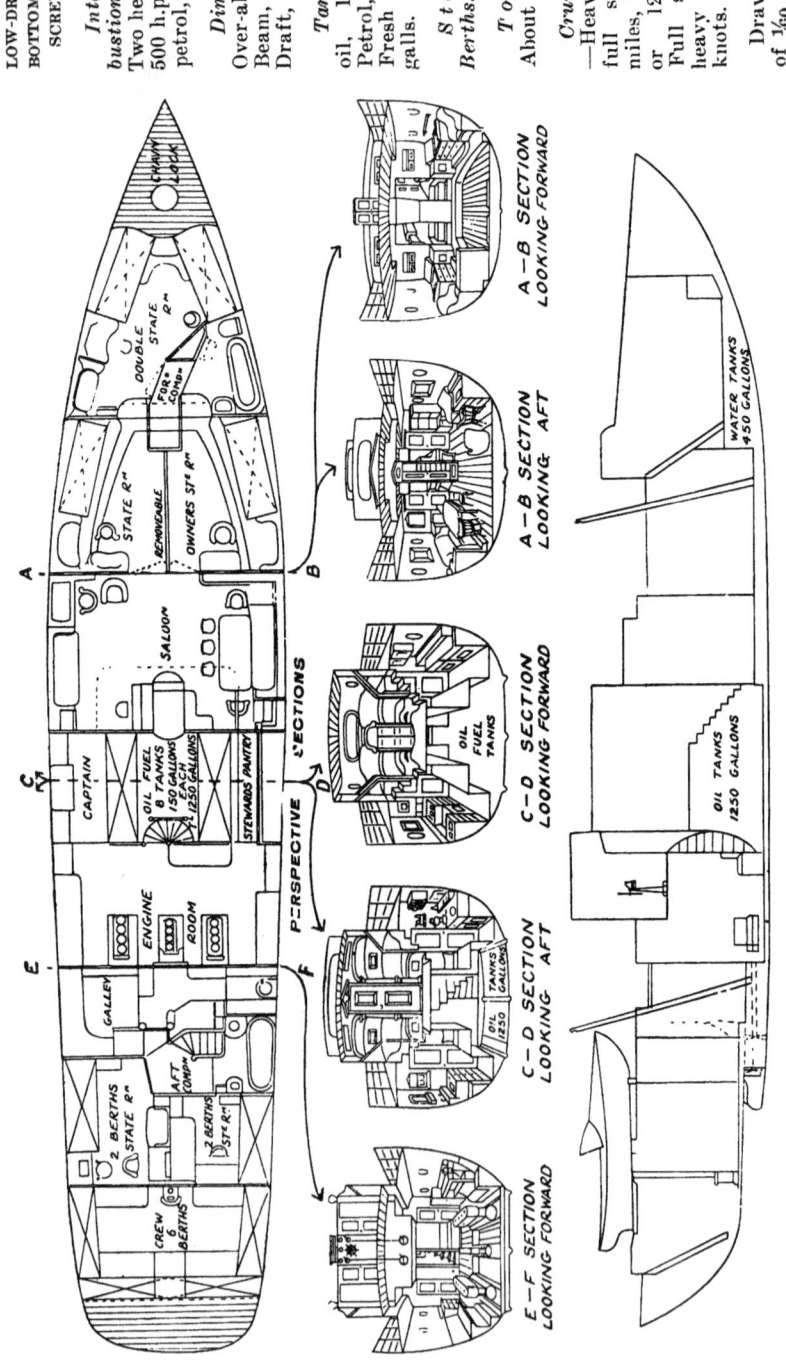

DETAIL OF SHALLOW-DRAFT, FLAT-BOTTOMED, TRIPLE-SCREW YACHT.

*Internal Combustion Engines.*—Two heavy oil, 250-500 h.p. each. One petrol, 40-80 h.p.

*Dimensions.*—Over-all, 80 feet. Beam, 15 feet. Draft, 4 feet.

*Tanks.*—Heavy oil, 1,250 galls. Petrol, 200 galls. Fresh water, 450 galls.

*State-room Berths.*—Eight.

*Tonnage.*—About 100 tons.

*Cruising Range.*—Heavy oil, at full speed, 2,000 miles, (*i.e.*, 5 days or 120 hours). Full speed, with heavy oil, 16.75 knots.

Drawn on scale of 1/60 or 5 feet to 1 inch, and reduced for reproduction.

The designs, drawings, and model took eight and a half months to complete

The corporal of the guard, when our small cheers died down, asked me what it was all about, and I had then the great satisfaction of telling him that it was our national "Bairam" (feast), and that we were cheering our "Padishah" (the King of England) and the British Army, *her zaman galeeb* (the ever-victorious)! On that I made my way back again to my room, thoroughly exhausted, but in a mood to defy and fight any Turk or any other man or beast, and so must have been feeling much the better for our glorious Christmas effort.

After this great day our lot became even worse, and in spite of all our efforts we were becoming despondent, when, on January 2nd, arrived a box, the only communication of any kind which we received from outside our prison walls during our long captivity. It was sent us by two kind women and one man, worthy representatives at Trezibond of the great and glorious American relief organization, whose matchless record of aid rendered to suffering humanity commands the admiration of all nations. They, by what means we never ascertained, contrived to get their gift through to us, though nothing reached us from any other quarter.

What the box may have contained originally we never knew, as, of course, it was opened by the guards, and all that reached us was an invaluable piece of bacon and some cigars; the former the guards would not touch, and the latter they were afraid to be seen smoking. We therefore received these safely, though all else had disappeared, except what we valued far more than all the rest, and that was a small card, on which was written:

> A Merry Xmas
> To Colonel Rawlinson,
> From the Americans in Trebizond.
> (*Signed*) ALMA B. KERR,
> JESSIE WHITE,
> ALBERT L. CHRISTIANSEN.

I wrote at once to thank them for their kind thought, but I fear that my letter never got farther than our guards, and if by chance any of those three kind-hearted citizens of the great American nation, whom I have been quite unable to trace, should be still alive and chance to see this book, I want them to know with what thankful feelings we received their good wishes, and how much we felt encouraged by the knowledge of their sympathy to face the troubles and privations which still lay before us; and in the name of my men, as well as in my own, I tender them our sincere and grateful thanks for their fellow-feeling in our sufferings.

We all at this time worked at making something, whatever our very meagre resources would allow. Ankers made a model of a motor tractor in wood; Carter made a plough, and also an excellent model of a native ox-cart, or araba, as the Turks call them, also in wood; whilst Leadbeater, who had been brought up as a watchmaker, produced a tiny brass coal-scuttle out of cartridge cases, which was quite a work of art.

I myself, rather ambitiously, designed a yacht, and produced scale-drawings of every detail, including the lines of the hull, finally constructing a model of the complete vessel in wood, with the aid of the one broken knife-blade which remained in my possession. This task took me eight and a half months of constant work, and the model and the drawings are amongst my most cherished possessions in my home to-day.

By these means we survived the month of January, and on February 1st, 1922, we were moved from our house to the common prison, that being the first time we had been outside the walls of our abode since March 16th, 1921, a period of ten months and fifteen days.

# CHAPTER IV

### THE PRISON

Some reflections—Armenian prisoners—The building—The new Commander—Our fellow-prisoners—The Armenian officers—Salah-a-din—A letter—My answer—Outside assistance—Another letter—The surprise—The search—Its result—Deprived of all literature—Salah-a-din's kindness—His books—Rumours of exchange—Visit of Headquarters Staff Officer—Order for our march to the coast—Our preparations—Lieutenant Hairie—Our lack of resources—Obtain credit from the "jobmaster"—Our departure—Ilija—"George's" lameness—The hovel at Pernikapan—The Khop—Baiburt—Khadrak—Gumush Khaneh—Zigana Khan—The pass—Hamsikeui—Trebizond—Our good treatment there.

In recalling the feelings with which I received the order that we were to be removed to the prison, I realize that all other sentiments were swallowed up in an overwhelming emotion of degradation and disgust that we, British soldiers who had done nothing but our duty, should be herded with the lowest criminals in the common gaol.

The bare fact itself brought home to me, with a bitterness which I am powerless to describe, the immensity of the fall which the prestige of my country had suffered through the vacillating weakness of those into whose hands the custody of that priceless national heritage had fallen since the proud days, a short twenty-eight months before, when our armies were everywhere victorious and the British uniform commanded respect throughout every country in the world.

I well knew, and had been brought up to be familiar with, the unremitting care and labour by which, during three centuries, the standing and credit of the British Flag had been built up throughout the East. Names of great men, for ever famous among my countrymen, flashed through my mind, who had devoted their life's work to this supreme object, and bitter thoughts surged up insistently as to what would have been the penalties exacted in days gone by for such an insult, which was probably destined now to be suppressed or ignored, or if, indeed, any reparation were demanded, its exaction would be confided to the futile efforts of Greeks or Armenians—sad champions indeed to uphold the prestige of the British Army.

The above may seem very bitter reflections, but no one could know better, or feel more deeply than I did, how the news of our imprisonment would run through every bazaar throughout the East, and how this defiance of the British by the Turks would be magnified and used for their own purposes by our enemies. In the feelings of sadness which then were mine there was never any thought as to what our own fate might be, but only an abiding sorrow that our great country should be made to appear so cheap and powerless in the eyes of ignorant Oriental populations.

On leaving our old quarters we first saw "Armenian prisoners." Those we saw were being used as labourers (slaves would be the proper word), and accustomed as I had become to see starvation, misery, and privations of every description, yet the appearance of these men gave me, even at that time, a shock such as I had never before experienced, and a memory which will remain with me whilst life lasts. It was then midwinter, the snow everywhere lying deep, the force and temperature of the arctic wind being beyond description; yet those miserable spectres were clothed, if that word can be applied to their condition, in the rottenest and filthest of verminous rags, through which their fleshless bones protruded in many places, so that it seemed *impossible* that humanity could be reduced to such extremities and live. In fact, the duration of their tragic misery depended only upon the individual vitality, which enabled some, possibly the least fortunate, to continue to exist longer than others, to whom death brought a speedier relief from their sufferings.

On arrival at the prison I was relieved to find that, though now used as such, it was originally a barrack, and was in very fair condition. A building of two floors faced the street, with an archway communicating with a yard in the interior, the east side of which consisted of a most ancient and interesting old mosque, now used for military stores. Along the north side ran a one-storied building, also used as stores, whilst on the west side was a two-storied building, with barred windows without glass, in which the Armenian officers were confined.

The ground floor of the main building, which occupied the

## THE ERZEROUM PRISON

The prison yard, with Armenian prisoners, taken from Col. R.'s cell

Leaving the prison—Col. R. shaking hands with Lt. Salah-a-din;
Lt. Hairie in black coat

south side of the courtyard, was used for the guards, and on the first floor was a corridor out of which opened four rooms on the south side and five on the north side. My three men were allotted one of these rooms and myself another, both on the north side, upon which the sun never shone. These rooms were fairly clean and had windows in which there were remains of glass. We were, however, allowed to bring from our house whatever we possessed, and the men were furnished with soldiers' beds, whilst I retained my camp-bed; and we were able presently to obtain a stove for each room and occasional wood for fuel, a most vital necessity, as the temperature fell constantly below zero.

Here, on the first morning of my arrival, I was visited by the new Commander of the fortress, a Lieut.-Colonel Emin Bey, whom I had previously known when he commanded a brigade on the frontier. He was quite civil, and, I should say, an efficient officer. His predecessor, to whose neglect of supervision our previous sufferings were directly due, had now, as it appeared, been deprived of his command, to which fact we owed our transfer to the prison, where supervision, of the treatment accorded to us, could be more effectively exercised by the new Commander.

On the whole, we were better off in the prison than we had been at our house, for although we were confined to our rooms and sadly missed the back-yard where we had been able to take exercise, yet this was largely compensated for by the fact that an officer was in charge of the prison and resident in the room opposite my own, to whom I was always at liberty to complain, and upon whose personality much depended. At the time of our arrival at the prison the officer in charge was a Lieutenant named Salah-a-din, with whom I got on very well, and who was very friendly and visited me in my room almost every day. I was indebted to him for many favours, and I did my best to teach him some English, which he was very anxious to learn. He remained in charge for six weeks after our arrival.

In the same corridor, on the opposite side, was also confined at this time a Kurdish Pasha, with the rank of a General in the Turkish Army. He had three attendants, officers of his own tribe, but I was never at liberty to speak to them, so that

I was unable to ascertain the reason of his confinement. I had reason, however, to surmise it was on account of his friendly attitude to the Allies. His name was Hussein Pasha, from the Zilanli tribe of Alashgird, and I had often heard of him previously, though I had never either been to his country or met him elsewhere.

The occupants of the other rooms at this time were not interesting, and the only distraction available was to look through the bars into the courtyard, from whence we could see the sun shining on the snow-mountains 30 miles away to the north, across the marsh, which served to remind us the world was still going on as usual outside our prison walls.

We also could see the Armenian officers, who were let out into the yard on the snow for about an hour every day. There were at this time nearly 200 of them, and they were in a bad way, so that their numbers gradually became automatically less. The mortality amongst them, however, bore no comparison to that amongst their men, who were confined elsewhere and of whom we only saw a few occasionally.

At this time I was reduced to the greatest straits for money, my reserve having nearly disappeared, and, as I was supplied with no rations, I was reduced to selling what little I had in order to buy food. In this matter the good-will of the officer Salah-a-din stood me in good stead, as he bought my fur coat from me himself, and saw to it that my other things were honestly sold in the town, and that we were not robbed unduly by the soldiers who were deputed to effect purchases for us. He also enabled us to purchase a small amount of wood for fuel, which was very difficult to obtain and was a matter of vital importance to our existence.

A fortnight or so after our arrival at the prison our officer obtained authority to permit one of my men to go daily to the market, accompanied by a guard, and thus we were able to economize still further by purchasing only what happened to be cheapest in the market at the moment. One day, about February 20th, the first "event" of our prison life occurred. On one of my men bringing me the purchases effected in the town, he gave me a short note which had been pushed into his hand in the market, and on opening it I found it was from someone whom I did not know, but who was evidently an Armenian, who asked if he could do anything to assist us.

Here was a development indeed, and one which caused me many hours of anxious deliberation. Naturally, I feared that this might be a manœuvre on the part of the Turks to entrap me into some move which would enable them to connect me with one of the Armenian plots which were constantly being discovered, in which case our situation would be infinitely worse than it was already. This seemed the more likely as at that time, although in entire ignorance of what might be happening in Europe, I had for some time past "sensed" a distinctly more unfriendly attitude towards us on the part of our gaolers. It was not, therefore, till after many hours' anxious thought that I finally decided to answer the letter at all, and even then only in a very guarded manner, saying that I was much interested in what he said, and asking him to communicate any proposition which he might desire to make.

This apparently reached its destination safely, as shortly afterwards I received a more elaborate epistle, which was handed to Corporal Ankers by an individual who seemed to be a Turk, and who had appeared in our corridor in a manner it would be unwise to describe, in case it might furnish the means for his identification. This letter was signed in a name I did not know, and asked me definitely what the writer could do to assist in or prepare for an attempt at our escape. I therefore wrote to say it would be necessary to purchase horses, by degrees, as if getting together a caravan, and that as soon as the snow rendered any passage of the mountains possible we could arrange further details. I was, however, careful not to disclose in which direction I thought of escaping.

The letter was the more interesting as my correspondent told me the bearer was absolutely to be trusted and had access to the prison at all times; also that one of our guards had been suborned and could be trusted, as he was in reality an Armenian. I was also told I could recognize this soldier at any time by the fact that he would have a piece of paper protruding out of a certain pocket. I was at this time allowed to go occasionally to my men's cell, which was two doors away from mine, a sentry with loaded rifle and fixed bayonet being always on duty day and night, outside my door in the corridor, to watch all my movements. Each time I now went into the corridor I saw a Turkish soldier lounging about, with the above described piece of paper protruding from his pocket. I therefore began to have more faith in my unknown correspondent outside and in the possibility of making use of his assistance.

Matters were in this state on February 26th, when, soon after midday, Ankers came to me and handed me another letter. This was still from my unknown friend, by the hand of the gentleman who had access to the prison, and to the effect that he had already begun to purchase horses, and that he was located at a certain village about 10 miles off, across the plain. It then went on to say that all his family had been massacred by the Turks, and that he himself wished to "drink the blood of the Turks," and also to establish Bolshevik committees and every other kind of horror all over the country. This gave me a terrible shock, as not only was it the most damnable and impossible nonsense, which did not interest me at all, but it was at the same time the most dangerous form of statement to commit to writing which it was possible to conceive, and the life of anyone having anything to do with it would not have been worth a moment's purchase if the Turks once got possession of such an excessively compromising document.

I was actually reading this most murderous and dangerous effusion before my window, 14 feet exactly from the door of my cell, when the said door burst suddenly open and in marched the second-in-command of the fortress, a Major Avni Bey, accompanied by three other officers, and I became at the same time aware that an armed guard of at least twenty-five men, with fixed bayonets, was drawn up in the corridor outside. I wheeled round instantly, and as I turned slipped the letter into my breeches pocket, where it at once seemed to *burn* like a red-hot coal. Nevertheless, with suitable politeness and unconcern, I said good-morning and asked to what fortunate event I was indebted for the pleasure of his unexpected visit. This very polite speech contained an absolute truth—namely, the unexpected nature of the visit, as it was indeed at that moment as unexpected as it was undesirable and unfortunate.

He replied that they had received information from Angora that I had sent a telegram to London (!), which had caused their Government great annoyance, and that orders had been received that all my papers were to be taken from me, and that I was not to be allowed to retain any books or writing materials in future, and also that my cell and myself were to be thoroughly searched forthwith.

Under these circumstances it may easily be imagined that the hot coal in my breeches pocket appeared to me to actually burst into flame. However, I retained what the sensational writers are pleased, as a rule, to refer to as the most perfect "sang-froid," and that at a moment when such a condition was most vitally necessary. During the few moments spent in going over the papers on my table, I was busy cudgelling my brains to devise a means whereby it might be possible for one man, surrounded by so many eager eyes all fixed upon him the whole time, to use his intelligence to such good purpose as to outwit so many observers. Upon the apparently impossible achievement of that feat all our lives were probably at that moment depending, as, for an absolute certainty, in any case, depended the life of our friend then waiting in the village ten miles off to "drink the blood of the Turk," and also that of his emissary in the passage outside, with regard to both of whom the blood-drinking process appeared likely to be infallibly and immediately reversed.

That being the position, I determined to do my best and to make use of what wits I had for all they were worth. I therefore proceeded to show them all my papers, including my diary, which I had carefully kept since the day of our arrest, and explained each paper to them with the utmost candour. This being concluded, I produced my portmanteau, which contained the greater part of my very meagre kit, saying they would doubtless wish to examine everything in it. On their assenting, I opened the portmanteau, and took my seat in a rickety old chair, which had once been covered in velvet, now hanging in tatters, the seat being furnished with springs, some of which still remained under the remnants of the velvet, and with the position of each and all of which I was thoroughly familiar. Sitting thus, sideways to the door, through which the guard outside were also observing me closely, I proceeded to take out each article of kit and to hold it up for their examination, passing it afterwards round all the four officers for their inspection also, after which it was placed on the floor beyond the portmanteau.

We soon came to my new tunic, which I was keeping against the happy day of my eventual release, and, as I expected and reckoned on, the appearance of this interesting and essentially military garment produced considerable curiosity on the part of all present, so that I was called upon to explain all the marks of rank, the respectable collection of chevrons, and particularly why one only was red and the rest blue; also as to the why and the wherefore of all the ribbons, etc. During this time, as each point was explained, the interest grew, and when we came to the decorations, to each of which I pointed with my finger, I felt pretty sure I had all their attention fixed on those objects, and I profited by that moment to slip the letter, or rather the blazing coal, out of my breeches pocket, jamming it instantly, whilst all eyes were fixed on the tunic, under a familiar protruding spring in the chair, under the tattered cover. That manœuvre having been successfully accomplished unobserved, I experienced a deep sense of relief, for, although I felt certain the chair was destined also to be thoroughly examined, yet a part, and that probably the most difficult, of my task had been triumphantly achieved. Before the examination of the portmanteau was complete, I found occasion to leave the chair and sit on the floor, apparently with the object of being in a better position to show them the construction of the trunk itself.

This completed, I went up to the Major and said I supposed he would be bound, according to his orders, to search *me* also, and on his answering, "Certainly," I commenced at once to undress, handing him for inspection each article as I took it off, and finally remaining in my vest only, and nearly frozen. As soon as the articles of my humble attire had been thoroughly examined, I lost no time in getting into them again, seating myself in my faithful relic of a chair for the purpose; and as soon as that hurried operation was complete, I pushed away the portmanteau and replaced it by my kit-bag, with the examination of which we then proceeded.

The articles here were of less interest. I had, however, reckoned upon my spurs in this instance to come to my assistance, for I had a pair of silver-plated spurs, which are quite unknown in Anatolia, and these had two peculiarities: first, they were furnished with silver-plated chains in place of straps, and, secondly, they were what we called "dummies," there being no rowels, nor even the usual slits provided to carry those rather barbarous contrivances.

I was in no sense mistaken in my estimate of the Turk and the interest he would take in these very European articles, for when I took out the first one and showed the silver chains, I was overwhelmed with questions about them, and when I handed them to the Major for him to examine, every eye followed them, whilst I took advantage of that instant to withdraw my "coal" of a letter from under the spring of the chair and to restore it once more to my pocket unobserved, as soon as possible afterwards taking up a position near the window, where the officers were busy packing up all my papers, books, etc., for removal, to answer the many questions which they asked about them. That operation concluded, they then turned their attention to the little furniture I had, and the poor old chair suffered a very drastic search, from which it never afterwards recovered, a matter of no consequence, however, seeing that it had already rendered a service more valuable to us all than fifty such chairs could ever have been, even when new and in immaculate condition.

Soon after the search-party's departure I received a visit from my men, all in a state of the greatest anxiety, as they knew, of course, I had received the letter, without knowing the dangerous nature of its contents, and they knew also that I could have had neither the time nor the means to destroy it. They therefore feared the worst, and could hardly believe me when I told them the story of how a little of that "sang-froid" already mentioned had enabled me to get the better of so many keenly watching eyes, under such apparently impossible conditions.

It was, however, a sad day indeed for us, and particularly for me. The others, being together, could talk and enjoy the benefit of each other's society, taking it also in turns to accompany our food-purchaser to the market; but for myself, I was rigorously confined to my cell and had no such means of passing the time, and had also lost many personal papers and records, quite irreplaceable, so that it needed indeed a stiff upper lip to keep up one's heart in the dreadful solitude that ensued. Everything had been taken from me, even to my steel mechanic's "rule," from which I had taken the scale dimensions to make the drawings of my model yacht; but the model itself and the drawings of it had, thanks to the intervention of my good friend Salah-a-din, been left to me. For this I was indeed grateful, and I commenced forthwith the construction of a new scale on a piece of stick, taking the dimensions from the drawings of the yacht, as from this scale I was determined at once to commence to design and construct a model of a house, which might some day be of service, and would at any rate serve to occupy my mind and to enable me to fight against the terrible mental trial which I knew now confronted me, and which in so many instances has proved fatal to the reason of those unfortunate individuals who have been subjected to solitary confinement.

Salah-a-din was at this time most sympathetic, constantly coming to see me and even lending me books, which were invaluable in occupying my mind, though the books themselves were few in number and of no great interest, the best being some plays of Racine and Fénelon's "Odyssey," both in French, the latter being remarkably heavy reading even for a prison.

English is quite unknown in the countries occupying the 3,000 odd miles which lie between Constantinople and the north-western frontier of India. In these wild parts all the most interesting literature is in Persian, with some Arabic, no Turkish, and a sprinkling only of French and Russian. Of the latter I was fortunate indeed in obtaining a copy of Tolstoi's "La Guerre et la Paix" in French, which was worth its weight in gold to me, and enabled me to while away many tedious hours in picturing the remarkable and extremely varied phases of life which he there depicts with such wealth of detail and excessive verbosity.

Salah-a-din also kept me informed of what little news he had as to happenings in Europe, and gave me to understand that negotiations of some sort were then actually taking place between the Angora Council and the Allies, from which I gathered that he considered it possible we might be exchanged for certain Turkish Pashas, four of whom he named, who were

## IN KEMALIST TURKEY 299

then prisoners at Malta. This was exceedingly encouraging news, and was more or less confirmed when about this time I received a visit from Kiazim's Chief of the Staff, acting, I understood, under instructions from Angora, the evident object of his visit being to ascertain, if possible, what my views generally were as to the Nationalist Movement, and also with regard to the Turkish relations with the Russians and Kurds. He was apparently most particularly anxious to find out how much I knew, in order to form an estimate as to what view I should be likely to put forward in England if released.

I had already received similar visits from representatives coming direct from Angora, previous to our transfer to the prison, and I had a good many more afterwards, but on each occasion, though I listened carefully to all that was said, I kept my own counsel as to how much I knew of affairs generally, confining myself in every instance to forecasts of the future based only on previous information in my possession before my arrest, since which date I affirmed I had received no information at all as to the course of events either in Europe or elsewhere. With this negative information they perforce had to be content, and I was able to gather very little at this time myself, beyond the one important fact that Réouf Bey was still a prisoner in our hands at Malta, and that they were excessively anxious to obtain his release, upon which they evidently placed a higher value than on that of all the other prisoners put together.

On the morning of March 24th I received a visit from Emin Bey, the Commander of the fortress and district, who informed me I was to be sent to the coast of Trebizond for exchange against certain prisoners then at Malta, amongst whom was Réouf Bey, Mustapha Kemal's great friend and the leader of the Nationalist Party in the Parliament which had assembled at Constantinople a year previously. This glorious news, in my then sadly weak and feeble condition, affected me so deeply that several long minutes passed before I was able to utter one word. As soon as I was able to speak, I proceeded to inquire as to how it was intended that we should travel, as the snow lay deep, and March and April are, of all the months in the year, probably the worst in which to take the road in those parts, as the sun begins to have more power at that time of the year, thawing the surface of the snow in the daytime sufficiently to make the use of sleighs impossible, except on the higher passes, and at the same time causing all torrents to run in flood, and avalanches and other unpleasant incidents, such as constant and heavy falls of rock, to be frequent amongst the mountains.

I was told that we should march under charge of an officer and an escort of six soldiers, who would accompany us all the way, and that two arabas (small native carts) would be provided for the party, and that the journey would be accomplished in ten days, supplementary guards being provided by the local gendarmerie where risky conditions might render them necessary. Having given me this outline of what was intended, the Governor left me, saying we should start on the 28th—namely in four days' time.

On his departure, my first proceeding was, of course, to communicate the news at once to the men, and I therefore staggered up the corridor to their room. On opening their door, I had no need to say anything at all, for one glance at my face told them all that I was finding it so physically difficult to convey to them, and we all then sat for some time in silence, our feelings all round being too deep for words. After a while, however, we "bucked up" a bit, and began to discuss what preparations it was possible and necessary for us to make for a journey that could not fail to be a terribly severe one.

We realized immediately that, as only two small arabas were to be provided for the whole party, they would at most contain only the men's kits and forage which would be required for the mules, the latter being necessarily a considerable amount, as none would be obtainable on the road. If by chance there should be any room left, it would obviously be our Turkish guards who would *ride*, and we should have to *walk*. This, in our then weak condition, I felt sure we should be unable to do. For though the men lately had each of them been able to walk as far as the bazaar for purchases, once every three days as their turn came round, I had not been out of my cell for two months, and for ten and a half months previously had not been outside the walls of our house; so that a 200 miles' march through the snow in four days' time would be, for me at any rate, an absolute impossibility. I was likewise at last literally at the end of my resources as regards ready money, and it would be necessary to buy food for the journey, or we should be in danger of starvation.

Under these circumstances we went through everything we had, to see what remained for us to sell, to enable us to do our best in the way of preparations. There was, alas! lamentably little left, and what we had were only little humble things, such as metal mugs and plates, a small lamp, and various trifles which, though valuable to us, were of pitifully small value in the market. We had, however, a few blankets, some puttees, and some odds and ends which we packed up, and which I decided to get Salah-a-din to have sold for us at once.

A short while afterwards our friend himself returned, full of sympathetic congratulations on our prospect of release, and I explained to him exactly how we stood and all I feared for the journey. He then made the suggestion that he should apply to the *arabaji* (jobmaster) of the town, to see whether he could not obtain a conveyance for me from him on credit, payable on our arrival at Trebizond. This was the more likely, as the man was in a large way of business and, of course, knew me well. Salah-a-din therefore went off at once to the town to fetch this interesting individual. He brought the man back with him shortly afterwards, and he agreed without difficulty to let me have what he called a "victoria," as well as a large four-horse araba, for the journey, on my undertaking to pay him 150 Turkish pounds (equal then to about £17) on my arrival at Trebizond. This I immediately agreed to, and wrote out and signed and sealed the necessary undertaking.

Salah-a-din then brought along the officer who was to go in charge of us, a Transport Lieutenant named Hairie, and a capital fellow in every way, certainly one of the nicest Turks it has been my lot to meet, and a man whom I should be glad to see again at any time. He (Hairie) fell in at once with our suggestion, which, of course, could only be carried out with his approval and consent, and it was agreed that he and I should ride in the victoria, and the men and their belongings in the large four-horse araba. I then sold my very last treasure, a small carpet I had "hung on to" and slept on all the time, as a last resource in case of urgent necessity. It was a very good one, worth, under ordinary conditions, at least 150 Turkish pounds in Erzeroum, but I was glad indeed to get 37 for it when submitted to auction in the open market, under Salah-a-din's supervision.

The 37 Turkish pounds received, amounting, as they did, to about £4, enabled me to buy certain provisions and to keep a small sum over to pay for accommodation on the road, as, of course, none would be provided for us, and sleeping in the snow would probably have finished us, even if the other hardships of the journey did not. All being at last ready, we left Erzeroum at 3 P. M. on March 28th, to go 8 miles to the village of Ilija that night.

The victoria turned out to be a vehicle quite beyond adequate description. It had once, indeed, been a kind of open victoria, but by dint of traversing the unspeakably rough roads of this terrible country under excessive loads the ironwork forming the floor of the carriage, and connecting the front portion with the back axle, had gradually given way and bent, so that the back was at an angle which made it only possible to sit in the seat when leaning forward, an excessively uncomfortable and tiring position. When to this was added the astonishingly cramped amount of space originally allowed for in its design, it will be readily understood that it was far from providing any kind of luxury as a conveyance over 200 miles of the roughest roads in winter.

Salah-a-din said good-bye to us at the prison gate, but even then could not make up his mind to leave us, insisting on accompanying us as far as the the entrance-gates of the fortress to bid us finally "Godspeed." So small, however, was the carriage that, although Hairie and myself had succeeded in stowing ourselves into it after a fashion, Salah-a-din could find no corner on which to sit, and was obliged to stand on the very rickety step. At last, however, we were out of the town in the open snow of the plain, and finally started on what we then fondly imagined was our homeward road.

The road in the plain of Erzeroum was so bad and the snow so deep that it took us two and a half hours to do the 8 miles to Ilija, although we had three horses to our light conveyance, which threatened every moment to fall to pieces on the way. Our poor old faithful "George," also, who had never left me in the prison, and whose loving sympathy had served on countless occasions to cheer and encourage me during the long and bitter nights, was obliged to follow afoot through the frozen snow, with the result that his poor feet were cut to pieces, though he came on steadily without a falter, even when lame in every leg and bleeding from all his feet.

On arrival at Ilija we found what, for Anatolia, was quite good accommodation, as there are hot springs there which have for centuries been used as sulphur-baths, and therefore certain unusual comforts are provided there for visitors. We obtained a small room with a stove, which we lit, and after attending to poor "George's" feet as best we could, we made some tea and ate some of the rolls we had made at Erzeroum for our journey, and so were soon asleep and warm again, having all been nearly frozen.

Next morning we started at 8 A. M., poor "George" travelling "jammed in" between my knees, where he was doubtless very uncomfortable, but infinitely better off than he would have been struggling through the frozen snow on his poor wounded feet. In this way, too, as so often before, he kept me warmer than I should otherwise have been in the terrible wind which blows across that dreary snow-covered plain.

The road here was slightly better than the day before, but was still deep in snow and very difficult. It took us over four hours to reach Karabuik, 16 miles distant from Ilija. This is the western railhead of the Russian war-time Decauville Railway, and there is no railway running from the Russian frontier farther west than this, all communications, westward towards Angora, being by the road which here branches from the Erzeroum-Trebizond road and runs through Erzingan to Sivas. I noticed a good deal of ammunition here at the railhead, though I was unable at that time to ascertain either its origin or its destination.

On leaving Karabuik, room was found for "George" in the four-horse araba with the men, and we soon afterwards crossed the Euphrates, then in high flood, by a good bridge, and reached Ashkala, 27 miles from Ilija, at 1.30 P. M.—very good travelling, under the existing conditions. After leaving Ashkala, the foot-hills of the Khop range commence, and progress there became infinitely more difficult. It took us four hours to cover the 7 miles to the village of Pirnikapan at the entrance to the

Khop Pass, where we arrived in the dark at 6 P. M., quite worn out, wet through from the snowdrifts, and frozen with cold. Here we found no accommodation at all, as, though there was one miserable caravanserai, it was crowded, every square inch of it, with the low-class Persian camel-drivers of the caravans waiting there at that time to get over the pass. "Hairie," however, was equal to the occasion, and, mustering his soldiers, he at once burst open the door of the reeking hovel, proceeding subsequently by main force to eject the occupants until he had cleared enough space for us within its forbidding recesses. This we occupied at once, and we were even able, as we were famished with hunger, to eat some more of our rolls, in spite of the nauseating atmosphere.

Much though I have travelled in rough places, I have never, either before or since, had to pass a night amongst such surroundings as we there experienced. When free, it has always been my custom to bivouac in the open, whatever may be the state of the weather, sooner than seek refuge in any of these pestilential underground hovels. This time we were unavoidably "in for it," and the best had therefore to be made of it. The hovel itself was underground and was, of course, without windows, the roof, not more than 6 to 7 feet high, being made of the trunks of trees, and the whole covered with several feet of earth and many feet of snow. The solitary room, if such it can be called, of which the hovel consisted was about 20 by 30 feet, an unusually spacious apartment, it is true, in that country. This was due to the fact that it afforded the only accommodation in the place, and that the village itself was situated on the main road at the foot of the pass, where travellers are perforce obliged frequently to halt for considerable periods whilst the pass above is blocked by snow.

Out of this fearsome cavity Hairie and his soldiers had already flung at least twenty stinking Persians, though when we entered there were at least twice as many more remaining, packed close together in their foul and steaming sheepskins, a small and smoky lamp serving to illumine the clouds of smoke which rose from the fire of *tezek* (dried cow-dung) which burnt and stank in a brazier in the centre. This most objectionable odour was, however, entirely overpowered by the natural effluvia which rose from the recumbent Persians, who alone remained

## ON THE ROAD TO THE COAST

The beginning of the Khop Pass. Col. R. on right

The Upper Khop Pass

## COMING DOWN TO THE SEA

The party and guards clear of the snow at last on the ninth day
Note—Col. R.'s beard has turned "white!"

The "Victoria" in which Col. R. travelled 200 miles through the snow in nine days

motionless in that horirble place, where all else was literally "moving" with every species of verminous life. All this caused me such nausea that it was thanks only to the emptiness of my stomach that I escaped, by the barest margin, the fate which attends bad sailors in a storm at sea. Like everything else, however, the night eventually passed, though I feel convinced the recollection of it will remain with us all for ever. Our guards were moving before daylight next morning, and, the horses having been fed, we were on our way up the pass before eight A. M., truly thankful at last to be able to breathe the pure fresh mountain air, however cold it might be.

I have described the Khop Pass before, and will not, therefore, depict it again, beyond saying that never have I had to pass it under worse conditions, the drifts being so deep that our progress was lamentably slow, for on many occasions the carts had to be held upright by hand, to prevent their turning over and rolling down the hillside, an unpleasant experience which is by no means uncommon, and which one vehicle did actually succeed in affording us on this occasion.

My men were obliged to walk, though I stuck to my victoria, and, as they took short cuts, they were soon out of my reach, before I had had time to warn them as to the necessity of smearing their faces with mud to ease the glare of the snow as soon as the sun was fairly up. When, therefore, I at last caught them up at Khop Khaneh, the village beyond the pass, at 4 P. M., having then taken just eight hours to do the 13 miles, I found them suffering agonies from their eyes and heads, all feeling very ill and being completely knocked up. We were fortunate indeed on this occasion to obtain one of the only two rooms which this place affords, and also to be able to buy some eggs, which are very rarely obtainable there, so that by next morning we were more or less capable of continuing our journey. Conditions were much better beyond the pass, and, leaving at 8 A. M., we reached Baiburt at 1 P. M., securing there a small but dry room, with a fire, and also obtaining the, to us, most unusual luxury of a hot dinner from the restaurant in the town with what was almost the last of my ready money.

Having rested well, all the afternoon, we were in much better condition next morning at 8 A. M., when we started to cross the Baiburt Plain for 17 miles to Khadrak, at the foot of the Vavok

Pass, arriving there at 3.30 P.M., it having taken us seven and a half hours to do these 17 miles through deep snow and, at times, even deeper mud.

We were now all suffering from the effects of the wind on the Khop Pass two days previously, which had been this time colder than ever, and, accompanied as it was by a bright sun, had burned us all so severely that our faces were no longer sensitive to the touch, and began shortly to peel wherever the skin had been exposed to the wind and sun. I was thankful on this occasion for my thick beard, which left only my nose and cheeks exposed and so saved me much of the suffering which the men went through.

We had a small but warm room at Khadrak, and left at 7.15 A.M. next day, in a heavy snowstorm. The climbing of the Vavok Pass was difficult, but once over the summit things were much better, and in the Kharshut Valley beyond the road was quite good, so that we eventually reached Gumush Khaneh, 32 miles from Khadrak, at 5.30 P.M. Here, in the sheltered valley, at only 3,800 feet altitude, the weather was very much better, and though the wind was still bitterly cold, yet there were signs of spring in the orchards by the river-bank, though the trees were not yet actually in leaf. We found bad quarters in the public room at Gumush Khaneh, but it was at any rate *not* a hovel, and all camel-drivers were excluded; we were therefore not too badly off, and felt indifferent to discomforts now, as we knew we were all the while getting nearer to the coast and Home.

We left Gumush Khaneh at 7.15 A.M. next day, in a bitter wind and snowstorm; but with a good road and not much snow underfoot we had no difficulty in climbing the Lower Zigana Pass, and in reaching Zigana Khan, a small hamlet at 4,200 feet, 24 miles distant from our starting-point, by 4.30 P.M. Here we found a weather-proof but very rickety wooden room, with a stove, and passed the night all right, with snow falling heavily round us. With the weather as it was, we now knew well we should have the greatest difficulty in getting over the Zigana Pass the next day, and we were therefore on the road well before daylight, at 5.30 A.M. Finally we *did get over*, and, not to weary the reader with so many incidents of mountain-travel under such heartbreaking conditions, I will quote from my dairy about this, the hardest day we had, as follows:

"Left 5.30 A. M. Hell of a day—over our waists in snow—horses down—carts overturned—icy wind—temperature below zero. Arrived Hamsikeui (18 miles) 7.30 P. M., all dead-beat."

Those 18 miles, therefore, took us fourteen hours' continuous labour, and when we got in we found only a *new mud* room, with the walls still oozing water, to sleep in. It is little wonder, therefore, that my note concludes with the words, "All ill-ish"! Little cared we, however, as we were now over the last of the ranges, with only 30 miles more to the coast, all downhill and getting warmer every moment.

We left our wet mud quarters at 6.30 A. M. and, 7 miles down the hill, met, to our inexpressible joy, a motor-lorry sent from Trebizond to meet us. It was much warmer here, with the snow all left behind us and the trees in full leaf. We therefore "shed" our snow-clothing and took some photographs, both of ourselves and our guards, before boarding the lorry, which landed us at Trebizond at 3.30 P. M. on April 5th, our ninth day out of Erzeroum, having been in the snow all the time until that morning.

In Trebizond our treatment was entirely different from any we had yet experienced, as we were given good furnished quarters in a fort by the sea-shore, one room being provided for the men and another for myself; and we were permitted to purchase our food from the restaurant and to go to the Turkish bath. A doctor also was provided for me, as I was in a sadly weak state, and the Turks did not like the look of me as a prospective "released prisoner" in Constantinople. I was also allowed to visit the Ottoman Bank, with an officer. The manager there immediately cashed my draft on the Command Paymaster at Constantinople, so that we were able to pay the jobmaster and also to procure ourselves some clothes, of which we stood sadly in need, as well as many of the little luxuries of civilization to which we had long been strangers.

Under these comparatively pleasant circumstances, we proceeded to endeavour to recover our health as quickly as might be possible, whilst waiting for news of our exchange, which we understood then to be imminent.

## CHAPTER V

### PRISON AGAIN

The Fort at Trebizond—Good treatment—We are told we are to return to prison—Our officer's offer to send a letter to Constant—My dispatch Our departure—Americans at Gumush Khaneh—Erzeroum Prison again—Kindness of the officer commanding the prison—My accounts and precautions—We are searched for money—Prince Toumanoff and his family—My model house—My dictionary—Permission to sit in the prison yard—The Bulgarian officer—The letter in a cigarette—Sketch of ancient mosque—Moonlight music—Visit from Nouri Pasha—Other visits—Ordered to the coast—Fighting on the Khop—"George's" speech —Billet at Trebizond—Maman—Colonel Baird arrives—We are taken on board H.M.S. *Somme*.

We remained confined in the fort at Trebizond for sixteen days, during which our treatment was *good,* and the fresh air and exercise which we were able to obtain did much to restore our health. The apparent imminence of our release, however, was, without doubt, the factor chiefly responsible for our recovery, as we were given to understand that at any moment a British ship might be expected to arrive for the purpose of embarking us.

A Turk Lieutenant was detailed to remain in charge of us, and occupied the room next to mine in the fort. He appeared very friendly, and I was permitted to accompany him into the town to effect purchases or visit the baths or restaurant; and so confident did I become of our approaching release that I visited the local barber and went through the very unpleasant operation of having my beard removed, having now worn it for over a year.

However, on April 16th, about midday, when going, as usual, for a walk with the officer, I became aware that he was very silent, and seemed overcome by emotion. I therefore asked him what was the matter—whether he had received any news. To this he replied that he had news, but that it was bad news, and that he hesitated to communicate it to me. This, of course, gave me a terrible shock, as I at once realized with dismay that some obstacle must have arisen in the carrying out of our exchange. However, I told him that I was neither a child, nor a man unable to face whatever adversity fate might yet have in store for him, and begged him to tell me his news at once, as shortly and plainly as possible.

He then told me orders had that morning been received by telegraph from Angora that we were to be sent back at once into the interior; he did not know to what destination, but that orders had already been given for the carts and guards to be got ready, and arrangements had been made for them to go at any rate as far as Baiburt. It appeared that at first it had been proposed that we should start that very afternoon, but it had finally been arranged to delay our departure till the next morning.

I will not attempt to describe what a terrible blow this was to me, as no words could be capable of conveying the effect of this sudden shattering of all my hopes, which in the last three weeks had gradually grown so strong and confident as to amount practically to a certainty of our approaching release. I trust, however, that I received this sentence with proper courage and self-control, saying that it would be necessary to return at once to the fort to communicate this sad news to my men, and to commence our preparations for the journey.

The young officer, who made this very unpleasant communication, displayed himself, I am glad to say, a great deal of feeling, for the possession of which I had by no means previously given him credit. On our way back to the fort he told me that he was terribly distressed at the unhappy turn events had taken, and that he would be prepared, if I so desired, to convey secretly any letter I might wish to write to my friends in Constantinople, undertaking to give it himself to the commander of an Italian vessel, then at anchor off the fort, which he had to visit that evening, and which was due to sail during the night. For this I thanked him most sincerely, and having called at the bank, where I drew a further 1,000 pounds Turkish (then worth about £120), we returned at once to the fort.

It is due to the two brave men, then in charge of the Ottoman Bank, to explain that, although they knew well that they risked their lives in supplying me with money, they did not for a moment hesitate to do so. Further, they undertook to honour any draft of mine which might reach them at any time, in future, from the interior; and this although a banker at Samsun, in a similar position to themselves, had, as they well knew, a short while previously paid with his life for a very similar action. I do not know these men's names, and even if I did, it would, in their interests, probably be unwise to publish them, but I made a point of reporting the action of the bank to the Commander-in-Chief at Constant, and of personally visiting the manager of the head office there, on my eventual release, to render my thanks, and to draw the attention of the board of directors to the very meritorious action of the employés, to whom I here once more tender my sincerest gratitude.

On arrival at the fort, my hardest task lay immediately before me—namely, to "tell the men." I have had in all my life no harder task than that. . . . Feelings were then stirred which were at the time, and are even now, far too deep for words, my one object being to do my utmost to assist and help them to meet the blow in a proper and soldier-like spirit, and, as far as in me lay, to set them the example which it was my duty and my privilege to do. But it was hard, and if, as I fear was the case, my voice trembled, it was small wonder, as my physical strength was at a sadly low level, and my own burden was a heavy one to bear.

The bad news was, however, spoken at last, and received with an absolute silence, far, far more expressive than any words; after which I did my best to help them to "face the music" and to get busy with our preparations. Before concluding this account of that most painful scene, I wish to take this opportunity of thanking my comrades once again for their help, and of saying, with deep respect and true appreciation of their courage, that *these were fine men,* tried and proved, and that I was proud indeed to be their commander.

The remainder of the day, and until the officer came for my packet at midnight, I was hard at work preparing the papers which were enclosed therein, and which consisted of—

1. A letter to the Commander-in-Chief, dated April 16th, 1921.
2. A summary of my original Diary, the full text of which had been taken from me at Erzeroum.
3. My accounts for the whole period, which had been returned to me before leaving Erzeroum.

# AWAITING EXCHANGE

Pte. Leadbeater with "George" in the Fort on the seashore at Trebizond

## THE JOURNEY BACK TO PRISON

The Upper Zigana Pass, April 20 (6,500 feet)

The Vavok Pass, April 22 (6,800 feet)

# IN KEMALIST TURKEY 311

4. Diary of our journey from Erzeroum to Trebizond, March 28th to April 5th.

No. 1 will be found below, and will itself explain, better than any other description could do, the sad position in which I felt we were placed, and the light in which I then regarded our future chances of survival.

"TREBIZOND, *April 16th,* 1921.

"MY DEAR GENERAL,

"Self and party have been here since 6th instant, awaiting exchange, and are now ordered to return to ERZEROUM to-morrow. I have obtained the promise of the officer in charge of us to send this letter, and I have every hope that he will do so, and also the accounts, which I send, as no papers are safe in our possession, and we are liable to be stripped at any moment. I have tried on many occasions to communicate, but fear I have been unsuccessful, notably through the Americans at Trebizond, under date of January 5th, January 10th, and February 24th, on which dates I was very doubtful whether we should survive. Now, however, we have been *fed,* and regained *some* strength, and I have obtained money, which is the most important of all, as, with it and the experience I have, I can employ it to great advantage, and, unless it is taken from me, we shall last till the winter comes again, if such is required of us. I have also arranged with the manager of the Ottoman Bank here to credit any draft in future, which he is quite prepared to do, and for which he deserves great thanks.

"My last communication received was mail-dated London, January 25th, 1920, and Constantinople, February, reaching me at Erzeroum March 12th, and newspapers to April 3rd, 1920, and half-dozen whisky, received from *you,* Sir, with our *very deepest thanks,* on June 10th. No news of any sort since.

"The extracts from my Diary, which were overlooked when all my other papers were taken on February 24th, 1921, will explain themselves, and you will see that our treatment since they took our cars—and I put them out of action first—has been a disgrace to any nation, and of a barbarity which I find it impossible to understand. I am told that it is largely on account of my having destroyed the cars and refused to say how, or to help the Turks, that they have treated us so badly; but we only did what it was our duty to do, and no maltreatment would have any effect on the gallant fellows I have here now, though the one Irishman could not stand it.

"My men are now—L/Corpl. ANKERS, No. 196424, 766 M. T. Coy. R.A.S.C.; Pte. H. CARTER, No. 97505, 85th Coy. M.G.C.; Pte. R. LEADBEATER, No. 59194, 66th Coy, M.G.C.; and I wish to say that they have all behaved splendidly in the face of the greatest hardships, and have done their utmost to maintain the best traditions of the British soldier. At no time has there been, nor, come what may, *will there be,* any treatment of the Turk by these men other than as an enemy.

"I attach a short statement to the Command Paymaster, in explanation of the accounts which go with this, and I shall be greatly relieved when they go, as they have been a great anxiety to preserve.

"I wish to say, in conclusion, Sir, that I can understand that it is more than possible, and, in fact, only too probable, that the Turks may have put such a price on our exchange that it may not be the country's interest to pay it, and that, under those circumstances, we return to our prison readily, and only trust that we may have the strength to carry out anything that our duty may demand of us, and we shall take pride in so doing, whatever it may be.

"To illustrate how they have treated us, I send you a snapshot of myself, taken by one of my men just over a year ago, since when we have been in much worse condition. However, I trust our trip to the seaside (!) may have given us a fresh reserve of strength, and, in any case, our hearts are in the right place, and we fear no Turk nor his atrocities.

"I have not the heart to write to my wife or brother, Sir, as this is a hard job to face as it is, but they are always in my thoughts, and you will please let them know, Sir, that I have every hope of coming through all right in the end, and that I fear nothing for myself—except to cause them pain and anxiety.

"Always yours sincerely,
"(*Signed*)   A. Rawlinson."

"P.S.—There are about 3,000 Armenian prisoners in the neighbourhood of Erzeroum, in terrible case and *starving*.

"P.P.S.—If this letter is very informal, Sir, please forgive, as I am still very weak, and to-day's news makes me so that I hardly know what I am doing, and the officer waits whilst I write—so very disconcerting!

"The whole country is now being combed *again* for men.

Parties are everywhere coming in on roads. Men are *young* and *good,* and are everywhere coming *willingly* (1 guard to 250 conscripts). Numbers are impossible to estimate, but met two or three parties of fifty and upwards during nine days' journey from Erzeroum.

"P.P.P.S—I hear it is possible we may be kept at Baiburt this time, but either from there or Erzeroum it would be possible to get away if we had *outside assistance,* horses, and a boat on the coast. In any case, 'Off,' between Rize and Trebizond, would be probably the best place to make for—over the Chorokh above Ispir. This is a feasible path and very unfrequented, and would not be suspected, but will hardly be passable much before June. Anyone to help should land at 'Off,' or, anyway, come over the hills from there, and it might be possible to ascertain at Trebizond where we were—either from Red Cross, or Bank, or Americans. There is no chance without horses, clothes, and help, and a *boat,* but we should have the strength if the chance came along. I *have* been in fear that they herded us with the Armenians in order to have an "accident" (!) by letting the townspeople in at them, and at us with them, as the prison looked prepared for that, and the townspeople would make a quick job of it; but the time had gone by when we left, and, for the time at any rate, there was less bloodthirsty feeling.

"*(Signed)* A. R."

I sealed this packet very carefully with my Turkish seal in various places on the thick cardboard cover in which it was enveloped, in the presence of the officer, who took it with him on board the Italian ship, for which I saw him embark at midnight from the little pier within the fort. I therefore had every right to conclude it was his intention to carry out his promise; and it gave me the greatest relief to think that, in all reasonable probability, the packet would reach its destination, and afford at last definite news as to our fate up to that time.

In the evening I had been presented to the officer who was to be in charge of our party, and had also seen the Trebizond jobmaster, from whom I obtained a victoria for the journey which, without being anything but a very inferior conveyance, was none the less an improvement upon the terrible contrivance in which I had arrived. The officer was very young, and impressed me chiefly by his excessive nervousness, as this was apparently the first "job" which he had ever been called upon to undertake on his own responsibility, and I therefore foresaw much unnecessary discomfort on the journey, which forecast subsequent events proved to be an absolutely correct one.

We finally left Trebizond at 10.30 A. M. on April 17th, accompanied by many more guards than had been considered necessary on our previous journey, and also by a party of mounted gendarmerie. I was not able to ascertain the reason for these excessive precautions, but I concluded it was considered that the many Greeks who had then already fled to the mountains, where they were in arms and in open revolt against the Turks, might possibly try to effect our rescue, of which laudable project, however, we saw no signs on the journey.

We reached Jeveslik, at 1,800 feet altitude and 17 miles from Trebizond, at 6.30 P. M., and found good quarters, or, at least, a small dry room to ourselves. The road was fair, but in the deep valley the heat was quite considerable—that is, much hotter than the hottest day of an English summer—this, of course, being caused by the powerful rays of the sun striking on the rocky walls of the confined valley. That night our very "jumpy" officer told me he intended next day to cross the Zigana and reach Zigana Khan, on the other side of the pass, and that we should be accompanied by a large detachment of mounted gendarmerie, who would scout ahead of us over the upper pass.

The distance from Jeveslik to Zigana Khan is 32 miles, and the summit of the pass is 5,600 feet above our starting-point, after which we should have to descend a further 2,500 feet to reach Zigana Khan. It was easy, therefore, to foresee that we were in for a terribly severe day, especially as the upper pass lay deep in snow. I was not surprised, therefore, when we were told we should start in the dark, at 4.30 A. M., which we did. There was much less snow on the pass than when we had come over it, in such high spirits, just fourteen days before, and we reached our destination at 7.30 P. M., having seen no signs of anyone but our numerous guards, my only comment in my notes on the journey being "A very long day," which description, I think, will be considered as amply justified by our fifteen hours' continuous march!

The next night we reached Gumush Khaneh, after ten hours' travelling, and on arrival the men told me they had seen and spoken to some Americans on entering the town. We were, as on our last halt at this place, quartered in the large common room, which serves the purpose, fulfilled in more civilized countries by an inn, of affording shelter for travellers; but on this occasion, thanks to the extreme nervousness of our young officer, all the public were ejected and we were hurried inside as quickly as possible. Before reaching the door, however, I saw an obvious American in the crowd, who shouted "Hulloa!" to which, however, I was only able to answer by a sign that I could not talk to him, as he was hurriedly shepherded off by Turkish soldiers, I being as hurriedly hustled into the building, where even the windows were promptly closed and covered. Our officer himself sat up the whole night to make sure that no communication should be possible between us and our American sympathizers in the town.

I understood that these gentlemen formed part of the American Relief staff, who had, to my knowledge, for long been doing their usual splendid work in relieving the starving Armenians in the Kars and Erivan districts. I gathered that they were now being forced to leave the country by the Turks, to whom, of course, any idea of philanthropy is hopelessly inexplicable, and who were inclined to treat these heroic workers in the cause of humanity as spies whose objects were to excite the sympathy of Europe and America in favour of the Christian minority, whom it is, and has long been, the deliberate policy of the Turkish Government to exterminate.

This party of Americans consisted of three men and three women, at least that was all I could see and count myself looking through a crack of a shuttered window as they left the town next morning. They had come from Kars via Sarikamish and Erzeroum and were the last representatives of their country left in the territories under the control of the Nationalist Turks. This final exodus by order of the Turkish Government, indicated the attitude of those in power in the country towards the Christian minorities who had so long been supported by the liberality of the American public. It was evident that the Government did not desire that they should receive further support from those humane people far away who sympathized so deeply with them, and who had made such great and successful efforts to alleviate their sufferings and to save their lives.

It was also to be inferred that whatever their unhappy fate might now be, it was preferred that the tragedy should take place unobserved and unreported by the evidence of independent American witnesses. It is this latter reason in particlar which urges me to record such facts as came under my own observation subsequent to the departure of the last members of the American organization.

With regard to the Armenian military prisoners, of whom 9,000 were taken at Kars in March 1921, by the date of my eventual departure from Erzeroum on October 5th of that year 746 only remained alive, and those were in a pitiable condition and their Commander rightly described them to me as '"spectres." The Armenian civilian population had long since "disappeared" from the districts which I traversed on my journeys to and from the coast, and at the time of our return to prison in April the country inhabited by the Greek Christians was also being cleared of those unfortunate people, who were being deported into the exclusively Moslem interior as slaves. At the time of our return journey to Trebizond in October, the hitherto prosperous and well cultivated coast valleys lay abandoned and deserted; the fields which had for centuries been carefully tended, and had supported a numerous and thriving population, then lay bare and unproductive, whilst the villages were desolate and in ruins, and an omnious silence reigned everywhere, emphasizing by its mute but most dramatic evidence the tragedy which had been enacted by the destruction of the entire Christian community.

This then was the result of the forced cessation of the supplies furnished and distributed by the American Near East Relief organization up to the time of their withdrawal, and thus perished many thousands who up to that time owed their lives to the generous and kind-hearted sympathy of the American public. Though such a tragedy must for ever be deplored, it serves to throw into even bolder relief the services rendered to Christian humanity by the generous citizens of the United States as long as it lay in their power to continue their glorious work. No after events can dim that brilliant record, which but shines the brighter by contrast with the subsequent tragedy, and forms a glorious page of history of which every American citizen may well be proud.

The morning after our arrival at Gumush Khaneh our departure was delayed, and we were not allowed outside, until the Americans had left the town on their way to Trebizond, when we continued our journey in the opposite direction. The Americans, however, had seen our party, and, having actually recognized me, were therefore able to report that fact on their arrival at Constantinople, from whence it was telegraphed home. This formed the first and only reliable news received as to my then being still alive, though on my way again to captivity in the interior.

The remainder of our journey was uneventful but exceedingly disagreeable, as the marches were long and our guards brutal to a degree, whilst the anxious young officer was a most unsuitable person for such duty. Above all else, we knew well with what misery we were now confronted, and therefore suffered even more in our minds than in our bodies.

On April 24th we finally reached Erzeroum, where the snow still lay deep and the wind was as bitter as ever, and returned to our prison, where we were given the same cells that we had previously occupied, and into which we were thrust without any kind of provision in the way of light, heat, or furniture of any kind, the cells being absolutely bare. I feel sure we shall all always remember that first night in the old prison which we had been so rejoiced to leave, as we thought, for ever, and the awful sensations of forsaken loneliness and misery with which our surroundings insistently oppressed us. However, we were, shortly after our arrival, visited by the officer then in charge of the prison in succession to Salah-a-din, who, to our infinite relief and joy, proved to be one whom we already knew well and much liked, but whose name, in his own interest, I am bound to withold.

His sympathy was of the utmost value, and I obtained readily his permission to send out to the restaurant in the town for food, and to have my men into my cell, so that we might all be together, at any rate during that dreadful night, for warmth and society. In the morning our prison Commander detailed a non-commissioned officer to effect purchases for us in the town, which now, having funds at our disposal, we were well able on this occasion to afford, and we indulged in stoves, lamps, cooking-pots, etc., so that we were much better off than we had been when last here, once the initial shock of the first night was past.

I also received an invaluable hint that, in all probability, we should be searched for our money, and we took immediate steps to safeguard this, to us, priceless treasure; by the following means. I was, of course, well aware that any search which might take place would be of the most rigorous nature, and I therefore again had recourse to an elaborate review of the situation, so as to utilize what experience of the limitations of our gaolers' intelligence I already had, in order to defeat our searchers by imagining myself to be in their position, and endeavouring by that means to determine exactly what they would be likely to do and how they would do it.

After some hours' hard thinking, I then proceeded to take the first step, by dividing our funds into nine different portions, of which six were comparatively small sums, two others were of more considerable amounts, and the last one was equal to the half of our total resources. These divisions were, of course, based upon the various positions in which I proposed to secrete our bank-notes, these positions, again, being determined with a view, first, to the possibility of our being separated or moved to other places of confinement; and, second, with a view to accessibility, so that small amounts might be readily available, whilst the larger amounts would be more permanently and safely concealed.

The men had made for themselves, long ago, slippers the soles of which consisted of the thick rubber from the inner tubes of our motor-car tyres, and these had been worn so long that the various thicknesses of which they consisted had become pressed practically into one solid piece of rubber. All these were now opened sufficiently to admit of certain of the smaller notes being inserted between them, and in this manner six of the smaller parcels of notes were disposed of in the six slippers of the three men, being not only easily accessible, but insuring that no man would be left penniless, even in event of us all being separated.

The next two parcels were of considerably higher value, and were more permanently concealed. As we still possessed two ordinary Service water-bottles, of which it was unlikely that we should be deprived, I proceeded to split the thick felt with which the outside of the bottles is covered, and inserted the notes therein, afterwards well damping the felt and submitting it to pressure, until the original slit became impossible to find, even when one knew where it had been made.

For the last and greatest treasure I had reserved a hiding-place which I considered would defy detection, however ingenious might be the searchers. For this purpose I made use of my old portmanteau, which was in a very dilapidated condition, all the linings, fittings, and stitchings having now perished or been torn away. The good English leather, however, was about a quarter of an inch thick, and this I split and inserted the notes in the interior of the leather, afterwards damping it and closing the slits by pressure when wet, so that it became absolutely impossible to conceive that anything could be concealed in the thickness of the material itself, where no opening could be found.

Having taken these precautions, I then proceeded to use my experience of the intellectual limitations of the Turks to even better purpose, without which further measure I have no doubt at all that none of the others previously taken would have been of any ultimate avail. It was my invariable custom, as the Turks well knew, to keep the most careful account of my expenditure and to take receipts for all payments. I therefore balanced my accounts carefully, showing the exact amount received from the bank at Trebizond (of which the Turks, I felt sure, would have already received accurate information), as well as the payments made by me, including a purchase of furs in Trebizond for dispatch to England, which payment, curiously enough, precisely corresponded with the amount of our concealed resources.

The account, which was quite clear and simple, showed finally a balance of 86 pounds Turkish in hand, as well as some small change which was in daily use as petty cash. These preparations completed, I was ready for the search, which we knew we might expect at any moment. As a matter of fact, although we had been very quick, yet even then we were barely in time, for on the afternoon of the third day after our return I received a visit from Avni Bey, a most interesting and original character, who, having risen from the ranks, was now, at the age of sixty, a Major of artillery, and Commandant of the "Merkez," or town and fortress headquarters. The moment I saw this old gentleman, whom I well knew to be a most efficient officer and one whose experience in this sort of business was probably unequalled in any country, I felt I had an opponent whom it would be a proud achievement to get the better of. I therefore, from the start, exhibited the utmost candour and played my part with the very greatest care, to the full extent of my ability.

One great advantage was mine from the beginning: *I knew what he had come for,* and he did not conceive or suspect that it was possible that I *could* know the purpose of his visit, as on receipt of his telegraphic personal orders he had come straight to my cell, and had spoken to no one on the way. I feel sure that, if the scene that then took place could be reproduced on the stage, it would afford my countrymen at home the greatest possible entertainment; and for myself, I cannot conceal that it afforded me, at the time, the purest joy.

Our most cunning old friend, on his arrival, was extremely polite, and sat down and talked on general subjects, our journey and so forth—of anything and everything, in fact, except the money he had come to find. And I, taking the bull straight by the horns, replied with childlike innocence that of course the journey and all the conditions had been much easier this time than before, as I had been able to draw some money from the bank at Trebizond. This news rather "hit him in the wind," though he gave no sign of it, merely replying: "Oh, is that so? And have you the money now?"

My answer was, "Of course I have," and, putting my hand in my pocket, I produced the piece of india-rubber in which I kept my notes rolled up, and handed it to him at once. He then asked me how much was there, and I said I thought it was 86 liras (Turkish pounds), and that I had some small notes also, which I produced from my breeches pocket, and got up to get my accounts, which I said would at once verify the amount which *should* be there, if he would kindly count. This he did, being obviously disconcerted at the absolutely straightforward nature of the whole proceeding. When he had finished counting, and found the total correct, he asked to see my accounts and then asked searching questions as to the "furs," of which some *had* actually been bought for me at Trebizond by some Greeks for dispatch home. This incident he also knew of, though providentially he had not been able to ascertain

## WOODEN MODEL OF HOUSE
### With plans of each floor made by Col. R. in prison

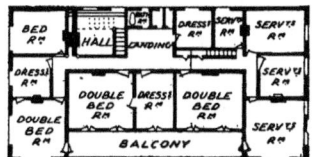

Plan of first floor

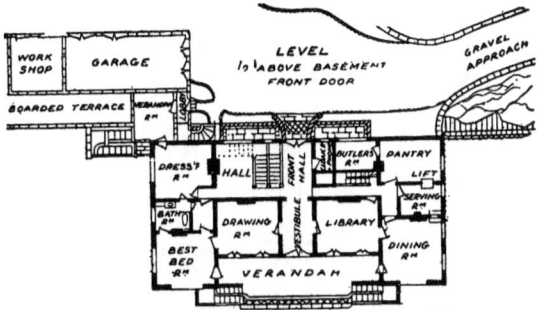

Plan of ground floor

Photograph of model

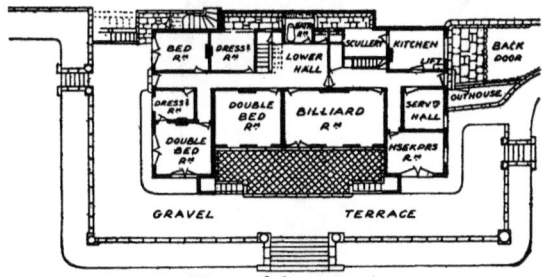

Plan of basement
Drawn at scale of 1/20, or 20 feet to 1 inch, and reduced for reproduction

## SKETCH OF THE ANCIENT MOSQUE ON THE EASTERN SIDE OF THE PRISON YARD AT ERZEROUM

The sign of the ancient god in the form of a bird with the sun and the palm-tree below establishes the date of the building as "Vannick"—viz., about 800 B.C. Window of Col. R.'s cell marked X

the actual amount, nor was he aware that I had not paid for them.

At this point this most interesting of cunning old barbarians dropped his mask, and told me he had orders to search me for the money which it was known I had drawn at Trebizond, and which I was not to be allowed to keep. I then told him I could easily comprehend that, but, as he had it already, I didn't understand what more he wanted, as he could see from my accounts, which he had already checked, that the amount was correct. This set the old fellow thinking hard, with the result that he presently handed me back my money, saying I was entitled to keep that, but that he must nevertheless search formally everywhere, for such were his orders.

I most politely agreed that of course he must carry out his orders, and search he did; but I am quite convinced that the "sting" had gone out of his keenness, and that his search, keen though it still was, was perfunctory only, compared to what it would have been had he not had "the wind taken out of his sails" before commencing; for it was evident to me that he now *expected* to find nothing, and, to my great relief, his expectations were in no way disappointed.

Although this very dangerous interview had finally reached such an entirely satisfactory conclusion, I was far from confident that, on reflection, further steps might not be taken. I therefore wrote a letter to Emin Bey, the Commander of the district, telling him that I had made arrangements for any drafts of mine to be honoured at the Ottoman Bank at Trebizond, and pointed out to him that, as I had brought very little money back with me, it would shortly become necessary for me to cash a cheque, asking him, at the same time, whether, if I drew it to *his* order, he would undertake to remit me the amount when received. To this he did not consent, but there was no further question of any search, and this had, of course, been the real object of my request.

On our return to prison the Kurd Pasha had been released, but his place had been taken by a Prince Toumanoff, a Russian, whose tragic story is too long to relate here, but who belonged to one of the best-known families in Imperial Russia, and whose dramatic fate had finally landed him in Erzeroum Prison, penniless, and accompanied by his charming wife and their child of two or three years of age. Their plight was terrible, as in order to avoid starvation this poor, delicate, and highly cultured lady, who was permitted to go out for the purpose, had to beg for needlework to do for the Turkish women, to enable her by that means to earn enough to keep life in the emaciated bodies of her husband and child.

About this time the snow began to disappear, and finally we were allowed to go out into the yard, at such times as the Armenian prisoners were not there, alternately with the Toumanoffs, which proved the greatest possible boon, and for which we have to thank our friend the Commander of the prison, who in this instance acted on his own responsibility, and subsequently incurred grave censure from his superiors for his humanity.

I now worked hard at my model house and drawings, and completed them, and also was able to purchase a very thirdrate Turkish-French dictionary, which I proceeded practically to learn by heart, and which I always took with me during the time I spent in the yard. This practice eventually became the means of my being able to establish communication with a Bulgarian officer who was confined with the Armenian officers in the building on the west side of the square, and who finally carried for me the only communication I was ever able to make to the outer world.

Our practice in communicating was difficult but exciting, as it necessitated my innocently taking my seat in the neighbourhood of the "field kicthen," where the Armenian officers' ration of wheat soup was boiled, and where several of the Armenian prisoners were always in attendance to see to the fire, amongst whom the Bulgarian would place himself. One of my men would then come and sit with me, and I would apparently proceed to read to him from my dictionary, whilst the Bulgarian, 15 yards away, would talk to one of his companions—at least, that is what *appeared* to be taking place; in reality, however, we were able to converse in this manner, as no one understood what we were saying; until, finally, one day he informed me he was to be released, and that he was prepared to take a letter for me to Constantinople, if I would recommend him to our Intelligence Branch there for employment. This I most readily consented to do, and told him I would drop a cigarette out of my window into the yard during the Armenian officers' roll-call parade that night, with my letter rolled inside it, and that he must endeavour to mark where it fell, and get hold of it before anyone else did. This was agreed to, and I wrote the following letter, which, alone of all my communications, reached its destination in safety.

"*To General Staff Intelligence, Allied Forces of Occupation, Constantinople.*
"IN ERZEBOUM PRISON,
*August 1st,* 1921.

"The bearer, a Bulgarian officer and fellow-prisoner, is to be trusted, and we are indebted to him for help under difficulties. He can give full information as to our sad state and hopes, and possible means of realizing same.

"I sent my accounts and receipts from Trebizond on April 16th, and also a letter to the C.-in-C., by hand of a Turk whom I had reason to trust, and who swore he gave them to the captain of the Italian ship which sailed for Constantinople that night. If they have failed to reach you, I consider it impossible to get away without outside assistance. Then it would be feasible, and if a *dak* (relays of horses) was laid over the hills and a boat of sorts provided, either at Off or in the lower Chorokh, we could get out and *succeed.*

"We were searched for money on our return from Trebizond, by order of G.H.Q., but I expected it, and they failed to find any.

"One of my men, Mahoney, of A.S.C., joined the Turks, and betrayed the fact of our having put our cars out of action, and disclosed the hiding-place of the parts. *Look after him, if you get him,* as he has been the cause of our disgraceful treatment, solitary confinement, starvation, and *misery.*

"Our health is wonderful, considering great privations and disgusting conditions, but we have kept our flag flying, and neither whined nor begged for anything. 'God Save the King!'
"(*Signed*) A. Rawlinson.

"P.S.—I have three men only left—Corporal ANKERS, A.S.C.; Privates CARTER and LEADBEATER, M.G.C. Please advise their people, and give my love to my wife and family, and brother, who are all constantly in my thoughts. All literature is denied us, but for the last two months we are allowed 'out' in prison-yard once a day. Never out before that. No news received since June, 1920, fourteen months; then received *Times* of April 20th."

This was dated August 1st, and was written very minutely on a small thin sheet of paper, and rolled in the centre of the tobacco contained in a cigarette. That evening I stood for some time, smoking cigarettes, at my window, until, choosing a moment when the arrival of a Turkish officer in the yard attracted the attention of both the guards and all the Armenian prisoners (who were by no means to be trusted), I was able at last to drop the all-important communication unobserved. We had agreed that in the event of his securing it safely the Bulgar was whistle "God Save the King," and our relief may be imagined when, a little later, we heard the strains of that glorious anthem, and knew that, this time at least, the chances were greatly in favour of our communication reaching its destination in safety.

The weather now was magnificent, and we spent all the time possible in the yard, where I made a sketch of the ancient mosque which formed one side of it, including the even older tower, inlaid with the old light-blue glazed tiles which form such a feature in ancient buildings of Mesopotamia. This tower is still in very fair repair, though the upper portion was destroyed by the great earthquake of 1859, when half the town was laid in ruins and many thousand lives were lost.

The nights on that upland plateau in August are beautiful beyond description, and I have spent many hours gazing through the bars at the distant mountains, which stand out in the bright moonlight even more clearly than by day, the slight haze which the sun raises from the marsh being then absent. At these times the Armenians would sing, and sing well, the old songs of their country, which sounded like hymns, but to which they would impart an amount of plaintive sorrow and sentimental pathos in proportion to the misery of their present condition and the hopelessness of their future prospects. Our own condition and weakness also, I feel confident, did much to enhance our appreciation of these moonlight concerts, so full of the purest melody and yet of such unutterable sadness.

My neighbour Toumanoff was the possessor of a violin, upon which he had the great gift of playing divinely, and on these occasions, as the quavering Armenian voices died gradually away, the low, sweet tones of that peerless instrument would steal out across the silent moonlit yard, gradually growing in volume and power till the whole building rang with the throbbing emotion of the supremely gifted musician, who then lay dying in his cell, where both he and his wife and child grew daily weaker, but who, when the spirit stirred him, would pour out his whole suffering soul in the purest melody of trembling sweetness, which was beautiful beyond description, though most pitifully sad.

After these very entrancing moments I would myself remain, sometimes for hours, as in a dream, with my eyes fixed on the far peaks of those glorious moonlit mountains and on the countless stars above and beyond them, lost entirely to my sordid surroundings, and, rising above them by the great gift of a fertile imagination, I passed the hours amidst visions of beautiful things and happy thoughts of home, till, when at last I became once more conscious of the vile realities around me, I found myself restored, and newly equipped with fresh courage to face the future, and to rise above the paltry physical misery which it was then our lot to endure.

There were certain rooms in our corridor which were kept for the accommodation of any Turkish officers who might be passing through Erzeroum, and I one day received a visit from three officers who had just arrived from the East, and were temporarily quartered in those rooms. I fancy they thought that I was destined to die in prison, as they were quite unusually communicative, and gave me most interesting information. They were, they said, officers of the Turkish Intelligence Branch at Angora, and were then on their return from the East. They had first gone to Cabul, the capital of Afghanistan, and, separating there, they had penetrated into India, one going to Delhi and the other two to the South, all being occupied in stirring up trouble amongst our Indian subjects and having a great deal to say as to the absence of any effective supervision of travellers in India, and as to the ease and success with which they had been able to carry out their mission. They also told me that others of their branch were similarly employed in Mesopotamia and Palestine, as well as in Egypt, where much good (?) work was being done.

I was disposed to disbelieve these "facts," and somewhat heated discussions ensued; but I was left, in the end, with very little doubt that they had good foundation for their story, as it was beyond question that the men themselves had been lately both to Cabul and to Delhi. About the other countries I could not be so certain, having no opportunity of cross-examining any officers other than these whom this remarkable chance thus threw in my way.

About this time, also, I received several interesting visits, the first of which occurred one afternoon in early August, when my door suddenly opened and a Turk in civilian dress entered, whom I had never seen before. He proceeded, to my infinite astonishment, to announce himself as Nouri Pasha, which was confirmed by the officer who accompanied him. Nouri Pasha I have always understood to be the elder brother of Enver Pasha, who was in reality responsible for Turkey's entry into the Great War, and who was the moving spirit of the old Turkish Committee of Union and Progress, the first outward sign of the forces of democratic revolution which have now finally destroyed the old Ottoman Empire of the Sultans. No one doubts, least of all the Turks themselves, that the vast sums of which Enver obtained possession were obtained by other fraudulent means in addition to whatever gigantic bribe he may have received from Berlin, and with these funds he has for the past four years been consolidating his influence amongst the Caucasian and Transcaspian States, as the Nationalist Turks, who know him well, will on no account agree to his return to his own country. Nouri Pasha was at one time a prisoner in the hands of the Allies, and was sentenced by court-martial to death for certain offences during the war and subsequent to the Armstice. He, however, succeeded in escaping from British custody at Batoum, and as he had, I knew, always acted as Enver's representative, I was immensely surprised to find him now at Erzeroum.

Under these circumstances I was most particularly anxious to hear what he had to say, and especially to learn why and wherefore he should come to see me. Our conversation was very long, three hours or more, but deeply interesting. From him I learned much that has no place here, but I found at once that he was then more or less a prisoner himself, and that he was endeavouring to reach Angora for the purpose of laying certain propositions on the part of Enver before the Angora Government, and was being detained at Erzeroum pending receipt of permission from Angora for him to proceed. Incidentally I afterwards heard that he left Erzeroum for Angora, but never arrived there, though whether or not his throat was cut on the road, as is quite probable, I never have been able to ascertain.

In the meanwhile, what interested me most was that, having many sources of information at his disposal, he assured me that I could not be much longer retained by the Turks, whose real object in confining me was to make use of me, both as a channel of communicating their views unofficially to the Allies and as a means of obtaining Réouf Bey's release by exchange; and that, although they had now come to the conclusion that I was of no service for their first purpose, yet they were certain to make use of me for the second, which could not be now long delayed. Having given me that information, he endeavoured to obtain a great deal from me, but without result, as I was able with absolute truth to assert my entire ignorance of the matters in question, though in the process I learned a great deal from him, and when he finally left me I was much pleased with all I had gained from his visit.

I also received a visit from General Rushdi Pasha, Kiazim's second-in-command on the Eastern front, whom I had known for a long time, and who also assured me I should soon be exchanged. Finally, in early September, arrived a staff officer from Angora, to once more sound me as to what attitude I was likely to adopt if released; he also got nothing out of me except an expression of ignorance as to all that had happened during my captivity. All this latter time we were much better off than we had before been, as we were now allowed to sit on the roof of the prison, where we spent all and every day in the open air, and as our funds were ample, we were able to have meat, which the men managed to eat, though my own digestion was too much destroyed to permit of my eating it myself. Still, I had soup every day, and, though weak, was certainly not then losing strength, though I am quite convinced I could never have survived another winter at Erzeroum. On October 2nd, I received a visit from Emin Bey, who told me orders had been received for us again to be sent to the coast, for exchange, and that we should leave on the 5th. Our preparations were soon made, and I obtained this time a different type of conveyance, of a model unknown in Europe, but in which one can lie down, and which has a roof; and in this peculiar chariot, accompanied by four arabas, we started on October 5th.

Although the snow was now down for the winter, the journey was neither difficult nor interesting, the only incident worth recording being the state of the Khop Pass, where many brigands were "out," and where an active engagement was actually in progress between them and the Turkish gendarmerie as we passed over under heavy guard. That night, on arrival at the miserable hovel at Khop Khaneh, at the foot of the pass, we were all worn out with fatigue, and both wet and cold as well as hungry.

A small mud room was given us to sleep in, and we begged our officer to obtain us food, for which we were well able to pay.

This was the one and only occasion on which our faithful "George" has ever been known to speak. When the officer returned he informed us, to our dismay, that no food of any kind was to be obtained, and that we should have to do without till we were able to reach Baiburt next day. On this "George" made his one remark, by saying in a loud voice "Aowe!" I believe he was really yawning, but if so, it was extraordinarily "apropos" at the moment, and made us all laugh, Turks included, thus tending to cheer us up a little at a moment when some brightening-up was sadly needed by us all.

On the Vavok Pass, also, an attack was expected by our party, which, however, failed to materialize, and we arrived without incident at Trebizond on October 14th, the tenth day after leaving Erzeroum. I noted, however, that the coast range and its fertile valleys, hitherto intensively cultivated by the Greeks, was at this time everywhere deserted, the villages being abandoned and the crops unreaped. Also I had not failed to observe the many gangs of Greek prisoners which we had passed on their way to the interior under guard, so that it was evident the Greek population were then being deported into the interior to replace the Armenian prisoners, of whom by this time very few remained alive.

We halted for the last night of our journey at Jevislik, where

## IN KEMALIST TURKEY 329

I received a telephone message from the Military Commander at Trebizond saying he would send a motor-car to bring me in the next day. I therefore remained where I was next morning till the car came for me, the remainder of the party leaving early, as usual. The car, when it arrived, contained a Turkish naval Sub-Lieutenant named Naffi, who had been detailed to be responsible for me, and a very agreeable and considerate companion he proved to be. The first thing he did on meeting me was to hand me a telegram from my wife in England telling me she was all right, and was waiting for me at Brighton. This, of course, was the first news I had had of her since my original arrest, twenty months previously, and nothing could have been more acceptable, as, in addition to the relief it was to me to know she was all right, it told me also that we were expected, and that obviously very special measures must have been taken to insure our release.

On arrival at Trebizond we were well received by the Commander, whom I saw now for the first time. He escorted me himself to a fine house in the town, the property of an old Greek widow lady, a Madame Cosvekis, upon whom we were to be billeted, the naval officer who had met me at Jevislik being ordered to remain both day and night with me, and a warrant officer of police being detailed for like duty with the men.

Our guards on this occasion were most sympathetic, and we were allowed to do almost as we pleased, provided they were always with us, my officer even exceeding his orders by sleeping in the opposite room to me instead of in my room, so that he might give me more freedom. Added to all this was the fact that nothing could possibly exceed the kindness of the old Greek lady herself and all her family, who racked their brains to devise any possible thing they could do in our service, and it will be understood how deep was our appreciation of their kindness after our past experiences of so opposite a nature.

We were, I fear, all both ill and weak, and afforded our hosts and our gaolers a good deal of anxiety, though for widely different reasons, as, whilst the Turkish orders undoubtedly were to be ready to deliver us in the best possible condition, the care of our Greek hosts sprang from a deep sympathy with our sufferings and a desire to do all in their power to assist in our recovery. So much was this the case that many times, when I happened to open my eyes during the night, I have found the dear old lady peeping through the partly open door, carrying in her hands a steaming cup of cocoa, to see if by chance I might be awake and willing to drink it.

As we were told once more that an English vessel might at any time be expected to take us "off," I was much concerned to know what possible means we could employ to demonstrate to this dear old lady our appreciation of all her kindness. I knew well beforehand that to make any attempt at payment in money would be to insult her, and I therefore decided we would get photographed for her especial benefit, ourselves and, perforce, our guards, not to forget "George," who had quickly become master of the entire household.

This photograph we all signed and had mounted and framed, and on it I wrote a suitable expression of our gratitude to our old "Maman," as we called her, for all her kindness, and it was then duly presented, on which occasion I, with the utmost difficulty, persuaded her to accept 150 Turkish pounds (about £20), a portion only of the expense which she must have incurred in our entertainment, for the benefit of her poor old countrywomen, who were everywhere in the deepest affliction, all the male population, as well as the younger females, having been deported to the interior.

During this time at Trebizond I received several telegrams of congratulation on my release. Amongst them was one from my kind friend Fred Stern, who had been my host at Cairo in 1918, when I was so ill there, and of whom I had heard nothing since that time, and also one from my old friend and Adjutant, both during the time of my command of the naval mobile A.A. Brigade and subsequently in the London A.A. Defences, who telegraphed from Alexandria. These were possibly a little premature, but were none the less extremely encouraging as to our prospects of exchange, and I felt very grateful to my kind friends for their sympathy.

After being in Trebizond about a week, however, an even more interesting event took place. One afternoon I was informed a Turkish officer was asking to see me, his visit being timed during the absence of the naval Sub-Lieutenant Naffi, who was my constant companion. As my visitor himself was

## LAST JOURNEY TO THE COAST

Ptes. Carter and Leadbeater in their "araba"

Col. R.'s conveyance for ten days' travelling. Pte. Carter on the right with "George"

## THE PARTY AT TREBIZOND BEFORE EXCHANGE
(Photo as signed and presented to Mme. Cosvekis)

Left to right—Back row: Pte. Leadbeater, Turkish Warrant Officer
of Police (in charge of men), Pte. Carter
Sitting: Sub.-Lt. Naffi, Turkish Navy (in charge of Col. R.), Col. R.,
Corpl. Ankers    In front: "George"

a member of the Headquarters Staff, he was at once admitted by my guards, and handed me, to my intense surprise, some English newspapers, for which I felt and expressed the deepest thanks. He then, first making certain that we were quite alone, handed me a small note, which had evidently been nailed up in the heel of someone's boot, as the marks of the nails were clear, and, having delivered it, he instantly disappeared without a word.

On opening this letter, I found, to my inexpressible relief, that it was from Constantinople, and signed by General Harington. He informed me that he had received my note in the Bulgarian's cigarette, and that he had at last obtained authority to take steps himself for our release, which matter had previously been in the hands of the Foreign Office, and that he felt sure he would eventually succeed in effecting our exchange. In the meantime he begged me to have patience, and, above all, to make no attempt to escape, and also informed me he was in communication both with my wife and my brother, who were both well, the former in England and the latter in India.

This was absolutely the first definite news I had as to anything which had been happening elsewhere during our imprisonment, and the moment I saw his name I understood that he must have become Commander-in-Chief at Constantinople, as to which I had previously had no information. I learnt also for the first time that my brother was in India, and therefore knew he must have become Commander-in-Chief there.

Further most interesting intelligence was to the effect that Mahoney was at Constantinople, and would be kept there till we arrived; so that the amount of information contained in so short a letter was really remarkable, as well as overpoweringly interesting. Having mastered the contents, I promptly destroyed the letter and imparted the information to the men, all of us being immensely encouraged by the confident tone in which it was couched, the outstanding fact, which I instantly appreciated myself and impressed upon them, being that our fate was now in the hands of the *military* authority on the spot, and, that authority being represented by one of the most capable and energetic of all our Generals, we could rest assured that a very different style and rate of progress would be achieved than had previously been the case during the many weary months during which the *civilian* element had been in charge of the negotiations.

On October 31st, after having been eighteen days in Trebizond, an officer visited me soon after midday, and told me a British warship had anchored that morning off the port, and that the Commander of the garrison wished us to pack our gear and to go at once to his headquarters. Actually within fifteen minutes of this notice we were all *en route* for headquarters, with all our possessions, "George" proudly leading the procession, and my famous new tunic having been specially donned for this long and deeply desired occasion.

Arrived at the headquarters, I was at once ushered into the Commander's room, where I found Colonel Baird, our military Attaché at Constantinople, waiting for me. It would be quite useless to try to convey to my readers the emotions with which I once more met a British officer, free and able to speak as the representative of the great nation and army which, in the past, I had myself been so proud to represent; but I found myself only able with the greatest difficulty to utter a word.

Baird at once came forward, his eyes shining with the deepest sympathy, and told me that he had come in a destroyer from Ineboli, some 500 miles farther west, where the exchange was to take place, and to which spot the Turkish prisoners had been sent from Malta, and were now waiting on board our ships for the exchange to be effected. At the same time he informed me that the Commander at Trebizond was not authorized to release me, but that he had prevailed upon him to allow me to proceed to Ineboli, he (Baird) passing his word that, in the event of the business not being completed, I should return to Turkish custody there.

Here, indeed, was an unexpected development, with which, however, I was at the moment by no means disposed to interfere. I therefore at once expressed my readiness to fall in with that proposal, and, advancing to the Commander, shook hands with him and thanked him for myself, and in the name of my men, for the courtesy and consideration which we had experienced at his hands at Trebizond. I also shook hands with the naval officer who had been responsible for me on this occasion, and also with the doctor, who had been most kind and attentive during our previous stay as well as during our present visit. That ceremony being concluded, we made our way to the pier, where the most glorious sight of all awaited us—namely, a steam launch manned by real British bluejackets, with smiles all over their faces, and the white ensign, that glorious emblem of the British Navy, floating proudly over the stern.

We were, of course, all very weak, and very naturally, at the moment, our feelings were too deep for words. I did not fail, however, to note the catch in the breath on the part of the sailors and the gripping of their hands, as they "took in" our appearance and condition (so different from that of the Turkish prisoners in *our* hands), and came forward to assist us with the utmost gentleness and care to climb on board the launch.

"George," I remember well, sat right against me and kept looking in my face, as if to ask who were these men in blue, whom he now saw for the first time, and who were evidently *not Turks*, as they were so kind and friendly. I could not, of course, tell him, but I dare swear that after the reception he received from the British Navy, both then and later, he would now go straight up to any British sailor at any time, in any place, with the certainty that, inside any British naval rig, he could count on finding a loyal friend.

We were soon on board the destroyer, the *Somme*, whose name recalled so many memories, and there, needless to say, once over the side, the great British Navy, from the highest to the lowest, just took entire charge of the whole lot of us, affording us an all too fleeting glimpse of that deep sympathy for suffering which is inseparable from true courage, and which forms the priceless attribute of all those who go down to the sea in ships, and especially of the British sailor.

For ourselves, the relief was wonderful beyond description, but the reaction was severe, and we were all, I think, more than content just to close our eyes in peace, knowing our work was done, and that, once more safe amongst our own people, all our troubles were over.

## CHAPTER VI

### EXCHANGE AND HOME

Turks return my papers and box—Arrangements for exchange—British expect to receive 140 prisoners—Three only are forthcoming besides ourselves—I board the cruiser—The High Commissioner cables authority to exchange—Constantinople once more—Colonel and Mrs. Gribbon's hospitality—Admiral Sir Reginald Tyrwhitt—His invitation—The Chief—Our interview—Dinner with Embassy Staff—Accumulated correspondence—The men are entertained at the Embassy—Luncheon with Sir Charles and Lady Harington—Chief's cable to War Office—Reasons for refusal to see reporters—Sail for Malta in the *Centaur*—The Achi Baba position in the Gallipoli Peninsula—Full-speed trial of *Centaur*—Malta—Lord and Lady Plumer's kindness—The Palace at Valetta—The castle—Cable from General Harington—Dinner with Sir John de Robeck—The *Somme* takes us to Naples—Entertain our liberators—"George's" railway tragedy—Paris—"George" rejoins—Arrive in London—Recommendation of men—Sir Henry Wilson—Collapse—Medical board's recommendations—New regulations—Visit to South of France—His Majesty receives our party at Buckingham Palace—Interviews with Lord Curzon at Foreign Office—Demobilization—Pensions.

Just before leaving the pier I was handed by the Turkish Commander's orders the box which I had left at Trebizond, when there in April, to be forwarded home by the officer who had undertaken also to forward my packet to Constantinople by the hand of the commander of the Italian vessel, but who, instead of doing so, had delivered them both to his superiors. The box, containing valuable furs as well as my pistols and other property, had of course been looted, and nothing of value remained in it. The packet, however, was still unopened, to my infinite relief, as no one had dared to break the Turkish seals with which it was sealed, not knowing, of course, who might have placed them there. It is to this fortunate chance that I owe the recovery of my Diary and of my letter of April 16th to the Commander-in-Chief, as well as other documents of considerable importance to me, for which I was most thankful.

On leaving Trebizond, Colonel Baird was able to give me an

## IN KEMALIST TURKEY

outline of the position with which we should find ourselves confronted on our arrival at Ineboli, which is the nearest point on the Black Sea coast from which a road runs to Angora, 150 miles distant inland. It appeared that at last our Foreign Office had consented to leave the matter of an exchange of prisoners in the most competent and energetic hands of Sir Charles Harington, then commanding-in-chief the Allied forces in the Near East. The immediate result of this long-delayed but extremely practical and intelligent decision had been that the Turkish prisoners whom it was proposed to exchange, over eighty in number, had been dispatched in a transport from Malta, and that Major-General Franks, then holding a staff appointment at Constantinople, had been placed in charge of the actual operations by which the business was to be effected.

The actual delivery of the prisoners was to take place at Ineboli, and General Franks had proceeded there on board the cruiser *Centaur,* accompanied by another war vessel, as well as by the transport which had brought the Turkish prisoners from Malta, the *Somme* having been detached to proceed to Trebizond to collect our party, and to then rejoin the other vessels at Ineboli. The arrangements, therefore, seemed at first sight to be extremely simple, and to offer no difficulty in their execution.

Colonel Baird also informed me that it was asserted that the Turks had in their possession about 140 British and Indian prisoners, and that our authorities had been supplied with a list of these, which he handed to me with an inquiry as to whether I was able to furnish any information about these most unfortunate people. This development, of course, placed an entirely different aspect on the situation, as one glance at the list was sufficient to convince me that, though one name was there of an officer who I knew had been alive at Koniah in Southern Anatolia within the last six months, yet the majority, if not the whole of the rest, had certainly been dead for at least a year. The only thing which could exceed Baird's surprise on learning this was my own on hearing that our people had accepted any Turkish assertion as to prisoners in their hands without previous verification of the fact of such persons' survival.

The most unpleasant fact, however, now remained to be faced

—namely, that our General was only empowered to exchange his Turks against the list of British prisoners which had been furnished as being in the hands of the Angora Government. As my party, if the exchange was not completed, would have to be handed back to Turkish custody, it will hardly be wondered at that I viewed the complications which could not fail to ensue on our arrival at Ineboli with very considerable concern and misgiving.

Ineboli is in no sense a port, but only an extremely open and exposed anchorage off a small and insignificant town, from whence the road runs inland through a deep gorge in the low but steep hills which there extend to the water's edge. On our arrival communication was at once made by signal with the cruiser *Centaur*, and Baird went on board that ship to report to the General. At that time it was blowing hard, and his transfer to the cruiser was a matter of great difficulty and danger. It was, however, safely carried out, and that only just in time, as the wind was increasing in force and any communication by boat was rapidly becoming impossible. Within half an hour of his boarding the cruiser I received a signal from the General to the effect that the Turks on shore were able to produce four prisoners only, and that they expressed absolute ignorance with regard to the existence of any others.

Under these circumstances I made up my mind that, if possible, I would myself also proceed on board the cruiser, leaving my men on the destroyer; and having explained the situation to Lieut.-Commander Archer, who commanded the *Somme*, and who had shown us all the greatest kindness and sympathy, he at once agreed that if the cruiser would send a boat he would contrive to get me on board it. We also agreed that, in the event of complications ensuing and preventing the completion of the exchange, it should be understood that, as the weather was becoming worse every moment, the *Somme* would soon be no longer able to remain where she was, and would be obliged to put to sea. The men therefore, in that case, would be safe, even in the unlikely event of their being considered to be included in the personal undertaking for our return given by Colonel Baird at Trebizond.

Signals were therefore made to the *Centaur*, and with the utmost difficulty a boat was sent; with still greater trouble I

## THE ENTRANCE TO THE DARDANELLES FROM THE ÆGEAN SEA

Taken from the summit of the Turkish position on Achi Baba. Cape Hellas, where British troops first landed in the Gallipoli peninsula, is marked X. The straits rapidly become narrow to the left of the picture

# RELEASED

At Constantinople—Left to right: Capt. Campbell, Corpl. Ankers, Gen. Sir Charles Harington, G.B.E., K.C.B., D.S.O. (Commander-in-Chief Allied Forces), Col. R., Pte. Carter. In front: "George"

On board H.M.S. "Centaur"—Standing: Pte. Leadbeater, Corpl. Ankers, Pte. Carter. Sitting: Capt. French, Col. R., Admiral Sir Reginald Tyrwhitt, Bt., K.C.B.

was then swung on board the boat at the end of a rope, and eventually arrived safely under the lee of the cruiser. There a rope-ladder was lowered, and I was expected to contrive to seize and climb it at the exact moment the small boat should be on the very crest of one of the heavy seas then running. Such an operation is by no means an easy one, even when a man is strong and well; it was therefore by no means surprising that in my weak state I made a pretty bad mess of it, and, my feet slipping, I remained in mid-air, hanging on to the rope-ladder like grim death by my hands only. Whilst I was in this most precarious position the boat, rising on the next wave, crushed my leg pretty severely against the side of the ship, making me think, as I hung there, that at last my time had come, and what rotten luck it was that a British ship should have come all that way to crack me like a nut against her side.

Many strong and willing hands, however, seized me instantly, and I was dragged quickly over the side before the boat had time to rise and catch me again, when it was found that I was unable to stand, and I was promptly put into a bunk and examined by the surgeon. It was discovered that the leg was crushed only, and that no bones were broken, so that such a trifle was of no interest at all compared to the other matters which then required urgent consideration.

General Franks was naturally much concerned at the unfortunate position which had arisen, although considerably relieved when I assured him that the Turks desired above all things Réouf Bey's release, and that as long as we "hung on" to *him* we were likely to remain masters of the situation. The General then proposed that he himself should surrender to the Turks in my place, to redeem Colonel Baird's pledge, and that the whole convoy should then return to Constantinople with the Turkish prisoners. To this, of course, I objected strongly, pointing out that if anyone had to go back it was obviously for me to do so, as we should then be no worse off than before, whilst his surrender would leave the Turks with the advantage of having gained possession of a General Officer in the place of a Lieut.-Colonel, and to this he was perforce obliged to assent.

It was finally agreed that a wireless communication should be sent to the High Commissioner at Constantinople, setting forth the exact situation, and stating that we should await further orders. This was done, and in due course instructions were received from Sir Horace Rumbold, the High Commissioner (acting, I understood, on his own responsibility), to "let all the Turks go," but to make sure that we received in exchange all British subjects who remained alive in Turkish hands. These instructions were carried out immediately, and to our disgust we saw all the Turkish prisoners go over the side into their native boats, knowing that there were amongst them scoundrels of the deepest dye, whose crimes, committed against British prisoners in their hands, had been of indescribable barbarity.

In exchange, in addition to my own party, we received only Captain Campbell, originally our Intelligence Officer at Koniah, who had been made prisoner there at the same time that my own party had been arrested at Erzeroum, and two civilians who claimed to be British subjects, though they were quite certainly not of British nationality. This operation completed, we immediately got under way for Constantinople, where we arrived on the evening of November 5th.

On our arrival Colonel Gribbon, then Chief of the Allied Headquarters Staff, whom I had previously known when he was a valued member of the Intelligence Staff at the War Office during the war, came on board; and with the greatest kindness invited me to stay at his house when I came ashore, until such time as I was in fit condition to undertake the journey home. This offer I most gladly accepted, saying I would come ashore the next morning, and no words of mine can adequately express my deep appreciation of the kindness I experienced at his hands and at those of his charming wife, all the time I was their guest before leaving for home.

I had passed the voyage confined to my bunk, and was still there early next morning, when I became aware that someone was in the doorway of my cabin. Hastily drawing aside the curtain, one glance was sufficient for me to appreciate the great honour which was being done me by the presence of such a distinguished visitor. I had never before had the honour of meeting him, but thanks to the excellence of our illustrated Press, all Englishmen know the features of Admiral Tyrwhitt, whose proud record during the war stands second to none on land or sea, and who was at that moment looking into the door of my cabin and inquiring as to my health. I have not the remotest notion what I may have said, but if, as I hope, I said what I felt, it was certainly that I considered it an honour to meet in person so distinguished an officer, and was deeply grateful for his kind inquiries.

After some conversation, he asked me what my plans were, and on my saying that I should have to put in ten days or a fortnight at Constantinople, to render my reports and to recover a little strength before proceeding home, he asked me, to my unbounded delight, whether I would come as his guest to Malta on the *Centaur* in about ten days' time. Needless to say, this kind and unexpected invitation was most gratefully accepted, and I understood that, with characteristic kindness, his invitation included both my three men and "George."

On going ashore I learned that Colonel Gribbon was now occupying the house, previously "A" mess, where I had been quartered during my last stay at Constantinople, and which was now, of course, infinitely more comfortable under the careful and competent supervision of its charming châtelaine, Mrs. Gribbon. Here I found every comfort and an unfailing kindness and consideration, which in my weak and nervous state did much to enable me to make a start in the recovery of my health. The next morning I had the honour of an interview with Sir Charles Harington, Commander-in-Chief, to whose efforts on our behalf, as we knew well, we certainly owed our freedom and probably our lives.

After giving me welcome news of my family, he told me that the only definite tidings he received of us, until the Bulgar had reached him with the famous cigarette, had been the report of the Americans that they had seen us at Gumush Khaneh, on our journey back to Erzeroum in April. He then asked me to bring in my men and "George," which I did, and proceeded to try to tell him, in their presence, how proud I felt of their conduct and bearing throughout all their trials; this, however, was beyond my powers, and I found, in my weakness, that my voice failed me, and that I was within an ace of breaking down completely.

The Chief, however, was, as he always is, kindness itself, and he told us we should get off home as soon as we were strong enough, and that he had got Mahoney, the Irish driver who joined the Turks, now in custody on another charge, and that we should have, in any case, to give evidence at the court-martial to be held on him before we left. It was also arranged that I should get on with the preparation of my report, by degrees, as my strength would allow, and a room was allotted to me at Headquarters to work in.

That night I dined at the Embassy with the staff, and the captain of the *Centaur*, Captain French, that most sympathetic of men and charming of hosts and companions, was also present. After dinner I was called upon to tell them incidents of our imprisonment, and I well remember that I told them the story of our Christmas dinner in Erzeroum, and added a few words about the men and their general behaviour, the whole being received by my audience with a sympathy and emotion which I very deeply appreciated.

For some days I was practically confined to my bed, as the nervous reaction of being once more at liberty and amongst friends was extremely trying, and it was only with great difficulty that I was able to complete my report, and that, I fear, only in a very inadequate manner. In the meanwhile I found at Constantinople stacks of letters which had been sent there during our confinement, in the hope that some communication with us might be possible; and amongst them over forty letters from my brother, which formed the most interesting history of the period, and which enabled me to learn a great deal of what had been happening in Europe during our imprisonment, as to all of which, of course, I was in the most profound ignorance.

I dined also at the Embassy with Sir Horace and Lady Rumbold, who, with the kindness and consideration which invariably distinguish them, invited me to bring the three men and "George" also to tea with them. That tea-party I shall never forget, as, although the men at first were naturally very shy, yet such was the natural charm of their hostess and the great interest unaffected sympathy displayed by the Ambassador himself, that a few moments after we were all seated round the tea-table the men found themselves completely at home, and were chatting away and telling stories and incidents of their experiences, perfectly naturally, in the same way as they would have done in their own home amongst their own families. It can easily be understood that all they had to say lost nothing of its interest from the atmosphere of sympathy and consideration with which they were surrounded; but to me, watching my comrades so carefully and knowing them so well, came a deep appreciation of the beauty of the sentiment which lay behind it all, and which enabled our gifted hosts at once to place these brave fellows completely at their ease, and to so insure their thorough enjoyment of their party. It was to me a very, very pretty incident, and I felt then, and still feel, deeply grateful to our host and hostess for their great kindness to us all.

I also had the honour of an invitation from the Chief to bring the men to lunch at his house, in which he was now established, some little distance outside the city. "George" also was invited, and Captain Campbell, who had returned from Ineboli with us; after luncheon photographs were taken, of which the Chief afterwards most kindly sent us copies. On this occasion I first had the pleasure of meeting Lady Harington, who had then lately arrived, and who from the moment of her arrival became at once the moving spirit in all the entertainments throughout the garrison, as, indeed, she continued to be until finally obliged by the political situation to return home, leaving behind her a gap impossible to fill.

A few days later the Chief told me he had received a wire from the War Office, inquiring as to our condition, and was kind enough to read me his cable reply. I then asked that I might be allowed to have an extract of the latter part of it to read to the men, which request was immediately granted, and below is the extract which I had the satisfaction of reading to them before our departure.

*"Extract from Cable from*
*Commander-in-Chief, Constantinople, to War Office,*
*London, dated November 15th, 1921.*

" . . . I have seen him and his men daily, and I am pleased and proud to say that I have not heard a word of complaint as to their treatment. . . . They had a bad time, but endured it with great bravery and fortitude, and deserve immense credit for the soldierlike spirit they are showing. . . . Their health has much improved since they arrived here. . . . They leave to-day."

The cause of these inquiries from home was that apparently certain articles had been published in the papers and questions asked in the House, and that an amount of interest was being created as to our treatment, which was then, and continued to be afterwards, extremely unpleasant to me. From the first moment of my arrival at Constantinople I had absolutely refused to see any of the many newspaper men who pursued me everywhere, or to give any information to anyone other than by my official report to the Commander-in-Chief. I even refrained from writing to my wife an exact account of our condition, in the fear that such information might transpire and be made use of to aggravate the already delicate political situation with regard to the Nationalist Turks.

I was then, and am still, of opinion that the inevitable policy of our country must always be to establish friendly relations with Turkey, if that be possible; and I had no idea of allowing our experiences to be made use of by any anti-Turk party, if that was by any possibility to be avoided. Further, I considered our treatment to be due to the ignorance and neglect of duty of subordinate officers, and under these circumstances it appeared to me that a much larger view should be taken of the whole question than one which would permit of any individual instances of neglect and ill-treatment being used to excite public feeling against a whole nation.

It appeared to me, also, that there is nothing new to be found in the bad treatment of their prisoners by the Turks, or in their traditional persecution of the Christian minorities, who have so long and with such difficuty still contrived to exist in many of the districts under Turkish rule; and that *unless* we were in a position to back up any agitation with respect to these matters by not only a display, but by an application, of *force* which would be capable of being followed up, if necessary, by serious and active military operations, it would be to the last degree unwise to bring such question forward at all. For these reasons I had taken every step, which it was open to me to take, to avoid, not only all interviews, but even appearing in public, in order that my indifferent state of health might not be made use of to in any way aggravate the situation; and I was therefore much concerned to learn that any publicity was being given at home to the matter of our detention and treatment. On November 15th, having said good-bye to my kind host and charming hostess and to their truly delightful children, with entirely inadequate expressions of my gratitude for all their great kindness, we finally embarked on the *Centaur* for our voyage to Malta.

This has been my one and only experience of a trip as an Admiral's guest on his flagship; it was an experience of which I shall for ever retain the most delightful recollections. My only fear, however, is that, as before leaving Constant I had been doing a great deal more work than I was in any way fit for, the state of my nerves was so bad that I am afraid I must on some occasions have said many things which I had no business to say, and drawn inferences which I had no right to draw, and so may possibly have annoyed my most courteous and delightful host, but whose kindness and consideration were such that he perhaps made allowances for my extremely "jumpy" state. However, in any case, I wish here once more to thank him for his extreme kindness to us all, and to myself in particular, for which we were all most deeply grateful.

We anchored off Cape Hellas, at the southern etxremity of the Gallipoli Peninsula, and as the Admiral had arranged to go ashore there for some shooting, I had, in passing Chanak, asked if the military authorities in charge of the cemeteries would be able to lend me a car to make the round of the Turkish positions. On arrival at our anchorage, therefore, I found a car waiting ashore, and, with a naval officer and one of the military staff of the Graves Commission, made the round of the landings, subsequently driving up the long 7 miles of gentle slopes through the village of Krithia, till we at last got out of the car and made our way on foot to the Turkish trenches on the summit of Achi Baba. That position dominates the whole slope to Cape Hellas, as well as the ground to the open sea on the right and to the Dardanelles on the left, each of them there not more than 2 miles distant.

I gazed long at that intensely interesting prospect, for the whole history of the dramatic landing, and subsequently heroic efforts of our immortal troops, is written in plain characters on the ground to-day, for all to read who have any experience of modern war. The trench systems on and about the summit are obviously of German design, similar to many with which we were familiar in France, the most interesting point being that at a glance it is apparent that, in laying out his trenches, the defender had evidently never for one moment contemplated the possibility of any serious attack being undertaken from the direction of the Cape itself, where our main landings were actually first effected, and which necessitated such a long advance over exposed ground.

The whole scheme of the defence was rather devised for the purpose, whilst incidentally commanding the long and gentle slope over which the main attack finally developed, of resisting the serious attacks which it had been evidently expected might be made up the ravines to be found on either flank, any of which afforded an amount of shelter from the defender's fire which was elsewhere absent, and at the same time necessitated an advance to the attack of not more than one-third of the distance which it was necessary to cover in a direct advance over the exposed ground from the Cape itself. It was impossible not to appreciate at once that the success or failure of any attack on the Achi Baba position must depend absolutely on the vital point as to whether or not the artillery preparation could be such as to dominate the enemy's fire from that commanding position, as without such a condition no successful attack would be possible, however heroically pushed home, against a well-armed enemy well entrenched there and adequately supplied with ammunition.

It was with astonishment, therefore, that on examining the works on the summit we found them practically untouched by artillery-fire; so much so was this the case that on the main position itself it was necessary to search about to find a shell crater, and that on a position which, had it existed on the Western front, would have been knocked to pieces by artillery-fire befor any serious attack would have been delivered against it.

That is the story told by the state of the ground on the position at Achi Baba to-day, and it was with great regret that we found we had not the time at our disposal to go farther and to examine the other positions subsequently attacked from Suvla Bay and Anafarta. It was, however, as a very silent and meditative party that we returned to the ship, each, no doubt, reconstructing in his own mind the state of affairs which the ground showed to have existed on the occasion of the original landing and subsequent attacks, though no one evinced the least disposition to make any remarks on the subject.

We left Cape Hellas that night for Malta, and next morning the cruiser was to do her full-speed trial, which she carried out successfully, in spite of a very considerable swell. I had the advantage of spending some part of the time during the trial on the upper bridge, and immensely enjoyed such an unusual experience. The speed attained was great; I dare not commit myself to an exact statement, as I made no note of it at the time, but it was, I know, even higher than was expected; and as the swell became worse as we proceeded, I know also that the question of being obliged to "ease down" was several times under consideration, although in the end the trial was continued for the full time laid down by the regulations.

The sight, as seen from the upper bridge, was quite an exceptional one, and as at that high speed the vessel occasionally plunged her nose deep into the oncoming swell, the whole forepart of the ship at such times disappeared in a white mass of seething, foaming water, the spray flying high above our heads even on the upper bridge, whilst every portion of the ship became dripping wet, and astern stretched a wake of boiling foam gradually broadening out until it showed our track as a great bar of silver on the dark background of the deep blue and glassy sea over which our course had lain. In the course of the trial we passed the battleship *King George the Fifth*. That ship had left Cape Hellas many hours before us, and some of her officers had undertaken to snap photographs of the *Centaur* at full speed as she passed them. The sun was bright and the light perfect, so that these photographs must have been splendid; but although I was told I should certainly have one, I had left Malta before they were available, and am therefore, much to my regret, unable to have this exceptional scene reproduced for the benefit of my readers.

On arriving at Malta the Admiral was on the bridge himself, and as all the formalities of entering the port and saluting the flag of the Commander-in-Chief of the Mediterranean Fleet were gone through, the sight was most impressive; particularly was it so to me, as here we once more entered a really British port, and evidence of the might of the Empire stood out on every hand, whilst the bugles rang out in salute, and all officers also saluted. It was, I think, the fact of all these evidences of the great disciplined power of our country, coming as such a contrast to our own previous misery and weakness, that effected me so deeply, for, to my astonishment, I found my eyes were wet, and there was such a lump in my throat I was quite unable to answer when spoken to, and sought my cabin as quickly as possible to recover my self-control, which threatened entirely to desert me. . . .

Soon afterwards the Governor's launch drew alongside, and one of Lord Plumer's aides-de-camp came to find me, telling me that a room was prepared for me at the Palace, and that I was to stay there as Lord Plumer's guest, he having then succeeded Lord Methuen as Governor of the island. I was therefore soon ashore and installed in most luxurious quarters in the Palace, where I promptly took to my bed till evening, when Lord Plumer, on his return, himself came to see me and showed me the utmost kindness.

That evening I had the pleasure of making Lady Plumer's acquaintance, and it would be impossible to imagine greater hospitality and goodness than we received from them both during the two more days we remained at Malta. The Palace, which stands in the centre of the town of Valetta, the capital of the island, was the medieval home of the Grand Masters of the ancient Order of the Knights of Malta, and is a beautiful building, the spacious marble corridors being lined by many suits of complete armour, and the many magnificent apartments profusely decorated with gilding, paintings, and tapestries, all dating from the great days of the Order in the fifteenth and sixteenth centuries. In the centre of the Palace is a courtyard in white marble, where are stately palms, and where reign a peaceful silence and a cool refreshing shade, forming a striking contrast to the noise and glare of the surrounding streets in the town.

Lord and Lady Plumer took me, both to their country Palace at San Antonio, which I have already described in Part I., and also to an ancient castle which they occupy in summer and which is quite different in style, but even more striking in appearance.

The castle in question was for many years the summer residence of the Grand Masters of the Order of the Knights of

Malta, and is built in the form of a large square tower, with smaller towers at the four corners. It stands high in lovely grounds and commands views on all sides of the island and the sea. The island in that part is more rocky even than elsewhere, but much trouble and care have been expended on the elaborate gardens and terraces, which are quite the feature of the place.

The castle itself is of exceptionally massive construction, and contains a great central hall, where the temperature is delightfully cool during the hottest days of the Maltese summer, and in the corner towers, as well as in the thickness of the great walls, are dungeons where, in times gone by, many prisoners have been confined, and where the old chains and fetters with which they were loaded can still be seen. My kind hosts also took me to the opera one night, which I much enjoyed, and which was a change indeed from Erzeroum.

Lord Plumer did my men the honour of receiving them one day at the Palace, and Lady Plumer then, with the greatest possible kindness, took them herself round the Palace and showed them many points of interest, which favour they most deeply appreciated. They were also sent round the island in a motor-car, accompanied by an officer, and had a delightful day, seeing all the sights, for which they were most grateful, and which, in their weak state, did their health much good.

The day before we reached the island a cable had arrived from Constantinople, asking that our return should be "expedited," as apparently questions were being asked at home about us, which it was desired we might be at hand to answer if necessary. The cable was handed to me, and is reproduced below:

"1276 16/11. For Governor, Malta. Will you please expedite journey home of Colonel Rawlinson and three men (who have been with him throughout), who left by H.M.S. *Centaur* yesterday for MALTA? Their behaviour has been splendid, and like true Englishmen they have come through severe hardships without complaint.

"GENERAL HARINGTON.
"1800. 16. 11. 20.

"*Copy to A. M. S. for H. E.*"

Admiral Sir John de Robeck, who was still Commander-in-Chief of the Mediterranean Fleet, and then in residence at

Malta, at the request of Lord Plumer, arranged, in accordance with the above cable, to send us to Naples in a destroyer, as that route would be far the quickest, and on my third night at Malta I had the pleasure of once more dining with that great and distinguished sailor, this time, however, on shore, at Admiralty House, where his hospitality was as lavish and as much appreciated by all as it had been on the *Iron Duke* when in the Bosphorus. After a most interesting and enjoyable evening I finally said good-bye to all my kind hosts, and went on board the destroyer which was to take us to Naples.

To our surprise and delight, when we reached the vessel we found her to be once more the *Somme,* which had brought us from Trebizond to Ineboli, to which ship's company we owed so much for all their care and attention. As we learned it was not strictly the *Somme's* turn to do dispatch work, we concluded that here was one more example of the kind consideration which we invariably experienced at the hands of the navy, which we greatly appreciated and for which we felt profoundly grateful. The voyage was uneventful, and the next evening we passed the island of Capri and enjoyed to the full the wonderfully beautiful prospect offered by the Bay of Naples when it is entered from the sea, the evening sun behind us showing up the rugged peak of Vesuvius on the right, and the glittering spires of the beautiful city of Naples on the left, as we glided over what is surely the bluest water in all the world.

On anchoring, we found our train did not leave till midnight, and we therefore had the chance of doing what we had hoped so much to have an opportunity to do—namely, to entertain our good friends and hosts of the *Somme.* We were able, I am glad to think, to arrange for the whole ship's company, consisting of about seventy, to go ashore, in two watches (batches) alternately, and to supply each rating (man) with a modest sum with which to enjoy himself. As the Italian exchange permits one shilling to become quite a considerable number of lire (the Italian coin), we had every reason to believe that they would, and did, have a good time, and that we were able to provide some enjoyment for them in return for all their kindness and consideration for us.

The officers, six in number, honoured me by dining with me at the Hôtel Excelsior, fronting on the bay, and as fine a hotel as

# THE PARTY AT BARON ROBERT DE ROTHSCHILD'S HOUSE IN PARIS

Left to right: Corpl. Ankers, Pte. Leadbeater, Col. R., "George," Pte. Carter

can be found in Europe, and we had a class of dinner quite in keeping with the place, and all, I think, thoroughly enjoyed it. The naval officers, after some persuasion, "took the floor" after dinner, in the ball-room of the hotel, with the Italian and other ladies who had the good fortune to be present there that night, and both the dancing and the gallant bearing of the navy were, as usual, in every way a credit to their service, as was also the behaviour of all the ship's company in the town. At last our time was up, and we repaired to the station, where our naval friends saw us off in great style, at the very last moment presenting me with a highly valued, photograph of H.M.S. *Somme*, signed by all the officers, which hangs beside me as I write.

Only one incident occurred on our voyage via Rome to Paris but that was a tragic one, and occurred in the following manner: About 8 A.M., when just approaching the mouth of the Mont Cenis Tunnel on the Italian side of the French-Italian frontier, the train came to a halt. "George," who at that time was sleeping, as usual, by my side, intimated to me that he would much like a run in the fresh mountain air. I therefore got up, having on my pyjamas only and being in my bare feet. Having then looked in both directions, up and down the line, seeing that we were on the open mountain-side and that there was no sign of any move on the part of the train, I opened the door and let him out.

As he leaped to the ground, to my horror the train started, and it became impossible to get him back on to the train. Such was my distress that it was only with the greatest difficulty that I refrained from jumping out after him myself, which, being without clothes or money and in my bare feet, would only have complicated the situation. I therefore shouted to him to "Otur," which means "Lie down" in Turkish, and proceeded to do my best to stop the train. This I succeeded eventually in doing, but not till we reached the next station, some miles farther on. Here we were fortunate enough to find a post of Italian Carabinieri (light infantry), and the officer in charge most kindly agreed to send back at once to get hold of "George" and to then send him on to the frontier at Modane, in charge of one of his own men, by the next train.

On arrival at Modane I was lucky enough to obtain the services of one of Mr. Cook's representatives, who undertook to bring "George" on to Paris, to Baron Robert Rothschild's house, whose guests we were once more to be on our arrival. On reaching Paris, my ever kind and charming friends and hosts gave us a great reception, and Baron Rothschild arranged that on "George's" arrival next morning his meeting with his friends should be photographed on the cinematograph, which was done, and it was hard to say who was happiest at meeting once more, whether "George" or the men or myself. We left Paris that morning; and as the weather was rough on going on board the boat we at once sought the cabin which had been reserved for us.

After a few moments, however, we were told that we must move, as we were in the wrong cabin, that one having been reserved by the Duke of Westminster, and, turning round, I found my old friend and very gallant comrade of the early days of the war at the door—a most unexpected and fortunate meeting, which made the crossing seem very short, as there was not time to tell him the half of my story. My son met me at Dover, and we reached Victoria at 7.30 P. M., where my wife, daughter, and sister-in-law appeared. Two officers from the War Office also came to welcome us home and to look after the men, who, however, were kind enough to remain as my guests that night, and a great home-coming we had. . . .

Next afternoon I reported at the War Office, and handed in a special report with regard to the conduct of the three men who returned to England with me, as below.

COPY OF REPORT FROM LIEUT.-COLONEL RAWLINSON.

*To Director of Military Intelligence, War Office, London.*
"L/Cpl. Ankers, No. 196424, 766th Coy. M.T., R.A.S.C.
"Pte. Carter, H., No. 97905, 85th Coy. M.G.C.
"Pte. Leadbeater, R., No. 59194, 66th Coy. M.G.C.
"SIR,
"With reference to the three B.O.R.s above mentioned, who were volunteers under my command in Eastern Anatolia in March, 1920, when my party was disarmed and confined by the Turkish Nationalist troops, I now have the honour to report as follows:
"I desire to call special attention to the steadfast courage and true soldierly bearing of these three men through a long period of great hardship, suffering, and persecution. It is

my opinion that the courage shown by them at all times throughout the long period when they were cut off from all communication and starved, persecuted, and frozen, is of a higher quality than that called for in the carrying out of any deed, however glorious, in the course of active operations.

"Where all are so worthy, it is invidious to make distinctions, but I consider that Lance-Corporal Ankers, being the senior, did much by his splendid example to strengthen the determination of the others, although he himself was suffering acute and long-continued agony from an injury to his right hand which finally necessitated the amputation of his thumb.

"At all times during a period of eighteen months, altuough their bodies were reduced to the last stage of exhaustion and weakness by sickness and starvation, the spirit of these men remained high and unbroken, and they are in every way a credit to the British Army.

"I have the honour to be, Sir,
"(*Signed*) A. RAWLINSON.
"(*Lieut.-Colonel*)."

NOTE.—The above men all subsequently received the Military Medal, awarded for acts of bravery in the field.

I also had a long interview with Sir Henry Wilson, who had already received my general report, which had been sent overland from Constantinople. General Thwaites, the Director of Intelligence, was also present, and the interview was a long one, as many questions were gone into with the map of the country before us.

My old friend the C.I.G.S. was most interested in all I had to say, and was, if possible, even kinder to me than usual, so that I found, on leaving, I had been there an hour and three-quarters, a very strenuous and anxious time for me, as I had so many things to report, and was so, perhaps unduly anxious to forget nothing, and, above all, on no account to give a wrong impression as to any of the particular facts and conditions which it was my duty to report. However, at last it was over, and I made my way home with the deepest feeling of relief that my report was finally made, and the time for rest had come at last.

The nervous reaction, however, was very great, and that night at dinner I suddenly collapsed, and remember no more for many hours, till I finally opened my eyes to find myself in bed, with a doctor by the bedside and my wife in attendance. I could see, and could also hear what was said, but was quite unable to speak, and very shortly afterwards relapsed again into unconsciousness. It appears that I lay for many hours senseless, from absolute exhaustion of the nervous system, which finally had failed entirely when my task was once over and finished, and the necessity for further effort no longer existed.

I was for some time allowed to see no one, and although His Majesty did me the honour to command me to Buckingham Palace, yet my medical advisers would not allow me to go, nor was I permitted to see Lord Curzon, who both wrote and sent to ask me to go and see him at the Foreign Office. I found on my return to England that the majority of my friends, and even my brother, had, after so long an interval without any news, practically given up hope of my survival. My wife, however, was always confident that I was still alive, and that I should return safely.

It was arranged that as soon as I was able to travel I should go to the South of France, where my old and kind friend the Duke of Westminster had invited me to stay at his château in the Landes beyond Bordeaux, and I was to start at the end of December, having reached London on November 24th.

In the meanwhile I had, on War Office instructions, attended a medical board, the president of which gave me a paper recommending me for three months' sick leave, after which I was to be re-examined; and this paper was marked as authorizing me to proceed "in expectation" of the completion of the formalities. I therefore proceeded to obtain a passport, which required some days, and on its completion I formally notified the War Office that I was proceeding abroad as authorized "in anticipation." This communication I made by telephone, just to make sure all was in order.

What, therefore, was my surprise to receive the answer that "No more sick leave was authorized under any circumsatnces, unless an officer was actually detained in a military hospital," and that unless I was re-employed I could only be granted two months' leave, and should then be automatically demobilized. This statement surprised me so much that I went to the War Office at once to check its correctness, but when I got there I was told that the statement was quite correct, but that in my case I was to be granted an extra month's ordinary leave, which would take me to March 23rd, and that then, if unemployed, I should be demobilized. On that I went off to France in search of peace and quiet and an opportunity of recruiting my strength, returning to England, considerably stronger, on February 1st, although I had been confined to my bed the greater part of the time during the interval.

On my return I had the honour of an interview with His Majesty the King at Buckingham Palace, where he also saw the men who came to London for the purpose, and whom I was proud indeed to present to him. His Majesty was most kind to us all, asking many questions as to our adventures, as well as examining the many photographs which we had brought back, and we all felt very grateful and very proud indeed of the honour of being received by our Sovereign, which more than repaid us for our long imprisonment.

The King also on this occasion presented me with a C.B.E., which had been awarded to me in respect of services previous to June, 1919, but which, of course, I had hitherto had no opportunity of receiving. I subsequently saw Lord Curzon twice; he was also full of sympathy for our sufferings, and told me he had on many occasions done his best to obtain our release or exchange, without success.

On March 23rd, there being no more "special stunts" upon which I could be employed, I was finally demobilized. I was at the same time granted the "substantive," (that is "permanent") rank, of Lieut.-Colonel in the British Army. Thus ended my *second* period of military service. This *second* period commenced on August 17th, 1914, and lasted for seven years and five months. During that period I was continuously employed on active service, and served upon six different Fronts. I was never for one moment out of uniform and neither asked for nor received ANY LEAVE AT ALL.

I am told that that constitutes a record in the British Army, and, if that be so, it is one that I am proud indeed to hold—and shall always remain *more than content,* if during that time I may have been able to render any service, of any kind, in any part of the world, which has been of any value to the great and glorious BRITISH EMPIRE, of which it is my pride to be a humble citizen.

**THE END**

www.ingramcontent.com/pod-product-compliance
Lightning Source LLC
Chambersburg PA
CBHW060449090426
42735CB00011B/1953